T0331850

Applications of Security, Mobile, Analytic, and Cloud (SMAC) Technologies for Effective Information Processing and Management

P. Karthikeyan
Thiagarajar College of Engineering, India

M. Thangavel
Thiagarajar College of Engineering, India

A volume in the Advances in Computer and
Electrical Engineering (ACEE) Book Series

Published in the United States of America by
> IGI Global
> Engineering Science Reference (an imprint of IGI Global)
> 701 E. Chocolate Avenue
> Hershey PA, USA 17033
> Tel: 717-533-8845
> Fax: 717-533-8661
> E-mail: cust@igi-global.com
> Web site: http://www.igi-global.com

Library of Congress Cataloging-in-Publication Data

Names: Karthikeyan, P., 1981- editor. | Thangavel, M., 1989- editor.
Title: Applications of security, mobile, analytic and cloud (SMAC)
  technologies for effective information processing and management / P.
  Karthikeyan and M. Thangavel, editors.
Description: Hershey, PA : Engineering Science Reference, [2018] | Includes
  bibliographical references.
Identifiers: LCCN 2017027302| ISBN 9781522540441 (hardcover) | ISBN
  9781522540458 (ebook)
Subjects: LCSH: Information technology. | Computer networks.
Classification: LCC T58.5 .A675 2018 | DDC 004--dc23 LC record available at https://lccn.loc.gov/2017027302

This book is published in the IGI Global book series Advances in Computer and Electrical Engineering (ACEE) (ISSN: 2327-039X; eISSN: 2327-0403)

British Cataloguing in Publication Data
A Cataloguing in Publication record for this book is available from the British Library.

For electronic access to this publication, please contact: eresources@igi-global.com.

Advances in Computer and Electrical Engineering (ACEE) Book Series

Srikanta Patnaik
SOA University, India

ISSN:2327-039X
EISSN:2327-0403

MISSION

The fields of computer engineering and electrical engineering encompass a broad range of interdisciplinary topics allowing for expansive research developments across multiple fields. Research in these areas continues to develop and become increasingly important as computer and electrical systems have become an integral part of everyday life.

The **Advances in Computer and Electrical Engineering (ACEE) Book Series** aims to publish research on diverse topics pertaining to computer engineering and electrical engineering. **ACEE** encourages scholarly discourse on the latest applications, tools, and methodologies being implemented in the field for the design and development of computer and electrical systems.

COVERAGE

- Applied Electromagnetics
- Computer Hardware
- Qualitative Methods
- Analog Electronics
- Optical Electronics
- Algorithms
- Programming
- Power Electronics
- Chip Design
- Circuit Analysis

IGI Global is currently accepting manuscripts for publication within this series. To submit a proposal for a volume in this series, please contact our Acquisition Editors at Acquisitions@igi-global.com or visit: http://www.igi-global.com/publish/.

Titles in this Series

For a list of additional titles in this series, please visit: www.igi-global.com/book-series

Soft-Computing-Based Nonlinear Control Systems Design
Uday Pratap Singh (Madhav Institute of Technology and Science, India) Akhilesh Tiwari (Madhav Institute of Technology and Science, India) and Rajeev Kumar Singh (Madhav Institute of Technology and Science, India)
Engineering Science Reference • copyright 2018 • 388pp • H/C (ISBN: 9781522535317) • US $245.00 (our price)

EHT Transmission Performance Evaluation Emerging Research and Opportunities
K. Srinivas (Transmission Corporation of Andhra Pradesh Limited, India) and R.V.S. Satyanarayana (Sri Venkateswara University College of Engineering, India)
Engineering Science Reference • copyright 2018 • 160pp • H/C (ISBN: 9781522549413) • US $145.00 (our price)

Fuzzy Logic Dynamics and Machine Prediction for Failure Analysis
Tawanda Mushiri (University of Johannesburg, South Africa) and Charles Mbowhwa (University of Johannesburg, South Africa)
Engineering Science Reference • copyright 2018 • 301pp • H/C (ISBN: 9781522532446) • US $225.00 (our price)

Creativity in Load-Balance Schemes for Multi/Many-Core Heterogeneous Graph Computing Emerging Research...
Alberto Garcia-Robledo (Center for Research and Advanced Studies of the National Polytechnic Institute (Cinvestav-Tamaulipas), Mexico) Arturo Diaz-Perez (Center for Research and Advanced Studies of the National Polytechnic Institute (Cinvestav-Tamaulipas), Mexico) and Guillermo Morales-Luna (Center for Research and Advanced Studies of the National Polytechnic Institute (Cinvestav-IPN), Mexico)
Engineering Science Reference • copyright 2018 • 217pp • H/C (ISBN: 9781522537991) • US $155.00 (our price)

Free and Open Source Software in Modern Data Science and Business Intelligence Emerging Research and...
K.G. Srinivasa (CBP Government Engineering College, India) Ganesh Chandra Deka (M. S. Ramaiah Institute of Technology, India) and Krishnaraj P.M. (M. S. Ramaiah Institute of Technology, India)
Engineering Science Reference • copyright 2018 • 189pp • H/C (ISBN: 9781522537076) • US $190.00 (our price)

Design Parameters of Electrical Network Grounding Systems
Osama El-Sayed Gouda (Cairo University, Egypt)
Engineering Science Reference • copyright 2018 • 316pp • H/C (ISBN: 9781522538530) • US $235.00 (our price)

Design and Use of Virtualization Technology in Cloud Computing
Prashanta Kumar Das (Government Industrial Training Institute Dhansiri, India) and Ganesh Chandra Deka (Government of India, India)
Engineering Science Reference • copyright 2018 • 315pp • H/C (ISBN: 9781522527855) • US $235.00 (our price)

701 East Chocolate Avenue, Hershey, PA 17033, USA
Tel: 717-533-8845 x100 • Fax: 717-533-8661
E-Mail: cust@igi-global.com • www.igi-global.com

Table of Contents

Detailed Table of Contents

    Kowsigan Mohan, Sri Krishna College of Technology, India
    P. Balasubramanie Palanisamy, Kongu Engineering College, India
    G.R. Kanagachidambaresan, Veltech Rangarajan Dr Sagunthala R&D Institute of Science
        and Technology, India
    Siddharth Rajesh, Sri Krishna College of Technology, India
    Sneha Narendran, Sri Krishna College of Technology, India

This chapter describes how security plays a vital role in cloud computing, as the name itself specifies the data can be stored from any place and can be owned by anyone. Even though the cloud offers many benefits such as flexibility, scalability and agility, security issues are still backlog the cloud infrastructure. Much research is being done on cloud security equal to the scheduling problems in the cloud environment. The customers under the cloud providers are very concerned about their data, which has been stored in the cloud environment. In this regard, it is essential for a cloud provider to implement some powerful tools for security, to provide a secure cloud infrastructure to the customers. Generally speaking, there are some foundational needs to be attained and some actions to be combined to ensure data security in both cloud, as well as, non-cloud infrastructure. This book chapter concentrates only on the security issues, security measures, security mechanisms, and security tools of the cloud environment.

    Swapnoneel Roy, University of North Florida, USA
    Sanjay P. Ahuja, University of North Florida, USA
    Priyanka D. Harish, University of North Florida, USA
    S. Raghu Talluri, University of North Florida, USA

In this chapter, we study the energy consumption by various modern cryptographic protocols for the cloud from the algorithmic perspective. The two categories of protocols we consider are (1) hash functions and (2) symmetric key encryption protocols. We identify various parameters that moderate energy consumption of these hashes and protocols. Our work is directed towards redesigning or modifying these algorithms to make them consume lesser energy. As a first step, we try to determine the applicability of the asymptotic energy complexity model by Roy on these hashes and protocols. Specifically, we try to observe whether parallelizing the access of blocks of data in these algorithms reduces their energy consumption based on the energy model. Our results confirm the applicability of the energy model on these hashes and protocols. Our work is motivated by the importance of cryptographic hashes and symmetric key protocols for the cloud. Hence the design of more energy efficient hashes and protocols will contribute in reducing the cloud energy consumption that is continuously increasing.

Chapter 3

Hemalatha J, Thiagarajar College of Engineering, India
KavithaDevi M.K., Thiagarajar College of Engineering, India
Geetha S., Vellore Institute of Technology Chennai, India

This chapter describes how ample feature extraction techniques are available for detecting hidden messages in digital images. In the recent years, higher dimensional features are extracted to detect the complex and advanced steganographic algorithms. To improve the precision of steganalysis, many combinations of high dimension feature spaces are used by recent steganalyzers. In this chapter, we present a summary of several methods existing in literature. The aim is to provide a broad introduction to high dimensional features space used so for and to state which the most accurate and best feature extraction methods is.

Chapter 4

Usha B. A., R V College of Engineering, India

Steganography is the art of hiding the fact that communication is taking place, by hiding information in other information. Many different carrier file formats can be used, but digital images are the most popular because of their frequency on the Internet. For hiding secret information in images, there exist a large variety of steganographic techniques some are more complex than others and all of them have respective strong and weak points.. As embedding data in an image, is independent of one another. Parallelism can be used to achieve considerable time gain. nography, although it has made communication safe, it has its own drawbacks. One among it is time required to embed data in pixels of the image. This problem is bugging computer scientists from long time. This paper discusses a method which makes OpenMP parallel library to parallelize embedding of data, which basically reduces the time by almost fifty percent and to achieve PSNR ranging from 30 to 50 after embedding data in the pixels of the image.

Chapter 5

Sushruta Mishra, C. V. Raman College of Engineering, India
Sunil Kumar Mohapatra, C. V. Raman College of Engineering, India
Brojo Kishore Mishra, C. V. Raman College of Engineering, India
Soumya Sahoo, C. V. Raman College of Engineering, India

This chapter describes how cloud computing is an emerging concept combining many fields of computing. The foundation of cloud computing is the delivery of services, software and processing capacity over the Internet, reducing cost, increasing storage, automating systems, decoupling of service delivery from underlying technology, and providing flexibility and mobility of information. However, the actual realization of these benefits is far from being achieved for mobile applications and open many new research questions. Together with an explosive growth of the mobile applications and emerging of cloud computing concept, mobile cloud computing (MCC) has been introduced to be a potential technology for mobile services. With this importance, this chapter provides an overview of mobile cloud computing in which its definitions, architecture, and advantages have been presented. It presents an in-depth knowledge of various aspects of Mobile Cloud Computing (MCC). We give a definition of mobile cloud computing and provide an overview of its features.

Chapter 6

Mobile Cloud Computing (MCC) which combines mobile computing and cloud computing, has become one of the industry ring words and a major conversation thread in the IT world with an explosive development of the mobile applications and emerging of cloud computing idea, the MCC has become a possible technology for the mobile service users. The concepts of Cloud computing are naturally meshed with mobile devices to allow on-the-go functionalities and benefits. The mobile cloud computing is emerging as one of the most important branches of cloud computing and it is expected to expand the mobile ecosystems. As more mobile devices enter the market and evolve, certainly security issues will grow as well. Also, enormous growth in the variety of devices connected to the Internet will further drive security needs. MCC provides a platform where mobile users make use of cloud services on mobile devices. The use of MCC minimizes the performance, compatibility, and lack of resources issues in mobile computing environment.

Chapter 7

This chapter describes how traditionally, Cloud Computing has been used for processing Internet of Things (IoT) data. This works fine for the analytical and batch processing jobs. But most of the IoT applications demand real-time response which cannot be achieved through Cloud Computing mainly because of inherent latency. Fog Computing solves this problem by offering cloud-like services at the edge of the network. The computationally powerful edge devices have enabled realising this idea. Witnessing the exponential rise of IoT applications, Fog Computing deserves an in-depth exploration. This chapter establishes the need for Fog Computing for processing IoT data. Readers will be able to gain a fair comprehension of the various aspects of Fog Computing. The benefits, challenges and applications of Fog Computing with respect to IoT have been mentioned elaboratively. An architecture for IoT data processing is presented. A thorough comparison between Cloud and Fog has been portrayed. Also, a detailed discussion has been depicted on how the IoT, Fog, and Cloud interact among them.

This chapter describes how we live in the era of data, where every event in and around us creates a massive amount of data. The greatest challenge in front of every data scientist is making this raw data, a meaningful one to solve a business problem. The process of extracting knowledge from the large database is called as Data mining. Data mining plays a wrestling role in all the application like Health care, education and Agriculture, etc. Data mining is classified predictive and descriptive model. The predictive model consists of classification, regression, prediction, time series analysis and the descriptive model consists of clustering, association rules, summarization and sequence discovery. Predictive modeling associates the important areas in the data mining called classification and prediction.

Chapter 9

This article describes how semantic annotation is the most important need for the categorization of labeled or unlabeled textual documents. Accuracy of document categorization can be greatly improved if documents are indexed or modeled using the semantics rather than the traditional term-frequency model. This annotation has its own challenges like synonymy and polysemy in the document categorization problem. The model proposes to build domain ontology for the textual content so that the problems like synonymy and polysemy in text analysis are resolved to greater extent. Latent Dirichlet Allocation (LDA), the topic modeling technique has been used for feature extraction from the documents. Using the domain knowledge on the concept and the features grouped by LDA, the domain ontology is built in the hierarchical fashion. Empirical results show that LDA is the better feature extraction technique for text documents than TF or TF-IDF indexing technique. Also, the proposed model shows improvement in the accuracy of document categorization when domain ontology built using LDA has been used for document indexing.

Chapter 10

This chapter describes how mobile advertisements are critical for both mobile users and businesses as people spend more time on mobile devices than on PCs. However, how to send relevant advertisements and avoid unnecessary ones to specific mobile users is always a challenge. For example, a concert-goer may like to visit restaurants or parks before the concert and may not like the advertisements of grocery stores or farmers' markets. This research tries to overcome the challenge by using the methods of location-aware data mining. Furthermore, privacy is always a great concern for location-based advertising (LBA) users because their location information has to be shared in order to receive the services. This chapter also takes the concern into serious consideration, so the user privacy will not be compromised. Preliminary experiment results show the proposed methods are effective and user-privacy is rigorously preserved.

Chapter 11

This chapter describes how in the digital data era, a large volume of data became accessible to data science engineers. With the reckless growth in networking, communication, storage, and data collection capability, the Big Data science is quickly growing in each engineering and science domain. This paper aims to study many numbers of the various analytics ways and tools which might be practiced to Big Data. The important deportment in this paper is step by step process to handle the large volume and variety of data expeditiously. The rapidly evolving big data tools and Platforms have given rise to numerous technologies to influence completely different Big Data portfolio.In this paper, we debate in an elaborate manner about analyzing tools, processing tools and querying tools for Big datahese tools used for data analysis Big Data tools utilize numerous tasks, like Data capture, storage, classification, sharing, analysis, transfer, search, image, and deciding which might also apply to Big data.

Chapter 12

This chapter describes how big data consist of an extreme volume of data, velocity, and more complex variable data that demands current technology changes in capturing, storage, distribution, management, analysis data. Business facing more struggles in identifying the pragmatic approach in capturing the data about customer, products, and services. Usage of big data mainly with the analytical method, but it specifically compares with features of an analytical method based on unstructured data contributed around 95% of big data. The analytical approach depends on heterogeneous data and unstructured data's like text, audio, video format. It demands new effective tool for predictive analysis for big data with the unstructured format. This chapter describes explanation of big data and characteristics of big data compress of Volume, Velocity, Variety, Variability, and Value. Recent trends in the development of big data that applies in real time application perspectives like health care agriculture, education etc.

Preface

The combination of security, mobile, analytics and cloud (SMAC) in one integrated stack maximizes the impact of each other in an organization. SMAC technology is spreading faster than any other in the recent past. Some experts in the field have predicted that by 2020 SMAC will account for $5 trillion of the total spending by customers. SMAC indeed takes more connective, collaborative, real-time and productive approach for innovations.

Big Data is an emerging term that describes any voluminous amount of structured, semi-structured and unstructured data that has the potential to be mined for information. Although big data doesn't refer to any specific quantity, the term is often used when speaking about petabytes and exabytes of data. These days' Big data is becoming a very essential component for the industries where large volume of data with large variety and at very high speed is used to solve particular data problems.

The Mobile Technologies and Internet of Things (IoT) have drawn great attention from both academia and industry since they offer to challenge the notion of creating the world where all the things, known as smart objects around us are connected, typically in a wireless manner to the Internet and communicate with each other with minimum human intervention.

Cloud computing is an increasingly popular technology that offers several advantages to IoT and it is based on the concept of allowing users to perform normal computing tasks using services delivered entirely over the internet. Cloud Computing has become a scalable services consumption and delivery platform in the field of Services Computing. The technical foundations of Cloud Computing include Service-Oriented Architecture (SOA) and Virtualizations of hardware and software.

The purpose of information security management in Mobile, Analytics, IoT & Cloud, is to ensure business continuity and reduce business damage by preventing and minimising the impact of security incidents. The Audit Commission Update report (1998) shows that fraud or cases of IT abuse often occur due to the absence of basic controls, with one half of all detected frauds found by accident. An Information Security Management System (ISMS) enables information to be shared, whilst ensuring the protection of information and computing assets.

This Book covers 4 major research areas:

1. **Big Data and IoT:** Big Data represents a major disruption in the business intelligence and data management landscape, upending fundamental notions about governance and IT delivery. With traditional solutions becoming too expensive to scale or adapt to rapidly evolving conditions, companies are scrambling to find affordable technologies that will help them store, process, and query all of their data. Innovative solutions will enable companies to extract maximum value from Big Data and create differentiated, more personal customer experiences.

As everything gets connected to everything, data is the commodity being transferred between the various IoT components and attempts to store all the data being generated as a result continues to push the boundaries of Big Data. The Internet of Things is the concept of everyday objects – from industrial machines to wearable devices – using built-in sensors to gather data and take action on that data across a network. IoT connects real world objects to the internet using tiny sensors or embedded devices. Simply put, the IoT is the future of technology that can make our lives more efficient. As sensors spread across almost every industry, the internet of things is going to trigger a massive influx of big data. IoT technology offers automated mechanisms for pulling machine data into data warehouses or Hadoop clusters, Spark and other big data platforms for analysis.

2.   **Mobile Technologies:** Mobile technology is the technology used for cellular communication. Mobile code division multiple access (CDMA) technology has evolved rapidly over the past few years. Since the start of this millennium, a standard mobile device has gone from being no more than a simple two-way pager to being a mobile phone, GPS navigation device, an embedded web browser and instant messaging client, and a handheld game console. Many experts argue that the future of computer technology rests in mobile computing with wireless networking. Mobile computing by way of tablet computers are becoming more popular. Tablets are available on the 3G and 4G networks.

Mobile application development is a term used to denote the act or process by which application software is developed for mobile devices, such as personal digital assistants, enterprise digital assistants or mobile phones. These applications can be pre-installed on phones during manufacturing platforms, or delivered as web applications using server-side or client-side processing (e.g., JavaScript) to provide an "application-like" experience within a Web browser. Application software developers also must consider a long array of screen sizes, hardware specifications, and configurations because of intense competition in mobile software and changes within each of the platforms. Mobile app development has been steadily growing, in revenues and jobs created. A 2013 analyst report estimates there are 529,000 direct app economy jobs within the EU 28 members, 60% of which are mobile app developers.

3.   **Cloud Computing:** The goal of Cloud Computing is to share resources among the cloud service consumers, cloud partners, and cloud vendors in the cloud value chain. The resource sharing at various levels results in various cloud offerings such as infrastructure cloud (e.g., hardware, IT infrastructure management), software cloud (e.g. SaaS focusing on middleware as a service, or traditional CRM as a service), application cloud (e.g., Application as a Service, UML modeling tools as a service, social network as a service), and business cloud (e.g., business process as a service). According to the Research and Markets' Global Security Services Market 2015-2019 report, the market for security products and services is growing globally and demand for cloud-based security is leading the charge.

4.   **Information Security:** "The future in now" a common phrase used by the technology spearheads has now become a thing to believe in. A technology which has been in the womb for almost a decade has now started to evolve and get into a prime shape. "Internet of things", "Cloud Computing", "Big Data" & "Mobile Technologies" - technologies which have the potential to reshape the very rules which we have been fundamentally following to live is ready to go. From environment to security, from sales to logistics and from industries to home automation, these technologies have a wide range of applications which can sweep the humanity of their feet.

OBJECTIVE OF THE BOOK

The book aims to promote high quality research by bringing together researchers and practitioners from academia and industry. It is a national forum to communicate and discuss various research findings and innovations in the areas including big data analytics, mobile communication and mobile applications, distributed systems and information security

ORGANIZATION OF THE BOOK

The book is organized into twelve chapters. A brief description of each of the chapters follows:

Chapter 1 discusses the essence and the need for Cloud Security. Security threats like data leakage, data loss, account hijacking, abuse of cloud service exist which has been discussed with proven mechanisms. These mechanisms include identity and access management, role based access systems, firewalls, zoning, encryption, IDPS etc. The concept of Governance, and its importance in Cloud Security has also been explained briefly in this book chapter.

Chapter 2 presents a detailed experimental evaluation of energy consumption for two distinct classed of cryptographic protocols used in the cloud. This chapter also discusses how to identify the main parameters of the protocols that impact their energy consumption. Then, provide a set of practical recommendations, derived from our experimental study, for energy-aware security protocol design.

Chapter 3 provides a brief study on high dimensional features used by current steganalyzers. One of the best idea that chapter recommends is to improve the accuracy of detecting stego images is using a combination of features extracted from various domains of images.

Chapter 4 proposes steganographic techniques to ensure secured communication between any two ends and exploiting parallelism concepts in data embedding and decrypting. This chapter also suggests to implement the proposed techniques through OpenMP parallel library to parallelize the embedding of data, through which the performance can be improved.

Chapter 5 discuss the challenges of migrating from mobile computing to mobile cloud computing like code/computation offloading, task-oriented cloud services, elasticity and scalability, security, and cloud pricing. The author have provided a survey of existing solutions toward each of these challenges and suggested future research directions.

Chapter 6 provides an summary of mobile cloud computing - definitions, security, issues and advantages. Data integrity has been identified as an most important issue related to security risks of cloud as well as MCC. The author have also proposed a scheme to solve the problem of data security, especially data integrity.

Chapter 7 establishes the need of fog computing for processing IoT data. The author have provided a fair comprehension of the various aspects of fog computing with the benefits, challenges and applications. Then, an architecture for IoT data processing and comparison between cloud and fog has been portrayed. The chapter also provides a detailed discussion on how the IoT, fog, and cloud interact in an application framework.

Chapter 8 reviews the prediction and classification algorithms in data mining. Prediction and classification algorithms have been discussed with equivalent pros and cons. The performance evaluation of the algorithms has been carried out by the authors. The author also suggests that The process of extracting knowledge from the large database plays a wrestling role in all the application like Health care, education and Agriculture etc.

Chapter 9 presents semantics based indexing or modeling for the improvisation of document categorization accuracy rather than the traditional term-frequency model. The author also comments that the model proposes to build domain ontology for the textual content so that the problems like synonymy and polysemy in text analysis are resolved to greater extent. The author have also proven that LDA is the better feature extraction technique for text documents than TF or TF-IDF indexing technique.

Chapter 10 proposes an effective method for location-based advertising. The challenge is sending more relevant advertisements to mobile users based on the current and past travel patterns of the users and others. The author also takes the privacy concern into serious consideration, so the users will be willing to receive the advertisements.

Chapter 11 elaborates the usage of analyzing tools, processing tools and querying tools for Big database tools used for data analysis Big Data tools utilize numerous tasks, like Data capture, storage, classification, sharing, analysis, transfer, search, image, and deciding which might also apply to Big data.

Chapter 12 discusses the recent trends in the development of big data that applies in real time application perspectives like health care agriculture, education etc. The chapter describes about big data tools under batch processing, stream processing, and interactive analysis. The author also points out different challenging aspects of big data for development sub-coordinate with both ethical and technical.

P. Karthikeyan
Thiagarajar College of Engineering, India

M. Thangavel
Thiagarajar College of Engineering, India

Acknowledgment

The editors would like to acknowledge the help of all the people involved in this project and, more specifically, to the authors and reviewers that took part in the review process. Without their support, this book would not have become a reality.

First, the editors would like to thank each one of the authors for their contributions. Our sincere gratitude goes to the chapter's authors who contributed their time and expertise to this book.

Second, the editors wish to acknowledge the valuable contributions of the reviewers regarding the improvement of quality, coherence, and content presentation of chapters. Most of the authors also served as referees; we highly appreciate their double task.

P. Karthikeyan
Thiagarajar College of Engineering, India

M. Thangavel
Thiagarajar College of Engineering, India

Chapter 1
Role of Security Mechanisms in the Building Blocks of the Cloud Infrastructure

Kowsigan Mohan
Sri Krishna College of Technology, India

P. Balasubramanie Palanisamy
Kongu Engineering College, India

G.R. Kanagachidambaresan
Veltech Rangarajan Dr Sagunthala R&D Institute of Science and Technology, India

Siddharth Rajesh
Sri Krishna College of Technology, India

Sneha Narendran
Sri Krishna College of Technology, India

ABSTRACT

This chapter describes how security plays a vital role in cloud computing, as the name itself specifies the data can be stored from any place and can be owned by anyone. Even though the cloud offers many benefits such as flexibility, scalability and agility, security issues are still backlog the cloud infrastructure. Much research is being done on cloud security equal to the scheduling problems in the cloud environment. The customers under the cloud providers are very concerned about their data, which has been stored in the cloud environment. In this regard, it is essential for a cloud provider to implement some powerful tools for security, to provide a secure cloud infrastructure to the customers. Generally speaking, there are some foundational needs to be attained and some actions to be combined to ensure data security in both cloud, as well as, non-cloud infrastructure. This book chapter concentrates only on the security issues, security measures, security mechanisms, and security tools of the cloud environment.

DOI: 10.4018/978-1-5225-4044-1.ch001

INTRODUCTION

The Internet is definitely one of the greatest inventions in the history of humankind, if not the greatest invention. It is a fact everyone agrees on as it has made our lives simpler and has made the entire world, a global village. The Internet has ensured that we enjoy the privileges offered by it such as fast and efficient communication, access to knowledge at our fingertips and so many offers that are more exciting. Today there are more than a billion devices connected to the World Wide Web (www), i.e., the Internet that shows its growth and the number of computers or so-called nodes is destined to increase in the upcoming years.

Since the advent of the Internet, storage and accessibility of data have been two major factors bothering the users and hence storage of files on the internet, which could be accessible by only the allowed users, was an idea, before it became reality in the 1960's. Robnett Licklider is the inventor of Cloud Computing, which allows users to store files online in storages called Clouds. These files, which were stored in the cloud, could be accessed later on any time thus saving the space on the physical hard disk of the user's computer.

Cloud Computing

Cloud Computing (Armbrust et al., 2010) is the term used to describe the delivery of computing services such as servers, storage, software and more, all over the Internet. Companies which provide such services are called cloud computing vendors. Some of the major vendors are Amazon (EC2), Google (Google Cloud Storage, Drop box), HP (Enterprise Services Cloud-Compute), IBM (SmartCloud), Microsoft (Azure), etc. Many of the scheduling problems in the cloud environment can be solved by using soft computing techniques such as auto associative memory network (Kowsigan, Balasubramanie, 2016). Metaheuristic approaches can also be used to solve scheduling problems in the cloud environment (Kowsigan et al., 2017). Probability distribution was used to schedule the jobs in a cloud environment (Kowsigan et al., 2017).

Cloud computing is being used by almost all the users of the Internet. Even the simplest and most often used tasks such as sending emails, editing documents, listening to songs online, etc., use cloud computing behind the scenes. Here are a few uses of cloud computing:

- Making new services and applications
- Storing and retrieving data
- Analyzing data to make predictions
- Hosting websites and blogs
- To provide software on demand
- Streaming the videos and audio clips

Cloud Security

The worldwide cloud computing market is expected to grow to $191 billion by the year 2020. Although it is universally known and agreed that cloud computing has numerous advantages, there is no denial that there are absolutely no disadvantages. Despite the number of advantages far outnumbering the disadvantages, it is necessary to keep in mind that the disadvantages have to be taken care of. A breach in the data displays the inefficiency of the cloud security and can damage and/or manipulate the data of the user(s) of that cloud service. The most particularly troubling breach is the LastPass breach, which has concerned IT departments throughout the world. In this type of breach, the hacker can access the user's entire website and cloud service passwords. With knowledge of these passwords, especially those belonging to administrators of an enterprise with extensive permissions of an organization's critical infrastructure, a cyber-criminal could launch a devastating attack (Kandukuri, et al., 2009).

There are various cloud-computing security risks faced by IT organizations. A few of them are:

- Loss of intellectual property
- Violation of compliance
- Account hijacking
- Injection of malware
- Data breaches
- Diminished customer trust
- Revenue losses
- Hacked interfaces and APIs

Information Security

Information security is a term that includes a set of practices, which protect information from unauthorized access (Loeb, Gordon, 2002). In short, it means the practices meant to keep the user data safe by preventing unauthorized access to it, which can manipulate or destroy the data.

The sole purpose of information security is to provide us:

- Confidentiality
- Integrity
- Availability

Key Information Security Terminology

- Confidentiality, integrity and availability (CIA)
- Authentication, authorization and auditing (AAA)
- Defense-in-depth
- Velocity of attack
- Information assurance
- Data privacy
- Data ownership

Confidentiality

Confidentiality is one of the most essential goals of information security. It along with integrity and availability is usually known as the security triad. Confidentiality provides the required data secrecy and ensures granting access to only authorized users. If there were no confidentiality of data, any person in an organization would be access the data stored and easily manipulate/destroy it which would be a data breach. Data confidentiality is a term, which usually refers to the user's agreement to store and share data to a group of authorized individuals.

Integrity

While data confidentiality prevents unauthorized users from accessing the data, integrity, as the name suggests, keeps all the data together and ensures that any unauthorized user is not able to modify the contents or delete the data. Integrity also checks when an authorized user accesses the data and makes unauthorized changes to its contents, and prevents it from happening. The main objective of ensuring integrity is to detect and protect against unauthorized alteration or deletion of information. It is also referred to as "data quality".

Availability

Availability ensures that the unauthorized users do not have any kind of access to the compute, storage, network and data resources. Data availability can be described as a term, which refers to the process of ensuring that the information is always available to the authorized users, whenever and wherever they need it. Availability itself refers to the condition that the stored data can be accessed by its authorized users whenever and wherever they need to. If any authorized user is unable to access the data at any point, it directly indicates a flaw in the cloud management system.

Data availability is done usually by implementing data redundancy such that authorized users during both normal and disaster recovery operations can access the data. Storage area networks (SAN), Network attached storage (NAS) and RAID-based (Redundant array of independent disks) storage systems are popular storage management technologies for ensuring data availability.

Authentication

Authentication (Dinesha & Agrawal, 2002) in an ATM money withdrawal process is to ensure the identity of the person making that transaction. It is a mandatory safety regulation. Similarly, authentication in data is a process to ensure that the users are who they claim to be. There has to be authentication/ verification for all users to check if they are who they claim to be and not some outsider who is trying to access the data under the name of an authorized person. In fact, there have been such malicious attacks by highly skilled persons who have used the identity and information of authorized persons to access their data by either phishing or using Trojan viruses on their computers and then modify/delete the data. Authentication process asks credentials, which are compared to the ones, stored on a file in the database or within an authentication server and if they match, access is granted.

Single-factor and multi-factor are the two types of authentication. Single-factor authentication involves the usage of only one factor, such as a password. Example: email login process, which requires a password. Multi-factor authentication uses more than one factor to authenticate a user. It is also known as "two step verification" and provides an extra layer of security to the data.

Authorization

Authorization (Ronald L. Krutz, Russell Dean Vines, A Comprehensive guide to secure Cloud Computing) can be defined as the process of determining what type of access privileges is offered to an authorized user for a particular resource. There are different levels of authorization depending upon the data. Authorization is done only after authentication. Only an authenticated user is subjected to authorization. The most common authentication and authorization mechanisms used in data centers and cloud environments are

- Windows Access Control List (ACL)
- UNIX Permissions
- Kerberos
- Challenge-Handshake Authentication Protocol (CHAP)

Auditing

Auditing refers to the logging of all transactions for assessing the effectiveness of security mechanisms. It helps to validate the behavior of the infrastructure components and to perform forensics, debugging and monitoring activities.

Defense-in-Depth

Defense in depth is a strategy in which there are numerous layers of security deployed throughout the entire cloud infrastructure in order to protect the data (Byres, 2012). Even if one layer of security is compromised, there will be various other security layers a hacker will have to pass through before he or she can access the data protected. Defense in depth strategy is also called "layered approach" and mainly relies on the efficiency of multiple firewalls between the protected computer systems and the internet. There are many different layers such as data, application, host, and internal network, and perimeter, physical and procedural layer.

Velocity of Attack

Velocity-of-attack (Chang, Kuo, 2016, pp. 24-41) refers to a situation, where there is already an existing security threat in the cloud infrastructure that can spread rapidly and have a greater impact. A typical cloud environment features homogeneity and standardization in terms of the components such as hypervisors, virtual machine file formats and guest operating systems. Since a cloud environment has numerous components, hence sometimes a minor breach in any random system goes unnoticed. This minor breach then can grow quickly and access data from other systems and then lead to data loss or data corruption. Security threats can be amplified and allowed to spread quickly when there are too many components in an environment.

Mitigating Velocity-of-Attack

Mitigating velocity-of-attack in a cloud infrastructure is a herculean task as there are numerous components in the cloud. The only way to mitigate is by employing strong and robust security enforcement mechanisms, which will scan the entire cloud infrastructure for even minor breaches.

Information Assurance

All cloud consumers need an assurance that all the other consumers operating on that cloud are given permission to access the data which only they have the rights to, and not any random user's data (Chakraborty et al., 2010). In simple words, IA ensures the confidentiality, integrity and availability of the user's data stored in the cloud. Confidentiality restricts access by placing restrictions on classified corporate data. Integrity ensures that those who are authorized to do so can only access the data. Availability ensures that the data stored is ready for usage by the user(s) who are permitted to access it.

Data Privacy

Data privacy is one of the major problems of cloud users (Chen & Zhao, 2012). All cloud consumers fear their personal data being stolen or misused, hence making all cloud vendors give major importance to data privacy. It is also known as Information privacy. Data privacy can be controlled by employing data encryption at all levels and through data shredding. Data security is also required in wireless sensor network, which has been managed by cloud computing nowadays (Kowsigan et al., 2017). The companies can define data privacy as the appropriate usage of data, where the user's data is entrusted to them. Data Security can be defined as the act of ensuring the confidentiality, availability and integrity of data.

Data Ownership

Data ownership can be described as the act of having legal rights and full control over a single piece or set of data (Subashini, Kavita, 2011). He/she has the legal rights over the data and it is the user's right to access and modify the data. While creating data, which is to be stored on a cloud environment, the determination on who owns the data depends upon:

- Terms of service, as defined in the service contract
- Type of information
- Name of the country in which it is created and stored

Security Threats in a Cloud Environment

According to the Cloud Security Alliance (CSA), the top threats in a cloud environment in the world right now are as follows:

- Data leakage
- Data loss

- Account hijacking
- Insecure APIs
- Malicious insiders
- Denial of service
- Abuse of cloud services
- Insufficient due diligence

Data Leakage

Data leakage is a term used to describe unauthorized access of any confidential data by a hacker (Clark, Hunt & Malacaria, 2012). Unauthorized user in case of a breach can access the data, which is stored on the cloud infrastructure and then that confidential data once accessed by a hacker can be very easily manipulated and even destroyed from the cloud infrastructure. Unauthorized access to confidential data of a user can be obtained by any of the following:

- Exploitation of poor application design
- Poor encryption implementation on the cloud infrastructure
- Using a Trojan virus to compromise the password database and get the details
- Through a malicious insider who knows the security protocols well

Although data leakage is definitely a nuisance for both the user and the cloud vendor, there are control measures to avoid data leakage. Although there are many ways to prevent data leakage, the best way is data encryption. The converted form is known as a ciphertext, which is difficult to interpret and therefore increasing security and making it impossible for unauthorized users (attackers) to access the data. Data encryption at both ends makes the data very secure by converting it as a ciphertext rather than the conventional plaintext.

Data Loss

Data loss can happen in the cloud infrastructure due to various reasons also including malicious attacks (Pearson, Benameur, 2010). It is an error condition in information system. Data loss occurs mostly due to system or hardware malfunctions in the storage infrastructure, which produces changes (unintended) to the original data, which destroys the data. Data corruption is also known to be one of the causes of data loss, which occurs during storage and produces unintended changes to the original data. Luckily, there are ways to protect the data from data loss such as data backup and replication. The original data, which is stored on the cloud, can be stored in various storages including physical memory banks as a backup in case there is any data loss. In addition, it is very essential to replicate the data stored on the cloud infrastructure as it can be destroyed during a natural disaster. Here data redundancy using RAID-based (Redundant Array of Independent Disks) mechanisms can be used to replicate the original data. It is a very efficient way to replicate data and store it in various locations, which can be easily retrieved later in case of any data loss.

Account Hijacking

It is possible for accounts on any cloud infrastructure to be hijacked once the attacker has the necessary security credentials to create a breach. In cloud account hijacking, (Khorsed et al., 2012) the account(s) of a single user or an entire organization is stolen by an attacker. The account once hijacked, can be used by the attacker to access its data to perform malicious activity. Account hijacking is one of the major concerns for data security provided by the cloud vendor and can be devastating as it depends on what the hijacker(s) can use the stolen data for. It destroys the reputation and company integrity of the organization and the confidential data stored can be leaked or manipulated which will significantly cost the business and lose them many of their customers. There are also legal implications for organizations. For example, account hijacking in a healthcare organization will lead to the exposure of confidential data of their clients and patients, which would be a disaster for that organization. Phishing is a type of account hijacking attack using the principles of social engineering where the user is deceived. It is done typically be spoofing emails, which appear as genuine addresses but are in fact a link to fake addresses, which ask for login details. Once the details are given, they are captured by the attacker which can be used later to take over the user's account(s).

Insecure APIs

Application Programming Interfaces (APIs) are extensively used in cloud infrastructures in order to perform resource provisioning and orchestration activities. There are two types of APIs. They are:

- Open
- Closed

Open APIs are also known as public APIs. APIs allow the network owner to grant universal access to customers, mostly developers. A closed API is not openly accessible anywhere on the internet and is known as a private API.

Denial of Service (DOS) Attack

A denial of service attack (Kevin J. Houle & George M. Weaver, Trends in Denial of Service Attack Technology) prevents the users from accessing the services of the network infrastructure. DOS attacks can be targeted against computer systems, networks and storage resources. In simple words, DOS attacks are attacks on online services and making them unavailable to the users by flooding it with traffic from multiple sources. It is possible to determine when a DOS attack is underway through the following indications:

- Inability to reach a particular website, even in multiple attempts
- Decrease in the network performance when trying to open websites
- Higher than usual volume of spam email

Distributed Denial of Service (DDOS) Attack

Distributed denial of service (DDOS) is a variant of DOS attack. DDOS attack (Felix Lau & Stuart H. Rubin, "Distributed Denial of Service Attacks") occurs when multiple systems flood the bandwidth and/or resources of a targeted system. An example of DDOS attack is a botnet flooding a web server with traffic from multiple sources. DDOS attacks cannot be avoided or escaped from without employing high capacity, stable and secure internet channels and distributed hardware equipment, which is clearly unaffordable by small businesses making these attacks un-avoidable as they are very expensive. Typical targets of DDOS attacks include financial institutions, e-commerce sites, news and media sites, public sectors and even entire countries.

Malicious Insiders

Cloud vendors are well aware of the number of threats issued by attackers, which are mostly outside the company, however insider attacks also occur, which are known as malicious attacks and are much more difficult to contain, as the insider would know the cloud infrastructure, required passwords, etc. Countermeasures such as firewalls and malware protection systems can minimize the risk of attacks from outsiders but it does not pose any kind of risk for an insider as he or she is familiar with the countermeasures and can easily pass through them and access the data. The various control measures to prevent such insider attacks are:

- Strict access control policies
- Regular security audit
- Disabling employee accounts immediately after contract termination
- Data encryption on both sides
- Role based access control
- Performing background checks on candidate before hiring them (Background investigation)

Abuse of Cloud Services

Cloud computing is indeed a boon to both customers and service providers, due to the several advantages it offers. However, individuals who perform illegal or unauthorized activities (Krutz & Vines, 2010) can misuse the services provided. Certain users who do not intend to use it for good purposes can use cloud services nefariously, which makes it one of the top threats identified by the Cloud Security Alliance (CSA). Cloud resources are often misused by performing unauthorized activities such as cracking an encryption key and by distributing pirated software. Many users mostly use the trial services offered by cloud vendors for their products and then use pirated software instead of buying original licensed software. In most cases, pirated software is not just used but also distributed which severely affects the sales of the original software, as most people in the world prefer to use free pirated software instead of paying for it when it is available free of cost.

Insufficient Due Diligence

Cloud Vendors must pay due diligence towards understanding the complete scope of the undertaking, while offering the customers with the cloud services. For example, in a hybrid cloud environment, where a cloud service provider connects to one or more cloud infrastructure(s) to leverage their capabilities, complete understanding of operational responsibilities is required. These responsibilities include incident response, encryption, governance, compliance, and security monitoring. Insufficient due diligence towards understanding these responsibilities may increase risk levels. Similarly, understanding operational responsibilities is very essential when a service provider may act as a broker by connecting to multiple cloud service providers to integrate their capabilities and offer services to the consumers. This risk can be reduced by thoroughly understanding and evaluating the cloud providers' services and their terms, and ensuring they provide security controls that can satisfy the consumers' security need. Further, it is important to understand the consumers' risk profile to ensure that the risks involved are within acceptable levels.

Case Study on Cloud Security Threats

Attack on Amazon EC2 cloud (Mosca, Wang, Zhang, 2014). Amazon's EC2 cloud was attacked in the year 2009. The Zeus Trojan horse was used to infect the machines and gain access through some other vulnerable domain. The cybercriminals behind the attack also plugged into Amazon's RDS (Relational Database Service) as backend alternative in case they failed to gain access to the original domain. Google, Facebook, Twitter, etc. have also experienced similar threats.

Existing Technologies in Cloud Security

RSA is a computer and network security company, founded in the year 1982. It is known for its security products like SecureID, which has experienced a phenomenal change in the last decade. Its products include threat detection and response, RSA SecureID suite, fraud prevention system, etc. Similarly, many other companies also provide cloud security services.

RSA SecureID

Identity and access management is an important assessment tool in order to permit or restrict an authority from accessing the data. The solution for this problem is provided by RSA SecureID suite. The fact that makes it stand apart is that it separates the concepts of access management and authentication. To access a resource, a user must combine both security PIN and a token code. This gives double assurance in terms of checking the identity of the authority trying to access the data.

RSA Adaptive Authentication

It is an authentication system, which measures the login as well as post-login activities by evaluating risk indicators. It provides transparent authentication by protecting online web portals, mobile applications, browsers, ATM's, SSL's and web-access management applications.

VMware Vcloud Networking and Security

It virtualizes networking and security to a greater agility, efficiency and extensibility in the data centre. It delivers software-defined networks and security with a broad range of services. The services include virtual firewall, virtual private network, load balancer and VXLAN.

Cloud Access Security Broker

A Cloud Access Security Broker (CASB) is cloud-based software, which sits right in-between the cloud service users and the cloud infrastructure, monitors all the activities, and enforces various security policies. A CASB can provide security services or management services as well as both.

IBM Dynamic Cloud Security

IBM Dynamic Cloud security offers protection from threats in the cloud environment through a range of solutions. It spans SaaS, laaS and PaaS, which is designed to work together with the organisation's existing security system and provide extra protection to the data. It also offers identity and access management, application, data security and security intelligence.

McAfee Cloud Security

McAfee allows organisations to customise their own security protocols. This further enables clarity, transparency and consistency. Constant data monitoring ensures regular checks on the critical data transfers. Deployment of this security mechanism could take place in a public, private or a hybrid cloud.

CipherCloud

Data transfer is made more secure through various approaches like malware detection, encryption, tokenisation, data loss prevention etc. Keys are generated and stored which provides authentication, which is further useful in businesses, which may encounter a series of risks. Thus, sensitive data could be safeguarded from threats.

Importance of Security Mechanisms at Various Levels of the Cloud Infrastructure

The Security Mechanisms are classified as administrative and technical. Administrative security is one, which is enabled by default and comprises of the standard procedures and policies to control the safe execution of operations. It activates the settings that enable a protection to the servers from an unauthorized access. Technical security also highlights the protection and authentication of sensitive data, which is prone to theft and is usually implemented through tools or devices deployed on computer systems, networks or storage. Security mechanisms in cloud infrastructure is deployed at three levels (Saini & Saini, 2014). They are:

- Compute level
- Network level
- Application level

Security mechanism at compute level includes security at a physical level i.e. to a server or a hypervisor. Security is provided to the hypervisor, as it is vulnerable to an attack. Security measures also include VM isolation and hardening which involves the changing of default settings. Antivirus should be implemented as well as updated.

Security mechanism(s) at network level includes a virtual firewall, which establishes a secure link between the VM's. This also ensures a secure traffic between the machines. An internal network could be vulnerable to attacks if exposed to an external network. Thus, a Demilitarized Zone (DMZ) is deployed which sets an additional logical or physical layer of security. Full disk encryption could be a method to provide security to the data-at-rest that resides at a particular location.

At application level, security of hardware and software must never be compromised. An intrusion detection system could be implemented which can be server-based, network-based or even an integrated system, which implements both a server based and network-based detection system.

Key Security Mechanisms

The key security mechanisms can broadly be classified as the following:

- Physical security
- Identity and access management
- Role-based access systems
- Network monitoring and analysis
- Firewall
- Intrusion detection and prevention system
- Port binding and fabric binding
- Virtual private network
- Virtual LAN and Virtual SAN
- Zoning and iSNS discovery domain
- Security hypervisor and management server
- Virtual machine hardening
- Securing operating systems and applications
- LUN masking
- Data encryption
- Data shredding

Authorization

Different types of job functions or entities access different type of data. However, each application service is logically separated from each other. Thus, should provide an efficient mechanism for accessing and control. Different entities are authenticated which further restricts accessibility and sharing of files and folders by other anonymous users. Types of authorization include Windows ACLs, UNIX permissions and OATH.

Windows ACLs

Access Control Lists (Yu et al., 2010) comprise of the set of rules that specify the access permissions given to users. A list involving the access control entries (ACEs) further identifies the trustees and highlights the rights given to them respectively. It can contain two types of ACLs: a DACL and a SACL.

If an object has a discretionary access control lists, access permissions are allowed explicitly by the access control entries in the DACLs. If the system does not have DACLs, the access permission is granted to everyone i.e. full access is given. If there are no ACEs in the DACLs, no permission is given to access to anyone. SACLs are used for implementing wider security policies for actions such as logging or auditing resource access. It creates an audit record when there is the access attempt either is successful or fails.

UNIX Permissions

These common permissions (Allison et al., 1998) depict whether a group, an owner and everyone else have the permission to read, write or execute a file. The access rights given to the users allow them to view, modify and also execute the contents of the file system.

OAuth

It (Hammer-Lahav, 2010) is an open authorization mechanism that allows a client to access protected resources from a resource server rather than accessing it from the resource owner. The entities that are

Figure 1. OAuth pictorial description

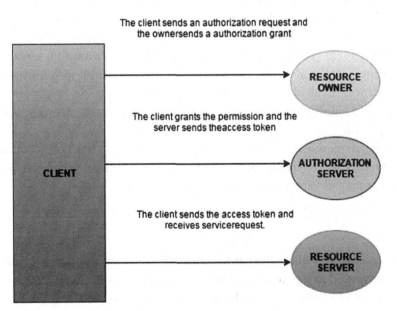

involved in authorization are the resource owner, the resource server, the client and the authorization server. The resource owners can authorize a third-party access to the information without exchanging any other credentials.

Authentication

It is a mechanism, which determines the user's credentials are compared to those given in a database. The process is carried out, if the credentials match otherwise the process is halted. It enables authentication among the clients and the servers. The types of authentication used are multi-factor authentication, CHAP, Kerberos, etc. Authentication is essential in order to safeguard data and to monitor its usage.

Multi-Factor Authentication

It is the process of granting access to a user by extracting several pieces of evidence depicting their identity. It can be something they know, something they own or something they are broadly classified as knowledge, possession and inherence (Quian, Lu, 2012).

Kerberos

It was created by MIT. It provides a solution to network security issues. A strong authentication is provided by using a secret-key cryptology. It is generally used for a client-server application. Encryption of communication is done in order to ensure private and secure data transmissions. A client and a server prove their identity using Kerberos. It can also be useful between server-server transmissions. Kerberos is very flexible, efficient and secure (Neumann, 1994).

Challenge Handshake Authentication Protocol

CHAP is a method, which is used to authenticate a user or a network to an authenticating entity by utilizing a private code. It is used periodically to verify the identity by a 3-way handshake.

A link is established between the initiator and the target. The initiator sends a "challenge message "or asks to initiate the login. The target sends a CHAP challenge (Simpson, 1994). The initiator reciprocates with a value calculated using "one-way hash" function and returns to the target. The target checks and compares with a calculated value of its own. If the hash values match, the authentication is acknowledged else the connection is terminated. At random intervals, the target sends a new challenge and this cycle is repeated.

The CHAP algorithm requires the password to be the length of at least one octet and also it should be a strong one, which cannot be easily guessed by anyone. A central server can be established in order to examine the responses and values.

OpenID

It is promoted by a non-profit foundation named OpenID Foundation. It is a mechanism in which one existing account can be used to sign in multiple websites. It does not require creation of new passwords for different websites. It is an open and standardized authentication protocol. The user has to create an account by selecting an OpenID identity provider. It is also a decentralized protocol i.e. it does not rely on any central authority to authenticate user's ID.

Role Based Access Control

This mechanism is useful in multiuser computing function. It is an approach where permission is given based on the individual's roles or job function (Sandhu, 1994). In an organization, roles are created based on qualification, responsibility and other criteria. Additionally, these roles can also be reassigned. Permissions and restrictions both are assigned to the specific roles as the system is upgraded or new system or applications are incorporated. Separation of duties is used to ensure that no single individual is able to specify an action as well as carry it out at the same time. Only certain roles are assigned certain privileges of performing the task associated with that role. Roles are considered a more stable concept in an organization than a task or a function.

Network Monitoring and Analysis

Network monitoring and analysis is a mechanism in which provides a detection of network failure or performance problems and further protect from such problems (Anderson et al., 2006). It is done in order to extract information about the type of data packets being transmitted, the uploading and downloading speeds, the data utilization etc. Any activity or transmission of malicious data packets can be identified and stopped from harming the system. This can be performed in two ways. They are:

- Active monitoring
- Passive monitoring

Active monitoring includes tools that can transmit data between two monitored ends. Passive monitoring depicts the information about a link or a device collected by probing the link or device. Active monitoring injects "test" traffic into the network whereas passive monitoring system is more of an observational test to analyze the already established network. Mechanisms used to monitor, detect and prevent the attacks are Firewalls, IDPS and network analysis systems.

Firewall

It is a security mechanism which is used to examine the data packets traversing a network and compare them with a set of filtering rules. It can either be hardware, software, or both. It is an essential part of the intranet security and is deployed at network level, compute level or a hypervisor level. It can also be used for the internal portion of organization's internal network, which implies protection from internal attacks. Its main function is to analyze the incoming packets and permit/restrict them, according to the configuration.

Intrusion Detection and Prevention System (IDPS)

IDPS is a process, which analyses the events of intrusion and prevents them. It is in fact, a security tool, which is used to automate the entire process of detecting and preventing events that can compromise the confidentiality, integrity, or availability of resources. There are two detection techniques. They are signature-based detection technique and anomaly-based detection technique. The signature-based detection technique scans for signatures to detect an intrusion event but is only effective for known threats. Anomaly-based detection technique scans and analyses events to detect if there are any abnormal events taking place. It can detect various events such as multiple login failures, excessive network bandwidth consumed by an activity. An anomaly based detection technique is able to detect most of the new attacks as these new attacks deviate from the already existing protocols. IDPS is implemented at three levels i.e. compute system level, network level and hypervisor level. The components of an IDPS include a sensor or an agent, a management server, a database server and a console. IDPS at network levels is used to monitor and analyze the network traffic, network devices and application protocol behavior. It is deployed in the form of appliance or software on the computer system and is usually isolated from malicious applications on computer systems. IDPS at hypervisor levels is used to monitor anomalies in a hypervisor.

Port Binding and Fabric Binding

Port binding limits the devices that can be attached to a specific switch port. It is rather the configuration, which determines the timing, and the destination of the message sent or received. It is supported in two environments. Firstly, FC SAN which maps a WWPN to a switch port. The WWPN login is rejected when illegitimate host is connected. Secondly, the Ethernet maps MAC and IP address of a computer system to a switch port. Fabric binding allows binding at the switch level. Additionally, it can used along with port and port-type locking capabilities.

Virtual Private Network (VPN)

It is the process, which provides an encrypted tunneling of the traffic. It can used to privatize and encrypt the flow until destination is reached. It extends a consumer's private network across a public network such as the Internet and enables the consumer to apply their internal network's security to the data transferred over the VPN connection (Ledesma, 2004).

There exist two methods to establish a VPN connection. They are:

- Remote access VPN connection
- Site-to-site VPN connection

In a remote access VPN connection, the remote client works by initiating a remote VPN connection request, which is gradually authenticated by the VPN server that grants access to the cloud network. In a site-to-site VPN connection, the remote site works by creating a site-to-site VPN connection and then access to the cloud network is granted by the server. There are two types of site-to -site VPN connection. They are:

- Intranet based
- Extranet based

Virtual LAN and SAN

A Virtual LAN (Yuasa, 2000) is software used to provide multiple networks in a single hub. VLAN has many advantages over LANs such as performance, simplicity, cost and security. They are widely used as they promise scalability and better security policies. Virtual SAN is provided by VMware, which gives the freedom of pooling our storage capabilities. VSAN is used as it reduces the cost and facilitates an easier storage and better management.

Zoning and iSNS Discovery Domain

The logical segmentation of node ports into groups is referred to as Zoning. Port zoning is used to reduce the risk of WWPN spoofing as it also provides higher security levels. In port zoning, we only work with switch domain or port number implying an efficient and easier use of it.

Internet Storage Name Service (iSNS) is a protocol that is used for automated configuration, management and discovery of iSCSI on any network. It functions identically to FC zones and enables a grouping of devices in an IP-SAN. Few benefits of iSNS include centralized management, scalability and flexibility.

Securing Hypervisor and Management Server

The security of the cloud depends upon the security of the hypervisors, which support their VMs. Compromising the hypervisor security places all VMs at risk. An attacker can access the information by attacking the hypervisor, as it is the backbone of any cloud infrastructure.

The control measures are given below as follows:

- Install security-critical hypervisor updates
- Harden hypervisor using specifications provided by CSI and DISA
- Restrict core functionality to only few selected administrators

Virtual Machine Hardening

It is a process used to change the default configuration of a VM. It removes or disables the devices that are not required. For example, disabling of the USB ports or CD/DVD drives. It is used to tune the configuration of VM features to operate in a secure manner such as disallowing changes to MAC address. In order to know the security baselines, VM templates should be hardened.

Securing Operating Systems and Applications

- Hardening OS and application
- Sandboxing

Hardening OS and Applications

Though anti-viruses and other protections cater to the needs of the system's security, they do not fulfill the complete needs of the operating system, in terms of protection. The main aim of system hardening is to provide better security and to prevent attacks. This is mainly done by the removal of unimportant or non-essential software, which may act as a gateway for the attackers to exploit the system. It may include reformatting the disks, configuring the components as per a hardening checklist provided by CIS and DISA. Benefits of hardening of OS include cost reduction as removal of non-essential software or hardware results to saving of money.

Sandboxing

Sandboxing is a mechanism, which tests non-trusted codes. It provides a tightly controlled set of resources on which the application executes. By implementing this, we can reduce or eliminate various risks, as it concentrates on damage containment. Most of the codes we run are sandboxed, for example, the web pages, the browser plug-in content, the mobile apps, etc.

LUN Masking

Logical Unit Numbering masking (H. Yoshida," LUN Masking", 1999) is a process, which deals with the assignment of numbers to ports. Thus, access is authorized to certain ports and unauthorized to the other. It refers to the assignments of LUNs to specific host bus adapter worldwide. However, more commonly at Host Bus Adapters (HBA) ports and are vulnerable to attacks. It improves management levels. Stronger variant of LUN masking uses source Fiber Channel address. In FC SAN, access controls done through zoning. These are used to identify the ports. In a cloud infrastructure, LUN masking can set policies at physical storage array and prevent data loss or intrusion.

Data Encryption

It is very important to protect our confidential data from hackers as there lays a threat of manipulation as misuse of it. Therefore, data is encrypted. Encryption (D. Coppersmith, "Data Encryption", 1994) simply means conversion of data. It is a cryptographic method by which data is encoded and made indecipherable to eavesdroppers or hackers. It is done for confidentiality and security reasons.

Data Shredding

It is impossible to also recover data from deleted files and folders. In order to prevent this, data shredding is implemented. Even emptying the system's recycle bin does not solve the issue of data theft. Data shredding is the process of deleting files and making them unrecoverable. Techniques for shredding data stored on tapes include overwriting tapes with invalid data. This primarily highlights the conversion of bit patterns i.e. 0's and 1's. This would make the recovery of the data stored previously in the disk hard.

Upcoming Security Mechanism Trends in Cloud Computing

Physical security deals with the implementation of measures to secure sensitive data. Deployment of these physical controls is useful in order to safeguard data from theft and provide an easy surveillance.

It is rather the foundation of IT security strategy. The upcoming technological trends in cloud computing promise better security. They are:

- **Securing Server-less Processes:** It involves the implementation of micro-services and virtual machines.
- **Security Through AI and Automation:** Artificial Intelligence and automation could be used to leverage the security by implementing predictive security postures across public, private and SaaS cloud infrastructure.
- **Micro-Segmentation:** It involves the usage of an identity management strategy to locate the end-point before it has any network visibility.

Security as a Service

Along with data comes the responsibility to secure it, efficiently and widely. This should also include the cost effectiveness and making it less vulnerable to attacks. According to the "Cloud Security Alliance", Security as a Service refers to the provision of security services via the cloud either to the cloud-based infrastructure and the software or from the cloud to the customer's on-premise systems. It enables the consumer to reduce the capital expenditure on security deployments and they also have a control on the security policies that are to be implemented.

Introduction to GRC

Data integrity can be maintained only by the trust between a Cloud Service provider (CSP) and a Cloud Service user (CSU). There need to be an appropriate check and maintenance of the information provided. GRC is the term which helps the organization ensure that its acts are ethically correct.

Governance

Cloud Governance highlights the implementations of policies by which an institution can be directed. Governance ensures the policies are agreed-upon and that the data is maintained properly and managed well. IT governance not only maintains a good database but also develops the understanding between the strategies set in by the providers and the infrastructure provided. The basic IT governance principle is to focus on policies related to managing and consuming cloud service.

Risk Management

Any business objective is accompanied by risks or an uncertainty. It is not possible to eliminate risks, but they can be managed. A systematic process needs to be followed to evaluate the consequences of each step, which is followed. This process is known as risk management. It includes the mechanism to assess the assets or data, evaluating its worth and creating a risk profile that is rationalized for each information asset across the business. The outages restrict the user to access the data for a certain amount of time but can cost the user heavily. Therefore, a framework needs to be designed to evaluate the cloud computing

Figure 2. Four corner stones of risk management

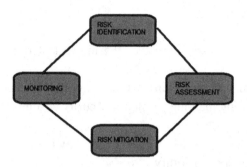

risks. The four key steps of risk management include risk identification, risk assessment, monitoring and risk mitigation. Risk identification is used to identify the source of the threat. Once the risk is identified, it is essential to assess and analyze the risk. Further, there are measures to be taken to minimize its impact. Thus, mitigating the risk is an important step that involves planning and deploying security mechanisms. After the securing of the system, it is necessary that we monitor the risk and its affects.

Compliance

The act of adhering to the laws, regulations and procedures is known as compliance. It demonstrates the act of embracement of the policies and demands of the service provider, the consumer 's demand and/or the demands of participating cloud providers. These policies may vary from one type of cloud to another i.e. public, private and hybrid. The primary purpose of compliance is to analyze the provider's policies so that it understands the controlling of it. There are two types' compliance policies that control IT operations i.e. internal policy compliance and external policy compliance. The internal policy compliance controls the nature of IT operations within an organization, whereas the external policy compliance controls the nature of the IT operations outside the organization. The compliance levels may differ based upon the type of information, business and so on.

CONCLUSION

The essence and the need for Cloud Security is discussed in this book chapter. The inclination of enterprises to the cloud for data storage is growing exponentially. This comes only with the trust that the data stored would be secure. Though there are many advantages of cloud computing, a breach in the data displays the inefficiency of the cloud security. Security threats like data leakage, data loss, account hijacking, abuse of cloud service exist which can be tackled only by implementing the above said and proven mechanisms. These mechanisms include identity and access management, role based access systems, firewalls, zoning, encryption, IDPS etc. Deployment of these security mechanisms ensure that the data will be stored in a secure manner in the cloud. The vulnerability to data theft can be reduced. The concept of GRC and its importance in Cloud Security has also been explained briefly in this book chapter. Concisely, the maintenance and security of data is the responsibility of the user who needs to choose the appropriate mechanism to safeguard it.

REFERENCES

Allison, B., Hawley, R., Borr, A., Muhlestein, M., & Hitz, D. (1998). File System Security: Secure Network Data Sharing for NT and UNIX. *Network Appliance, 16.*

Anderson, B. D. O., & Vongpanitlerd, S. (1973). *Network Analysis and synthesis.* Prentice-Hall.

Armbrust, M., Fox, A., Griffith, R., Joseph, A. D., Katz, R., Konwinski, A., ... Zaharia, M. (2010). A view of cloud computing. *Communications of the ACM, 53*(4), 50–58.

Byres, E. J. (2012). *Defense in Depth. InTech Magazine.* Nov-Dec.

Chakraborty, R., & Reddy, S. (2010, March). The Information Assurance Practices of Cloud Computing Vendors. *IT Professional, 12*(4), 29–37. doi:10.1109/MITP.2010.44

Chang, V., Kuo, Y. H., & Ramachandran, M. (2016). Cloud computing adoption framework: A security framework for business clouds. *Future Generation Computer Systems, 57,* 24–41.

Chen, D., & Zhao, H. (2012). Data Security and Privacy Protection issues in Cloud Computing. In *International Conference on Computer Science and Electronics Engineering.* 10.1109/ICCSEE.2012.193

Clark, D., Hunt, S., & Malacaria, P. (2002). Quantitative Analysis of the leakage of Confidential Data. Elsevier Electronic Notes in Theoretical Computer Science, 59(3), 238-251.

Coppersmith, D. (1994). The Data Encryption Standard (DES) and its strength against attacks. IBM journal of research and development, 38(3), 243-250. doi:10.1147/rd.383.0243

Dinesha, H. A., & Agrawal, V. K. (2012, February). Multi-level authentication technique for accessing cloud services. In *2012 International Conference on Computing, Communication and Applications (ICCCA).* IEEE. doi:10.1109/ICCCA.2012.6179130

Gordon, L. A., & Loeb, M. P. (2002). The economics of information security investment. *ACM Transactions on Information and System Security, 5*(4), 438–457.

Hammer-Lahav, E. (2010). *The OAuth 1.0 Protocol.* Internet Engineering Task Force.

Houle, K. J., & Weaver, G. M. (2001). *Trends in Denial of Service Attack Technology (v1.0).* Carnegie Mellon University.

Kandukuri, B. R., & Rakshit, A. (2009, September). Cloud security issues. In *IEEE International Conference on Services Computing SCC '09* (pp. 517-520). IEEE. doi:10.1109/SCC.2009.84

Khorshed, M. T., Ali, A. S., & Wasimi, S. A. (2012). A survey on gaps, threat remediation challenges and some thoughts for proactive attack detection in cloud computing. *Future Generation Computer Systems, 28*(6), 833–851.

Kowsigan, M., & Balasubramanie, P. (2016). An Improved Job Scheduling in Cloud Environment using Auto-Associative-Memory Network. *Asian Journal of Research in Social Sciences and Humanities, 6*(12), 390–410.

Kowsigan, M., Kalicharan, S., Karthik, P., Manikandan, A., & Manikandan, R. M. (2017). An Enhanced Job Scheduling in Cloud Environment Using Probability Distribution. *IACSIT International Journal of Engineering and Technology*, *9*(2), 1374–1381.

Kowsigan, M., Rajkumar, S., Seenivasan, P., & Kumar, C. V. (2017). An Enhanced Job Scheduling in Cloud Environment using Improved Metaheuristic Approach. *International Journal of Engineering Research and Technology*, *6*(2), 184–188.

Kowsigan, M., Rubasri, M., Sujithra, R., & Banu, H. S. (2017). Data Security and Data Dissemination of Distributed Data in Wireless Sensor Networks. *International Journal of Engineering Research and Applications*, *7*(3 part 4), 26–31.

Krutz, R. L., & Vines, R. D. (2010). *Cloud security: A comprehensive guide to secure cloud computing.* Wiley Publishing.

Krutz, R. L., & Vines, R. D. (2010). Cloud security: A comprehensive guide to secure cloud computing. Wiley Publishing.

Lau, F., Rubin, S. H., Smith, M. H., & Trajkovic, L. (2000). Distributed denial of service attacks. In 2000 IEEE International Conference on Systems, Man, and Cybernetics (Vol. 3, pp. 2275-2280). IEEE. doi:10.1109/ICSMC.2000.886455

Ledesma, S., Aviña, G., & Sanchez, R. (2008). Practical considerations for simulated annealing implementation. In *Simulated Annealing*. InTech.

Lu, H. K. (2014). U.S. Patent Application No. 13/729,070.

Mosca, P., Zhang, Y., Xiao, Z., & Wang, Y. (2014). Cloud Security: Services, Risks, and a Case Study on Amazon Cloud Services. *International Journal of Communications. Network and System Sciences*, *7*(12), 529.

Neuman, B. C., & Ts'o, T. (1994, September). Kerberos: An authentication service for computer networks. *IEEE Communications Magazine*, *32*(9), 33–38. doi:10.1109/35.312841

Pearson, S., & Benameur, A. (2010). Privacy, Security and Trust Issues Arising from Cloud Computing. In *IEEE Second International Conference on Computer Science and Technology*. 10.1109/CloudCom.2010.66

Rajeshkumar, J., & Kowsigan, M. (2011). Efficient Scheduling in Computational Grid with an Improved Ant Colony Algorithm. International Journal of Computer Science and Technology, 2(4), 317-321.

Saini, H., & Saini, A. (2014). Security Mechanisms at different Levels in Cloud Infrastructure. International Journal of Computer Applications, 108(2).

Sandhu, R. S., Coyne, E. J., Feinstein, H. L., & Youman, C. E. (1996). Role-based access control models. *Computer*, *29*(2), 38–47.

Simpson, W. A. (1996). *PPP challenge handshake authentication protocol.* CHAP.

Subashini, S., & Kavita, V. (2011). *A survey on security issues in service delivery models of cloud computing. Elsevier Journal of Network and Computer Applications.*

Yoshida, H. (1999). *LUN security considerations for storage area networks (Paper-XP, 2185193).* Hitachi Data Systems.

Yu, S., Wang, C., Ren, K., & Lou, W. (2010, March). *Achieving secure, scalable, and fine-grained data access control in cloud computing. In 2010 proceedings IEEE Infocom.* IEEE.

Yuasa, H., Satake, T., Cardona, M. J., Fujii, H., Yasuda, A., Yamashita, K., . . . Suzuki, J. (2000). U.S. Patent No. 6,085,238. Washington, DC: U.S. Patent and Trademark Office.

KEY TERMS AND DEFINITIONS

Authentication: The process of validating someone's identity.

Authorization: An act of granting permission to somebody.

Cloud Security: The set of rules, regulations and policies that are created to adhere to compliance rules to protect enterprises assets like data, information associated with cloud.

Data Encryption: The translation of the data into another form so that a third party cannot understand or extract it.

Data Loss: The information stored is destroyed, due to various reasons in an error condition.

Data Privacy: An aspect which considers the fact whether the data could be shared a third party or not.

Integrity: The maintenance and the assurance of the accuracy and the consistency of data.

Chapter 2
Energy Optimization in Cryptographic Protocols for the Cloud

Swapnoneel Roy
University of North Florida, USA

Sanjay P. Ahuja
University of North Florida, USA

Priyanka D. Harish
University of North Florida, USA

S. Raghu Talluri
University of North Florida, USA

ABSTRACT

In this chapter, we study the energy consumption by various modern cryptographic protocols for the cloud from the algorithmic perspective. The two categories of protocols we consider are (1) hash functions and (2) symmetric key encryption protocols. We identify various parameters that moderate energy consumption of these hashes and protocols. Our work is directed towards redesigning or modifying these algorithms to make them consume lesser energy. As a first step, we try to determine the applicability of the asymptotic energy complexity model by Roy on these hashes and protocols. Specifically, we try to observe whether parallelizing the access of blocks of data in these algorithms reduces their energy consumption based on the energy model. Our results confirm the applicability of the energy model on these hashes and protocols. Our work is motivated by the importance of cryptographic hashes and symmetric key protocols for the cloud. Hence the design of more energy efficient hashes and protocols will contribute in reducing the cloud energy consumption that is continuously increasing.

DOI: 10.4018/978-1-5225-4044-1.ch002

INTRODUCTION

Motivation to consider energy efficiency in delivering information technology solutions for the Cloud comes from: 1) the usage of data centers in the Cloud with strong focus on energy management for server class systems; 2) the usage of personal computing devices in the Cloud such as smartphones, handhelds, and notebooks, which run on batteries and perform a significant amount of computation and data transfer; and, 3) Cloud providers expecting to invest in equipment that will form an integral part of the global network infrastructure. On the other hand, information security has become a natural component of all kinds of technology solutions for the Cloud. Security protocols consuming additional energy are often incorporated in these solutions. Thus, the impact of security protocols on energy consumption needs to be studied. Ongoing research in this context has been mainly focused on energy efficiency/consumption on specific hardware and/or different systems/platforms. Very little is known or has been explored regarding energy consumption or efficiency from an "applications" perspective, although apps for smartphones and handhelds abound.

Cryptography has evolved from the earliest forms of secret writing to current era of computationally secure protocols, addressing range of security issues. In modern age, cryptography is not only about encryption, but it has larger objective of ensuring data protection from adversary's activities. Scope of modern cryptography also includes techniques and protocols to achieve authentication, nonrepudiation, and integrity objectives. Complexity of cryptology methods and its applications have continuously increased and evolution of computers has given a completely new dimension to this. Now cryptography problems/algorithms are measured in terms of computational hardness. In this journey, cryptography has always received a threat of getting obsolete because of rapidly increasing computational capabilities.

However, cryptography techniques still have great relevance and importance for the cloud, and the cloud enabled industry to keep them protected from dynamically changing threat scenarios (Jasim et al., 2013; Li et al., 2013; Somani et al., 2010; Li et al., 2010; Muñoz et al., 2016).

Energy has become a first-class parameter now days. This has been triggered with the ever-increasing energy generation by the data centers, and with the advent of the hand-held battery-driven devices like laptops, PDAs, etc. Cryptographic protocols have become an integral part of these devices to make them secured. Also, the cryptographic protocols are generally very expensive in terms of their energy consumption. Therefore, especially for hand held devices, the protocols drain out a lot of battery power while operating. A network flooding attack with the intention of causing a simple denial of service by depleting the battery life of the device has been illustrated in (Salerno et. al 2011). They show that these flooding attacks can be carried out utilizing a smartphone as the aggressor in order to attack other mobile devices and that the procedure for such attacks is not difficult. A simple tool has been developed in order to carry out these attacks and to show that even though these attacks are relatively simple, they can have profound effects.

Therefore, the necessity of reducing the energy consumption of cryptographic protocols comes into picture. As mentioned, we have considered two classes of cryptographic protocols to implement a parallelism technique based on the energy model of (Roy et al., 2013) that leads to reduction in their energy consumption.

Objectives of This Chapter

This research illustrated in this chapter makes a few key contributions. We first, present a detailed experimental evaluation of energy consumption for two distinct classed of cryptographic protocols used in the cloud. The first is the hash functions in which we cover MD2, MD5, SHA-1, and SHA-2 hashes. The second is symmetric key encryption in which we cover Blowfish, DES, 3DES, and AES ciphers. Our work experimentally validates the applicability of the energy model proposed in (Roy et al., 2013) on these classes of cryptographic protocols. We also present a generic way to achieve any desired degree of memory parallelism for a given protocol (hash or symmetric key), which can be employed by software engineers to implement energy efficient cryptographic protocols. We observe that the increased parallelism reduces running time along with energy. Second, we identify the main parameters of the protocols that impact their energy consumption. Our final contribution is a set of practical recommendations, derived from our experimental study, for energy-aware security protocol design.

BACKGROUND

Work has been done to show that hash functions are computationally intensive and are used in mobile devices. In this (Damasevicius et al., 2012) paper, the authors have analyzed the energy efficiency versus quality characteristics of several hash functions. They perform Avalanche and Chi-square test to analyze the energy usage in Java-enabled smart phone. With the result obtained, the authors propose the best cryptographic and non-cryptographic algorithms that can be used in mobile devices (Damasevicius et al., 2012).

The impact of various parameters at the protocol level (such as cipher suites, authentication mechanisms, and transaction sizes, etc.) and the cryptographic algorithm level (cipher modes, strength) on overall energy consumption for secure data transactions has been investigated in (Potlapally et al., 2003). Based on their results, the authors discuss various opportunities for realizing energy-efficient implementations of security protocols. Further work on these lines has been done in (Toldinas et al., 2015; Potlapally et al., 2006; Elminaam et al., 2010; Prasithsangaree et al., 2003; Kaps & Sunar 2006; Nie et al., 2010).

However, in our opinion, the recommendations proposed above for energy reductions in cryptographic protocols though very nice, stop short of making energy minimization a primary goal of security protocols design. In other words, the works do not address the questions: "(1) How do we design secured cryptographic protocols that are energy optimal? (2) How do we modify existing cryptographic protocols to make them energy optimal?" The main impediment for pursuing this direction is a to prove the applicability of a realistic model of energy consumption at the algorithm design by (Roy et al., 2013) on some of these protocols. We believe that our work will complement this body of existing work.

Cryptography and the Cloud

Data in motion and data at rest are best protected by cryptographic techniques. Any data that is hosted by cloud providers should be protected with encryption. This is because when data is hosted in the cloud users does not have physical control over their data. So cryptographic measures are needed to secure data in the cloud with cryptographic keys in the control of the cloud user. This is more so for any confidential data relating to medical and financial applications. To secure data at rest in the cloud a cloud user may encrypt data before uploading to cloud storage or they may rely on the cloud provider to encrypt data for them when the cloud provider receives it, with the former being the preferred approach. At the very least a cloud provider needs to provide encrypted connections such as HTTPS or SSL to ensure that data is secured in transit. A comprehensive platform for cloud security also needs to have strong access controls and key management capabilities (Lord, 2017). A challenge in cloud-based cryptography has to do with the key management process because data has to be able to be decrypted in the cloud in order to execute the functions that a cloud user needs to have performed and then re-encrypted for storage. Data should remain encrypted up to the moment of use and that both the decryption keys and the clear-text versions of the data should be available in the clear only within a protected transient memory space. Another option is to use homomorphic encryption to perform operations on encrypted data without decryption as proposed by Ustimenko et al in (Ustimenko & Wroblewska, 2013). In this case the cloud user initiating the request can only decrypt the retrieved encrypted data. Searchable encryption is another approach that allows the user not only to retrieve data privately but also to search it in the cloud (Agudo et al., 2011).

Energy Optimization in Clouds

Energy is a big factor in cloud computing environments. High energy costs and huge carbon footprints are incurred due to the massive amount of electricity needed to power and cool the numerous servers hosted in cloud data centers. The increasing energy consumption of the cloud raised concerns about the impact on CO_2 emissions and global warming. Placing VMs in data centers that use green energy sources is an important way to mitigate this problem. There is a need to shift focus from optimizing data center resource management for pure performance alone to optimizing for energy efficiency while maintaining high service level performance. An efficient solution is to use green clouds, which provides a power efficient model at the data center level of cloud environments (Ahuja & Muthiah, 2017). Green Cloud computing is envisioned to achieve not only efficient processing and utilization of computing infrastructure, but also minimize energy consumption. As a solution to reduce power usage and carbon emission, a middleware tool "Green Cloud Broker", which is intermediate between the cloud users and providers, that facilitates managing, responding and providing services to end users (Thakur & Chaurasia, 2016). The broker maintains information like carbon emission level of a system and greener cloud for the request service. It analyzes user requirements, calculates cost and carbon footprint of services, and performs carbon aware scheduling. The various modules involved are scheduler, task selector, cost calculator, application profile, green resource information database, and carbon emission calculator. The green cloud middleware architecture looks for greener clouds and processes the service request by computing the schedule with the lowest carbon emission based on application requirements.

General Computing Techniques for Energy Optimization

In this section we briefly survey the work done in energy optimization in various levels of computing. We divide the levels into Hardware, Virtual Machines, Operating Systems, System Software, and Application. However, we point out the work done in a particular level is of both kinds. There has been work done in a particular level which treat the other levels as black boxes; while there also has been work done in a particular level, which is very much inter related with another level, and cannot really be categorized as work on a single level.

Hardware

A recent hardware level work by (Ranganathan et. al, 2006) on energy optimization has been mostly the budgeting of power consumption over several heterogeneous systems (termed an ensemble of systems). Their work was the first to manage and enforce a peak power budget across a server ensemble, e.g., a blade enclosure. In their work, they discuss algorithms to redistribute the power budget in two contexts: 1. Strict constraints for power delivery; 2. Looser constraints for heat dissipation.

They use the notion of setting and enforcing a power budget, but their work differs from the prior work e.g. (Brooks & Martonosi, 2001), and (Felter et al., 2005) in its focus on trends across multiple systems, and, all these optimizations can be used together on future systems. Prior to their work, at a single-server level, (Brooks & Martonosi, 2001) proposed setting a thermal threshold and enforcing it from a cooling point of view while (Felter et al., 2005) suggest dynamic shifting of power within the processor and memory components of a single server.

At a cluster level, (Femal & Freeh 2004) discuss how, for a given cluster power budget, one can choose different permutations of the quantity and size of individual nodes to better improve throughput, by optimizing for the different power-performance efficiency curves. Individual nodes are responsible for determining their power limits and the environment assumes an explicit trust model between nodes. Other previous work has evaluated algorithms to turn off or turndown individual servers when they are not used (Chase et al., 2001). These have been mainly focused on reducing electricity consumption in such environments.

Many papers have studied the resource demand profiles of competing workloads through time in order to evaluate the performance impact of resource sharing. For example, one recent study examines several workloads and concludes that overbooking resources for a shared hosting platform may increase a hosting provider's revenue while meeting probabilistic service level agreements (Urgaonkar et al., 2002).

Ranganathan et al., use a similar idea to constrain the power budget for a shared ensemble of servers, with little performance impact. Their use of dynamic voltage scaling to throttle CPU power consumption dynamically is similar to GRACEOS (Yuan & Nahrstedt, 2003), which profiles CPU usage in conjunction with soft real-time CPU scheduling to conserve battery power while bounding missed deadlines. They leverage a similar insight at the OS level: all processes will not demand cycles at the same time.

Virtual Machines

In this section, we mainly focus on explaining a recent technique called server consolidation (Verma et al., 2009) to reduce the energy costs of a data center. We also mention about related work along these lines.

Server consolidation tries to maximize the utilization of available server resources all of the time. This involves techniques like co-locating applications, perhaps in individual virtual machines. Thus, it allows for a reduction in the total number of physical servers, minimizes server sprawl as well as the total data center space requirements.

Server consolidation can be loosely broken into static, semi-static and dynamic consolidation. In static consolidation, applications (or virtual machines) are placed on physical servers for a long time period (e.g. months, years), and not migrated continuously in reaction to load changes. Semi-static refers to the mode of consolidating these applications on a daily or weekly basis. On the other hand, dynamic consolidation spans a couple of hours and requires a runtime placement manager to migrate virtual machines automatically in response to workload variations. (Verma et al., 2009) is the first such work on consolidation that utilizes correlation between workloads in a systematic way for determining the most effective static consolidation configuration.

In (Verma et al., 2009), the authors present the first systematic server workload characterization of a large data center from the perspective of medium (semi-static) or long-term (static) consolidation. They study the distribution of the utilization and occurrence of the peak utilization on servers relative to various percentiles and average metrics. They discover that the tail of the distribution does not decay quickly for most servers implying that sizing applications based on average utilization has high degree of risk. They further observe significant correlation between applications hosted on different servers. They make the important observation that certain metrics like the 90-percentile as well as cross correlation between applications are fairly stable over time. They next use the insights obtained from their workload characterization to design two new consolidation methodologies, namely: 1. Correlation Based Placement (CBP), 2. Peak Clustering based Placement (PCP).

They implement the methodologies in a consolidation-planning tool and evaluate the methodologies using traces from a live production data center. Their evaluation establishes the superiority of the proposed algorithms in their work. They also bring out the various scenarios in which each methodology is effective and show how to tune various parameters for different workloads.

Prior and contemporary to the work of (Verma et al., 2009), the existing research in workload modeling can be classified into 1. Aggregate workload characterization, 2. Individual server utilization modeling. Aggregate workload characterization of a web server by (Iyenger et al., 1999) and workload models of a large-scale server farm by (Bent et al., 2006) fall in the first category. Individual server utilization has been studied in (Bobroff et al., 2007). Bohrer et al., (2002) use peak-trough analysis of commercial web servers to establish that the average CPU utilization for typical web servers is fairly low. Similar observations on the peak-trough nature of enterprise workloads have been made in (Gmach et al., 2007). In (Bobroff et al., 2007), the authors perform trace analysis on commercial web servers and outline a method to identify the servers that are good candidates for dynamic placement.

Operating System

Managing power and thermal issues has been addressed extensively for single platforms, particularly their processor components. (Brooks & Martonosi, 2001) propose mechanisms to enforce thermal thresholds on the processor. For memory-intensive workloads, dynamic voltage and frequency scaling (DVFS) during memory-bound phases of execution has been shown to provide power savings with minimal performance impact. Solutions based on this premise include hardware-based methods (Li et al., 2003) and OS-level techniques that set processor modes based on predicted application behavior (Isci et al., 2006. Power budgeting of SMP systems with a performance loss minimization objective has also been implemented via CPU throttling (Kotla et al., 2005).

Another work by (Nathuji et al., 2007) in this area called the VirtualPower approach to online power management attempts to 1. Support the isolated and independent operation assumed by guest virtual machines (VMs) running on virtualized platforms, 2. Make it possible to control and globally coordinate the effects of the diverse power management policies applied by these VMs to virtualized resources. To attain these goals, VirtualPower extends to guest VMs 'soft' versions of the hardware power states for which their policies are designed. The resulting technical challenge is to appropriately map VM-level updates made to soft power states to actual changes in the states or in the allocation of underlying virtualized hardware. An implementation of VirtualPower Management (VPM) for the Xen hypervisor addresses this challenge by provision of multiple system-level abstractions including VPM states, channels, mechanisms, and rules.

System Software

A recent survey by (Albers, 2010) discusses various theoretical techniques in the system software (and application) levels to reduce energy consumption. We highlight some of these techniques in this section.

Power Down Mechanisms

We all have encountered this if we have a computer. If we leave out computer idle, it goes into a sleep mode. The system consumes low power while in this mode. The following natural question arises: Is it possible to design strategies that determine such thresholds and always achieve a provably good performance relative to the optimum solution? This section discusses certain algorithmic techniques that attempt to address this question.

The above power management problem is an online problem, that is, at any time a device is not aware of future events. More specifically, in an idle period, the system has no information when the period ends. Is it worthwhile to move to a lower-power state and benefit from the reduced energy consumption, given that the system must finally be powered up again at a cost to the active mode? An algorithm ALG is compared with the optimal offline algorithm OPT in this setting. Online algorithm ALG is called c-competitive if for every input, such as, for any idle period, the total energy consumption of ALG is at most c times that of OPT.

For systems with two states (an active or a sleep), we have a deterministic and a randomized online algorithm in the literature. The deterministic algorithm has a competitive ratio of 2 and this ratio of 2 is provably optimal for any deterministic online algorithm for this problem. The randomized algorithm however achieves a competitive ratio of 1.58 (Karlin, 1994). For systems with more than two states, again it has been proved that the best a deterministic algorithm achieves is a ratio of 2. There is an advanced probabilistic algorithm, which achieves a ratio of e/(e-1) (Irani ei. al., 2003).

Dynamic Speed Scaling

If a processor runs at speed s, then the required power is s^α, where $\alpha > 1$ is a constant. Obviously, energy consumption is power integrated over time. The goal in dynamic speed scaling is to dynamically set the speed of a processor so as to minimize energy consumption, while still providing a desired quality of service.

We refer the reader to (Albers, 2010) for a detailed description of some problems and techniques on scheduling, which arose from dynamic speed scaling. The problems include:

1. Scheduling with Deadlines
2. Minimizing Response Time
3. Extensions of the above

Another prominent area of such theoretical system software development mentioned in (Albers, 2010) is a wireless network. The reader is again referred to the paper for details.

Application

Energy optimization from the application or algorithms perspective has been first modeled by (Roy et al., 2013) where the authors proposed an energy complexity model to bind the energy consumption of an algorithm in terms of its input size. Their model was later extended by (Tran & Ha, 2016) to cover multi-threaded processors.

ENGINEERING CRYPTOGRAPHIC ALGORITHMS FOR ENERGY EFFICIENCY

This section describes the general techniques to engineer the protocols to make them energy efficient.

The Energy Complexity Model

An asymptotic energy complexity model for algorithms was proposed in (Roy et al., 2013). Inspired by the popular DDR3 architecture, the model assumes that the memory is divided into P banks (M_1, M_2, ..., M_p) each of which can store multiple blocks of size B. Each bank M_i has its own cache C_i that can hold exactly one block. A block can be accessed only when it is in the cache of the bank it belongs to. Therefore, only one block of a particular bank can be accessed at a particular time. But P blocks in P different memory banks can be accessed in parallel. The main contribution of the model in (Roy et al., 2013) was to highlight the effect of parallelizability of the memory accesses in energy consumption. In particular, the energy consumption of an algorithm was derived as the weighted sum T+(P*B)/I, where T is the total time taken and I is the number of parallel I/Os made by the algorithm. However, this model measures the energy consumption asymptotically and in particular, ignores constants in order to derive the simple model above.

P-Way Parallelism for Blocks

In the both classes of cryptographic algorithms we consider for energy efficiency (hashes and symmetric key), the input (plaintext) is in a vector form, and it is divided into blocks of a given size B, which are then processed. In this section, we describe a generic technique we adopt to parallelize the input blocks to the cryptographic algorithms based on the results in (Roy et al., 2014).

Figure 1. The energy complexity model

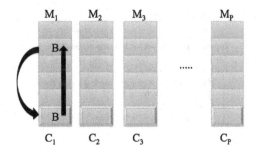

Given any input data (vector), we created a logical mapping, which ensures access to the vector in P-way parallel fashion, where P ranges from 1 to 8. As we mentioned before, the input data (vector) for both the classes of algorithms are accessed block-wise with predefined sized blocks. Consider an input vector V size of N. Our mapping function logically converts V into a matrix M of dimensions (N/B)*B, where B is the size of each block.

We then define a page table vector T of size N/B that contains the ordering of the blocks. The ordering is based on the way we want to access the blocks (P-way would mean a full parallel access). Picking blocks with jumps populates the page table. For a 1-way access, we select jumps of P ensuring the consecutive blocks are in the same bank. For a P-way access, we selected jumps of 1 i.e. the blocks are picked from banks in round robin order. Figure. 2 presents an example with 4-way and 2-way parallel access.

The division of the input into blocks is done differently for hashes and symmetric key algorithms respectively. The specifics of the mappings for each of them will be discussed when we illustrate each one in detail.

Figure 2. Memory layout for achieving various degree of parallelism for P=4

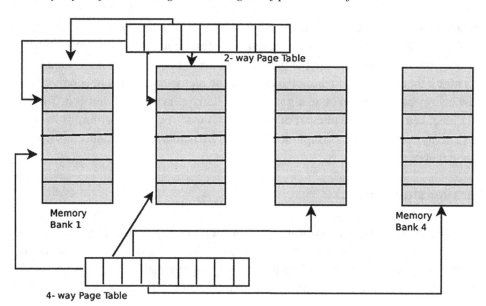

Figure 3. The function to create an ordering among the blocks

```
Input: Page table vector V, jump amount jump.
factor = 0;
for i = 0 to N/B - 1 do
    if i > 1 and ((i × jump) (mod N/B) = 0) then
        factor = factor + 1;
    end
    Vi = (i × jump + factor) (mod N/B);
end
```

Code Optimization

As the memory layout scheme is implemented on top of the algorithm, it might lead to additional overhead, negatively impacting the energy savings. Hence, we incorporated some optimization techniques to reduce this overhead.

- **Usage of Spatial Locality:** For every memory access we need to call the map function, which creates an overhead. We used the concept of Spatial Locality (consecutive elements in a logical stride are placed on consecutive memory locations) to reduce the overhead.
- **Bit Shifts:** We replaced operations like multiplication, division and mod with bit shifts wherever possible.
- **Register Variables:** To reduce runtime, we utilized Register variables when a variable had to be computed numerously.

The benchmark code was written in C and was compiled using gcc compiler.

Experimental Setup and Methodology

The two sets of cryptographic protocols we chose to experiment on are hashes and symmetric key encryption protocols.

Protocols Studied

We considered a mix of hashes and symmetric key protocols. We experimented on a few old ones, and the most recent ones.

Our experiments are primarily designed to test whether the energy model of (Roy et al., 2013) is applicable to these protocols. In other words, can we observe a variation in the energy consumption of these protocols by varying the degree of parallelism of their inputs? Hence, we implement variants of the protocols that allow us to use 1, 2, 4, or 8 memory banks in parallel on DDR3 memory with 8 memory banks.

Below we list the benchmarks used in this study.

1. **Hashes:** The hashes we consider are MD2, MD5, SHA-128, and SHA-256.
2. **Symmetric Key Protocols:** The protocols we consider are Blowfish, DES, 3-DES (triple DES), and AES.

Each experiment has been repeated 100 times and the means are reported in this work. The variations in the energy readings that is, deviations from the average values were small (less than 4%) for all the experiments performed.

Hardware Setup

The experiments were run on a Mac notebook with 4 Intel cores, each of which operates at a frequency of 2 GHz. The laptop has 4GB DDR3 memory with 8 banks and is running Mac OS X Lion 10.7.3. The sizes of L2 Cache (per Core), and L3 Cache are respectively 256 KB and 6 MB. The disk size of the machine is 499.25 GB. During any experimental run, all non-essential processes were aborted to ensure that the power measured by us could be attributed primarily to the application being tested. We measured the (total) power drawn using the Hardware Monitor tool (Software-Systeme, 2015) which include the processor power, memory (RAM) power, and a background (leakage) power. The Hardware Monitor tool reads sensor data directly from Apple's System Management Controller (SMC), which is an auxiliary processor independent of the main computer. Hence, energy consumed by the monitoring infrastructure does not add to the sensor readings, ensuring that the reported measurements are fairly accurate.

Calculation of Energy Consumption by Each Algorithms

Based on the model described, the total energy consumption for each algorithm is calculated by taking the product of the execution time of the algorithm and the total power consumed by the algorithm during its execution (obtained from Hardware Monitor reading).

The Hash Functions

Table 1 lists the hashes considered along with the sizes of their output, and any known vulnerabilities.
    The output sizes specifications suggest, the output is always of that size irrespective of the size of the input.

P-Way Parallelism for Hashes

Energy optimal algorithms proposed in (Roy et al., 2013) require data to be laid out in memory with a controlled degree of parallelism. We first propose a way to ensure desired memory parallelism for a given input M to the hash algorithm.

Merkle–Damgård Construction

All of the hashes we consider (MD2, MD5, SHA-1, and SHA-2) are based on the Merkle–Damgård construction (Damgård 1990; Merkle 1990).
    In this construction, the given input M is padded with a few bits at the end to make it a multiple of a chosen block size B. Applying a chosen function f on each block, and combining the result then produce the hash.

Table 1. The hash functions considered

Hash	Output Size (bits)	Vulnerabilities
MD2	128	Preimage and collision.
MD5	128	2^{64} complexity collision.
SHA-1	160	2^{80} complexity collision.
SHA-256	256	None.

As described in Figure 4, the algorithm starts with an initial value, the initialization vector (IV). The IV is a fixed value (algorithm or implementation specific). For each message block, the compression (or compacting) function f takes the result so far, combines it with the message block, and produces an intermediate result.

The last block is padded with zeros as needed and bits representing the length of the entire message are appended.

Implementing the Parallelism

For the message M, which is a multiple of blocks of B bytes, we created a logical mapping, which ensures access to the blocks in P-way parallel fashion, where P ranges from 1 to 8.

More specifically, when P=1, (almost) all the blocks of B bytes are clustered in a single bank. While for P=8, the blocks are evenly spread across all 8 banks to ensure the maximum degree of parallelism of the access to the input (M). We also experiment for P=2, and P=4.

To achieve the above, we create a mapping function, which maps the physical input M into the logical input that defines the degree of parallelism (Figure 5). In other words, we define an ordering among the blocks of B bytes, which defines the logical input (and the degree of parallelism). We change the order of processing of the blocks to ensure the change in parallelism of the input M. So e.g. for 1-way parallelism, every eight consecutive block accesses would be in the same bank; whereas for 8-way parallelism, every eight consecutive block accesses would be spread across the 8 different banks.

Symmetric Key Encryption Protocols

Table 2 lists the symmetric key protocols considered along with the sizes of their input blocks, keys, and any known vulnerabilities.

P-Way Parallelism for the Symmetric Key Protocols

Each of the protocols considered (Blowfish, DES, 3-DES, and AES) are block ciphers operating on fixed-length groups of bits, called blocks (of size B), with an unvarying transformation that is specified by a symmetric key.

Figure 4. The Merkle–Damgård construction

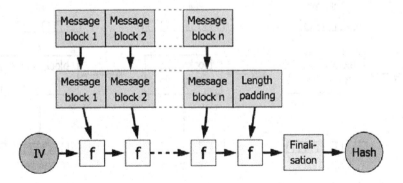

Figure 5. Implementing parallelism for hashes

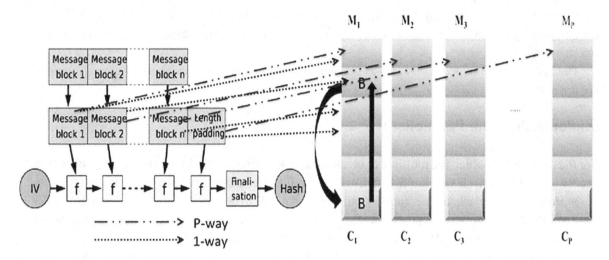

Table 2. The symmetric key protocols considered

Protocol	Input Block Size (bits)	Key Size (bits)	Vulnerabilities
Blowfish	64	32-448	Weakness in key selection
DES	64	56	Brute forcing over keys
3-DES	64	168	Computationally inefficient
AES	128	128, 192, 256	None

Figure 6 describes how each of the protocols (block ciphers) work.

Implementing the Parallelism

We treat each symmetric key algorithm (protocol) as a black box. Given an input M, the protocol divides M into blocks of B bytes and processes each block for encryption to produce the ciphertext (Figure 6).

Figure 6. Block ciphers

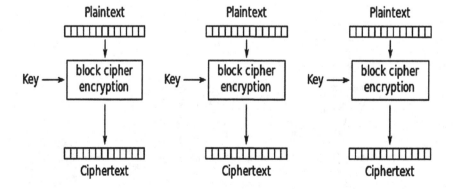

For the message M that is a multiple of blocks of B bytes, we created a logical mapping, which ensures access to the blocks in P-way parallel fashion, where P ranges from 1 to 8. More specifically, when P=1, (almost) all the blocks of B bytes are clustered in a single bank. While for P=8, the blocks are evenly spread across all 8 banks to ensure the maximum degree of parallelism of the access to the input (M). We also experiment for P=2, and P=4.

To achieve the above, we create a mapping function, which maps the physical input M into the logical input, which defines the degree of parallelism. In other words, we define an ordering among the blocks of B bytes, which defines the logical input (and the degree of parallelism). We change the order of processing of the blocks to ensure the change in parallelism of the input M.

Figure 7. Implementing parallelism for symmetric key protocols

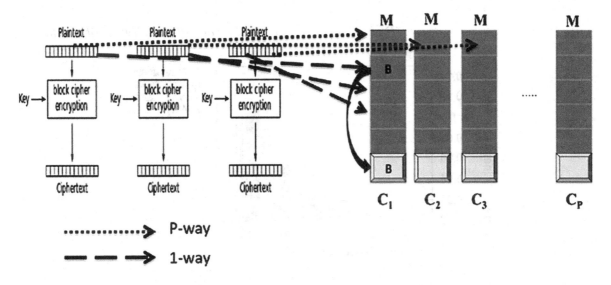

Figure 8. Energy consumption by MD2 hash for various input sizes on different degrees of parallelism

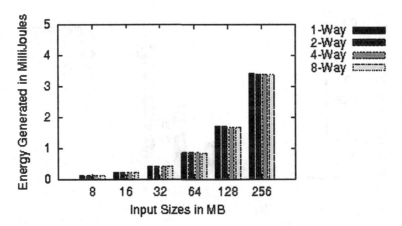

Effect of Parallelism on Hash Functions

In our first set of experiments, we compare the hash functions MD2 and MD5. We observe (Figure 8 and Figure 9) that memory parallelism has significant impact on energy consumption for MD2 and MD5. That is, we observe that energy consumption of these hashes decreases with the increase in the degree of parallelism of the blocks. This is in line with energy model proposed in (Roy et al., 2013). Interestingly the MD5 hash shows more significant reductions in energy consumption for different degrees of parallelism.

Next, we compare the hash functions SHA-1 and SHA-2. (Figure 10 and Figure 11) show a similar trend in the energy consumption as before that is again along the expected lines with the energy model of ~ (Roy et al., 2013).

Figure 9. Energy consumption by MD5 hash for various input sizes on different degrees of parallelism

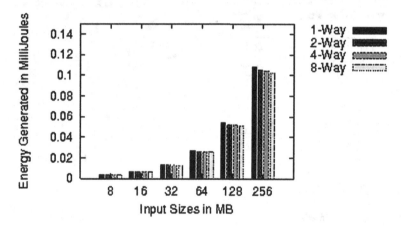

Figure 10. Energy consumption by SHA1 hash for various input sizes on different degrees of parallelism

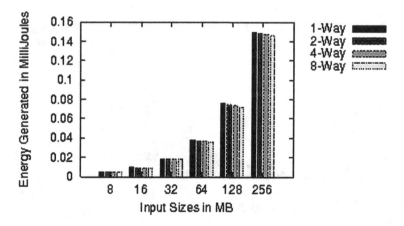

Figure 11. Energy consumption by SHA2 hash for various input sizes on different degrees of parallelism

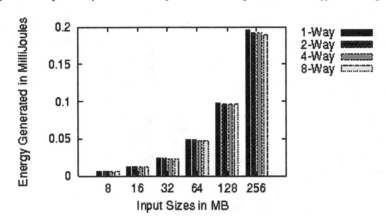

Effect of Parallelism on Symmetric Key Encryption Functions

For the symmetric key protocols, we first compare the DES and 3DES. We observe (Figure 12 and Figure 13) that memory parallelism again has significant impact on energy consumption for DES and 3DES. Also, as expected 3DES consumes about thrice the amount of energy DES consume

Next we compare the symmetric key protocols AES and Blowfish. (Figure 14 and Figure 15) show a similar trend in the energy consumption as before that is again along the expected lines with the energy model of~(Roy et al., 2013). We use a 256-bit key for AES in the experiments.

For symmetric key protocols in general the variations in energy consumption is bigger for larger size inputs (e.g. 256 MB); whereas we see little variations for small inputs (e.g. 8MB). This is due to the fact that small size inputs fit into the caches nullifying the effect of memory parallelism in the RAM on the energy consumption. Also, in general, the energy consumption variations seem to work better for the symmetric key protocols than on the hash functions.

Figure 12. Energy consumption by DES for various input sizes on different degrees of parallelism

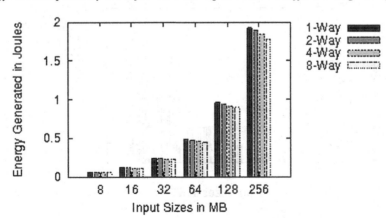

Figure 13. Energy consumption by 3DES for various input sizes on different degrees of parallelism

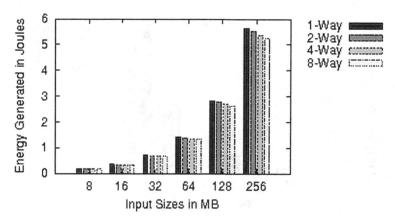

Figure 14. Energy consumption by AES for various input sizes on different degrees of parallelism

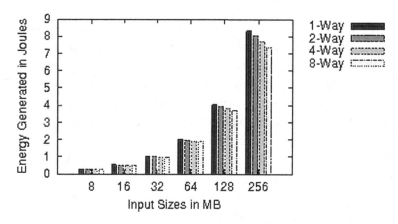

Figure 15. Energy consumption by Blowfish for various input sizes on different degrees of parallelism

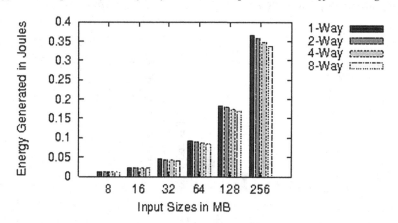

Comparison of Energy Consumed

We also compare the energy consumed by various hash functions, and symmetric key protocols.

As we see from Figure. 16, MD2 consumes way more energy than the other three, which consumes comparable amount of energy. For the symmetric protocols, (Figure. 17), AES consumes more energy than 3DES because of the fact we work with a 256 bit key for AES as compared to a 168 bit key for 3DES. The interesting observation is how light Blowfish is in terms of energy consumption.

ANALYSIS OF RESULTS

Applicability of the Energy Complexity Model

Our experimental study establishes variations in energy consumed for both the classes of cryptographic algorithms with the variations in parallelization of their block accesses. Overall, these results establish

Figure 16. Energy consumption by hashes for a fixed input size

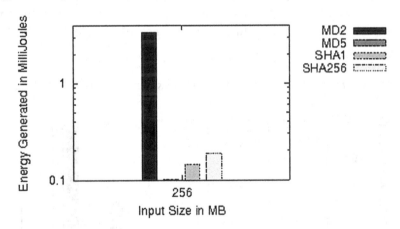

Figure 17. Energy consumption by symmetric key protocols for a fixed input size

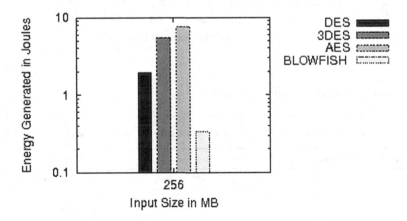

the applicability of the energy complexity model proposed in (Roy et al., 2013) on these classes of cryptographic algorithms. One of the key aspects highlighted by our experiments is the reduced impact of parallelism, when the input data is small. This was due to the fact that smaller inputs fit into the cache. The memory controller then applies smart techniques to perform write backs to make the accesses more efficient (esp. during low parallelism), and in the process, negates the effect of parallelism.

Analysis for Hashes

With the applicability of the energy model established we further conducted micro experiments to compare the energy consumption of SHA-2 during our best case of parallelism, (8-way) with that during we have no parallelism at all (Figure 18).

We see differences in energy consumption, but the difference at the moment is not very significant. However, as before, the difference becomes more significant with larger inputs. Hence, we can conclude that if the data is large, using the 8-way parallel technique is more energy efficient than not using any parallelism at all (just the regular implementation).

Recommendations for Hash Usage

Figure 16 shows MD5 to be the most efficient in terms of energy consumption. But from Table 1, we know MD5 is vulnerable to the collision attack, whereas no vulnerabilities for SHA-2 are currently

Figure 18. Energy consumption of SHA-2 with no parallelism and 8-way parallelism

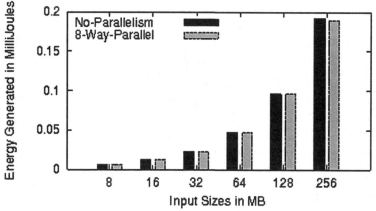

Table 3. Time required performing collision attacks

Hash	Vulnerabilities	Time Required at 10^9 Comparisons/s	Time Required at 10^{13} Comparisons/s
MD5	2^{64} complexity collision.	2^{64} ns $\approx$ 584.5 years	6 months
SHA-1	2^{80} complexity collision.	2^{80} ns $\approx$ 3.83*10^7 years	38000years
SHA-2	None	--	--

known. To further investigate if MD5 might be still usable to conserve energy in some places (and it is still in use), we estimated the numbers in Table 3.

What we would like to conclude from the numbers is, the reason why MD5 is still in use is it is not very likely for any adversary to have a supercomputer of the capacity to perform the collision attack on it in a reasonable amount of time (based on the numbers we get). Hence, we recommend the use of MD5 over SHA-2 to conserve energy if the user is mostly sure of the strength of the probable adversary.

Analysis for Symmetric Key Protocols

In a similar way, we further conducted micro experiments to compare the energy consumption of AES during our best case of parallelism, (8-way) with that during we have no parallelism at all (Figure 19).

Again, we see differences in energy consumption, but the difference at the moment is not very significant. However, as before, the difference becomes more significant with larger inputs. Hence, we can conclude that if the data is large, using the 8-way parallel technique is more energy efficient than not using any parallelism at all (just the regular implementation).

Recommendations for Symmetric Key Protocols Usage

Figure 17 shows Blowfish to be the most efficient in terms of energy consumption. But Blowfish becomes computationally intense when it comes to key replacement. We have not conducted how expensive is the key replacement for Blowfish in terms of energy consumption. We would recommend the usage of Blowfish over the other protocols if the user were not required to change the keys too often.

Hashes vs. Symmetric Key Protocols

There is a fundamental difference in how we parallelized the hashes and the symmetric key protocols. In case of the hashes, the parallelization of the block is done inside the hash function in the phase of the Merkle–Damgård construction, where the blocks are formed and accessed. Whereas in case of the symmetric key protocols, we do the parallelization of the blocks before they are applied for encryption

Figure 19. Energy consumption of AES with no parallelism and 8-way parallelism

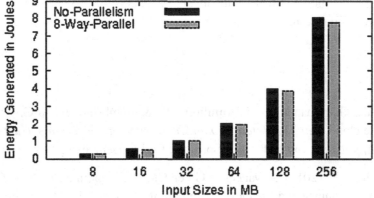

(as a preprocessing phase). Comparing the results of hashes with that of the symmetric key protocols, we observe, the parallelization for the symmetric key protocols appear to be more effective. In other words, the symmetric key protocols exhibit larger variations in energy consumption than the hashes by applying parallelization.

CONCLUSION AND FUTURE RESEARCH DIRECTIONS

To summarize, we have proved the applicability of the energy model by~(Roy et al., 2013) on two important classes of cryptographic protocols, which is our main result. Additionally, we have discovered a few things that might be instrumental towards designing energy aware secured cryptographic protocols. A few questions worth pursuing are:

1. Can we develop more efficient techniques to parallelize block accessed in hashed and symmetric key protocols?
    a. **Using Meta-Blocks:** To throw some light on this point, the machine we used had a version of DDR3 RAM where the banks had a block size of 256 bits. Therefore, a single block of DES (size of 64 bits) AES (size of 128 bits) does not entirely fill up a single block in the memory banks. We define a meta-block to be formed of one or more blocks. Therefore, for example in the case of AES, we could work with meta-blocks of size 256 bits, where each meta-block would contain two AES blocks. We believe this additional level of abstraction to help further reduce the energy consumption in symmetric key protocols.
2. Is the energy model by~(Roy et al., 2013) applicable on public key protocols?
    a. Public key protocols depend on the computational hardness of one-way functions like modular-exponentiation or elliptic curve cryptography (ECC). It will be interesting to investigate whether we can parallelize computations for those operations, and whether parallelization reduces energy consumption in public key protocols like RSA or Diffie-Helman.
3. We have only considered encryptions for the symmetric key protocols. Do the decryption techniques for these protocols show the similar results?
    a. Decryption process in some symmetric-key ciphers (e.g. DES) is exactly the same operation(s) as encryption. But ciphers like AES have different decryption operation(s) than encryption. We have applied the energy model to the encryption processes of the symmetric-key ciphers, our belief is the model will be applicable to the decryption processes as well, and we expect to observe similar results.

REFERENCES

Agudo, I., Nuñez, D., Giammatteo, G., Rizomiliotis, P., & Lambrinoudakis, C. (2011, June). Cryptography goes to the cloud. In *FTRA International Conference on Secure and Trust Computing, Data Management, and Application* (pp. 190-197). Springer, Berlin, Heidelberg.

Ahuja, S. P., & Muthiah, K. (2017). Advances in Green Cloud Computing. In Green Computing Strategies for Competitive Advantage and Business Sustainability. Hershey, PA: IGI-Global.

Albers, S. (2010). Energy-efficient algorithms. *Communications of the ACM*, *53*(5), 86–96. doi:10.1145/1735223.1735245

Bent, L., Rabinovich, M., Voelker, G. M., & Xiao, Z. (2006). Characterization of a large web site population with implications for content delivery. *World Wide Web (Bussum)*, *9*(4), 505–536. doi:10.100711280-006-0224-x

Bobroff, N., Kochut, A., & Beaty, K. (2007, May). Dynamic placement of virtual machines for managing sla violations. In *10th IFIP/IEEE International Symposium on Integrated Network Management IM'07* (pp. 119-128). IEEE. 10.1109/INM.2007.374776

Bohrer, P., Elnozahy, E. N., Keller, T., Kistler, M., Lefurgy, C., McDowell, C., & Rajamony, R. (2002). The case for power management in web servers. In Power aware computing (pp. 261-289). Springer US. doi:10.1007/978-1-4757-6217-4_14

Brooks, D., & Martonosi, M. (2001). Dynamic thermal management for high-performance microprocessors. In *The Seventh International Symposium on High-Performance Computer Architecture, HPCA '01* (pp. 171-182). IEEE. 10.1109/HPCA.2001.903261

Chase, J. S., Anderson, D. C., Thakar, P. N., Vahdat, A. M., & Doyle, R. P. (2001). Managing energy and server resources in hosting centers. *Operating Systems Review*, *35*(5), 103–116. doi:10.1145/502059.502045

Damasevicius, R., Ziberkas, G., Stuikys, V., & Toldinas, J. (2012). Energy consumption of hash functions. *Elektronika ir Elektrotechnika*, *18*(10), 81–84. doi:10.5755/j01.eee.18.10.3069

Damgård, I. (1990). A design principle for hash functions. In Advances in Cryptology—CRYPTO'89 Proceedings (pp. 416-427). Springer Berlin/Heidelberg. doi:10.1007/0-387-34805-0_39

Elminaam, D. S. A., Abdual-Kader, H. M., & Hadhoud, M. M. (2010). Evaluating the performance of symmetric encryption algorithms. *International Journal of Network Security*, *10*(3), 216–222.

Felter, W., Rajamani, K., Keller, T., & Rusu, C. (2005, June). A performance-conserving approach for reducing peak power consumption in server systems. In *Proceedings of the 19th annual international conference on Supercomputing* (pp. 293-302). ACM. 10.1145/1088149.1088188

Femal, M. E., & Freeh, V. W. (2004, December). Safe overprovisioning: Using power limits to increase aggregate throughput. In PACS (pp. 150-164).

Gmach, D., Rolia, J., Cherkasova, L., & Kemper, A. (2007, September). Workload analysis and demand prediction of enterprise data center applications. In *IEEE 10th International Symposium on Workload Characterization IISWC '07* (pp. 171-180). IEEE. 10.1109/IISWC.2007.4362193

Irani, S., Shukla, S., & Gupta, R. (2003). Online strategies for dynamic power management in systems with multiple power-saving states. *ACM Transactions on Embedded Computing Systems*, *2*(3), 325–346. doi:10.1145/860176.860180

Isci, C., Contreras, G., & Martonosi, M. (2006, December). Live, runtime phase monitoring and prediction on real systems with application to dynamic power management. In *Proceedings of the 39th Annual IEEE/ACM International Symposium on Microarchitecture* (pp. 359-370). IEEE Computer Society. 10.1109/MICRO.2006.30

Iyengar, A. K., Squillante, M. S., & Zhang, L. (1999). Analysis and characterization of large-scale Web server access patterns and performance. *World Wide Web (Bussum)*, *2*(1), 85–100. doi:10.1023/A:1019244621570

Jasim, O. K., Abbas, S., El-Horbaty, E. S. M., & Salem, A. B. M. (2013). Cloud Computing Cryptography. World Academy of Science, Engineering and Technology, International Journal of Computer, Electrical, Automation. *Control and Information Engineering*, *7*(8), 1161–1164.

Kaps, J. P., & Sunar, B. (2006, August). Energy comparison of AES and SHA-1 for ubiquitous computing. In *International Conference on Embedded and Ubiquitous Computing* (pp. 372-381). Springer Berlin Heidelberg. 10.1007/11807964_38

Karlin, A. R., Manasse, M. S., McGeoch, L. A., & Owicki, S. (1994). Competitive randomized algorithms for nonuniform problems. *Algorithmica*, *11*(6), 542–571. doi:10.1007/BF01189993

Kotla, R., Ghiasi, S., Keller, T., & Rawson, F. (2005, April). Scheduling processor voltage and frequency in server and cluster systems. In *Proceedings. 19th IEEE International Parallel and Distributed Processing Symposium*. IEEE. 10.1109/IPDPS.2005.392

Lawton, S. (2015) Cloud Encryption: Using Data Encryption In The Cloud, tomsitpro.com. Available at: http://www.tomsitpro.com/articles/cloud-data-encryption,2-913.html

Li, H., Cher, C. Y., Vijaykumar, T. N., & Roy, K. (2003, December). VSV: L2-miss-driven variable supply-voltage scaling for low power. In *Proceedings. 36th Annual IEEE/ACM International Symposium on Microarchitecture MICRO-36* (pp. 19-28). IEEE.

Li, J., Wang, Q., Wang, C., Cao, N., Ren, K., & Lou, W. (2010, March). Fuzzy keyword search over encrypted data in cloud computing. In INFOCOM, 2010 Proceedings IEEE. IEEE. doi:10.1109/INFCOM.2010.5462196

Li, M., Yu, S., Zheng, Y., Ren, K., & Lou, W. (2013). Scalable and secure sharing of personal health records in cloud computing using attribute-based encryption. *IEEE Transactions on Parallel and Distributed Systems*, *24*(1), 131–143. doi:10.1109/TPDS.2012.97

Lord, N. (2017). Cryptography in the Cloud: Securing Cloud Data with Encryption. *digitalguardian.com*. Retrieved from https://digitalguardian.com/blog/cryptography-cloud-securing-cloud-data-encryption

Merkle, R. (1990). A certified digital signature. In Advances in Cryptology—CRYPTO'89 Proceedings (pp. 218-238). Springer Berlin/Heidelberg. doi:10.1007/0-387-34805-0_21

Merkle, R. C., & Charles, R. (1979). Secrecy, authentication, and public key systems.

Muñoz, C., Rocci, L., Solana, E., & Leone, P. (2016). Performance Evaluation of Searchable Symmetric Encryption in Wireless Sensor Networks. In *Internet of Things. IoT Infrastructures: Second International Summit, IoT 360° 2015*, Rome, Italy, October 27-29, 2015. Revised Selected Papers, Part I (pp. 40-51). Springer International Publishing.

Nathuji, R., & Schwan, K. (2007, October). Virtualpower: Coordinated power management in virtualized enterprise systems. *Operating Systems Review*, *41*(6), 265–278. doi:10.1145/1323293.1294287

Nie, T., Song, C., & Zhi, X. (2010, April). Performance evaluation of DES and Blowfish algorithms. In *2010 International Conference on Biomedical Engineering and Computer Science (ICBECS)*. IEEE. 10.1109/ICBECS.2010.5462398

Potlapally, N. R., Ravi, S., Raghunathan, A., & Jha, N. K. (2003, August). Analyzing the energy consumption of security protocols. In *Proceedings of the 2003 international symposium on Low power electronics and design* (pp. 30-35). ACM. 10.1145/871506.871518

Potlapally, N. R., Ravi, S., Raghunathan, A., & Jha, N. K. (2006). A study of the energy consumption characteristics of cryptographic algorithms and security protocols. *IEEE Transactions on Mobile Computing*, *5*(2), 128–143. doi:10.1109/TMC.2006.16

Prasithsangaree, P., & Krishnamurthy, P. (2003, December). Analysis of energy consumption of RC4 and AES algorithms in wireless LANs. In *Global Telecommunications Conference GLOBECOM'03* (Vol. 3, pp. 1445-1449). IEEE. 10.1109/GLOCOM.2003.1258477

Ranganathan, P., Leech, P., Irwin, D., & Chase, J. (2006, June). Ensemble-level power management for dense blade servers. In ACM SIGARCH *Computer Architecture News*, *34*(2), 66–77. doi:10.1145/1150019.1136492

Roy, S., Rudra, A., & Verma, A. (2013, January). An energy complexity model for algorithms. In *Proceedings of the 4th conference on Innovations in Theoretical Computer Science* (pp. 283-304). ACM.

Roy, S., Rudra, A., & Verma, A. (2014, September). Energy aware algorithmic engineering. In *2014 IEEE 22nd International Symposium on Modelling, Analysis & Simulation of Computer and Telecommunication Systems (MASCOTS)* (pp. 321-330). IEEE. 10.1109/MASCOTS.2014.47

Salerno, S., Sanzgiri, A., & Upadhyaya, S. (2011). Exploration of attacks on current generation smartphones. *Procedia Computer Science*, *5*, 546–553. doi:10.1016/j.procs.2011.07.071

Software-Systeme. (n.d.). Hardware Monitor. Retrieved 2015-07-01 from http://www.bresink.com/osx/HardwareMonitor.html

Somani, U., Lakhani, K., & Mundra, M. (2010, October). Implementing digital signature with RSA encryption algorithm to enhance the Data Security of cloud in Cloud Computing. In *2010 1st International Conference on Parallel Distributed and Grid Computing (PDGC)* (pp. 211-216). IEEE. 10.1109/PDGC.2010.5679895

(2011). Stave 2011. *Communications in Computer and Information Science*, *187*, 190–197.

Thakur, S., & Chaurasia, A. (2016, January). Towards Green Cloud Computing: Impact of carbon footprint on environment. In *2016 6th International Conference on Cloud System and Big Data Engineering (Confluence)* (pp. 209-213). IEEE.

Toldinas, J., Štuikys, V., Ziberkas, G., & Naunikas, D. (2015). Power awareness experiment for crypto service-based algorithms. *Elektronika ir Elektrotechnika*, *101*(5), 57–62.

Tran, V. N. N., & Ha, P. H. (2016, December). ICE: A general and validated energy complexity model for multithreaded algorithms. In *2016 IEEE 22nd International Conference on Parallel and Distributed Systems (ICPADS)* (pp. 1041-1048). IEEE. 10.1109/ICPADS.2016.0138

Urgaonkar, B., Shenoy, P., & Roscoe, T. (2002). Resource overbooking and application profiling in shared hosting platforms. *ACM SIGOPS Operating Systems Review*, *36*, 239-254.

Ustimenko, V., & Wroblewska, A. (2013, July). On some algebraic aspects of data security in cloud computing. In Proceedings of Applications of Computer Algebra ACA 2013 (p. 155).

Verma, A., Dasgupta, G., Nayak, T. K., De, P., & Kothari, R. (2009, June). Server workload analysis for power minimization using consolidation. In *Proceedings of the 2009 conference on USENIX Annual technical conference* (pp. 28-28). USENIX Association.

Yuan, W., & Nahrstedt, K. (2003, October). Energy-efficient soft real-time CPU scheduling for mobile multimedia systems. *Operating Systems Review*, *37*(5), 149–163. doi:10.1145/1165389.945460

Chapter 3
A Recent Study on High Dimensional Features Used in Stego Image Anomaly Detection

Hemalatha J
Thiagarajar College of Engineering, India

KavithaDevi M.K.
Thiagarajar College of Engineering, India

Geetha S.
Vellore Institute of Technology Chennai, India

ABSTRACT

This chapter describes how ample feature extraction techniques are available for detecting hidden messages in digital images. In the recent years, higher dimensional features are extracted to detect the complex and advanced steganographic algorithms. To improve the precision of steganalysis, many combinations of high dimension feature spaces are used by recent steganalyzers. In this chapter, we present a summary of several methods existing in literature. The aim is to provide a broad introduction to high dimensional features space used so for and to state which the most accurate and best feature extraction methods is.

INTRODUCTION

The tremendous communication technology growth and unrestricted practice of internet have significantly smoothed the data transfer. In spite of this practice, it makes the communication channels more vulnerability to data security terrorizations and initiating the unauthorized information access. To provide a solution to this problem, data hiding concepts such as steganography, watermarking are emerged. Steganography is an art of hiding the data in an innocuous cover medium such as image, audio, video and text, firewall, protocols, etc. This technology can be misused by terrorists and criminals for scheduling and synchronizing the felonious activities. The idea of a way to do this is, the secret messages are em-

DOI: 10.4018/978-1-5225-4044-1.ch003

bedded in digital images and post it in public spots so that the others are not known about the message existence. Later this chapter will discuss about the types of steganography, tools existing for hiding the secret messages, applications of steganography, misuse of steganography, etc. In contrast, steganalysis is an art of sensing the data hidden in the digital media. The aim is to gather adequate proof since a cover image is hidden by a secret message. The purpose of using the digital image as a carrier file is wide availability of high-resolution pixels. Fundamentally three common image formats are used for the hiding purpose; they are JPEG, BMP, and GIF. Each format will perform differently when it is embedded by a hidden message. Consequently, various steganalysis algorithms are there for each image format.

For the GIF (Graphics Interchange Formats) image format, palette based image steganalysis is used predominantly. It encourages only 8 bpp (bits per pixel), pixel colors are indicated from the color palette table. It contains 256 distinct colors and it will be mapped to the 24-bit RGB color image. The hiding algorithm strength lies in lessening the probability of the color palette change and also in lessening the visual distortion about the occurrence of the hidden message.

On the other hand, JPEG image format is the most popular cover choice for hiding the stego content. With the background of JPEG images, some standard steganographic algorithms are available such as JSTEG, F5 (Westfeld et al., 2001), Outguess (outguess), etc. In the JPEG image format, each image is divided into 8 by 8 blocks; in each block first component is the DC component remaining is the AC components. In F5 algorithm matrix embedding is used to embed the message bits in the DC coefficients. Likewise, in the starting age of steganography and steganalysis Fridrich et al. (Fridrich et al., 2003) proposed a practice for appraising the unaltered histogram to calculate the number of changed bits and the hidden message length. To calculate this initially the image has been cropped by four columns and then the image has been recompressed by the quantization table. The preceding histogram of DCT coefficients will very close to the original image. Also in (Fridrich et al., 2003) technique has been proposed for attacking the outguess algorithm.

In the ancient day's steganalysis done by visual analysis: detection has been done with the naked eye or analyzing the bit planes of an image separately for any scarce appearance in an image. Then the steganographers are very clever in designing the steganography tools and algorithms since it cannot be distinguished with visual attacks. Later steganalysis did by statistical analysis: examining the statistical properties of an image, whether the properties are changed due to steganographic embedding. This statistical steganalysis can be categorized into specific and universal/blind. In the case of specific steganalysis, the detection can be done only if the embedding steganographic algorithms are previously known. While in universal/blind steganalysis, the stego objects can be detected when it is embedded with any steganographic algorithms.

Most of the recent techniques for blind steganalysis are depending on two phases. In the first phase, the statistical features are extracted with reducing the dimensionality. In the second phase train the classifier with the set of clean and stego images, the decision has to be carried out for detecting the stego images from the extracting features. In the earlier days, the statistical features space is in fewer dimensions, the existing classifier has been achieved good performance. To increase the recognition rate of modern steganographic systems, the feature dimension has to be extensively increased.

Steganalysis consistency is strongly influenced by the cover source. In the prisoner's problem, choosing a cover source should be a better mask for hiding the secret message. In Eve's problem, even a single-bit message hidden also eves should successfully detect the message.

In this chapter, we look at some of the recent steganalysers working with the high dimensional features. The rest of the chapter is organized as follows. Before discussing the high dimensional features, briefly, see about the types of steganalysis, feature construction, the feature sets available for stego anomaly detection. The Later section starts with the explanation of high dimensional features extracted from spatial domain and then proceeds with the explanation of the high dimensional features extracted from transform domain. Finally, the conclusion is explained in the last Section.

STEGANOGRAPHY AND ITS TYPES

Image steganography has three terminologies they are i) cover image: for message entrenching, original image is chosen as a cover image, ii) Message: Message is a piece of data which can be either text or an image to hide in an image, iii) stego image: an image generated, after hiding the secret message is called a stego image, iv) stego key: To embed a secret message in to a cover image or extracting the secret message from a stego images is done by the stego key.

Basically, image steganography is an information hiding method which generates a stego image and it can send to the trusted party with a known medium and it doesn't known to the third party that this is a stego image and it bears a concealed message. Once the stego image is received then the message can be extracted by using stego key or without using stego key. A steganographic algorithm or method is considered to be the best when it satisfies the parameters i) High capacity: Maximum amount of data can be embedded in an image file ii) Perceptual limpidity: Once the message is hidden in a cover image then the perceptual quality of an image will not be degraded iii) Robustness: if the stego image undergoes some transformation such as scaling, filtering, cropping; data should be stay intact iv) Temper Resistance: once the message has embedded then it may difficult to alter the message.

Domain used for message hiding:

- **The Strength of Steganography:** Rather than the parameters discussed above, domain used for hiding the message is also important. Image steganography techniques can be falls under two domains, namely a) spatial domain b) Transform domain
- **Spatial Domain:** Spatial steganography, it alters some bits of the image pixels directly. For example, LSB – steganography, it is the very famous and easiest hiding method and it hides the secret message in the LSB bits of pixel values without noticing any changes in an image. Some of the spatial domain techniques are listed below
  - Pixel Value Differencing
  - Least Significant Method
  - Random Pixel Embedding
  - Edge based Embedding
  - Pixel Intensity based hiding
  - Texture based hiding
  - Labeling or connectivity based scheme
  - Histogram shifting
  - Mapping pixel based method

- **Pixel Value Differencing:** PVD offers good imperceptibility to the stego image and it selects two successive pixels following with designing a quantization table range to find the payload (calculating by subtracting the values among the successive pixels). Also, PVD conveys large number of payloads and it maintains image consistency.
- **Least Significant Bit Method:** When using LSB hiding method image degradation will be less and it can convey large payload.
- **Random Pixel Embedding:** in the case of LSB embedding, the group of bits embedded can be found that effects in sudden alterations in the bits statistics and this can outcome in detection. But in the case of random pixel embedding, there are no such grouping because the bits are embedding in a scatter manner in a cover image. So detection process is very difficult. Random pixel embedding is also a variation of LSB embedding. To embed the message, pseudo random number generator (PRNG) can be used to choose the random pixels of an image. The key what we are chosen is inserted in to the pseudo random number generator and it can find an order of random numbers. The generated random numbers indicate some of the pixels in a cover image where the message can be embedded in the LSB bit of those pixels. In such case, where the absence of secret key, it is very difficult to find the target pixels. Hence, it makes the system more secure and the receiver should know the secret key and the random embedding locations.
- **Edge Based Embedding:** Pixels in textured area and noisy area are shown to be best area for data embedding, because it may difficult to model. Likely, pixels in edges are looks like noisy because of high or low intensities due to immediate changes in the coefficient gradient than the neighboring pixels. Edges are difficult to model because of sharp changes in the statistical and visual properties of an image. Hence choosing edges for steganography hiding is an optimal choice than the other part of an image.
- **Transform Domain:** Hiding information in transform domain is more complex than the information hiding in the spatial domain. Likewise, the data hiding process in frequency domain signal is stronger than the time domain. Transform domain techniques are broadly categorized as follows.
  - Discrete Fourier Transformation based hiding (DFT-based Hiding)
  - Discrete Cosine Transformation based hiding (DCT –based Hiding)
  - Discrete Wavelet Transformation based hiding (DWT- based Hiding)
  - Lossless and reversible based hiding
  - Data embedding in the coefficients bits of an image.

STEGANALYSIS

Steganalysis is an art of detecting the stego images. Basically, in steganalysis we are having two approaches: named as blind/universal and targeted/specific steganalysis, i.e., attacking on unknown and known embedding method.

1. Targeted/Specific Steganalysis

In Specific steganalysis, feature vectors are built from an understanding of the hiding algorithm. On the other hand, the feature vectors constructed in blind steganalysis are built in such a manner as it should be able to detect all the possible steganographic algorithms and also to detect the future algorithms. The specific steganalysis method works well with single scalar feature whereas the blind steganalysis methods involves large feature sets and are implemented by means of machine learning algorithms.

Feature Construction for Targeted Steganalysis

There are various strategies are there in feature construction for targeted steganalysis. As we discussed earlier feature vectors are built from the hiding algorithm knowledge and also it is quite easy to find such features from the known values of cover and stego images.

S1: [Stego Testing] Find a feature that achieves a targeted known value f_α on particular stego image but gets changed values on the cover images. Then hypothesis stego testing problem is given in Eq. (1).

$$Hypothesis1: \quad f = f_\alpha,$$
$$Hypothesis2: \quad f \neq f_\alpha \tag{1}$$

In the above formula α refers the rate of change and f_α denotes that it is the feature calculated from a stego image attained by change rate.

$$\alpha = \frac{number\ of\ embedding\ changes}{number\ of\ elements\ in\ the\ cover\ image} \tag{2}$$

S2: [Property of known cover] from the available set of features in a natural image, find a feature f that undergoes with data embedding $f_\alpha = \Psi(f_0; \alpha)$; then $f_0 = \Psi^{-1}(f_\alpha; \alpha)$ with the assumption of known function $F(f_0 = 0)$ for $F: R^d \rightarrow R^k$, then from $F\left(\Psi^{-1}(f_\alpha; \hat{\alpha})\right) = 0$ calculate $\hat{\alpha}$. Then evaluate the below hypothesis

$$Hypothesis1: \quad \hat{\alpha} = 0$$
$$Hypothesis2: \quad \hat{\alpha} > 0 \tag{3}$$

From the above hypotheses, *Hypothesis*1 is for stego image and *Hypothesis*2 for cover image.

S3: [Calibration] Calibration is a process of estimating the feature value from the stego image and also compares, what the feature value would be, when it is estimated from the cover image.

For example: Assume that $\hat{f}_0$ be the feature computed from the cover image, and f_α be the compute of stego feature, then the embedding feature allows f_α is a function of f_0, α. Then again calculate α from $f_\alpha = \phi(\hat{f}_0; \hat{\alpha})$, then again test the following hypothesis.

$$Hypothesis1: \quad \hat{\alpha} = 0$$
$$Hypothesis2: \quad \hat{\alpha} > 0 \tag{4}$$

We like to give one practical example. Here we attempt to attack an LSB embedding steganographic method. The attack based on histogram features. For an 8-bit grayscale image, the histogram values of cover image $h[2x]$ is undergone into $h[2x+1]$ when it undergone with the Least Significant Bit embedding.

$$h[2x] \approx h[2x+1], x = 0, 1, 2...127 \tag{5}$$

Now we are going to formulate the hypothesis testing problem, consider the feature vector the histogram h, then the hypothesis will be as follows

$$For\, cover\, Hypothesis1: \quad h[2x] = \frac{h[2x] + h[2x+1]}{2}, x = 0, 1, 2...127$$
$$For\, stego\, Hypothesis2: \quad h[2x] \neq \frac{h[2x] + h[2x+1]}{2}, x = 0, 1, 2...127 \tag{6}$$

This Least Significant Bit problem was solved using Pearson's chi-square test (Fridrich et al., 2002; Moerland et al., 2003; Westfeld et al., 1999).

Yet again we enter into the principles of the calibration process. Calibration is a process of tries to calculate the chosen macroscopic quantities of the cover from the steganogram. The detection of JPEG (Joint Photographic Expert Group) image steganographic embedding is a tedious process because distortion is very small when the message is embedded in the quantized DCT coefficients. This calibration process starts with decompress the steganogram into spatial domain and then crop the image by 4×4 rows and columns. Finally using the same quantization table again recompression process will be done. The resulting JPEG and the cover image will be visually same, and also the resulting quantized DCT coefficients are not influenced by the embedding. The reason is compression was almost done on the 8×8 matrix transferred by four pixels similar to the 8×8 matrix in the cover image. Hence, the decompression process erased the footprint effects of steganographic embedding. And also, the histograms of macroscopic quantities are almost equal to the histogram of the cover image. Likewise, other than cropping technique, all the image transformation such as scaling, rotation can also be used in the attack on watermarking/ steganographic schemes. Hence it is called Stirmar (Kutter et al., 1999).

From all the above discussed points, we conclude that the features constructed for the specific steganalysis is modeled by analyzing the embedding schemes of a targeted embedding operation and its dimensions also within the range of lower space.

2. Quantitative as a Type of Steganalysis

Most of the specific steganalysis schemes are used to estimate the embedding change rate. Likewise, quantitative steganalysis is a method of estimating the change rate of embedding and it is the most wanted practice in forensic steganalysis. Anyhow the change rate given by a quantitative steganalysis is not a satisfied one because; on the assumption basis only the estimator was derived. In (2014) Li et al. proposed the message embedding rate estimation for LSBMR (Least significant bit matching revisited) steganography method. Their experimental results show that LSBMRCP method, actively detects the other existing methods. In (2006) Bohme et al. proposed the quantitative steganalysis method. Their findings found the error rate of detecting the steganalysis, found the weight. Also, they analyzed the local variance effect, cover saturation on the different sources of error. Likewise, in (2017) Chutani et al. proposed the framework and calculated the payload ratio when evaluated using ensemble method and hence it is called ensemble based universal quantitative steganalyzer. Similarly, in (Kodovský et al., 2013; Kodovský et al., 2010; Guan et al., 2010; Pevny et al., 2009) the authors proposed the quantitative steganalysis method and also compared their error rates with other existing methods.

3. Blind Steganalysis

Blind steganalysis is a type of detecting any steganographic schemes irrespective of its embedding. In targeted steganalysis, the process will do with the entire image, but in the case of blind scheme, transform the entire image into lower dimensional feature space.

Idea of Choosing Good Features

The idea of embedding the message is, as like adding the noise with some specific properties. Hence, a lot of modeled features are very sensitive to adding noise but insensitive to the content of image

- **Noise:** To separate the noise from the image content, transformation of an image spatial domain into curvelet, wavelet, Fourier is an adaptable method. Calculate the statistical characteristics of the noise signal will automatically increase the SNR (signal to noise ratio).
  Calibration: Find a feature f, that probably changes with message embedding then calibrate it. That is, calculate a difference $f_\alpha - \hat{f}_0$. Here calibration is used for twofold, and allows the feature nearly zero mean on the cover set $E_{I_c}\left[f_\alpha(X - \hat{f}_0(X)\right] \approx 0$ and decrease the variance as $Var_{I_c}\left[f_\alpha(X - \hat{f}_0(X)\right]$. To make the features works in an effective manner, it is advisable to construct such features, from the same domain where the message embedding occurs. For instance, suppose we planned to design features for detecting the steganographic method that embeds in JPEG- quantized DCT coefficients, which it is advisable to compute features exactly from the quantized DCT coefficients of JPEG images.
- **Known Cover Properties:** Consider the known covers that satisfy some of the known statistical properties, (example- DCT histogram symmetry) then it is advisable to consider that also when designing a feature set.

CLASSIFICATION

Once the feature set is ready, then eve has two options exclusively to construct the detector.

Option 1: Cover feature sets are described by the proper mathematical probability distribution and then test the hypothesis.

For example – For the sample distribution of cover feature set, fit the parametric model $\hat{I}_c$, following that test the hypothesis as follows

$$
\begin{aligned}
Hypothesis\,1 &: X \sim \hat{I}_c \\
Hypothesis\,2 &: X \not\sim \hat{I}_c
\end{aligned}
\tag{7}
$$

Option 2: Designing a large database of images with few known steganographic methods with some payload (uniformly distributed) and later fit another distribution $\hat{I}_s$, via the data obtained from experiment. Now eve has easily face the below hypothesis testing problem.

$$
\begin{aligned}
Hypothesis\,1 &: X \sim \hat{I}_c \\
Hypothesis\,2 &: X \sim \hat{I}_s
\end{aligned}
\tag{8}
$$

1. Idea of Using IQM (Image Quality Metrics) as Features

IQM is abbreviated as Image Quality Metrics. In finding the quality of the image, IQM plays a major role and it could be very accurate and consistent. In the steganalysis scenario, accuracy is stated as with minimum error, it should be accurate in detecting the hidden message presence. Likewise, consistency referred as providing consistently accurate predictions. To classify the stego images from the clean images analysis of variance (ANOVA) technique is used as the feature sets. Multivariate regression classifier is trained and tested based on the quality metrics. Basically, in (Avcibas et al., 2003) Image Quality Metrics are classified into the following groups and is explained as follows.

- **Measures Based on Pixel Difference:** Measures depends on mean square error, pixel neighborhood error, pixel multi resolution error, mean absolute error, etc.
- **Measures Based on Correlation:** Measures depends on image fidelity, normalized cross correlation, mean angle similarity, magnitude similarity, correlation on czenakowsi.
- **Measures Based on Edges:** Measures based on Pratt edge and stability of edges.
- **Measures Based on Spectral Distance:** Measures such as spectral phase error, block spectral phase and magnitude error, etc.
- **Context Based Measures:** Measures such as Spearman rank correlation, Matusita distance, Hellinger distance, and rate distortion.
- **Measures Based on Human Visual Systems:** Measures depends on human visual system weighted spectral alteration or dissimilar basis.

In (Geetha et al., 2008) Image Quality Metrics are calculated on the image dataset containing clean and steganogram images, then genetic x means classifier has been used on the selected feature set and the stego image detection accuracy has been compared with the artificial neural network (ANN).In (Bo et al., 2007) 26 image quality measures encapsulated by Avcibas et al. are analyzed and then extracted the eight sensitive features from the four domains such as ICA, DCT, DWT and spatial. From the original and Gaussian filtered version images the feature scores are calculated. Using multi class support vector machine as a classifier the feature vectors are trained and tested the clean and stego images. In (Sabnisa et al., 2016) Image Quality Metrics are used as a feature set for detecting the wavelet based fusion hiding method. In (Celik et al., 2004) they propose the steganalysis scheme for detecting the stochastic embedding. The feature vector has been formed by extracting the features such as Mean Square Error, Mean Absolute Error, Weighted mean square error (Image Quality Metrics). This feature vector is trained and tested by using Bayesian Classifier and their experimental results showed that comparison has been made with different data hiding schemes. In (Geetha et al., 2009) proposed the steganalysis scheme to improve the performance of Steganalyzer such as maximizing the sensitivity and specificity of the system by means of content independent Image Quality Metrics.

2. Idea of Using Higher Order Statistics

Recent many works stated that higher order statistics are more accurate in detecting the stego images. In (Farid et al., 2002) a steganalysis method has been proposed based on first and higher order statistics. From the wavelet decomposition first order means and higher order statistics such as variance, skewness, and kurtosis are extracted to construct a feature vector. Similarly, in (Harmsen et al., 2003) mass center of the histogram characteristic functions are extracted as the first moment feature vector. Likewise, in (Candes et al., 2004; Holotyak et al., 2005; Shi et al., 2005), higher order statistics are used as a feature in accurately detecting the stego images from the image dataset. In (Pathak et al., 2014) blind steganalysis technique has been proposed. The input image has been divided into RGB components and each component has been transformed by spatial, frequency and wavelet. The features such as mean, Skewness, variance, global histogram, kurtosis, co-occurrence matrix, etc. are extracted from each domain and the resultant feature vector is given as input to the SVM classifier. Clear and stego images have been detected by the designed support vector machine classifier. In (Battikh et al., 2014) the security of the chaos steganographic method has been analyzed by extracting the higher order statistical features from the wavelet multi resolution. A Fisher Linear Discriminant (FLA) classifier has been used to analyze chaotic EA-LSBMR strength. In (Swagota Bera et al., 2016) the author proposed an enhancement technique due to the dissimilarity effect of JPEG steganographic embedding by manipulating the different discrete wavelet transform 2D array among the 4 directions. With the choice of existing a relationship between the nearest neighbor pixels, the DWT difference has been caught by using two step Markovian process. Then from the predicted and calculated difference higher order statistical features are calculated and then it is trained and tested using support vector machine.

3. Spatial Domain: High Dimensional Features

Naturally, the noises in the images are high dynamic range other than the pixels, along with that; the stego signal uses a larger SNR (Signal to Noise Ratio). Likewise designing a model for noise residuals is easier than the pixels. The dimensionality of the noise residuals is very high that it is proportional to the dimension of the original image. Therefore, it is not an advice model a histogram from the noise residuals; instead, it is necessary to capture the joint statistic. As a result, the co-occurrence matrix/sample joint probability mass function can be formed by quantizing the residuals into a lesser number of samples. The key problem with co-occurrence matrix is the number of bins increases with matrix dimensionality in terms of exponential and also with quantizer centroids in terms of the polynomial.

In the recent few years, all the steganalyzers converged that the very strong statistical detector in the spatial domain is a Spatial Rich Model (SRM). SRM features are modeled by four-dimensional co-occurrence matrix of quantized residuals. The dimensionality of SRM is 12, 753 (SRMQ1) with single quantization step. Selection- channel – aware (max SRM) (Denemark et al., 2014) merged with SRM and makes the dimension of 34,671. SRM features have both linear and nonlinear pixel predictors.

We will see some brief knowledge about the spatial rich model features. All the linear pixel predictors are realized as shift invariant finite impulse captured by 5×5 the kernel or above (Kodovsky et al., 2011). The usage of linear predictors is based on the idea of the content of the image locally follows a polynomial model. For instance

$$predictor(x_{ij}) = x_{i,j+1} \Big/ \left(x_{i,j-1} + x_{i,j-1} \right) \Big/ 2 \Big/ \left(x_{i,j-1} + 3x_{i,j-1} - x_{i,j+2} \right) \Big/ 3 \tag{9}$$

Here the assumption is that the content of the image is linear, constant and quadratic.

The steganalysis methods utilize the information that embedding by noise addition modifies dependencies among pixels. In this scenario, stego noise is considered as the noise. To model, the differences among neighbor pixels the SPAM (Subtractive Pixel Adjacency Matrix) features are introduced. The idea is to suppress the content of the image and exposes the stego noise. SPAM features have been modeled by Pevny et al. (2010). First order and second order markov chains are used to model the difference between the neighbor pixels and transition probability matrix is used as features. The dimension of the SPAM features is 686 and it has been used to detect LSB matching. Support vector machine has been used for training and testing the model. SPAM features are, the more promising blind image steganalyzer in the spatial domain.

Hao Zhang et al. (2014) extended the SPAM features and generated the new feature set by merging the SPAM feature with additional parallel subtractive pixels. Also, the dimension of the SPAM feature is reduced by extracting the features from spatial as well as grayscale inverted image and made the symmetrical feature matrices. In addition to that adjacency matrix has used to further reduce the dimension. The detection performance has been better at detecting the LSB matching and YASS (Yet Another Steganographic Scheme) algorithm. The experimental results showed that the proposed steganalyzer outperforms the SPAM features introduced by Pevny et al. (2010).

Min et al. (2016) proposed the universal steganalysis based on SPAM features. Optimal dimension of feature vector has been determined using principal component analysis. The optimal subset has been generated with Fisher linear discriminant for achieving better results and lowers the computational complexity. Chikkara et al. (2016) proposed the improved firefly algorithm for reducing the dimension of SPAM features and Cartesian Calibrated features. Experimental results show that the redundant features in SPAM and Cartesian Calibrated (transform domain) are removed and computation time also reduced with hybrid DyFA (Dynamic Firefly Algorithm) than hybrid GLBPSO through dynamic adaptation. Likewise, Chikkara et al. (2016) suggested the improved particle swarm optimization – hybrid filter-wrapper approach to improving the stego detection accuracy using SPAM and Cartesian Calibrated feature set. In the first stage of this feature selection method two filters are taking place: to discriminate the stego image from clear, t-test and multi-regression are used for selecting the features based on discrimination ability. Followed within the second stage using improved PSO the features selected from the initial phase is further reduced. The experiment has done with support vector machine and results shown that the dimensions are drastically reduced and accuracy also has been greatly improved.

Another high dimensional feature used in the spatial domain is SRM – Spatial Rich Model features. Kodovsky et al. (2012) proposed the rich model of DCT coefficients for stego image detection. The model has been constructed as a combination of smaller sub models formed as DCT coefficient joint distribution of adjacent pixels and its frequencies. Similarly, Fridrich et al. (2012) proposed the rich models for stego detection. Due to high dimensionality ensemble classifier has been used and demonstration was done with three steganographic algorithms such as HUGO (Highly Undetectable Stego), edge adaptive algorithm, optimally coded ternary ±1 (LSB – Least Significant Bit) embedding. Noise residuals are considered to be the high-frequency components. The SRM features are extracted features from the neighboring noise residuals for capturing the dependency changes occurred due to embedding. Following that Wang et al. (2016) examined the residuals effectiveness. From the FLD perspective, neighboring residual samples are categorized as ineffective, effective and highly effective. Ineffective residuals still remain it does not undergo any changes with steganographic modification. It may affect the stego detection once it's mixed with the feature vector. Depends on the neighboring noise residual samples, pure SRM features are extracted. The experiment has been done with three content adaptive steganographic algorithms, and the results shown are more promising than the SRM. In (2016) Liao et al. proposed the content adaptive steganalysis scheme for color images. Instead of extracting features from the entire image, SRM features are extracted from each RGB channel and from the pixels color rich model features are extracted. For locating the pixels first embedding costs of each channel has been calculated, then the pixel subset with smaller embedding costs is selected. The performance has been better than the other existing color image steganalysers. Holub et al. (2013) proposed the PSRM (Projection Spatial Rich Model) - random projections on local neighborhoods, for high adaptive steganography. In (2015) Holub et al. rather than using co-occurrence matrix, neighboring residual samples on the random vectors and its histogram projections have been taken as features called PSRM. Feature dimensionality has been greatly reduced because of not using co-occurrence matrix. The key problem in PSRM features is, it needs thousands of convolutions among image noise residuals. This makes the implementation time-consumed. To overcome this Ker et al. (2014) suggested implementing the PSRM features on GPU hardware which utilize parallelism. As a result, with a single GPU, feature calculation time and detection power has been greatly reduced.

Wang et al. (2016) proposed a feature normalization method for Spatial Rich Model (SRM) based on random feature sub-sets. Subset normalization has been done by per- sample rescaling method for making the entire feature subset image as the same norm. Experimental results have been shown that normalized feature subsets achieved better detection performance. Song et al. (2016) proposed the specific steganalysis method based on 2D- Gabor filter richer feature for content adaptive steganography. Gabor rich feature (GRF) comprises histogram features as well as the co-occurrence features from the filtered coefficients at neighboring scales, positions, intra and inters block neighboring positions. Since GRF feature has very large in dimension, the feature selection has been applied. The dimensionality of the GRF feature has been greatly reduced with 31, 756 dimensions after applying the feature selection. The proposed feature has been analyzed with CC-PEV, CHEN, LIU, CC-JRM (Cartesian Calibrated JPEG domain rich model), DCTR (Discrete. Cosine Transform Residual), PHARM (Phase Aware Projection Model).

4. Transform Domain: High Dimensional Features

Some steganalyzers worked under JPEG domain only. Generally, in image processing JPEG images are described via DCT (Discrete Cosine Transform) coefficients. The images are divided into 8 by 8 blocks where the first coefficient is the DC component the remaining 63 are said to be AC coefficients and also it is an output of high pass filter. Hence, they are considered as quantized noise residuals. When constructing the features, need to make a difference between noise residuals and DCT coefficients. JRM (JPEG Rich Model) features is a collection of two dimensions inter and intra block co-occurrences of absolute DCT coefficient values. This JRM features set is more promising in detecting the older steganographic techniques. Likewise, some other feature set such as DCTR (Discrete Cosine Transform Residual) (Holub et al., 2013) of dimension 8,000, CF* (Kodovsky et al., 2012) of dimension 7,850, PHARM (Phase Aware Projection Model) (Holub et al., 2015) of dimension 12,600, and CC-JRM (Cartesian calibrated JPEG Rich Model) merged with SRMQ1 namely (JSRM) of dimension 35,263 features.

From the decompressed JPEG images Holub et al. (2010) extracted the first-order quantized noise residuals. The JPEG image has been decompressed using 64 kernels of DCT. This low complexity feature is a counterpart for the PSRM feature because of its low computational complexity, lower dimension, and improved performance.

Shakeri et al. (2014) proposed the steganalysis method using contourlet transform, for showing that the embedding process can affect the contourlet coefficient statistics. Contourlet sub-band coefficient is used as features and absolute Zernike moment & contourlet characteristic function moment has been used to distinguish the stego images. The extracted features have been given as input for the non-linear SVM with RBF kernel for classifying the stego images.

Zong et al. (2012) proposed an idea of extracting features from inter and intra wavelet sub band correlations. After doing the two level decomposition, the joint probability density of each sub band from neighboring coefficients is extracted. Then the entropy and energy are extracted from the joint probability density function. Also from the each sub band wavelet coefficient probability density function has extracted. The feature vector has been formed by combining all the three kinds of features and detection has been done.

Desai et al. (2016) proposed an idea for reducing the dimension of the merged feature set used by Fisher criterion and ANOVA (Analysis of Variance). The merged feature vector has been formed by extracting the features such as statistical features from wavelet sub band and binary similarity measures form DCT coefficients. Once the feature vector has been applied with Fisher criterion and ANOVA, the features have been selected given by the feature selection methods as a reduced feature set. Support Vector Machine (SVM) classifier with RBI kernel has used to train and test the images.

Laimeche et al. (2017) proposed the universal steganalysis technique with wavelet transform and Zip's law. Features are calculated from statistical characteristics of curves of Zipf at each sub band. A random classifier has been used for distinguishing the stego images from the clean images.

SUMMARY OF THE CHAPTER

In this chapter, we presented our claim that the higher dimensional features work better and gives a high promising result in detecting the stego files other than the old feature extraction techniques. Recent high dimensional features are fighting against the recent steganographic techniques for finding the stego images. In addition to that the classifier such as support vector machine, neural networks, etc., is quite difficult in handling high dimensional features. Many authors reported that Random forest gives the excellent result in handling high dimensional features, more number of training examples. Also, the accuracy rate of detecting stego images is also high while using random forest because of generating a random subspace.

We are interested in scrutinizing some parameters of steganalytic systems done in the literature. Table 1 and 2 shows some interesting factors such as targeted embedding designs, steganographic applications, feature extraction domain, the dimension of features. We also evaluated the accuracy rate, detection error, machine learning classifier used by various authors, etc. We observed that many authors used the spatial rich model and subtractive pixel adjacency matrix as a base because of giving the promising result. Also, some of the authors tried to reduce the dimension of the existing feature set using some feature selection method. Some of them used normalization, projections for reducing and making the feature set more optimal.

Table 1. Summarization of works with high dimensional features in spatial domain

Steganalytic Systems	Feature Dimension	Feature Extraction Domain	Targeted Embedding Scheme	Payload of Stego Images	Classifier Used for Training and Testing	Accuracy of Detection
Pevny et al. (2012) (SRM feature)	34,671	Spatial	HUGO, edge adaptive algorithm, ± embedding	0.05-0.40 bpp	Ensemble	97%
Pevny et al. (2010) (SPAM feature)	686	Spatial	LSB Matching (spatial), F5, nsF5, MB1, JP Hide & Seek, MMx, Steghide, (PQ)	0.25-0.50 bpp	Support vector machine with Gaussian kernel	95%
Zhang et al. (2014)	400	Spatial	LSB Matching, YASS	0.25- 0.5 bpp	Support vector machine with Gaussian kernel	89.41%
Wang et al. (2016) (NRS_Order4)	34,671	Spatial	HUGO, WOW, UNIWARD	0.1-0.4 bpp	LCLSMR	96%
Song et al. (2016) (GRF feature)	31,756 (110 feature units)	spatial	UED, J-UNIWARD, SI-UNIWARD	0.05-0.5 bpac	Ensemble	96.23

Table 2. Summarization of works with high dimensional features in transform domain

Steganalytic Systems	Feature Dimension	Feature Extraction Domain	Targeted Embedding Scheme	Payload of Stego Images	Classifier Used for Training and Testing	Detection Error
Holub et al. (2015) (DCTR feature)	8000	JPEG	J-UNIWARD, ternary coded UED, nsF5	0.05-0.40 bpp	Ensemble	0.1523%
Zhang et al. (2012)	126	DWT	F5, Jsteg, Outguess, Jphide	30%, 50%,100%	Back propagation neural network	4.67%
Laimeche et al. (2017)	56	DWT	2LSB, SM2LSB, YASS, Outguess	0.02- 0.10 bpac	Random Forest	10.01%

CONCLUSION

The idea of steganalysis is to reveal the presence of hidden messages in a given cover objects. The attainment of the steganalysis is increased by integrating forensic evidence at the detector. For instance, when a computer is grasped the stego tool may installed in the computer, then it has a pair of cover/stego images and it may assist in recovering the stego key and stego image. In this paper, we have given a brief study on high dimensional features used by current steganalyzers. One of the best ideas to improve the accuracy of detecting stego images is using a combination of features extracted from various domains of images. Moreover, we have shown that many steganalyzers pointed that Spatial rich model (SRM) is the most promising method for detecting the steganogram. Hence the future hope lies in modeling high dimensional features for detecting all the existing steganographic methods blindly.

REFERENCES

Chhikara, R. R., Sharma, P., & Singh, L.(2016). An improved dynamic discrete firefly algorithm for blind image steganalysis. *International Journal of Machine Learning and Cybernetics*.

Avcibas, I., Memon, N., & Sankur, B. (2003). Steganalysis using Image Quality Metrics. *IEEE Transactions on Image Processing*, *12*(2), 221–229. doi:10.1109/TIP.2002.807363 PMID:18237902

Battikh, D., El Assad, S., Bakhache, B., Deforges, O., & Khalil, M. (2014). Steganalysis of a chaos-based steganographic method. In *Proceedings: of 10th International Conference on Communications (COMM)*, Bucharest, Romania. 10.1109/ICComm.2014.6866665

Bo, X., Wang, J., Liu, X., & Zhe, Z. (2007). Passive steganalysis using image quality metrics and multi-class support vector machine. In *Proceedings of IEEE third international conference on natural computation* (pp. 215–220).

Bohme, R., & Kerb, A. D. (2006). *A Two-Factor Error Model for Quantitative Steganalysis. In proceedings of: SPIE 2006: Security, Steganography, and Watermarking of Multimedia Contents VIII*.

Candes, E. J., & Donoho, D. L. (2004). New tight frames of curvelets and optimal representations of objects with C2 singularities. *Communications on Pure and Applied Mathematics*, *57*(2), 219–266. doi:10.1002/cpa.10116

Celik, M. U., Sharma, G., & Tekalp, A. M. (2004). Universal Image Steganalysis Using rate- distortion curves. In Proceedings of SPIE: Security, Steganography, and Watermarking of Multimedia Contents VI, San Jose, CA (pp. 19-22).

Chhikara, R. R., Sharma, P., & Singh, L. (2016). A hybrid feature selection approach based on improved PSO and filter approaches for image steganalysis. *International Journal of Machine Learning and Cybernetics*, *7*(6), 1195–1206. doi:10.100713042-015-0448-0

Chutani, S., & Goyal, A. (2017). Improved universal quantitative steganalysis in spatial domain using ELM ensemble. *Multimedia Tools and Applications*. doi:10.100711042-017-4656-3

Denemark, T., Sedighi, V., Holub, V., Cogranne, R., & Fridrich, J. (2014). Selection-channel-aware rich model for steganalysis of digital images. In *Proceedings of IEEE International Workshop on Information Forensics and Security (WIFS)* (pp. 48–53).

Farid, H. (2002). Detecting hidden messages using higher-order statistical models. In *Proceedings of International Conference on Image Processing*, Rochester, NY (pp. 905–908). 10.1109/ICIP.2002.1040098

Fridrich, J., & Goljan, M. (2002). Practical steganalysis of digital images-state of the art. In *Proc. SPIE Photonics West, Electronic Imaging, Security and Watermarking of Multimedia Contents*, San Jose, CA.

Fridrich, J., Goljan, M., Hogea, D., & Soukal, D. (2003). Quantitative Steganalysis of Digital Images estimating the Secret Message Length. *ACM Multimedia Systems*, *9*(3), 288-302.

Geetha, S., Sindhu, S. S. S., & Kamaraj, N. (2008). StegoBreaker: Defeating the steganographic systems through genetic Xmeans approach using image quality metrics. In *Proceedings: of the 16th IEEE International Conference on Advanced Computing and Communication* (pp. 382–391).

Geetha, S., Sivatha Sindhu, S. S., & Kamaraj, N. (2009). Blind image steganalysis based on content independent statistical measures maximizing the specificity and sensitivity of the system. *Computers & Security*, *28*(7), 683–697. doi:10.1016/j.cose.2009.03.006

Guan, Q., Dong, J., & Tan, T. (2010). Blind Quantitative steganalysis Based on Feature Fusion and gradient boosting. In *Proceeding of Digital Watermarking: 9th International Workshop, IWDW*.

Harmsen, J. J. (2003). Steganalysis of Additive Noise Modelable Information Hiding [Master dissertation]. Rensselaer Polytechnic Institute, Troy, NY.

Holotyak, T., Fridrich, J., & Voloshynovskiy, S. (2005). *Blind statistical steganalysis of additive steganography using wavelet higher order statistics*. doi:10.1007/11552055_31

Holub, V., & Fridrich, J. (2015). Low Complexity Features for JPEG Steganalysis Using Undecimated DCT. *IEEE Transactions on Information Forensics and Security*, *10*(2), 219–228. doi:10.1109/TIFS.2014.2364918

Holub, V., Fridrich, J., & Denemark, T. (2013). Random Projections of Residuals as an Alternative to Co-occurrence in Steganalysis. In *Proceedings of SPIE, Electronic Imaging, Media Watermarking, Security and forensics XV*, San Francisco, CA. 10.1117/12.1000330

Holub, V., & Fridrich, J. (2015). Phase-aware projection model for steganalysis of JPEG images. In *Proceedings of Media Watermarking, Security, and Forensics 2015*, San Francisco, CA, February 9-11.

Holub, V., & Fridrich, J.(2013). Random Projections of Residuals for Digital Image Steganalysis. *IEEE Transactions on Information Forensics and Security*, *8*(12), 1996-2006.

Jessica Fridrich, J. Kodovsky. (2012). Rich Models for Steganalysis of Digital Images. IEEE Transactions on Information Forensics and Security, 7(3).

Ker, A. D. (2014). *Implementing the projected spatial rich features on a GPU. SPIE 9028*. Media Watermarking Security, and Forensics.

Kodovsky, J. Jessica Fridrich. (2012). Steganalysis of JPEG images Using rich Models. In *Proceedings of SPIE, Electronic Imaging, Media Watermarking, Security, and Forensics XIV*.

Kodovsky, J., & Fridrich, J. (2010). Quantitative steganalysis of LSB embedding in JPEG domain. In *MM&Sec '10 Proceedings of the 12th ACM workshop on Multimedia and security* (pp. 187-198). 10.1145/1854229.1854265

Kodovsky, J., Fridrich, J., & Holub, V. (2011). On dangers of overtraining steganography to incomplete cover model. In *Proceedings of 13th ACM Multimedia and security workshop*, Niagara Falls, New York (pp. 69-76). 10.1145/2037252.2037266

Kodovsky, J., Fridrich, J., & Holub, V. (2012). Ensemble classifiers for steganalysis of digital media. *IEEE Transactions on Information Forensics and Security*, *7*(2), 432–444. doi:10.1109/TIFS.2011.2175919

Kodovský, J., & Fridrich, J. (2013). Quantitative Steganalysis Using Rich Models. In *Media Watermarking, Security, and Forensics XV*, San Francisco, CA, February 3-7.

Kutter, M., & Petitcolas, F. A. P. (1999). A fair benchmark for image watermarking systems. In E. J. Delp, & P. W. Wong (Eds.), *Proceedings SPIE, Electronic Imaging, Security and Watermarking of Multimedia Contents I*, San Jose, CA (pp. 226–239). 10.1117/12.344672

Laimeche, L., & Merouani, H. F. & Mazouzi, S. (2017). A new feature extraction scheme in wavelet transform for stego image classification. Evolving Systems.

Li, W., Zhang, T., Wang, R., & Zhang, Y. (2014, February 18). Quantitative steganalysis of least significant bit matching revisited for consecutive pixels. *Journal of Electronic Imaging*, *23*(1), 013025. doi:10.1117/1.JEI.23.1.013025

Madhavi B. Desai, S. V. Patel, Bhumi Prajapati. (2016). ANOVA and Fisher Criterion based Feature Selection for Lower Dimensional Universal Image Steganalysis. *International Journal of Image Processing*, *10*(3), 145- 160.

Min, L., Ming, L., Xue, Y., Yu, Y., & Mian, W. (2016). Improvement of Universal Steganalysis Based on SPAM and Feature Optimization. In *Proceedings Second International conference ICCCS*, Nanjing, China.

Moerland, T. (2003). Steganography and Steganalysis. *Leiden Institute of Advanced Computing Science*. Retrieved from http://www.liacs.nl/home/tmoerl/privtech.pdf

Outguess – Universal Steganography. (n.d.). Retrieved from http://www.outguess.org

Pevny, T., Bas, P., & Fridrich, J. (2010). Steganalysis by Subtractive Pixel Adjacency Matrix. *IEEE Transactions on Information Forensics and Security*, *5*(2), 215–224. doi:10.1109/TIFS.2010.2045842

Pevny, T., & Jessica Fridrich, A. D. Ker. (2009). From Blind to Quantitative Steganalysis. In *Proc. SPIE, Electronic Imaging, Media Forensics and Security XI*, San Jose, CA, January 18-22.

Pritesh Pathak, S. (2014). Blind Image Steganalysis of JPEG images using feature extraction through the process of dilation. *Digital Investigation*, *11*(1), 67–77. doi:10.1016/j.diin.2013.12.002

Sabnisa, S. K., & Awale, R. N. (2016). Statistical Steganalysis of High Capacity Image Steganography with Cryptography. *Procedia Computer Science*, *79*, 321–327. doi:10.1016/j.procs.2016.03.042

Shakeri, E., & Ghaemmaghami, S. (2014). An Extended Feature Set for Blind Image Steganalysis in Contourlet Domain. *The ISC International Journal of Information Security*, *6*(2), 169-181.

Shi, Y. Q., Xuan, G., Yang, C., Gao, J., Zhang, Z., Chai, P., . . . Chen, W. (2005). Effective steganalysis based on statistical moments of wavelet characteristic function. In *Proceedings of IEEE International Conference on Information Technology: Coding and Computing* (Vol. 1, pp. 768–773). 10.1109/ITCC.2005.138

Song, X., Liu, F., Zhang, Z., Yang, C., Luo, X., & Chen, L. (2016). 2D Gabor filters-based steganalysis of content-adaptive JPEG steganography. *Multimedia Tools and Applications*.

Swagota Bera, S. Subramanya Sikhar, AtulDwivedi. (2016). An efficient blind steganalysis using higher order statistics for the neighborhood difference matrix. In Proceedings: of wireless communications, signal processing and Networking (WiSPNET).

Wang, P., Wei, Z., & Xiao, L. (2016). Pure spatial rich model features for digital image steganalysis. *Multimedia Tools and Applications*, *75*(5), 2897–2912. doi:10.100711042-015-2521-9

Wang, P., Wei, Z., & Xiao, L. (2016). Spatial rich model steganalysis feature normalization on random feature-subsets. *Soft Computing*.

Westfeld, A. (2001). F5 – A Steganographic Algorithm. In International workshop on information hiding, *LNCS* (Vol. *2137*, pp. 289–302). doi:10.1007/3-540-45496-9_21

Westfeld, A., & Pfitzmann, A. (1999). Attacks on steganographic systems. In *Proceedings of Third International Workshop on Information Hiding*, Dresden, Germany, September 28–October 1 (pp. 61-75).

Xin, L., Chen, G., & Yin, J. (2016). Content- adaptive steganalysis for color images. *Security and Communication Networks*, *9*(18), 5756–5763. doi:10.1002ec.1734

Zhang, H., Ping, X. J., ManKun, X., & Wang, R. (2014). Steganalysis by subtractive pixel adjacency matrix and dimensionality reduction. *Science China. Information Sciences*, *57*(4), 1–7. doi:10.100711432-014-5073-0

Zong, H., Liu, F., & Luo, X. (2012). Blind image steganalysis based on wavelet coefficient correlation. *Digital Investigation*, *9*(9), 58–68. doi:10.1016/j.diin.2012.02.003

Chapter 4
High Efficient Data Embedding in Image Steganography Using Parallel Programming

Usha B. A.
R V College of Engineering, India

ABSTRACT

Steganography is the art of hiding the fact that communication is taking place, by hiding information in other information. Many different carrier file formats can be used, but digital images are the most popular because of their frequency on the Internet. For hiding secret information in images, there exist a large variety of steganographic techniques some are more complex than others and all of them have respective strong and weak points.. As embedding data in an image, is independent of one another. Parallelism can be used to achieve considerable time gain. nography, although it has made communication safe, it has its own drawbacks. One among it is time required to embed data in pixels of the image. This problem is bugging computer scientists from long time. This paper discusses a method which makes OpenMP parallel library to parallelize embedding of data, which basically reduces the time by almost fifty percent and to achieve PSNR ranging from 30 to 50 after embedding data in the pixels of the image.

INTRODUCTION

In today's generation, hackers are intelligent enough to crack the normal encrypting algorithms. So there exists a need for a better way to communicate the critical data between the two ends, without being exposed to the hackers. Steganography is one such technique, which really helps to achieve this, by embedding the data in pixels of an image. Although it is not an entirely different way of communication, it helps us to embed the critical data and helps us to achieve better security.

Digital information hiding was inherent with the advent of digital technology. These days, steganography systems use distinctive sorts of computerized media like text, image, audio, video, binary, or html files. Modern steganography techniques rely on data hiding techniques using current media. Steganography varies from cryptography; cryptography focuses on keeping the substance of a message riddle and safe

DOI: 10.4018/978-1-5225-4044-1.ch004

while steganography deals with keeping the vicinity of a message mystery. Cryptography provides data security by applying encryption/decryption techniques.

An encrypted message is susceptible to eavesdroppers' attacks, if they know of its presence. The superlative resolution is to hide the message reality by implanting it into cover media. Therefore, the role of steganography is clear and strong with use of cryptography. Both techniques provide more secure communication between sending and receiving ends.

Embedding data is independent of all other things; this gave us motivation to exploit parallelism concepts and achieve significant time difference. With parallel embedding of data, high volume data embedding is promising.

Over the last decade, novel techniques have been applied and developed for Image Steganography. Image steganography is a very upcoming hiding technique since the robustness offered by the algorithms to the steganalytic attack is appealing high and, therefore, ensures secure data transmission both when data hidden is critical and sensitive. Text, images, audio data have been tried as secret messages to be hidden in the Image. Some of the latest developments in the field of Image Steganography have used artificial intelligence techniques, sudoku puzzle, hybrid fusion techniques, cognitive science and many more.

There are two main objectives for this application. They are as below:

- Ensuring secured communication between any two ends, using steganographic techniques.
- Exploiting parallelism concepts in data embedding and extraction, this gives us significant time gain in processing.

The common requirements to rate the performances of steganographic techniques are as follows.

- **Invisibility:** The invisibility of a steganographic algorithm is the first and foremost requirement, while the strength of steganography lies in its capability to be unobserved by the human eye. The moment that one can see that a picture has been messed with, the algorithm is compromised.
- **Payload Capacity:** As opposed to watermarking, which in turn would need to introduce merely a bit of copyright data, steganography is aimed at undetectable connection and for that reason demands adequate embedding ability.
- **Robustness Against Statistical Attacks:** Measurable steganalysis is the act of identifying hidden data through applying factual tests on image information. Numerous steganographic calculations leave a "mark" while installing data that can be effectively distinguished through measurable investigation. To have the capacity to go by a supervisor without being recognized, a steganographic algorithm must not leave such an imprint in the picture that is measurably large.
- **Robustness Against Image Manipulation**b In the correspondence of a stego picture by trusted frameworks, the picture may experience changes by a dynamic supervisor trying to uproot concealed data. Image manipulation, such as cropping or rotating, can be performed on the image before it reaches its destination. According to the manner in which the information will be inlayed, these types of manipulations may eliminate the concealed information. It is ideal for steganographic algorithms to be vigorous against either malicious or accidental changes to the image.
- **Independence of File Format:** With a wide range of picture record arrangements utilized on the Internet, it may appear to be suspicious that one and only kind of document configuration is consistently conveyed between two gatherings. The most intense steganographic calculations in this way have the capacity to implant data in a document. This additionally takes care of the issue

of not continually having the capacity to locate a suitable picture at the right minute, in the right arrangement to use as a spread picture.

- **Unsuspicious Files:** This prerequisite incorporates all attributes of a steganographic calculation that may bring about pictures that are not utilized ordinarily and may bring about suspicion. Unusual document size, for instance, is one property of a picture that can bring about further examination of the picture by a supervisor.

This chapter covers the idea of efficient data embedding technique using parallel programming. The development of such an algorithm overcomes the shortcomings of serial data embedding process in terms of effective bandwidth utilization. This chapter includes the importance of design; an algorithm used in the present work and also explains the implementation and other features. The chapter concludes with the results obtained.

BACKGROUND

Lots of research has been carried out in the field of Image steganography, which basically suggests different way of transmitting secret information between any two ends. About 10 papers are referred and these papers help to understand the basics of steganography.

The paper titled 'An Overview of Image Steganography' (Hamid et al., 2012) intends to give an overview of image steganography, its uses and techniques. It also attempts to identify the requirements of a good steganographic algorithm and briefly reflects on which steganographic techniques are more suitable for which applications.

The paper titled 'A Survey of Image Steganography Techniques – SERSC' (Hussain & Hussain, 2013) gave idea about different techniques like Least Significant Bit Insertion and other Machine Learning Algorithms. It elaborates how data can be embedded in least significant bits of every pixel and it also gives reason why we choose least significant bits for data embedding.

The paper published by Computer Science Department, Virginia (Juneja & Sandhu) on least significant insertion gives us information about how digital images are being represented by an array of values. These values represent the intensities of the three colors red, green and blue, where a value for each of the three colors describes a pixel (this color model is called the RGB model). Least significant bit insertion is the most obvious but also the most known approach for hiding information in images. As the name already indicates, you literally put the information in the least significant bits of the pixel values.

The paper titled 'Information Hiding Using Least Significant Bit Steganography and Cryptography' (Gupta, Goyal, Bhushan, 2012) gave us information about the implementation of least significant bit insertion. As this method is vulnerable to steganalysis so as to make it more secure the raw data is encrypted before embedding it in the image. Though the encryption process increases the time complexity, but at the same time provides higher security also. This paper uses two popular techniques Rivest, Shamir, Adleman (RSA) algorithm and Diffie Hellman algorithm to encrypt the data. The result shows that the use of encryption in Steganalysis does not affect the time complexity if Diffie Hellman algorithm is used instead of RSA algorithm

The paper titled 'Steganography and its application in Security' (Kumar & Pooja, 2010) gave us information about steganography and how these steganographic techniques help in providing secrecy.

This paper also gives information about its application, which in turn helps us to understand the real-world application of Steganography

The paper titled 'A Study of Various Steganographic Techniques Used for Information Hiding' (Sumathi, Santanam, Umamaheswari, 2013) compared various techniques available for embedding data inside an image and also helps us to choose the algorithm accordingly. This paper compared steganographic algorithms and plotted graph for every algorithm. By making use of those graphs, it infers best algorithm.

The paper titled 'Searching For Hidden Messages: Automatic Detection of Steganography' (Berg et al., 2003) deals with testing, whether the image contains embedded data in it or not. Usually in order to do so, they run all possible decrypting algorithms on the image which they get. Task level parallelism can be exploited here.

The paper by Prof. Guevara, on fundamentals of cryptographic algorithms (Noubir, n.d.) focuses on the basics of cryptography and encryption algorithms for text. This paper discusses about AES encryption algorithm, RSA algorithm and other famous encryption techniques. This paper also discusses the drawbacks of these algorithms.

The paper by Wiley publishers (Schaathun, 2012) deals with how best the machine learning techniques can be used in Steganalysis. This paper also provides information about how neighboring pixel's brightness, color and contrast are considered, while choosing pixels, for embedding data in them. These techniques makes a hacker's job difficult, and it is hard to decipher them, as there is uncertainty in the pixels, which has hidden data in them.

Cybercrime report done by KPMG (2014), gives details about the cyber-attacks, which happened in the year 2014. This clearly shows hackers are getting intelligent day by day. This paper also focuses on the techniques they use to hack and it has also discussed about the ways to protect data, from those kinds of attacks. This paper gave information about the statistics of cyber-attacks and it also reveals the fact that there is necessity for better data transmission techniques.

MAIN FOCUS OF THE CHAPTER

Steganography finds its application in secret transmission of data between the two ends. Steganography, although it has made communication safe, it has its own drawbacks. One among it is time required to embed data in pixels of the image. This problem is bugging computer scientists from long time. This application discusses a method which makes OpenMP parallel library to parallelize embedding of data, which basically reduces the serial data embedding time by almost fifty percent and to achieve good PSNR.

Issues

In today's generation, hackers are intelligent enough to crack the normal encrypting algorithms. So there exists a need for a better way to communicate the critical data between the two ends, without being exposed to the hackers. Steganography is one such technique, which really helps to achieve this, by embedding the data in pixels of an image. Although it is not an entirely different way of communication, it helps us to embed the critical data and helps us to achieve better security.

Embedding data is independent of all other things; this gave us motivation to exploit parallelism concepts and achieve significant time difference. With parallel embedding of data, high volume data embedding is promising.

Objectives

There are two main objectives for this mini project. They are as below

- Ensuring secured communication between any two ends, using Steganographic techniques.
- Exploiting Parallelism concepts in data embedding and decrypting, this gives us significant time gain in processing.

Difficulties Encountered and Strategies Used to Tackle

Following are problems encountered and actions taken to solve it.

1. **Selection of Programming Language:** The important constraint is the selection of the programming language, which helps us to parallelize things easily. Preferably C, C++ or Python (which has built in Image libraries). Not all programming languages are suitable for parallel computing.
2. **Image Size:** The main constraint of this project is Image size. If the image size is not more than the threshold value, parallel execution will take more time than serial execution. This is because of the overhead in creating and executing threads. So the primary objective is to make sure that cover image's size is greater than threshold value.
3. **Allocation of Memory:** Allocation of bit memory to all the bits to be embedded and extracted is a difficulty since allocation of huge memory is not supported in C/C++. So, "Boost C++" library is used to support the allocation of huge memory.

METHODOLOGY ADOPTED

The main constraint of implementing this work is to identify the maximum number of bits that can be embedded in an image, without affecting the quality of the stego image. In order to meet this constraint, it is required to calculate and maintain PSNR value of an image.

The second important constraint is the selection of the programming language, which helps us to parallelize things easily. Preferably C, C++ or Python (which has built in image libraries) can be used. Not all programming languages are suitable for parallel computing.

System Architecture for Embedding and Extraction of Data

Figure 1 shows the system architecture for embedding module, which takes image and data as input. It converts image into its bitmap and first encrypts text using any encryption algorithm. It converts encrypted data into its bit equivalent. It processes pixels of the image in parallel, embeds a bit of the text data in the least significant bits of the pixel. It exploits parallelism concepts here and helps in achieving significant time gain.

Following are the steps involved in embedding process

Step 1: The cover image is input from the user (preferably png image)
Step 2: The secret data to be embedded is input from the user.

Figure 1.

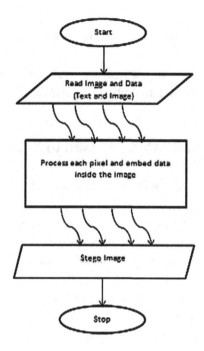

Step 3: The text is converted into bits.

Step 4: Pixel data of the image is extracted in terms of pixel byte values (RGB pixel bytes)

Step 5: Every pixel is looped over, each time inserting the specified number of bits to be inserted in each pixel byte.

Step 6: The new pixel data is converted back to an image (Stego image)

Step 7: The password is given to the user to be used while decrypting.

Extraction module processes every pixel of the stego image in parallel, extracts least significant bits of every pixel. Reordering is must, as it does this in parallel. Extract hidden message from these extracted bits.

Following are the steps involved for extraction process

Step 1: The Stego image is input from the user.

Step 2: The password is input from the user and necessary values are extracted from it.

Step 3: Pixel data of the image is extracted in terms of pixel byte values. (RGB pixel bytes)

Step 4: The pixel byte values are looped over and necessary number of bits are extracted from each byte.

Step 5: The bit values are grouped into characters.

Implementation Features

Implementation makes use of the models which are developed in the designing phase, and uses programming language which has been selected in the designing phase. It involves defining classes on the basis of architecture of the model, which has been built.

Figure 2. The module for data extraction process

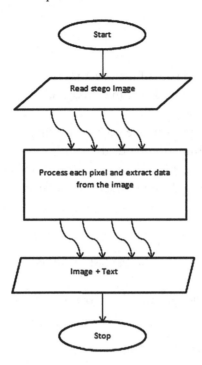

Implementation makes use of the models which are developed in the designing phase, and uses programming language which has been selected in the designing phase. It involves defining classes on the basis of architecture of the model, which has been built.

Programming Language Selection

Selection of programming language is a very important aspect when trying to implement 'Image steganography using HPC'. That programming language should support parallel constructs. Because of all these constraints, C/C++ is selected as a programming language, along with Gd Image Library and OpenMP parallel library.

Platform Selection

QT creator is used to create the User interface. Gd image manipulation library and OpenMP parallel library is used with C++ to achieve the task. QT interface modules are used in conjunction with these libraries to complete the project.

Code Convention

This section discusses the naming Convention, classes used and the user interface details in the implementation.

Naming Convention

Below are the variables used.

- **Imagepath:** This is the selected path of the cover image
- **Textpath:** The text file to be embedded in the cover image
- **Text:** The text read from the textpath file
- **Noofbits:** The number of bits in each pixel to be embedded
- **Textbitsize:** Number of bits from the text read
- **Bitarray:** An array of bits for storing the bits extracted from the text
- **Img:** The data structure holding the pixel values of the image
- **W:** Width of the image
- **H:** Height of the image
- **Actualw:** Number of columns to loop till
- **Actualh:** Number of pixels to loop till in the last column
- **Pass:** Password generated
- **Colors[3]:** An array storing the rgb value bytes of a pixel
- **T:** Time taken for execution

EXPERIMENTAL ANALYSIS AND RESULTS

Experimental analysis and results are the two important things, which, helps us to draw inferences and cross verify whether system is working as per expectations.

Evaluation Metrics

The evaluation metrics used in this application are:

- Serial execution time
- Parallel execution time
- PSNR calculation

Experimental Dataset

Images with different resolution are used as cover images in this work. They are: 1585 x 1142, 2688 x 1345 and 3168 x 3543. Along with this, text files of 1.2 MB, 1.8 MB, 2.4 MB, 3.6 MB, 4.8 MB, 5.4 MB and 10.1 MB are used as secret data.

Result Analysis for Embedding Data

Figure 3 shows the data embedding for the image of resolution 1585 x 1142 and same is computed in Table 1.

Figure 3.

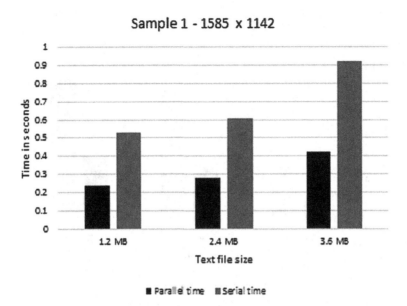

Table 1. Result analysis on resolution of the image is 1585 x 1142

Text Size in MB	Parallel Time in Second	Serial Time in Second	No of Bits Encoded per Byte	PSNR
1.2 MB	0.235713	0.526804	2	43.2932
2.4 MB	0.282216	0.603721	4	29.7348
3.6 MB	0.425145	0.922503	6	17.4752

Figure 4 shows the data embedding for the image of resolution 2688 x 1345 and same is computed in Table 2.

Figure 5 shows the data embedding for the image of resolution 3168 x 3543 and same is computed in Table 3. The tables below also shows the result of different sizes of secret data getting embedded in an image of given resolution. Serial and Parallel execution time are recorded. The number of bits of data embedded in every pixel and corresponding PSNR is also calculated.

Result Analysis for Extracting Hidden Data From Stego Image

Figure 6 shows the data extraction for the Image of resolution 1585 x 1142 and same is computed in Table 4.

Figure 7 shows the data extraction for the image of resolution 2688 x 1345 and same is computed in Table 5.

Figure 8 shows the data extraction for the image of resolution 3168 x 3543 and same is computed in Table 6. Tables also shows the result of different sizes of secret data getting extracted from stego image of different resolution. Serial and Parallel execution time are recorded.

Figure 4.

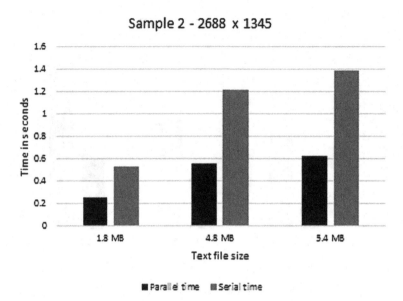

Table 2. Result analysis on resolution of the image is 2688 x 1345

Text Size in MB	Parallel Time in Second	Serial Time in Second	No of Bits Encoded per Byte	PSNR
1.8 MB	0.249431	0.528877	1	44.9728
4.8 MB	0.552323	1.21362	2	30.2407
5.4 MB	0.626806	1.38682	4	29.6558

Figure 5.

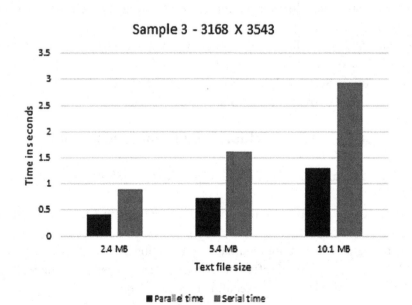

Table 3. Result analysis on resolution of the image is 3168 x 3543

Text Size in MB	Parallel Time in Second	Serial Time in Second	No of Bits Encoded per Byte	PSNR
2.4 MB	0.410078	0.889421	1	53.6882
5.4 MB	0.732206	1.61464	2	45.4695
10.1 MB	1.30879	2.93899	3	37.3667

Figure 6.

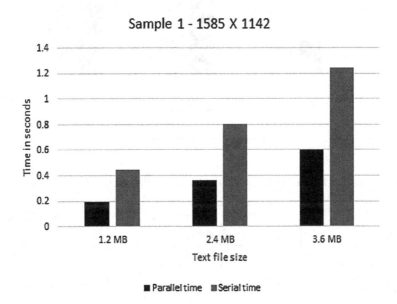

Table 4. Result analysis on extracted data with resolution of the image 1585 x 1142

Text Size in MB	Parallel Time in Second	Serial Time in Second
1.2 MB	0.193386	0.444544
2.4 MB	0.359936	0.803301
3.6 MB	0.596339	1.24128

Inference From the Result

Image steganography is achieved in parallel, which is groundbreaking; no material exists on the internet which boasts successful parallel implementation of image steganography. Parallel is found to take approximately 40% of the serial time. But as the size of the image increases, more improvement in execution time can be expected.

Figure 7.

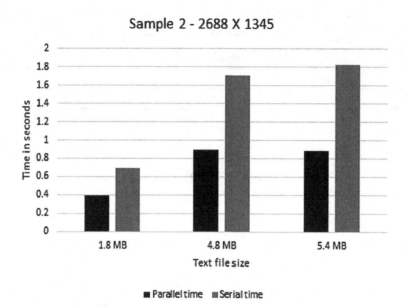

Table 5. Result analysis on extracted data with resolution of the image 2688 x 1345

Text Size in MB	Parallel Time in Second	Serial Time in Second
1.8 MB	0.395855	0.692053
4.8 MB	0.889018	1.70461
5.4 MB	0.88321	1.82758

Figure 8.

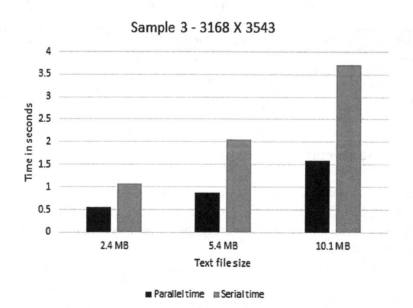

Table 6. Result analysis on extracted data with resolution of the image 3168 x 3543

Text Size in MB	Parallel Time in Second	Serial Time in Second
2.4 MB	0.549181	1.06278
5.4 MB	0.868594	2.05291
10.1 MB	1.58697	3.70948

CONCLUSION

This chapter gave a perception on the performance of the application by analyzing the experimental results. From the experimental analysis done, it can be inferred that, parallel data embedding process took approximately 40% less time than of the serial time. Parallelism is used to achieve considerable time gain. But as the size of the image increases, more improvement in execution time can be expected. OpenMP parallel library is used to parallelize embedding of data, PSNR achieved was ranging from 30 to 50 dB after embedding data in the pixels of the image.

Number of bits, which is considered for embedding the data bits, is also important. It should be less. It is optimal if it is one bit and it should not cross four bits. This is because if it crosses four bits for embedding data, color of that pixel will vary which makes it noticeable for hacker and creates backdoor for him. So, the number of pixels, which is considered for embedding, is also limited.

Future Enhancements

Hackers are becoming intelligent, day by day. They are becoming good at Steganalysis too. So better algorithms are needed which make use of machine learning algorithms for embedding data in an image. These machine learning algorithms actually make use of brightness and pixel values of the neighboring pixels before embedding data. Future scope of this project includes the development of these algorithms, which makes hackers job difficult and also ensures secured data communication.

REFERENCES

Berg, G., Davidson, I., Duan, M., & Paul, G. (2003). Searching For Hidden Messages: Automatic Detection of Steganography. In *Proceedings of the Fifteenth Conference on Innovative Applications of Artificial Intelligence*, Acapulco, Mexico, August 12-14.

Gupta, S., Goyal, A., & Bhushan, B. (2012). Information Hiding Using Least Significant Bit Steganography and Cryptography. *International Journal of Modern Education and Computer Science*, 4(6), 27.

Hamid, N., Yahya, A. R., Ahmad, B., & Al-Qershi, O. M. (2012). *Image Steganography Techniques: An Overview. International Journal of Computer Science and Security,* 6(3).

Hussain, M., and Hussain M. (2013). A Survey of Image Steganography Techniques. *International Journal of Advanced Science and Technology,* 54.

Juneja, M., & Sandhu, P. S. (2013). An Improved LSB Based Steganography Technique for RGB Color Images. *International Journal of Computer and Communication Engineering*, 2(4).

KPMG. (2014). Cybercrime Survey Report 2014. Retrieved from https://cyberlawin.files.wordpress.com/2014/09/kpmg_cyber_crime_survey_report_2014.pdf

Kumar, A., & Pooja, K.M. (2010). Steganography: A Data Hiding Technique. *International Journal of Computer Applications*, 9(7).

Noubir, G. (n.d.). Fundamentals of Cryptography: Algorithms, and Security Services. Retrieved from http://www.ccs.neu.edu/home/noubir/Courses/CSU610/S06/cryptography.pdf

Schaathun, H. G. (2012). *Machine Learning in Image Steganalysis*. Hoboken: Wiley-IEEE Press. doi:10.1002/9781118437957

Sumathi, C.P., Santanam T., & Umamaheswari, G. (2013). A Study of Various Steganographic Techniques Used for Information Hiding. *International Journal of Computer Science & Engineering Survey,* 4(6).

Chapter 5
Analysis of Mobile Cloud Computing:
Architecture, Applications, Challenges, and Future Perspectives

Sushruta Mishra
C. V. Raman College of Engineering, India

Sunil Kumar Mohapatra
C. V. Raman College of Engineering, India

Brojo Kishore Mishra
C. V. Raman College of Engineering, India

Soumya Sahoo
C. V. Raman College of Engineering, India

ABSTRACT

This chapter describes how cloud computing is an emerging concept combining many fields of computing. The foundation of cloud computing is the delivery of services, software and processing capacity over the Internet, reducing cost, increasing storage, automating systems, decoupling of service delivery from underlying technology, and providing flexibility and mobility of information. However, the actual realization of these benefits is far from being achieved for mobile applications and open many new research questions. Together with an explosive growth of the mobile applications and emerging of cloud computing concept, mobile cloud computing (MCC) has been introduced to be a potential technology for mobile services. With this importance, this chapter provides an overview of mobile cloud computing in which its definitions, architecture, and advantages have been presented. It presents an in-depth knowledge of various aspects of Mobile Cloud Computing (MCC). We give a definition of mobile cloud computing and provide an overview of its features.

DOI: 10.4018/978-1-5225-4044-1.ch005

INTRODUCTION TO CLOUD COMPUTING

Cloud is a huge collection of effortlessly approachable imaginary like utilities that can be used and accessed from anywhere, (for example software, hardware, advanced operating environments and applications). These operating environments and applications could be alterably re-designed to get accustomed to a varying burden, permitting likewise for best environment utilization. These environments and facilities are ordinarily known to be a per utilization payment arrangement where in insurances are guaranteed by the service issuer by method of altered service level agreements. This means truly that more information technology services, applications and technology are outsourced to outside sources over the Web, which finally will prompt a change in the conventional businesses where it is private cloud arranged to a virtual undertaking. This virtual endeavor, taking into account primarily cloud facilities, could be what's to come point of view. Then associations are investigating business process outsourcing, which includes the assignment of a whole business procedure to an unbiased gathering supplier, incorporating its supporting services. We utilize the internet to exchange data between any computing gadgets on the planet that are associated with the internet, however up to this point the greater part of the genuine computing we do has been performed mainly on the units themselves or on corporate networks. Right away, with an internet association and cloud computing, we can connect remotely with rich and effective, unbiased gathering, electronic frameworks, and utilize clearly unrestricted preparing power as though they were as of now incorporated with the nearby computing mechanisms, from anyplace at any time.

Cloud computing can be defined as a model for enabling convenient, on-demand network access to a shared pool of configurable computing resources (for example, networks, servers, storage, applications, and services) that can be rapidly provisioned and released with minimal management effort or service provider interaction. Some of the important properties of cloud computing are:

1. **Resource Efficiency:** Computing and network resources are pooled to provide services to multiple users. Resource allocation is dynamically adapted according to user demand.
2. **Elasticity:** Computing resources can be rapidly and elastically provisioned to scale up, and released to scale down based on consumer's demand.
3. **Self-Managing Services:** A consumer can provision cloud services, such as web applications, server time, processing, storage and network as needed and automatically without requiring human interaction with each service's provider.
4. **Accessible and Highly Available:** Cloud resources are available over the network anytime and anywhere and are accessed through standard mechanisms that promote use by different types of platform (e.g., mobile phones, laptops, and PDAs) Cloud computing is a computing paradigm, where a large pool of systems are connected in private or public networks, to provide dynamically scalable infrastructure for application, data and file storage. With the advent of this technology, the cost of computation, application hosting, content storage and delivery is reduced significantly. It is a practical approach to experience direct cost benefits and it has the potential to transform a data center from a capital-intensive set up to a variable priced environment. Enterprises can choose to deploy applications on Public, Private or Hybrid clouds. Cloud Integrators can play a vital part in determining the right cloud path for each organization. There are four primary cloud deployment models:

a. **Public Cloud:** Public clouds are owned and operated by third parties; they deliver superior economies of scale to customers, as the infrastructure costs are spread among a mix of users, giving each individual client an attractive low-cost, "Pay-as-you-go" model. All customers share the same infrastructure pool with limited configuration, security protections, and availability variances. These are managed and supported by the cloud provider. One of the advantages of a Public cloud is that they may be larger than an enterprises cloud, thus providing the ability to scale seamlessly, on demand.

b. **Private Cloud:** Private clouds are built exclusively for a single enterprise. They aim to address concerns on data security and offer greater control, which is typically lacking in a public cloud. There are two variations to a private cloud:

    i. **On-Premise Private Cloud:** On-premise private clouds, also known as internal clouds are hosted within one's own data center. This model provides a more standardized process and protection, but is limited in aspects of size and scalability. IT departments would also need to incur the capital and operational costs for the physical resources. This is best suited for applications which require complete control and configurability of the infrastructure and security.

    ii. **Externally Hosted Private Cloud:** This type of private cloud is hosted externally with a cloud provider, where the provider facilitates an exclusive cloud environment with full guarantee of privacy. This is best suited for enterprises that don't prefer a public cloud due to sharing of physical resources.

c. **Hybrid Cloud:** Hybrid Clouds combine both public and private cloud models. With a Hybrid Cloud, service providers can utilize 3rd party Cloud Providers in a full or partial manner thus increasing the flexibility of computing. The Hybrid cloud environment is capable of providing on-demand, externally provisioned scale. The ability to augment a private cloud with the resources of a public cloud can be used to manage any unexpected surges in workload.

d. **Community Cloud:** The cloud infrastructure is shared by several organizations and supports a specific community that has shared concerns (e.g., mission, security requirements, policy, and compliance considerations).

Cloud Computing vs. Mobile Cloud

The terms like "mobile cloud" and "cloud computing" are being used interchangeably. So a number of confused thoughts have resulted for most people, because although the two Technologies depend on the cloud but their functions may differ. There are a number of unique features that separate cloud computing from the mobile cloud, right from storage, computing capacity and even tolerance. In fact, the only connection between the two technologies is that they both run on the cloud, and employ the use of wireless systems to transmit data, encrypted or otherwise. Both technologies also have their fair share of pros and cons, but to make the difference clear, here is a comparison of cloud computing with the mobile cloud.

While cloud computing refers explicitly to the design of new technologies and services that enable wireless, or hardwired data sharing over distributed networks, the mobile cloud refers to the development of new hardware and interfaces. Cloud computing uses wireless connections to secure data at remote locations that are typically operated by third-party vendors, who cater to multiple web clients. The development of today's generation of smartphones and tablet PCs to outperform traditional computing devices, are all products of the mobile cloud. Apart from remote accessibility, mobile cloud computing functions involve granting users' access to the Internet via mobile browsers that support an array of software applications. These systems typically run on a core operating system that sends and receives multiple data types. Mobile cloud computing is typically designed for customer facing services, including operating systems and themes. But cloud computing is something is typically employed by businesses, both small and large. The basic premise of cloud computing is that it offers businesses to liberty to access services and functionalities that were previously only available through wired connection. The mobile cloud, however, is dedicated to making services available via mobile network operators (MNOs). This covers any aspect of mobile computing, including the numerous apps that perform location, messaging, shopping, gaming, and other functions. But instead of being limited to a fixed amount of storage space that comes with a physical mobile device, users are free to store as much data on a flexible cloud system. Cloud computing and the mobile cloud can only seem similar because of the common use of the word "cloud". However, now that you know the inherent differences between these cloud-based platforms, it is also important to remember that both technologies are in their relative infancy, and will see more improvements over current versions. And with the mobile cloud offering standalone cloud services, the day isn't far when cloud computing and the mobile cloud will blend together to provide a number of cutting edge features to web developers, including improved location services and high-security encryption for subscriber data.

EVOLUTION OF MOBILE CLOUD COMPUTING

With the emergence of cloud computing and mobile computing, mobile cloud computing came into picture in the year 2009. From a simple perspective, mobile cloud computing can be thought of as infrastructure where data and processing could happen outside of the mobile device, enabling new types of applications such as context-aware mobile social networks. As a result, many mobile cloud applications are not restricted to powerful smartphones, but to a broad range of less advanced mobile phones and, therefore, to a broader subscriber audience. MCC can be simply divided into mobile computing and cloud computing. The mobile devices can be laptops, PDA, smartphones and so on, which connect with a base station or a hotspot by a radio link such as 3G, Wi-Fi or GPRS. Although the client is changed from PCs or fixed machines to mobile devices, the main concept is still cloud computing. Mobile users send service requests to the cloud through a web browser or desktop application. The management component of cloud then allocates resources to the request to establish connection, while the monitoring and calculating functions of mobile cloud computing are implemented to ensure the QoS until the connection is completed. It is the combination of mobile computing, cloud computing and wireless networks to bring high quality computational resources to network operators, mobile users, and cloud computing providers (Abolfazli et al., 2014; Liu et al., 2013). MCC is a new platform for combining the mobile devices and cloud computing to create a new infrastructure. It refers an infrastructure where both the data storage and the data processing happen outside of the mobile device (Perez, 2009). In this architecture, cloud performs the heavy lifting of computing-intensive tasks and store large amounts of data. The rapid emergence of mobile computing (MC) (Satyanarayanan, 2010) becomes a powerful trend in the development of information technology. However, the mobile devices in mobile computing are facing many problems in their resources (e.g., battery life, storage, and bandwidth) and communications (e.g., mobility and security) (Tavel, 2007). Due to major application model in the era of Internet, mobile cloud computing has become a significant research topic of the scientific and industrial communities. Its application is becoming more popular day by day. Therefore, different applications based on mobile cloud computing have been developed and served to users, such as Google's Maps, Gmail, and Navigation systems for Mobile, Voice Search, and various applications on an Android platform, MobileMe from Apple and Moto Blur from Motorola. Mobile cloud applications move the computing power and data storage way from mobile phones and into the cloud. Aepona (2010) describes mobile cloud computing as a new paradigm for mobile applications where data processing and storage are moved from mobile device to powerful and centralized computing platforms located in clouds over the internet. All these centralized applications are then accessed over the wireless connection based on a thin native client or web browser on the mobile devices. Alternatively, mobile cloud computing can be defined as a combination of mobile web and cloud computing (Christensen, 2009; Liu et al., 2010) which is the most popular tool for mobile users to access applications and services on the Internet.

Now days, both hardware and software of mobile devices get greater improvements than before, some smartphones such as iPhones, Android serials, window mobile phones and blackberry, are no longer just traditional mobile phones with conversation, SMS, Email and website browser, but are daily necessities to user. However, at any given cost and level of technology, considerations such as weight, size, battery life, ergonomics and heat dissipation exact a severe penalty in computational resources such as processor speed, memory size, and disk capacity. The following approaches are used for mobile cloud applications:

- Extending the access to cloud services to mobile devices
- Enabling mobile devices to work collaboratively as cloud resource providers
- Augmenting the execution of mobilize applications on portable devices using cloud resources

As the mobile devices have certain resource constraints, there arises a need to get resources from external sources. One of the ways to overcome this problem is getting resources from a cloud, but the access to such platforms is not always guaranteed or/and is too expensive. Huerta-Canepa (2010) presents the guidelines for a framework that mimics a traditional cloud provider using mobile devices in the vicinity of users. The framework detects nearby nodes that are in a stable mode, meaning that will remain on the same area or follow the same movement pattern. If nodes in that state are found, then the target provider for the application is changed, reflecting a virtual provider created on the-fly among users. Collaboration of mobile devices to work as a unit in a networked environment is a good solution for a common task. But sometimes work cannot be distributed among mobile devices and has to be offloaded to a resource rich platform. Ricky et al. (2012) proposed stack-on demand asynchronous exception execution mechanism for offloading of work to a nearby cloud. In this mechanism, a stack is being maintained for the storage of execution state and only the recent execution state that is on top of the runtime stack will be migrated. In recent years, researchers have explored an era; in which offloading is being done partly to the cloud and rest is completed at mobile side. Chunim, Ihm, Maniatis, Naik, and Patti (2011) defined an approach Clone Cloud, with aim of offloading execution blocks from mobile device to the cloud dynamically to modify the execution performance of a mobile device. Two of the major advantages of clone cloud are enhanced performance of smartphones and reduced battery consumption as smartphones do not use its CPU frequently.

Mobile Cloud Computing is emerging to be a dynamic force:

- Mobile devices face many resource challenges (battery life, storage, bandwidth etc.)
- Cloud computing offers advantages to users by allowing them to use infrastructure, platforms and software by cloud providers at low cost and elastically in an on-demand fashion.

Mobile cloud computing provides mobile users with data storage and processing services in clouds, obviating the need to have a powerful device configuration (e.g. CPU speed, memory capacity etc.), as all resource-intensive computing can be performed in the cloud.

EMERGENCE OF MOBILE CLOUD COMPUTING

Mobile devices allow users to run powerful applications that take advantage of the growing availability of built-in sensing and better data exchange capabilities of mobile devices. As a result, mobile applications seamlessly integrate with real-time data streams and Web 2.0 applications, such as mashups, open collaboration, social networking and mobile commerce (Wright, 2009; Kovachev, Renzel, Klamma, and Cao, 2010). The mobile execution platform is being used for more and more tasks, e.g., for playing games; capturing, editing, annotating and uploading video; handling finances; managing personal health, micro payments, ticket purchase, interacting with ubiquitous computing infrastructures. Even mobile device hardware and mobile networks continue to evolve and to improve, mobile devices will always be resource-poor, less secure, with unstable connectivity, and with less energy since they are powered by battery. Resource poverty is major obstacle for many applications (Satyanarayanan, Bahl, Caceres, and Davies, 2009). Therefore, computation on mobile devices will always involve a compromise. Mobile devices can be seen as entry points and interface of cloud online services. The cloud computing paradigm is often confused about its capabilities, described as general term that includes almost any kind of outsourcing of hosting and computing resources. The combination of cloud computing, wireless communication infrastructure, portable computing devices, location-based services, mobile Web, etc., has laid the foundation for a novel computing model, called mobile cloud computing, which allows users an online access to unlimited computing power and storage space. Mobile Cloud Computing refers to an infrastructure where both the data storage and data processing happen outside of the mobile device. Mobile cloud applications move the computing power and data storage away from the mobile devices and into powerful and centralized computing platforms located in clouds, which are then accessed over the wireless connection based on a thin native client. Mobile cloud computing provides mobile users with data storage and processing services in clouds, obviating the need to have a powerful device configuration (e.g. CPU speed, memory capacity, etc.), as all resource-intensive computing can be performed in the cloud. Mobile cloud computing is a technique or model in which mobile applications are built, powered and hosted using cloud computing technology. A mobile cloud approach enables developers to build applications designed specifically for mobile users without being bound by the mobile operating system and the computing or memory capacity of the smartphone. Mobile cloud computing centered are generally accessed via a mobile browser from a remote webserver, typically without the need for installing a client application on the recipient phone. Most applications built for smartphones requires intensive computing power and software platform support for application execution. Many low-end but browser-enabled mobile phones are unable to support such applications. With the advent in mobile cloud computing, the resources in terms of computing, storage and plat from support required to execute these applications are available through the cloud and, in theory, a greater number of devices can be supported.

APPLICATIONS OF MOBILE CLOUD COMPUTING

Some of the applications reinforced by the mobile cloud computing is as follows:

1. **Mobile Commerce:** It means buying and selling of products using mobile devices. M-commerce applications are normally used to achieve some tasks that require mobility like mobile transactions and payments, mobile ticketing and messaging. They have to face a lot of complications like low network bandwidth, high complexity configurations of mobile devices and security. Therefore m-commerce applications are integrated with cloud computing environment to solve these problems.
2. **Mobile Learning:** It refers to electronic learning and mobility. The classical m-learning applications had various limitations like high cost of devices and network, low network data rate and limited educational resources. Cloud based m-learning applications are meant to solve these issues. For example, utilizing a cloud with a large storage capacity and powerful processing ability, the applications offer the learners with much comfortable services in terms of information size and processing speed.
3. **Mobile Healthcare:** Mobile cloud computing in medical applications is used to minimize the limitations of traditional medical treatment like small physical storage, security and privacy and medical errors. M-healthcare offers mobile users with appropriate help to access resources easily. It provides the health care organizations a diversity of on-demand services on clouds rather than existing applications on local servers.
4. **Mobile Banking:** It is an uprising in traditional banking services where the users can avail the bank services through their mobile irrespective of location and time. Transaction can be done even if the user is busy in his routine work via SMS or mobile internet. Also, the special applications can be downloaded to the mobile device.
5. **Mobile Game:** It is a prospective market producing income for service providers. M-game can completely offload game requiring large computing resource to the server in the cloud and the gamers can only interact with the screen interface on their devices which demonstrates that offloading can save energy for mobile devices thereby increasing the playing time of games on the mobile devices.

Other Miscellaneous Applications of MCC

With scalable computation and large data storage, cloud computing facilitates MCC applications to be run on ultra-thin mobile devices. In this section, we first discuss existing MCC applications. Then we discuss emerging and future MCC applications.

Existing MCC Applications

We have witnessed a number of MCC applications in recent years, including mobile commerce, multimedia sharing, mobile learning, mobile sensing, mobile healthcare, mobile gaming, mobile social networking, location-based mobile service, and augmented reality. Mobile commerce, such as e-banking, e-advertising and e-shopping, uses scalable processing power and security measures to accommodate a high volume of traffic due to simultaneous user access and data transaction processing. Multimedia sharing provides secure viewing and sharing of multimedia information stored on smartphones while providing administrative controls to manage user privileges and access rights necessary to ensure security. Mobile learning allows a thin terminal to access learning materials on the cloud any time and any place. Mobile sensing utilizing sensor-equipped smartphones to collect data will revolutionize many MCC applications including healthcare, social networking, and environment/health monitoring. Mobile healthcare allows an enormous amount of patient data to be stored on the cloud instantaneously. A doctor can conveniently look at the patient records on his/her mobile device for remote diagnosis or monitor a patient's status for preventive actions. Mobile gaming achieves scalability by leveraging scalable computation and instantaneous data update on the cloud side and screen refresh at the mobile device side. Mobile social networking allows a group of mobile users to upload audio/video/multimedia data for real-time sharing, with cloud computing providing not only storage for data, but also security to protect secrecy and integrity of data.

Emerging and Future MCC Applications

Future MCC applications must leverage unique characteristics of MCC. Due to limitation of power, intensive data processing on mobile devices is always costly. With the technology advancement, however, mobile devices are equipped with more functional units, such as high-resolution camera, barometer, light sensor, etc. Future MCC applications must leverage deep sensing capability of smartphones for data collection. Data can be uploaded to the cloud and the cloud can integrate pieces of observations from mobile devices and utilize data analytics techniques to mine and visualize trends or patterns embedded in massive data collected in parallel at runtime from millions of mobile devices. For instance, given a severe natural disaster, people nearby can send photos taken from the cameras in their smartphones to the cloud, and the cloud server can process these data, analyze possible crucial points, and plot a detailed map, covering not only visible objects but also invisible physical phenomena, such as the presence of poisonous air to help facilitating the rescue mission. With potentially unlimited storage and processing power, MCC brings out potential killer applications. Table 1 lists emerging and future applications that can power from MCC. Initial efforts toward building these killer MCC applications are also cited in the table.

PROS AND CONS OF MCC

Advantages of Mobile Cloud Computing

1. **Flexibility/Elasticity:** Users can rapidly access provision computing resources without human interaction. User Capabilities can be rapidly and elastically provisioned, in some cases dynamically, to quickly scale out or up.

Table 1. Emerging and future MCC applications

Type of Application	References
Crowdsourcing (crowd computing)	(Campbell et al., 2008) (Satyanarayanan, 2010) (Yang, Xue, Fang, and Tang, 2012)
Collective Sensing	(Lane et al., 2010) (Cheng, Sun, Buthpitiya, and Griss, 2012) (Lu, Pan, Lane, Choudhury, and Campbell, 2009) (Sensorly, 2016.)
Traffic/ Environment Monitoring	(Thiagarajan et al., 2009) (Herring et al., 2009) (Hunter et al., 2011) (Mun et al., 2009)
Mobile Cloud Social Networking	(Khalid, Khan, Khan, and Zomaya, 2014) (Wang, Wu, and Yang, 2013) (Miluzzo et al., 2008)
Mobile Cloud Healthcare	(Cimler, Matyska, and Sobeslav, 2014) (Wu, Wang, and Wolter, 2013) (Consolvo et al., 2008)
Location-Based Mobile Cloud Service	(Tamai and Shinagawa, 2011) (La and Kim, 2010)
Augmented Reality and Mobile Gaming	(Kangas and Oning, 1999) (Luo, 2009)

2. **Scalability of Infrastructure:** In the physical servers, new nodes can be added or dropped from the network with limited modifications to infrastructure set up and software. According to demand mobile cloud architecture can scale horizontally or vertically easily.

3. **Improving Data Storage Capacity and Processing Power:** Storage capacity is also a constraint for mobile devices. MCC is developed to enable mobile users to store/access the large data on the cloud through wireless networks. First example is the Amazon Simple Storage Service (Amazon S3) which supports file storage service. Another example is Image Exchange which utilizes the large storage space in clouds for mobile users. This mobile photo sharing service enables mobile users to upload images to the clouds immediately after capturing. Users may access all images from any devices. With cloud, the users can save considerable amount of energy and storage space on their mobile devices since all images are sent and processed on the clouds.

4. **Real Time Data Availability:** Another advantage of mobile cloud computing is that you can get access to real time data, whenever and wherever you want. Given that the data and applications are managed by a third party, updating your data as well as accessing it in real time is easily possible. Moreover, it can be accessed by multiple persons simultaneously.

5. **Broad Network Access:** User capabilities and ability are available over the network and can be accessed through standard mechanisms that promote use by heterogeneous platforms like mobile phones, laptops, and PDAs etc.

6. **Location Independence:** There is a sense of different location independence where customer generally has no control or knowledge over the exact location of the provided resources. But it may be able to specify location at a higher level of abstraction from country, state, or data center.

7. **Reliability:** Through the use of multiple redundant site reliability can be improved and this makes cloud computing worthier for disaster recovery applications and business continuity.
8. **Economies of Scale and Cost Effectiveness:** In order to take advantage of economies of scale mobile cloud implementations, regardless of the deployment model, tend to be as large as possible. Large number of mobile cloud deployments may be located close to cheap power stations and low-priced real estate, for lower costs.

Disadvantages of Mobile Cloud Computing

1. **Low Bandwidth:** As the mobile network resource is much smaller than the traditional networks, bandwidth is one of the major issues in the mobile cloud environment.
2. **Security and Privacy in the Cloud:** When establishing a remote cloud base infrastructure certainly any organization will give away private data and information which might be sensitive and confidential. Therefore, it has been a biggest concern.
3. **Prone to Attack and Vulnerability:** Nothing on the internet is completely protected. Sensitive data and information may be stolen on the internet as many hackers and malicious users always look for the chances.
4. **Looking for Vendor and Dependency:** It becomes really painful when one user wants to switch from one service provider to another because he has to transfer a lot of data from the previous provider to the new one. Therefore, one has to be careful enough while selecting a vendor.
5. **Limited Control and Flexibility:** Since all the applications are running on virtual or remote environments, users have limited control over the function and execution of the hardware and software.

TECHNICAL CHALLENGES OF MCC

As discussed in the previous section, MCC has many advantages for mobile users and service providers. However, because of the integration of two different fields, i.e., cloud computing and mobile networks, MCC has to face many technical challenges.

Issues in Mobile Communication Side

1. **Low Bandwidth:** Bandwidth is one of the big issues in MCC since the radio resource for wireless networks is much scarce as compared with the traditional wired networks.
2. **Availability:** Service availability becomes more important issue in MCC than that in the cloud computing with wired networks. Mobile users may not be able to connect to the cloud to obtain service due to traffic congestion, network failures, and the out-of-signal.
3. **Heterogeneity:** MCC will be used in the highly heterogeneous networks in terms of wireless network interfaces. Different mobile nodes access to the cloud through different radio access technologies such as WCDMA, GPRS, WiMAX, CDMA2000, and WLAN. As a result, an issue of how to handle the wireless connectivity while satisfying MCC's requirements arises (e.g., always-on connectivity, on-demand scalability of wireless connectivity, and the energy efficiency of mobile devices).

ISSUES IN COMPUTING SIDE

1. **Computing Offloading:** As explained in the previous section, offloading is one of the main features of MCC to improve the battery lifetime for the mobile devices and to increase the performance of applications.
2. **Security:** Protecting user privacy and data/application secrecy from adversary is a key to establish and maintain consumers' trust in the mobile platform, especially in MCC. In the following, the security related issues in MCC are introduced in two categories: the security for mobile users and the security for data. Also, some solutions to address these issues are reviewed.
3. **Enhancing the Efficiency of Data Access:** With an increasing number of cloud services, the demand of accessing data resources (e.g., image, files, and documents) on the cloud increases. As a result, a method to deal with (i.e., store, manage, and access) data resources on clouds becomes a significant challenge.
4. **Context-Aware Mobile Cloud Services:** It is important for the service provider to fulfill mobile users' satisfaction by monitoring their preferences and providing appropriate services to each of the users. A lot of research work try to utilize the local contexts (e.g., data types, network Status, device environments, and user preferences) to improve the quality of service (QoS).

OPEN ISSUES AND FUTURE RESEARCH DIRECTIONS

Several research works contribute to the development of MCC by tackling issues as presented in the previous section. However, there are still some issues which need to be addressed. This section presents several open issues and possible research directions in the development of MCC.

1. **Low Bandwidth:** Although many researchers propose the optimal and efficient way of Band width allocation, the bandwidth limitation is still a big concern because the number of mobile and cloud users is dramatically increasing.
2. **Network Access Management:** An efficient network access management not only improves link performance for mobile users but also optimizes bandwidth usage. Mobile users in MCC must be able to detect this radio resource availability (through spectrum sensing) while ensuring that the traditional services will not be interfered.
3. **Quality of Service:** In MCC, mobile users need to access to servers located in a cloud when requesting services and resources in the cloud. However, the mobile users may face some problems such as congestion due to the limitation of wireless bandwidths, network disconnection, and the signal attenuation caused by mobile users' mobility. They cause delays when users want to communicate with the cloud, so QoS is reduced significantly.
4. **Pricing:** Using services in MCC involves with both mobile service provider (MSP) and cloud service provider (CSP). However, MSPs and CSPs have different services management, customer's management, methods of payment and prices. Therefore, this will lead to many issues, i.e., how to set price, how the price will be divided among different entities, and how the customers pay.
5. **Service Convergence:** The development and competition of cloud service providers can lead to the fact that in the near future these services will be differentiated according to the types, cost, availability and quality. Moreover, in some cases, a single cloud is not enough to meet mobile

user's demands. Therefore, the new scheme is needed in which the mobile users can utilize multiple clouds in a unified fashion. In this case, the scheme should be able to automatically discover and compose services for user.

CURRENT STATUS IN MOBILE APPLICATIONS

Offline Applications

Most of the applications available for modern mobile devices fall into this category. They act as fat client that processes the presentation and business logic layer locally on mobile devices with data downloaded from backend systems. There is periodical synchronization between the client and backend system. A fat client is a networked application with most resources available locally, rather than distributed over a network as is the case with a thin client. Offline applications, also often called native applications, offer:

- Good integration with device functionality and access to its features
- Performance optimized for specific hardware and multitasking
- Always available capabilities, even without network connectivity

Table 2. MCC application challenges, existing solutions, and future research areas

Limitations	Current Feasible Solutions	Future Work Flow
Code/ Computation Offloading	• **Static Partitioning:** (Hunt et al., 1998), (Giurgiu et al., 2009), (Cooper, Lindley, Wadler, and Yallop, 2007), (Yang, Shanmugasundaram, Riedewald, and Gehrke, 2006) • **Dynamic Profiling:** (Chun, Ihm, Maniatis, Naik, Patti, 2011), (Cuervo, Balasubramanian, Wolman, Saroiu, Chandra, and Bahl, 2010), (Kemp, Palmer, Kielmann, and Bal, 2012), (Kosta, Aucinas, Hui, Mortier, and Zhang, 2012) • **Local/Cloud Processing Decision:** (Rudenko, Reiher, Popek, and Kuenning, 1999), (Newhouse and Pasquale, 2004)	Automation of code / computation offloading
Task-Oriented Mobile Services	• **Mobile Data as a Service:** (Guo, Yan, and Aberer, 2012) • **Mobile-Computing as a Service:** (Hao, Lakshman, Mukherjee, and Song, 2009) • **Mobile-Multimedia-as-a-Service:** (Zhu, Luo, Wang, and Li, 2011), (Ferretti, Ghini, Panzieri, and Turrini, 2010), (Nan, He, and Guan, 2011), (Altamimi, Palit, Naik, and Nayak, 2012) • **Location-Based Services:** (Tan, Chu, and Zhong, 2014), (Cho, Myers, and Leskovec, 2011), (Stuedi, Mohomed, and Terry, 2010)	Creating human-centric task-oriented mobile services
Elasticity and Plasticity	• **Data Intensive Computation:** (Ananthanarayanan, Douglas, Ramakrishnan, Rao, and Stoica, 2012) • **Resource Allocation:** (Rai, Bhagwan, and Guha, 2009) • **Scheduling:** (He, Elnikety, Larus, and Yan, 2012), • (Tumanov, Cipar, Ganger, and Kozuch, 2012) • **VM Migration:** (Shen, Subbiah, Gu, and Wilkes, 2011)	Design and validation of resource allocation/ scheduling algorithms using valid traffic models for MCC Applications
Security	• **Authentication:** (Harbitter and Menasc´e, 2001), • (Al-Muhtadi, Ranganathan, Campbell, and Mickunas, 2002), (Bonneau, Herley, van Orschot, and Stajano, 2012), (Recordon and Reed, 2006), (Parno, Kuo, and Perrig, 2006) • **Authorization:** (Sun and Beznosov, 2012), (Chari, Jutla, and Roy, 2011), (Pai, Sharma, Kumar, Pai, and Singh, 2011), (Hueniverse, n.d.), (Miculan and Urban, 2011) • **Data/Code Integrity:** (van Dijk, Juels, Oprea, Rivest, Stefanov, and Triandopoulos, 2012), (Chen and Wang, 2012)	Cloud-to-mobile Authentication Authorization without releasing user credential Code integrity Verification
Cloud Service Pricing	• **Auctioning/Bidding:** (Zaman and Grosu, 2011), (Wang, Li, and Liang, 2012), (Zafer, Song, and Lee, 2012), (Tang, Yuan, and Li, 2012) • **Game Theory Based:** (Li and Li, 2011)	Empirical Validation Pricing Optimization

On the other hand, the native applications have many disadvantages:

- No portability to other platforms
- Complex code
- Increased time to market

Online Application

An online application assumes that the connection between mobile devices and backend systems is available most of the time. Smartphones are popular due to the power and utility of their applications, but there are problems such as cross-platform issues. Here Web technologies can overcome them; applications based on Web technology are a powerful alternative to native applications. Mobile has the potential to overcome some of the disadvantages of offline applications because they are:

- Multi-platform
- Directly accessible from anywhere
- Knowledge of Web technologies is widespread among developers, greatly minimizing the learning curve required to start creating mobile applications

However, mobile Web applications have disadvantages:

- Too much introduced latency for real-time responsiveness,
- (Even 30 msec. latency affects interactive performance)
- No access to device's features such as camera or motion detection
- Difficulties in handling complex scenarios that require keeping communication session over longer period of time

Issues With Offline and Online Mobile Applications

Current applications are statically partitioned, i.e. most of the execution happens on the device or on backend systems. However, mobile clients could face wide variations and rapid changes in network conditions and local resource availability when accessing remote data and services. As a result, one partitioning model does not satisfy all application types and devices. In order to enable applications and systems to continue to operate in such dynamic environments, mobile cloud applications must react with dynamical adjusting of the computing functionality between the mobile device and cloud depending on circumstances. In other words, the computation of clients and cloud has to be adaptive in response to the changes in mobile environments.

MCC Architecture

Figure 1 presents the general scenario of a Mobile Cloud Computing.

- Mobile devices are connected to the mobile networks via base stations that establish and control the connections and functional interfaces between the networks and mobile devices.

Figure 1. General framework of MCC

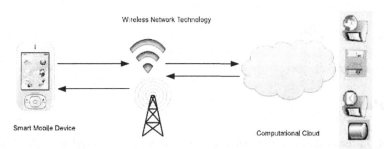

- Mobile users' requests and information are transmitted to the central processors that are connected to servers providing mobile network services.
- The subscribers' requests are delivered to a cloud through the Internet.
- In the cloud, cloud controllers process the requests to provide mobile users with the corresponding cloud services.

The general architecture of MCC can be shown in Figure 2, In this figure mobile devices are connected to the mobile networks via base stations (e.g., base transceiver station (BTS), access point, or satellite) that establish and control the connections (air links) and functional interfaces between the networks and mobile devices. Mobile users' requests and information (e.g., ID and location) are trans-

Figure 2. MCC architecture

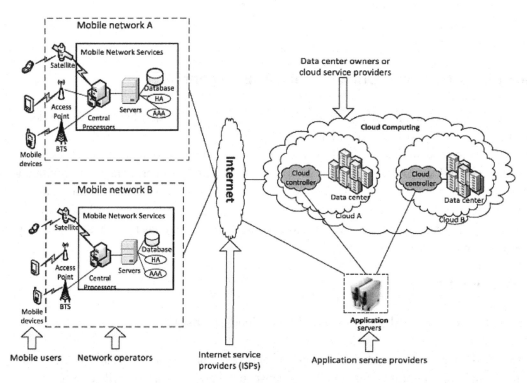

mitted to the central processors that are connected to servers providing mobile network services. Here, mobile network operators can provide services to mobile users as AAA (for authentication, authorization, and accounting) based on the home agent (HA) and subscribers' data stored in databases. After that, the subscribers' requests are delivered to a cloud through the Internet. In the cloud, cloud controllers process the requests to provide mobile users with the corresponding cloud services. These services are developed with the concepts of utility computing, virtualization, and service-oriented architecture (e.g., web, application, and database servers).

Application Models for Mobile Cloud Computing

Mobile cloud computing could be described as the availability of cloud computing services in a mobile ecosystem, i.e. worldwide distributed storage system. To leverage the full potential of mobile cloud computing we need to consider the capabilities and constraints of existing architectures.

Augmented Execution

To overcome the limitations of smartphones in terms of computation, memory and battery augmented execution is used.

The mobile phone hosts its computation and memory demanding applications. However, some or all of the tasks are offloaded in the cloud where a cloned system image of the device is running. The results from the augmented execution are reintegrated upon completion. This approach for offloading intensive computations employs loosely synchronized virtualized or emulated replicas of the mobile device in the cloud. Thus, it provides illusions that the mobile user has a more powerful, feature-rich device than actually in reality, and that the application developer is programming such powerful device without having to manually partition the application or provision proxies. Instantiating device's replica in the cloud is determined based on the cost policies which try to optimize execution time, energy consumption, monetary cost and security.

Figure 3 Shows categorization of possible augmented execution for mobile phones:

Figure 3. Clone Cloud categories for augmented execution

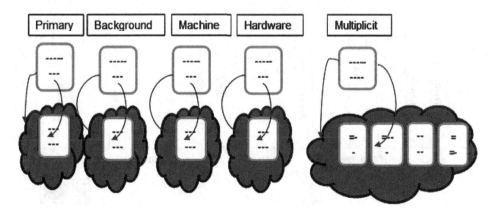

1. Primary functionality outsourcing (more like a client-server application)
2. Background augmentation (good for independent separate process that can run in background like a virus scanning)
3. Mainline (in-between primary and background augmentation)
4. Hardware (the replica runs on more powerful emulated VM, and (5) multiplicity – helpful for parallel executions)

Elastic Partitioned/Modularized Applications

Running applications in heterogeneous changing environments like mobile clouds requires dynamic partitioning of applications and remote execution of some components. Applications can improve their performance by delegating part of the application to remote execution on a resource-rich cloud infrastructure. The AlfredO framework allows developers to decompose and distribute the presentation and logic layer of the application, while the data layer always stays on the server side. The minimal requirement is the UI of the application to run on the client side.

Elasticity in software can be observed as the ability to acquire and release resources on demand. Modules are units of encapsulation and units of deployment that compose the distributed application. The underlying runtime module management platform hides most of the complexity of distributed deployment, execution, and maintenance.

Application Mobility

The mobile cloud is accessed through heterogeneous devices. In order to provide seamless user experience same applications, need to run on different devices. The application mobility plays a crucial role in enabling the next generation mobile applications. Application mobility is the act of moving application between hosts during their execution. Basically, application mobility is migrating running application

Figure 4. AlfredO architecture

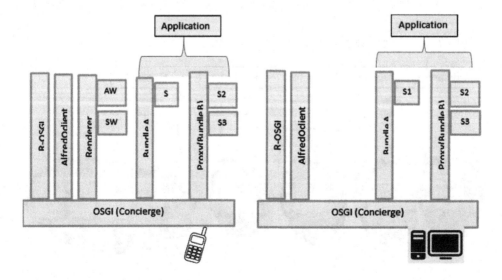

Figure 5. Reference architecture for elastic applications

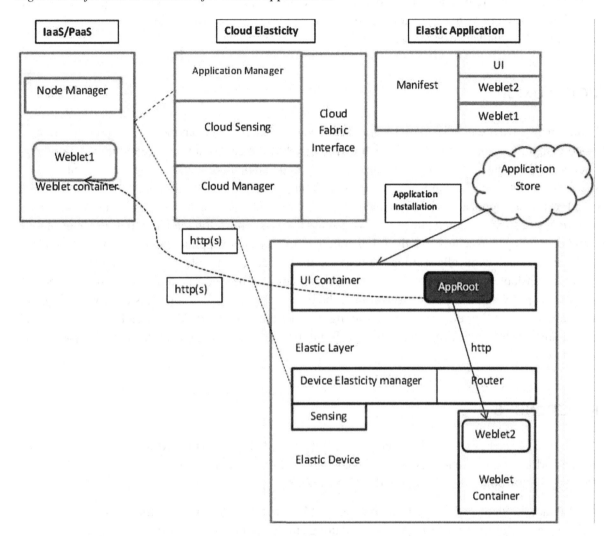

states from one device to another to which the user has an immediate access. Application mobility is closely related to process migration. Process migration is an operating system capability that allows a running process to be paused, relocated to another machine, and continued there. It represents seamless mobility at the granularity of individual processes, and has been the research focus of many experimental projects. However, application mobility involves more than process migration, e.g. migration tasks to different architectures.

Ad-Hoc Mobile Clouds

An ad-hoc computing cloud represents a group of mobile devices that serve as a cloud computing provider by exposing their computing resources to other mobile devices. This type of mobile cloud computing becomes more interesting in situations with no or weak connections to the Internet and large cloud providers. Offloading to nearby mobile devices save monetary cost, because data charging is avoided, especially favored in roaming situations. Moreover, it allows creating computing communities in which users can collaboratively execute shared tasks.

CONCLUSION

In this chapter we discussed perspectives and challenges of migrating from mobile computing to mobile cloud computing. We surveyed existing and speculated future generation mobile cloud computing applications. We identified various challenges, namely, code/computation offloading, task-oriented cloud services, elasticity and scalability, security, and cloud pricing, for building the next generation mobile cloud computing applications. We provided a survey of existing solutions toward each of these challenges and suggested future research directions. We discussed some application models and its usage in Mobile cloud computing. We believe that the full potential of mobile cloud applications lies in between the two extremes, while dynamically shifting the responsibilities between mobile device and cloud. Moreover, due to the unstable mobile environments, many factors need to be incorporated in a cost model, and fast predictive optimizing algorithms decide upon the best application execution. To simplify the development a convenient, but effective, programming abstraction is required. Mobile cloud computing will be a source of challenging research problems in information and communication technology for many years to come.

REFERENCES

Abolfazli, S., Sanaei, Z., Ahmed, E., Gani, A., & Buyya, R. (2014). Cloud-based augmentation for mobile devices: Motivation, taxonomies, and open challenges. *IEEE Communications Surveys and Tutorials, 16*(1), 337–368. doi:10.1109/SURV.2013.070813.00285

Al-Muhtadi, J., Ranganathan, A., Campbell, R., & Mickunas, M. (2002). A flexible, privacy-preserving authentication framework for ubiquitous computing environments. In *International Conference on Distributed Computing Systems Workshops* (pp. 771-776). 10.1109/ICDCSW.2002.1030861

Altamimi, M., Palit, R., Naik, K., & Nayak, A. (2012). Energy-as-a-service (EaaS): On the efficacy of multimedia cloud computing to save smartphone energy. In *IEEE 5th International Conference on Cloud Computing* (pp. 764–771). 10.1109/CLOUD.2012.72

Ananthanarayanan, G., Douglas, C., Ramakrishnan, R., Rao, S., & Stoica, I. (2012). True elasticity in multi-tenant data-intensive compute clusters. In *ACM Symposium on Cloud Computing*. 10.1145/2391229.2391253

Bonneau, J., Herley, C., van Oorschot, P., & Stajano, F. (2012). The quest to replace passwords: A framework for comparative evaluation of web 25 authentication schemes. In *IEEE Symposium on Security and Privacy* (pp. 553–567). 10.1109/SP.2012.44

Campbell, A., Eisenman, S., Lane, N., Miluzzo, E., Peterson, R., Lu, H., ... Ahn, G. (2008). The rise of people centric sensing. *IEEE Internet Computing*, *12*(4), 12–21. doi:10.1109/MIC.2008.90

Chari, S., Jutla, C. S., & Roy, A. (2011). Universally Composable Security Analysis of OAuth v2. 0. *IACR Cryptology EPrint Archive*.

Chen, I., & Wang, Y. (2012, October). Reliability analysis of wireless sensor networks with distributed code attestation. *IEEE Communications Letters*, *16*(10), 1640–1643. doi:10.1109/LCOMM.2012.091212.121454

Cheng, H., Sun, F., Buthpitiya, S., & Griss, M. (2012). *Sensorchestra: Collaborative sensing for symbolic location recognition. In Mobile Computing, Applications, and Services* (pp. 195–210). .

Cho, E., Myers, S. A., & Leskovec, J. (2011, August). Friendship and mobility: user movement in location-based social networks. In *Proceedings of the 17th ACM SIGKDD international conference on Knowledge discovery and data mining* (pp. 1082-1090). ACM.

Christensen, J. H. 2009. Using RESTful web-services and cloud computing to create next generation mobile applications. In *Proceedings of the 24th ACM SIGPLAN conference companion on Object oriented programming systems languages and applications* (pp. 627-634). ACM. 10.1145/1639950.1639958

Chun, B. G., Ihm, S., Maniatis, P., Naik, M., & Patti, A. (2011). Clone Cloud: Elastic execution between mobile device and cloud. In *Proceedings of EuroSys* 2011.

Chun, B.-G., Ihm, S., Maniatis, P., Naik, M., & Patti, A. (2011). Clone Cloud: elastic execution between mobile device and cloud. In *ACM Conference on Computer systems* (pp. 301–314).

Cimler, R., Matyska, J., & Sobeslav, V. (2014). Cloud based solution for mobile health care application. In *ACM 18th International Database Engineering and Applications Symposium.*

Consolvo, S., McDonald, D. W., Toscos, T., Chen, M. Y., Froehlich, J., Harrison, B., ... Smith, I. (2008, April). Activity sensing in the wild: a field trial of ubifit garden. In *Proceedings of the SIGCHI Conference on Human Factors in Computing Systems* (pp. 1797-1806). ACM.

Cooper, E., Lindley, S., Wadler, P., & Yallop, J. (2007). *Links: Web programming without tiers. In Formal Methods for Components and Objects* (pp. 266–296). Springer. doi:10.1007/978-3-540-74792-5_12

Cuervo, E., Balasubramanian, A., Cho, D. K., Wolman, A., Saroiu, S., Chandra, R., & Bahl, P. (2010). Maui: Making smartphones last longer with code offload. In AMC international conference on Mobile systems, applications, and services (pp. 49-62).

Ferretti, S., Ghini, V., Panzieri, F., & Turrini, E. (2010). Seamless support of multimedia distributed applications through a cloud. In *IEEE 3rd International Conference on Cloud Computing* (pp. 548–549). 10.1109/CLOUD.2010.16

Giurgiu, I., Riva, O., Juric, D., Krivulev, I., & Alonso, G. (2009). Calling the cloud: Enabling mobile phones as interfaces to cloud applications. *Middleware*, *2009*, 83–102.

Guo, T., Yan, Z., & Aberer, K. (2012). An adaptive approach for online segmentation of multi-dimensional mobile data. In *ACM International Workshop on Data Engineering for Wireless and Mobile Access*. 10.1145/2258056.2258059

Hao, F., Lakshman, T. V., Mukherjee, S., & Song, H. (2009, August). Enhancing dynamic cloud-based services using network virtualization. In *Proceedings of the 1st ACM workshop on Virtualized infrastructure systems and architectures* (pp. 37-44). ACM.

Harbitter, A. & Menasc´e, D.A. (2001). The performance of public key enabled Kerberos authentication in mobile computing applications. In *ACM conference on Computer and Communications Security* (pp. 78–85).

He, Y., Elnikety, S., Larus, J., & Yan, C. (2012). Zeta: scheduling interactive services with partial execution. In *ACM Symposium on Cloud Computing*. 10.1145/2391229.2391241

Herring, R., Hofleitner, A., Amin, S., Nasr, T., Khalek, A., Abbeel, P., & Bayen, A. (2009). *Using mobile phones to forecast arterial traffic through statistical learning*. Transportation Research Board.

Hueniverse. (n.d.). Oauth 2.0 (without signatures) is bad for the web. Retrieved from http://hueniverse.com/2010/09/oauth-2-0-without-signatures-isbad- for-the-web/

Huerta-Canepa, G., & Lee, D. (2010). A Virtual Cloud Computing Provider for Mobile Devices. In *ACM Workshop on Mobile Cloud Computing & Services: Social Networks and Beyond. MCS'10*. 10.1145/1810931.1810937

Hunt, G., & Scott, M. (1998). The coign automatic distributed partitioning system. ACM Operating systems review, 33, 187–200.

Hunter, T., Moldovan, T., Zaharia, M., Merzgui, S., Ma, J., Franklin, M., ... Bayen, A. (2011). Scaling the mobile millennium system in the cloud. In *ACM Symposium on Cloud Computing 2011* (p. 28). 10.1145/2038916.2038944

IEEE. (2009). Cloud computing drives mobile data growth. Retrieved from http://spectrum.ieee.org/telecom/wireless/cloudcomputing-drives-mobile-data-growth

Immagic. (n.d.). Compromising twitter's oauth security system. Retrieved from http://www.immagic.com/eLibrary/ARCHIVES/GENERAL/GENPRESS/A090903P.pdf

Intel. (2012). Int. cloud services platform beta location-based services. Retrieved from http://software.intel.com/enus/articles/cloud-services-location-based-api-overview

Kangas, K., & Röning, J. (1999, August). Using code mobility to create ubiquitous and active augmented reality in mobile computing. In *Proceedings of the 5th annual ACM/IEEE international conference on Mobile computing and networking* (pp. 48-58). ACM.

Kemp, R., Palmer, N., Kielmann, T., & Bal, H. (2012). Cuckoo: A computation offloading framework for smartphones. In *Mobile Computing, Applications, and Services, LNICSSITE* (Vol. *76*, pp. 59–79) . *Springer*.

Khalid, O., Khan, M., Khan, S., & Zomaya, A. (2014). Omni Suggest: A Ubiquitous Cloud based Context Aware Recommendation System for Mobile Social Networks. *IEEE Transactions on Services Computing*, *7*(3), 401–414. doi:10.1109/TSC.2013.53

Kosta, S., Aucinas, A., Hui, P., Mortier, R., & Zhang, X. (2012, March). Think Air: Dynamic resource allocation and parallel execution in the cloud for mobile code offloading. In IEEE INFOCOM (pp. 945-953).

Kovachev, D., Renzel, D., Klamma, R., & Cao, Y. (2010). Mobile Community Cloud Computing: Emerges and Evolves. In *Proceedings of the First International Workshop on Mobile Cloud Computing (MCC)*, Kansas City, MO. 10.1109/MDM.2010.78

La, H., & Kim, S. (2010). A conceptual framework for provisioning context aware mobile cloud services. In *IEEE 3rd International Conference on Cloud Computing* (pp. 466–473). 10.1109/CLOUD.2010.78

Lampe, U., Siebenhaar, M., Papageorgiou, A., Schuller, D., & Steinmetz, R. (n.d.). Maximizing cloud provider profit from equilibrium price auctions [pre-print].

Lane, N., Miluzzo, E., Lu, H., Peebles, D., Choudhury, T., & Campbell, A. (2010). A survey of mobile phone sensing. *IEEE Communications Magazine*, *48*(9), 140–150. doi:10.1109/MCOM.2010.5560598

Li, H., & Li, H. (2011). A research of resource provider-oriented pricing mechanism based on game theory in cloud bank model. In *IEEE International Conference on Cloud and Service Computing* (pp. 126–130). 10.1109/CSC.2011.6138509

Liu, F., Shu, P., Jin, H., Ding, L., Yu, J., Niu, D., & Li, B. (2013). Gearing resource-poor mobile devices with powerful clouds: Architectures, challenges, and applications. *Wireless Communications, IEEE*, *20*(3), 14–22. doi:10.1109/MWC.2013.6549279

Liu, L., Moulic, R., & Shea, D. 2010. Cloud service portal for mobile device management. In *2010 IEEE 7th International Conference on e-Business Engineering (ICEBE)* (pp. 474-478). IEEE. 10.1109/ICEBE.2010.102

Lu, H., Pan, W., Lane, N., Choudhury, T., & Campbell, A. (2009). Sound sense: scalable sound sensing for people-centric applications on mobile phones. In *International conference on Mobile systems, applications, and services* (pp. 165–178).

Luo, X. (2009, July). From augmented reality to augmented computing: A look at cloud-mobile convergence. In *International Symposium on Ubiquitous Virtual Reality* (pp. 29–32). 10.1109/ISUVR.2009.13

Ma, R. K. K., & Wang, C.-L. (2012). Lightweight Application level Task Migration for Mobile Cloud Computing. In *Proceedings of 26th IEEE International Conference on Advanced Information Networking and Applications*. 10.1109/AINA.2012.124

Miculan, M. & Urban, C. (2011). Formal analysis of Facebook connects single sign-on authentication protocol. *SOFSEM*, *11*, 22–28.

Miluzzo, E., Lane, N. D., Fodor, K., Peterson, R., Lu, H., Musolesi, M., . . . Campbell, A. T. (2008). Sensing meets mobile social networks: the design, implementation and evaluation of the cenceme application. In ACM conference on Embedded network sensor systems (pp. 337-350).

Mobilecommercedaily. (2011). AT&T to launch cloud-based lbs mobility data offering. Retrieved from http://www.mobilecommercedaily.com/attto-launch-cloud-based-lbs-mobility-data-offering

Mun, M., Reddy, S., Shilton, K., Yau, N., Burke, J., Estrin, D., . . . Boda, P. (2009). Peir, the personal environmental impact report, as a platform for participatory sensing systems research. In ACM international conference on Mobile systems, applications, and services (pp. 55-68).

Nan, X., He, Y., & Guan, L. (2011). Optimal resource allocation for multimedia cloud based on queuing model. In *IEEE 13th International Workshop on Multimedia Signal Processing*. 10.1109/MMSP.2011.6093813

Newhouse, T., & Pasquale, J. (2004). Resource-controlled remote execution to enhance wireless network applications. In *Workshop on Applications and Services in Wireless Networks* (pp. 30-38). 10.1109/ASWN.2004.185152

Oauth2.0. (n.d.). Retrieved from http://oauth.net/2/

Pai, S., Sharma, Y., Kumar, S., Pai, R., & Singh, S. (2011). Formal verification of oauth 2.0 using alloy framework. In *IEEE International Conference on Communication Systems and Network Technologies* (pp. 655–659). 10.1109/CSNT.2011.141

Paper, W. (2010). *Mobile Cloud Computing Solution Brief*. AEPONA.

Parno, B., Kuo, C., & Perrig, A. (2006). *Pool proof phishing prevention*. In *Financial Cryptography and Data Security*.

Perez, S. (2009, August 4). Why cloud computing is the future of mobile. *Readwriteweb*. Retrieved February 2015 from http://www.readwriteweb.com/archives/why_cloud_com.puting_is_the_future_of_mobile.php

Rai, A., Bhagwan, R., & Guha, S. (2012). Generalized resource allocation for the cloud. In *ACM Symposium on Cloud Computing*.

Recordon, D. & Reed, D. (2006). Open id 2.0: a platform for user-centric identity management. In *ACM workshop on Digital identity management* (pp. 11–16).

Rudenko, A., Reiher, P., Popek, G. J., & Kuenning, G. H. (1999, February). The remote processing framework for portable computer power saving. In *Proceedings of the 1999 ACM symposium on Applied computing* (pp. 365-372). ACM.

Satyanarayanan, M. (2010). Mobile computing: the next decade. In *Proceedings of the 1st ACM Workshop on Mobile Cloud Computing & Services: Social Networks and Beyond (MCS)*.

Satyanarayanan, M. (2010). Mobile computing: the next decade. In *ACM Workshop on Mobile Cloud Computing Services: Social Networks and Beyond*.

Satyanarayanan, M., Bahl, P., C'aceres, R., & Davies, N. (2009, October). The Case for VM-Based Cloudlets in Mobile Computing. *IEEE Pervasive Computing, 8*(4), 14–23. doi:10.1109/MPRV.2009.82

Sensorly. (2016). Retrieved from http://www.sensorly.com/

Shen, Z., Subbiah, S., Gu, X., & Wilkes, J. (2011). Cloud Scale: elastic resource scaling for multi-tenant cloud systems. In *ACM Symposium on Cloud Computing.*

Sociallipstick. (n.d.). Under the covers of oauth 2.0 at Facebook. Retrieved from http://www.social-lipstick.com/?p=239

Stuedi, P., Mohomed, I., & Terry, D. (2010, June). Wherestore: Location-based data storage for mobile devices interacting with the cloud. In *Proceedings of the 1st ACM Workshop on Mobile Cloud Computing & Services: Social Networks and Beyond*. ACM.

Sun, S.-T. & Beznosov, K. (2012). The devil is in the (implementation) details: an empirical analysis of oauthsso systems. In *ACM conference on Computer and communications security* (pp. 378-390).

Tamai, K., & Shinagawa, A. (2011). Platform for location-based services. *Fujitsu Scientific and Technical Journal, 47*(4), 426–433.

Tan, Z., Chu, D., & Zhong, L. (2014). Vision: cloud and crowd assistance for GPS urban canyons. In Proceedings of the fifth international workshop on Mobile cloud computing & services (pp. 23-27). ACM. doi:10.1145/2609908.2609950

Tang, S., Yuan, J., & Li, X. (2012). Towards optimal bidding strategy for amazon ec2 cloud spot instance. In *IEEE 5th International Conference on Cloud Computing* (pp. 91–98). 10.1109/CLOUD.2012.134

Tavel, P. (2007). *Modeling and Simulation Design*. AK Peters Ltd.

Thiagarajan, A., Ravindranath, L., LaCurts, K., Madden, S., Balakrishnan, H., Toledo, S., & Eriksson, J. (2009). Vtrack: accurate, energy-aware road traffic delay estimation using mobile phones. In *ACM Conference on Embedded Networked Sensor Systems* (pp. 85–98). 10.1145/1644038.1644048

Tumanov, A., Cipar, J., Ganger, G. R., & Kozuch, M. A. (2012). alsched: algebraic scheduling of mixed workloads in heterogeneous clouds. In *ACM Symposium on Cloud Computing*. 10.1145/2391229.2391254

Van Dijk, M., Juels, A., Oprea, A., Rivest, R. L., Stefanov, E., & Triandopoulos, N. (2012, October). Hourglass schemes: how to prove that cloud files are encrypted. In *Proceedings of the 2012 ACM conference on Computer and communications security* (pp. 265-280). ACM.

Wang, W., Li, B., & Liang, B. (2012). Towards optimal capacity segmentation with hybrid cloud pricing. In *IEEE 32nd International Conference on Distributed Computing Systems* (pp. 425–434). 10.1109/ICDCS.2012.52

Wang, Y., Wu, J., & Yang, W. S. (2013). Cloud-Based Multicasting with Feedback in Mobile Social Networks. *IEEE Transactions on Wireless Communications, 12*(12), 6043–6053. doi:10.1109/TWC.2013.102313.121508

Wright, A. (2009). Get Smart. *Communications of the ACM, 52*(1), 15–16. doi:10.1145/1435417.1435423

Wu, H., Wang, Q., & Wolter, K. (2013). Mobile Healthcare Systems with Multi cloud Offloading. In *IEEE 14th International Conference on Mobile Data Management* (pp. 188-193). 10.1109/MDM.2013.92

Yang, D., Xue, G., Fang, X., & Tang, J. (2012). *Crowdsourcing to smartphones: incentive mechanism design for mobile phone sensing*. In *ACM MobiCom*. doi:10.1145/2348543.2348567

Yang, F., Shanmugasundaram, J., Riedewald, M., & Gehrke, J. (2006). Hilda: A high-level language for data driven web applications. In *IEEE International Conference on Data Engineering* (pp. 32).

Zafer, M., Song, Y., & Lee, K. (2012). Optimal bids for spot vms in a cloud for deadline constrained jobs. In *IEEE 5th International Conference on Cloud Computing* (pp. 75–82). 10.1109/CLOUD.2012.59

Zaman, S., & Grosu, D. (2011). Combinatorial auction-based dynamic vm provisioning and allocation in clouds. In *IEEE Third International Conference on Cloud Computing Technology and Science* (pp. 107–114). 10.1109/CloudCom.2011.24

Zhu, W., Luo, C., Wang, J., & Li, S. (2011). Multimedia cloud computing. *IEEE Signal Processing Magazine, 28*(3), 59–69. doi:10.1109/MSP.2011.940269

Chapter 6
Mobile Cloud Computing:
Applications Perspective

Parkavi R
Thiagarajar College of Engineering, India

Priyanka C
Thiagarajar College of Engineering, India

Sujitha S
Thiagarajar College of Engineering, India

Sheik Abdullah A
Thiagarajar College of Engineering, India

ABSTRACT

Mobile Cloud Computing (MCC) which combines mobile computing and cloud computing, has become one of the industry ring words and a major conversation thread in the IT world with an explosive development of the mobile applications and emerging of cloud computing idea, the MCC has become a possible technology for the mobile service users. The concepts of Cloud computing are naturally meshed with mobile devices to allow on-the-go functionalities and benefits. The mobile cloud computing is emerging as one of the most important branches of cloud computing and it is expected to expand the mobile ecosystems. As more mobile devices enter the market and evolve, certainly security issues will grow as well. Also, enormous growth in the variety of devices connected to the Internet will further drive security needs. MCC provides a platform where mobile users make use of cloud services on mobile devices. The use of MCC minimizes the performance, compatibility, and lack of resources issues in mobile computing environment.

INTRODUCTION

Today's mobile phone users can execute a wide range of tasks by downloading applications to their receiver from online stores. These applications are called resident applications exact to the mobile operating system and they use the computing power and memory restricted in the device to run the application. In complicated applications which requires more dealing out power and memory is not suited

DOI: 10.4018/978-1-5225-4044-1.ch006

to run on these devices. Hence it poses a dispute for the mobile application developers to build different versions of the same application for multiple mobile operating systems and more complicated applications involve robust computing power and memory in the receiver. Cloud computing, a developing trend with which we can access a variety of services over the internet, can bring exceptional sophistication in mobile ecosystem. It can influence the power of handsets by executing the applications on the cloud as an alternative of locally running them on the mobile device. This give rise to the new term called mobile cloud computing. Mobile cloud applications can not only be accessed by smart phones, but they can also be accessed by low cost featured phones where the processing power and memory is restrained. Several views exist on mobile cloud computing. From one perspective, mobile cloud computing can be defined as an architecture where the data processing and storage happens outside of the mobile device. Mobile cloud applications move the computing power and data storage away from mobile phones into the cloud, bringing the apps and mobile computing to not just Smartphone users but a much broader range of mobile subscribers. On the other way round, mobile cloud computing can be thought of as a cloud where the cloud is formed by a group of mobile devices that share their computing power to run applications on them. By this way mobile cloud computing can bring tremendous benefits to the feature phone enabled users as equivalent to the smart phone users. Mobile computing can also mean using moveable devices to run stand-unaccompanied applications and/or accessing remote applications via wireless networks.

Nowadays, both hardware and software of mobile devices get better development than before, some smart phones such as iphone 4S, Android serials, Windows Mobile serials and Blackberry, are no longer just established mobile phones with conversation, SMS, Email and website browser, but are daily necessities to users. Meanwhile, those smart phones include various sensing modules like direction-finding, optics, significance, orientation, and so on which brings a suitable and intelligent mobile experience to users. In 2010, Google CEO Eric Schmidt described mobile cloud computing in a discussion that 'based on cloud computing service development, mobile phones will become more and more complicated, and evolve in the direction of a transportable super computer. In the face of a variety of mobile cloud services provided by Microsoft, Apple, Google, HTC, and so on, users may be puzzled about what mobile cloud computing exactly is, and what its features are. Mobile Cloud computing at its simplest refers to an communications where both the data storage and the data handing out happen outside of the mobile device. Mobile cloud applications move the computing power and data storage space away from mobile phones and into the cloud, bringing applications and mobile computing to not just smart phone users but a much broader range of mobile subscribers.

LITERATURE SURVEY

An Anonymous End-to-End Communication Protocol for Mobile Cloud Environments

The increasing unfold of mobile cloud computing paradigm is dynamically the quality mobile communication infrastructure. Mobile cloud introduces new privacy risks, since personal information of the human action users is distributed among several parties (e.g., cellular network operator, cloud provider) throughout this paper, they tend to propose a solution implementing academic degree end-to-end anonymous communication protocol between two users inside the network that leverages properties of social tend to trust academic degree person model, where each party observant a number of the communication most likely colludes with others to uncover the identity of human action users. And they extensively analyze the security of proposed protocol and thus the anonymity preserved against on high adversaries. Most importantly, they tend to assess the performance of proposed solution by comparing it to on a real tested of thirty-six smart phones and relative clones running on Amazon EC2 platform. (Claudio et al., 2014)

A Privacy-Aware Authentication Scheme for Distributed Mobile Cloud Computing Services

Privacy aware authentication scheme for distributed mobile cloud computing service is proposed and the scheme provides security for mobile users to multiple services using only a single private key. The security strength of the proposed scheme is bilinear paring system. In one mobile user authentication session, only targeted cloud service provider needs to interact with the service requestor. For distributed cloud service providers and mobile clients the trusted SGC serves as secure key. In the proposed scheme the trusted SCG service is not involved in individual user authentication processing time required by interaction and calculation between cloud service providers and traditional trust third party services (Tsai & Lo, 2015). They propose a new anonymous authentication scheme for distributed mobile cloud services environment. Proposed scheme supports mutual authentication, key exchange, user anonymity, user untraceability. The trusted SCG service is not involved individual user authentication process. They also reduce authentication processing time required by communication and computation between cloud service provider and traditional trusted third-party services.

A Mobile Payment Mechanism With Anonymity for Cloud Computing

In this work transactions have been replaced by electronic transactions. To guard the security of the electronic connections, a variety of electronic payment (e-payment) mechanism has been proposed. They have found the previous e-payment mechanisms do not make available the non repudiation requirement in the client side. Thus, a malevolent customer can easily reject the business and the businessmen may not get the payment. In addition, these mechanisms cannot be applied to the mobile payment for cloud computing due to large computation and communication costs. To solve the above problems, suggest a new mobile payment mechanism with anonymity for cloud computing in this paper (Yang & Lin, 2016). The proposed device not only reduces the calculation cost but also provides the non-repudiation condition in the client side. Compared with the related works, the proposed mechanism is securer, fairer, and extra efficient. Therefore, the proposed mobile payment mechanism is additional suitable and practical for the cloud computing.

An Efficient and Secure Anonymous Mobility Network Authentication Scheme

The demands of Internet users are progressively increasing. Many users access Internet services through mobile devices via wireless networks. To avoid disclosure of private data, researchers have proposed a variety of anonymous roaming authentication schemes which apply different technologies to give integral security properties, such as symmetric and asymmetric encryption etc. Regrettably, a few of these schemes still reveal safety and competence issues. In order to provide tripartite authentication and enhance efficiency, they propose an efficient and secure anonymous authentication scheme for mobility networks. Performance and security analysis, they can prove that the proposed scheme is capable to improve efficiency and improve security in comparison to previous schemes. In this paper, they proposed an efficient and secure anonymous roaming authentication scheme for mobility networks. Instead of symmetric and asymmetric system they proposed scheme which utilizes hash functions and point operations to maintain secure advantages. Comparing security and performance, proposed scheme improve the performance during the roaming authentication phase for mobility networks and also it has more security properties in comparison with previous schemes. This method uses point operations which are independent in that these operations do not rely on an external framework for support and it does not rely on the assumptions or structure of asymmetric cryptography (Wen-Chung Kuo et al., 2014).

BACKGROUND

Mobile cloud computing can be consideration of as infrastructure where data and handing out could happen outside of the mobile device, enabling new types of applications such as framework-aware mobile social networks. As a result, many mobile cloud applications are not constrained to powerful smart phones, but to a broad range of less highly developed mobile phones and, therefore, to broader subscriber spectators. MCC can be separated into mobile computing and cloud computing. The mobile devices can be laptops, PDA, smart phones and so on, which connect with a base station or a hotspot by a radio link such as 3G, Wi-Fi or GPRS. Although the client is distorted from PCs or permanent machines to mobile devices, the main concept is unmoving cloud computing. Mobile users send service needs to the cloud through a web browser or desktop application. The organization component of cloud then allocates resources to the request to ascertain connection, while the monitoring and manipulative functions of mobile cloud computing are implemented to ensure the QoS until the connection is completed. The cloud model as defined by NIST promotes accessibility and is composed of five important characteristics, three service models. As a development and addition of Cloud Computing and Mobile Computing, Mobile Cloud Computing, as a new phrase, has been devised since 2009. In order to help us avaricious better understanding of Mobile Cloud Computing, let's start from the two previous techniques: Mobile Computing and Cloud Computing.

Mobile Computing

Mobility has become a very popular word and rapidly increasing part in today's computing area. An incredible growth has appeared in the development of mobile devices such as, Smartphone, PDA, GPS Navigation and laptops with a variety of mobile computing, networking and security technologies. In addition, with the improvement of wireless technology like WiMax, Ad Hoc Network and WIFI, users may be surfing the Internet much easier but not limited by the cables as before. Thus, those mobile devices have been accepted by more and more people as their first choice of working and entertainment in their daily lives. It is described as a form of human-computer interaction by which a computer is expected to be transported during normal usage. Mobile computing is based on a collection of three major concepts: hardware, software and communication. The concepts of hardware can be considered as mobile devices, such as Smartphone and laptop, or their mobile components (Kaur & Kaur, 2014). Software of mobile computing is the numerous mobile applications in the devices, such as the mobile browser, anti-virus software and games. The communication issue includes the infrastructure of mobile networks, protocols and data delivery in their use. They must be transparent to end users.

Features

1. Mobility Mobile nodes in mobile computing network can establish connection with others, even fixed nodes in wired network through Mobile Support Station (MSS) during their moving.
2. Diversity of network conditions Normally the networks using by mobile nodes are not unique, such network can be a wired network with high-bandwidth, or a wireless Wide Area Network (WWAN) with low-bandwidth, or even in status of disconnected.
3. Frequent disconnection and consistency as the limitation of battery power, charge of wireless communication, network conditions and so on, mobile nodes will not always keep the connection, but disconnect and consistent with the wireless network passively or actively.
4. Dis-symmetrical network communication Servers and access points and other MSS enable a strong send/receive ability, while such ability in mobile nodes is quite weak comparatively. Thus, the communication bandwidth and overhead between downlink and uplink are discrepancy.
5. Low reliability due to signals is susceptible to interference and snooping, a mobile computing network system has to be considered from terminals, networks, database platforms, as well as applications development to address the security issue.

Challenges

Compared with the traditional wired network, mobile computing network may face various problems and challenges in different aspects, such as signal disturbance, security, hand-off delay, limited power, low computing ability to the wireless environment and numerous mobile nodes. In addition, the Quality of Service (QoS) in mobile computing network is much easier to be affected by the landforms, weather and buildings.

Cloud Computing

In the era of PC, many users found that the PCs they bought 2 years ago cannot keep pace with the development of software nowadays; they need a higher speed CPU, a larger capacity hard disk, and a higher performance Operation System (OS).That is the magic of 'Moore's Law' which urges user upgrading their PCs constantly, but never ever overtaken the development of techniques. Thus, a term called 'Cloud Computing' burst upon our lives. However, there is no consensual definition on what a Cloud Computing or Cloud Computing System is, due to dozens of developers and organizations described it from different perspectives. Major function of a cloud computing system is storing data on the cloud servers, and uses of cache memory technology in the client to fetch the data. Those clients can be PCs, laptops, smart phones. Perspective of marking that cloud computing is a parallel and distributed computing system, which is combined by a group of virtual machines with internal links. Such systems dynamically offer computing resources from service providers to customers according to their Service level Agreement (SLA). However, some authors mentioned that cloud computing was not completely new concept (Youseff et.al, 2008) from UCSB argue that cloud computing is just combined by many existent and few new concepts in many research fields, such as distributed and grid computing, Service-Oriented Architectures (SOA) and in virtualization.

Essential Characteristics

On-demand self service A consumer can unilaterally provision computing capabilities, such as server time and network storage, as needed automatically without requiring human interaction with each service provider.

Broad network access Capabilities are available over the network and accessed through standard mechanisms that promote use by heterogeneous thin or thick client platforms like mobile phones, laptops, PDAs etc.

Resource pooling the provider's computing resources is pooled to serve multiple consumers using a multi-tenant model, with different physical and virtual resources dynamically assigned and reassigned according to consumer demand. The customer does not have control or knowledge over the exact location of the provided resources. Examples of resources include storage, processing, memory, network bandwidth and virtual machines.

Rapid elasticity Capabilities can be rapidly and elastically provisioned, in some cases automatically, to quickly scale out and rapidly released to quickly scale in.

Measured Service Cloud systems automatically control and optimize resource use by leveraging a metering capability at some level of abstraction appropriate to the type of service (e.g. storage, processing, bandwidth and active user accounts).

Service Models

- **Software as a Service (SaaS):** The capability provided to the consumer is to use the provider's applications running on a cloud infrastructure. The applications are accessible from various client devices through a thin client interface such as a web browser (e.g., web-based email). The consumer does not manage or control the underlying cloud infrastructure with the possible exception of limited user-specific application configuration settings.
- **Platform as a Service (PaaS):** The capability provided to the consumer is to deploy onto the cloud infrastructure consumer created or acquired applications created using programming languages and tools supported by the provider. The consumer does not manage or control the underlying cloud infrastructure including network, servers, operating systems, or storage, but has control over the deployed applications and possibly application hosting environment configurations.
- **Infrastructure as a Service (IaaS):** The capability provided to the consumer is to provision processing, storage, networks, and other fundamental computing resources where the consumer is able to deploy and run arbitrary software, which can include operating systems and applications.

Deployment Model

- **Public Cloud:** It is most popular type of model. In public cloud third party provides the space for data storage and computing power for all applications. Service providers make resources which are available to the whole public over internet. Amazon and Google apps is an example of public cloud computing.
- **Private Cloud:** It is infrastructure operated only for single organization but it is managed by third party. All data center is to be set up and have to bear all installation and maintenance cost. But organization has complete control on data. In private cloud there is more security.

- **Community Cloud:** It shares applications between some organizations which have common type of needs. Community cloud can be managed internally or by the third party.
- **Hybrid Cloud:** It comprises of two or more clouds. Clouds in hybrid remain unique but are linked together so it's easy to move data from one deployment model to another.

MOBILE CLOUD COMPUTING

Mobile Cloud Computing (MCC) is the combination of cloud computing, mobile computing and wireless networks to bring rich computational resources to mobile users, network operators, as well as cloud computing providers. The ultimate goal of MCC is to enable execution of rich mobile applications on a plethora of mobile devices; with a rich user experience. MCC provides business opportunities for mobile network operators as well as cloud providers. More comprehensively, MCC can be defined as "…a rich mobile computing technology that leverages unified elastic resources of varied clouds and network technologies toward unrestricted functionality, storage, and mobility to serve a multitude of mobile devices anywhere, anytime through the channel of Ethernet or Internet regardless of heterogeneous environments and platforms based on the pay-as-you-use principle…" Cloud computing Is an emerging concept combining many fields of computing. The foundation of cloud computing is the delivery of services, software and processing capacity over the Internet, reducing cost, increasing storage, automating systems, decoupling of service delivery from underlying technology, and providing flexibility and mobility of information.

Mobile Cloud Computing (MCC) is the combination of cloud computing, mobile computing and wireless networks to bring rich computational resources to mobile users, network operators, as well as cloud computing providers (Qi & Gani, 2012). The ultimate goal of MCC is to enable execution of rich mobile applications on a plethora of mobile devices, with a rich user experience. MCC provides business opportunities for mobile network operators as well as cloud providers.[5][6] More comprehensively, MCC can be defined as "a rich mobile computing technology that leverages unified elastic resources of varied clouds and network technologies toward unrestricted functionality, storage, and mobility to serve a multitude of mobile devices anywhere, anytime through the channel of Ethernet or Internet regardless of heterogeneous environments and platforms based on the pay-as-you-use principle. Mobile cloud computing uses cloud computing to deliver applications to mobile devices. These mobile apps can be deployed remotely using Speed and flexibility and development tools. On the Mobile cloud applications can be built or revised quickly using cloud services. They can be delivered to many different devices with different operating systems, computing tasks and data storage. Thus, users can access applications that could not otherwise be supported.

In today's world handheld devices such as, smartphone, tabletPCs have emerged as an integral part of human life as they are very convenient and effective tools for communication at any place and at any time. The users have the expectation that all the information should be accessible at their finger tips anytime anywhere. But, compared to conventional processing devices such as PCs and laptops mobile devices have lack of resources (e.g. bandwidth, storage and battery life).For overcoming the limitations of handheld devices a new technology named mobile cloud computing has emerged which combines both cloud computing and mobile computing. The concept of mobile has been introduced not much after the launch of cloud computing in mid 2007. Since mobile cloud computing reduces the cost for development and running of mobile applications, it has attracted the attention of large number of industrialist.

Key Features

- Facilitates the quick development, Shared resources of mobile apps.
- Supports a variety of development approaches and devices.
- Improves reliability with information backed up and stored in the cloud.
- Applications use fewer device resources because they are cloud-supported.
- Mobile devices are connected to services delivered on API architecture.

MOBILE CLOUD SERVICES NEEDED BY CLIENT

The client provides mobile-oriented features like data synchronization, real-time push, and mobile RP etc.

- **Sync:** Sync is a service to synchronize data on to cloud. Any changes made to data or application will be synchronized to open up next time according to your settings.
- **Push:** all the notifications being sent by cloud server are managed by push. Users need not check or update necessarily any notification.
- **Offline App:** Offline App is platform to co ordinate between low level services. Users need not to program for any synchronization. Offline App automatically manage synchronization. Users just need to click for sync.
- **Network:** Network is just a channel that establishes connection between mobile network and cloud server. User need not to know underlying functioning of network.
- **Mobile RP:** Remote Procedure Call Simple Mobile RPC (Remote Procedure Call) exposes your server-side coarse grained business services. These services are invoked via a simple RPC mechanism without any low-level programming like http-client code, client side REST library, etc on the part of the App developer. There is a RPC API that is used for making these calls.
- **Database:** Database store data for Apps .Database provide safe concurrent access to apps.

MOBILE CLOUD SERVICES NEEDED BY SERVER

A Cloud Server is located in the 'Cloud'. The server A Cloud Server is located in the 'Cloud'. The server provides mobile-oriented features like data synchronization, real-time push, and mobile RPC etc. Cloud server is intermediate between the mobile device and the actual cloud data services being provided to mobile devices.

- **Sync:** All your app data is automatically managed by the on-device cloud stack. Any operations that have occurred in offline mode are auto-tracked. When the platform detects network connectivity, it auto-syncs the information back with the cloud. In the sync process, it brings in any new information that may have appeared on the cloud while you were disconnected. Server Sync service synchronizes device side App state changes with the backend services where the data actually originates. It also must provide a plug-in framework to mobilize the backend data.
- **Push:** The Push mechanism uses a pure network/socket based approach instead of clunky out of band methodologies like sms alerts, text message, or email alerts. The Push notifications happen

inside the app's environment Server Push service monitors data channels (from backend) for updates. The moment updates are detected, corresponding notifications are sent back to the device. If the device is out of coverage or disconnected for some reason, it waits in a queue, and delivers the push the moment the device connects back to the network.

- **Secure Socket-Based Data Service:** Depending on the security requirements of the Apps this server-side service must provide plain socket server or a SSL-based socket server or both.
- **Security:** Security component provides authentication and authorization services to make sure mobile devices connecting to the Cloud Server are in fact allowed to access the system. Every device must be first securely provisioned with the system before it can be used. After the device is registered, it is challenged for proper credentials when the device itself needs to be activated. Once the device is activated, all Cloud requests are properly authenticated/authorized going
- **Management Console:** Every instance of a Cloud Server must have a Command Line application.

ADVANTAGES OF MCC

1. **How Battery Lifetime Can Be Extended by MCC:** Battery is main component of mobile devices. Structure of battery need a change to co- operates with present applications. Secondly, application cost for mobile users is also issue of concern. So, MCC is solution to problem. The solution is offloading technique in MCC. Offloading: computation offloading technique transfer large computations and complex processing from device which have limited resources like mobile devices to machines which have full resources that is cloud server in cloud. This will result in less power consumption because offloading technique will avoid long application execution time on mobile device.

2. **Storage Capacity:** Challenge in storage capacity is today user need more and more capacity on mobile devices to save information that is essential or for his/her entertainment sake, but as the storage capacity increase weight of device also increases. Then what could be the solution to save large amount of data on low weight devices?

Again, the solution is MCC. MCC is developed to enable mobile users to store the large amount of data on cloud through network server. Some best examples of such kind of service are Flicker, Google Derive, Amazon S3, Gmail etc.

3. **Reliability:** Of course, every user needs a reliable backup for their data. MCC provide a reliable source to store data that is cloud. User need not to worry about loss of data on crash of device or loss of device. Storing data or running applications on cloud is very safe way to improve reliability since data is automatically backed up on cloud.

4. **Dynamic Provisioning:** Dynamic on-demand provisioning of resources on a fine-grained, self-service basis No need for advanced reservation. A dynamic service provisioning, i.e. dynamic resource allocation and dynamic deployment of services in a distributed environment enables high flexibility and optimized usage of the infrastructure. Cloud provisioning is the allocation of a cloud provider's resources to a customer. When a cloud provider accepts a request from a customer, it must create the appropriate number of virtual machines (VMs) and allocate resources to support them. The process is conducted in several different ways: advance provisioning, dynamic provisioning

and user self-provisioning. In this context, the term provisioning simply means "to provide." With advance provisioning, the customer contracts with the provider for services and the provider prepares the appropriate resources in advance of start of service. The customer is charged a flat fee or is billed on a monthly basis. With dynamic provisioning, the provider allocates more resources as they are needed and removes them when they are not. The customer is billed on a pay-per-use basis. When dynamic provisioning is used to create a hybrid cloud, it is sometimes referred to as cloud bursting. With user self-provisioning (also known as cloud self-service), the customer purchases resources from the cloud provider through a web form, creating a customer account and paying for resources with a credit card. The provider's resources are available for customer use within hours, if not minutes.

5. **Scalability:** Mobile applications can be performed and scaled to meet the unpredictable user demands Service providers can easily add and expand a service.

DISADVANTAGES OF MCC

1. **Security:** One of the major concerns with cloud computing is the security of Data. Often mobile users will provide sensitive information through the network, and if not protected, can lead to major damages in the case of a security breach.
2. **Performance:** Another major concern with mobile cloud computing is with regard to its performance. Some users feel performance is not as good as with native applications. So, checking with your service provide rand understanding their track record is advisable.
3. **Connectivity:** Internet connection is critical to mobile cloud computing. So, you should make sure that you have a good one before opting for these services.

APPLICATIONS OF MCC

1. **Mobile Commerce:** Mobile commerce usually known as M-commerce is a model for commerce on mobile devices. Mobile Commerce, or m-Commerce, is about the explosion of applications and services that are becoming accessible from Internet-enabled mobile devices. It involves new technologies, services and business models. As the numerous products and applications are provided through m-commerce, but there are various challenges associated with m-commerce like low network bandwidth availability, high complexity in mobile device configurations, and the major issue is of security/privacy. As a result, m-commerce applications are used through computing environment to solve these issues. But PKI (public key infrastructure) can be solution to this problem. PKI mechanism uses an encryption-based access to ensure users private and secure access to the cloud stored data.
2. **Mobile Learning:** Mobile learning techniques is rapidly adopted by youth. M-learning is combination of e-learning and mobility. Any data can be downloaded on mobile while busy in work. As we see, traditional e-learning has limitation of slow transmission rate, resources that are used for traditional learning are limited in number, also the devices which are used for traditional m-learning are high cost, so, the solution to theses traditional e-learning problem is cloud based learning. Through m-learning remote resources can be accessed (Afolabi, 2014).

3. **Mobile Healthcare:** In traditional medical treatment small storage, medical errors are some problems that occur to users. Through M-healthcare mobile users can continentally access resources whenever user is in need of healthcare. Many of healthcare services are provided on clouds which are on-demand. The advantages of healthcare to access healthcare information and manage expenses on health.

    a. Some comprehensive healthcare services are provided to users which help to monitor users ate anywhere anytime through mobile device.

    b. Intelligent emergency management system manages and co-ordinate the fleet of emergency vehicles effectively and in time when receiving calls of accident.

    c. Health aware mobile devices detect blood pressure, pulse rates and level of alcohol to alert healthcare emergency systems.

    d. Pervasive access to healthcare information allows patients or healthcare providers to access the current and post information.

    e. Healthcare expenses and other related charges can be managed through pervasive lifestyle incentive management.

4. **Mobile Gaming:** As with advanced deployment of wireless network, new possibilities are opened to play internet games developed for pc's on wireless mobile devices. According to developers of Mobile System Design due to constraint on hardware, memory and graphics processing, goal might be difficult to achieve using current client server architecture. But this is also the fact that mobile gaming is main source of generating, revues for service providers. Mobile games need to be offloading to save energy. According to offloading devices can save energy for mobile devices so the time for mobile game playing increases. According to offloading is a solution to augment these mobile system capabilities by migrating computations to more resourceful computers. For better solution on energy saving proposes a MAUI (Mobile Assistance Using Infrastructure) MAUI system helps in fine grained energy aware offloading of mobile code to cloud. MAUI divides application code at runtime based on communication network and processor to maximize energy savings.

5. **Melog:** It is MCC applications that enable mobile users to share real time experience. The mobile users are supported by several cloud services such as guiding a trip, slowing images and videos and showing maps etc. Video based mobile locations search capture a short video clip of surrounding buildings. The information is used in matching algorithm run on cloud to search for location of these buildings. One hour translation is a translation service in which you choose language such as English to French, upload material and select expertise. It helps mobile users to receive information translated in their language through mobile device.

MCC CHALLENGES AND ISSUES

In mobile cloud computing environment, the limitations of mobile devices, such as limited computing capability and energy resource, quality of wireless communication, to deploy complicated application, storage capacity, network bandwidth and support from cloud computing to mobile are all important factors that affect assessing from cloud computing. The following are the challenges and some solutions about mobile cloud computing:

Limitations of Mobile Devices

The processing capacity, storage, battery time, and communication of those smart phones will be limited when compared to desktop systems. Computation offloading techniques migrate the large computations and complex processing from resource limited devices to resourceful devices, thus avoiding mobile devices to take a large execution time.

The Virtual machine migration technology to offload execution blocks of applications from mobile devices to Clone Cloud either fully or partly extending the Smartphone-based execution to a distributed environment. In Clone Cloud system, the Smartphone is cloned (virtualized) as an image in distributed computing environment. Then it is passes computing or energy-intensive blocks to cloud for processing. Once execution completed, the output will be passed back to the Smartphone. Though it reduces battery consumption, it fails in handover delay and bandwidth limitation.

Quality of Communications

The dynamic changing of application throughput, mobility of users, and even weather will lead to changes in bandwidth and network overlay. Thus, the handover delay in mobile network is higher than in wired network. Network bandwidth performance can be improved by regional data centers or other means to bring content closer to mobile broadband. Network latency can be reduced by moving Application processor to the edge of mobile broadband. Cloudlet is presented by M. Satyanarayanan from Carnegie Mellon University, which provides rapidly instantaneous customized service to mobile devices using virtual machine (VM) technology for solving bandwidth-induced delay between devices and cloud, and so on. Cloudlet is deployed as a 'Micro Cloud' to be accessed by mobile devices with high bandwidth low delay.

Division of Application Services

The mobile devices have inherently limited resources. Thus, the applications have to be divided in order to achieve a particular performance target (low latency, minimization of data transfer, fast response time etc.)

Considering the demands of MCC, the essential factors for delivering 'good' cloud services have been enumerated below:

- Optimal partition of application services across cloud and mobile devices
- Low network latency in order to meet application and code offload interactivity
- High network bandwidth for faster data transfer between cloud and mobile devices
- Adaptive monitoring of network conditions to optimize network and device costs against user perceived performance of the Cloud application.

SOME OF THE ISSUES

Though mobile cloud makes the application accessing and storing data easier but still there some issues that need to solved, like low bandwidth. Wireless radio transmission sources are scarce as compared to wired transmission. This is hazard in application service because downloading and uploading is severally affected with speed of transmission. A solution was proposed that users which are located in same area and are accessing same type of content should share bandwidth. But this will be possible only if users are involved in same type of content. Availability and heterogeneity are also the major issues need to be solved out. Availability is limitation of resources or inability to connect to server due to traffic congestion or low bandwidth. Heterogeneity problem occur when mobile devices interact through different radio access technologies (Zohreh et al., 2013). These were the issues on server side. Some computing side issues could be offloading in static and dynamic environment, in static offloading can consume more energy to process short codes compared to local processing. In dynamic problem of offloading data ca not reach to destination or data can be lost while returning to user. Second issue that can be discussed can be security issue. Privacy of data is main issue while using LBS(location based services) to provide private data on cloud and integration of data while using application is necessary issue to be handled .these are just some of issues many more issues need concern like data access, quality of service etc.

1. **Security:** The absence of standards poses a serious issue specifically with respect to security and privacy of data being delivered to and from the mobile devices to the cloud.
2. **Better Service:** The original motivation behind MCC was to provide PC-like services to mobile devices. However, owing to the varied differences in features between fixed and mobile devices, transformation of services from one to the other may not be as direct.
3. **Task Division:** Researchers are always on the lookout for strategies and algorithms to offload computation tasks from mobile devices to cloud. However, due to differences in computational requirement of numerous applications available to the users and the variety of handsets available in the market, an optimal strategy is an area to be explored.
4. **Pricing:** MCC involves with both mobile service provider (MSP) and cloud service provider (CSP) with different services management, customers management, methods of payment and prices. This will lead to many issues. The business model including pricing and revenue sharing has to be carefully developed for MCC.
5. **Service Convergence**: Services will be differentiated according to the types, cost, availability and quality. A single cloud may not be enough to meet mobile user's demands. New scheme is needed in which the mobile users can utilize multiple clouds in a unified fashion. The scheme should be able to automatically discover and compose services for user.

MOBILE CLOUD SECURITY

In addition to the aforementioned concerns, securing a mobile cloud introduces the following challenges propose a security model for elastic applications made up of 'web lets' that can be migrated to and from a cloud to a mobile device:

1. Authentication between the web lets that would be distributed between the cloud and the device.
2. Authorization for weblets that could be executing on relatively untrusted cloud environments to access sensitive user data, and
3. Establishment and verification of trusted web let execution cloud nodes.

Their security framework is based on the assumption that the cloud elasticity service (CES), including the cloud manager, application manager, cloud node manager, and cloud fabric interfaces (CFI), is trustworthy (Mane & Devadkar, 2013). The security threats are categorized as threats to mobile devices, threats to cloud platform and application container, and threats to communication channels. The authors propose a framework with the following security objectives: Trustworthy weblet containers (VMs) on both device and cloud, authentication and secure session management needed for secure communication between web lets and multiple instantiation concurrently, authorization and access control enforcing web lets on the cloud to have the lowest privileges, and logging and auditing of weblets. Mobile Cloud aims to provide a security services architecture for MANET clouds in three ways:

Acting as an Intermediary for Identity, Key, and Secure Data Access Policy Management

Identity management is supported by Attribute-Based Identity Management (ABIDM), which supports user-centric identity management schemes also known as Identity 2.0. They propose ABKM, a system for key management, which is an extension of identity-based cryptography. However, in ABKM, the Trust Authority (TA) generates private key components for each user depending on their public attributes, and the key exchange protocol is not required. Therefore, this is effective for delay tolerant MANETs where the source and the destination do not usually talk prior to sending the data (Huang, D.et al., 2011).

Protect Information Belonging to Mobile Users by Means of Security Isolations

Mobile Cloud has Virtual Trusted and Provisioning Domains (VTaPD), which are virtual domains enforced with resource isolation. A VTaPD contains various nodes corresponding to different physical systems. Nodes in the same VTaPD support the secure Mobile Cloud communication system when passing messages to each other. A cryptography based approach is used to enforce data access control and information isolation.

Assess Risks by Monitoring MANET Status

The centralized data collection and processing in the MANET is used by the risk management service to identify malicious nodes and take preventive measures according to estimated risks.

Privacy

As the recent incident regarding CarrierIQ being installed and collecting information from mobile phones, it is important for mobile phone users to have transparency and choice (Chaturvedi, M.et al., 2011). Users need to be aware of what personal information is exactly visible to the public, and to have control over their personal data that is stored on their smart phones. It is vital that any personal data that is shared is done so with user consent, and that they can choose to opt out of any data collecting program at any time present the following requirements of a mobile and ubiquitous system that satisfies user privacy: protection against misuse, identification of pirated datasets, adjustment of laws (to provide additional security under certain circumstances), and ease of use. These are valid requirements for a mobile cloud as well. In a mobile cloud where mobile device share work with other mobile devices, a primary concern is malicious devices. In a setting where the device users are unknown and the mobile cloud is formed opportunistically, this is a most serious concern. Although the Public Key Infrastructure (PKI) is an appropriate method for the security issue, the problem is that it draws a high operational overhead that is not practical on resource constraint mobile devices. Furthermore, the connections between the devices in a mobile cloud are highly dynamic, and adaptive. At a given moment, new devices may be joining while current devices may be leaving. In such a scenario, the frequency of user authentication requests will increase to such an extent that it could result in insufficient resources to perform asymmetric key operations and transmit heavy messages. A solution to this problem is proposed in, in which PKASSO, a PKI based authentication protocol is introduced. To solve the resource constraint problem, PKASSO offloads the complicated PKI operations from the mobile device, to a remote resource rich server. Although this is a valid option in hybrid clouds that have connectivity to Internet, this is not viable in cases that long range connectivity is a problem. However, the cloudlet concept is useful in this scenario: cloudlets could operate as the local infrastructure to which the PKI operations can be offloaded. Techniques of anonymous routing such as onion routing can also be used to provide privacy for mobile nodes in a decentralized mobile cloud. Examples exist in the p2p domain. However, there are certain overheads and a risk of unreliable delivery associated with most anonymous p2p routing protocols. As a solution, the degree of anonymity should be flexible and depend on the context. For an example, a mobile cloud operating in a public environment where the potential for malicious nodes are high, should have a high level of privacy, but this would incur higher transmission (e.g.: longer paths) and computation costs (e.g.: cryptography processing overheads). In addition to an authorization scheme, users of the mobile cloud should also have the ability to change their privacy settings and dictate what information can be seen. For example, a mobile cloud participant may not want other devices to record his/her location information. In propose such a system, called the Privacy Rights Management for Mobile Applications (PRiMMA) project. PRiMMA's key objectives are to provide the users with a tool to control and add privacy policies, resolve inconsistencies between user privacy policies, and predict the privacy requirements using monitoring mechanisms.

Security

Before convincing more mobile users to run MCC applications, many security issues must be resolved. On the cloud side, it is a must to make sure a user accessing cloud resources is the one it claims to be. Cloud servers must be secure themselves and protect data from intrusion. On the user side, a mobile user needs to authenticate the cloud; that is, the cloud is the one it claims to be; secondly, it needs assurance of data/code integrity; third, it needs assurance that the user application will run only with permission.

Authentication

The foremost security challenge for MCC applications is authentication. Authentication is bidirectional, i.e., the mobile client must authenticate to the cloud (called mobile-to-cloud authentication) and the cloud must authenticate to the mobile client (called cloud-to-mobile authentication).In the literature, analyzed the performance of Kerberos-based mobile-to-cloud authentication with a proxy created between the mobile client and the cloud (Dinh, H. T.et al., 2013). They discovered that the proxy is a performance bottleneck. Another problem of Kerberos-based authentication is its vulnerability to attacks due to password only protection. Mobile-to-cloud authentication framework for ubiquitous computing environments using wearable devices, such as active badges, smart jewelry, smart watches, and biometrics. This provides a better protection for authenticating a mobile user's identity than password only protection. Focusing on both security and usability, web authentication the end user tends to carry more than one mobile device they proposed an authenticating scheme by which the same password may be used for several devices, as long as one of them passes authentication. The password is encrypted by a master password which is stored in the cloud and is effective for all other devices belonging to the same end user. The merit of this protocol is usability. However, protecting the secrecy of the master password is vulnerability. Another mobile-to-cloud authentication protocol by which a server asks for other available servers to serve as trusted identity servers to authenticate mobile users. OpenID possesses the advantage of usability but not security. It is subject to cookie stealthy and phishing attacks. Phool proof is another authentication protocol without the need of a trusted third party. It is specifically designed for mobile banking applications utilizing PKI technology based on the assumption that mobile devices are operated by the intended mobile users. All prior work cited above is for mobile-to-cloud authentication. While the literature is abundant in mobile-to-cloud authentication protocol design, there is little research done in cloud-to-mobile authentication. This deserves more research attention as MCC authentication must be bidirectional.

Authorization

Another major security issue for MCC applications is authorization. Authorizing an application to access user data without releasing the user's credential can save energy of mobile devices and reduce data transportation overhead. OAuth 2.0 with single sign-on (SSO) is widely applied in Google, Facebook and Twitter. Prior studies have verified its security. Hammer-Lahav reveals that OAuth 2.0 without signature is risky for users when sending the request to a wrong server. And Sheppard analyzed the implementation of OAuth in Face book. Analyzed the misuse of OAuth 2.0 in Twitter. Sun et al. studied its vulnerability by tracing SSO credentials. They discovered that the access token embedding scope and timeout information for authorization is subject to copying attacks. That is, if another entity has a copy, it will be authorized to accessing user data.

Data/Code Integrity

A classic method for securing data integrity is to store encrypted data on the remote server. It is feasible for a desktop computer to encrypt data before uploading it to the cloud. However, due to the computation cost for running the encryption algorithm, it is not practical to encrypt data on a Smartphone. Developed a protocol allowing a mobile user to encrypt and store data in the cloud. The mobile user needs to store the encryption key on the cloud and upload the plaintext to the cloud for encryption. The user data is divided into equal length blocks, each being encrypted using the encryption key provided, and an image is made out of each encrypted block. A mobile user verifies whether its data are encrypted properly by randomly selecting a block and challenging the cloud server to return the image of the block selected as a response. If the cloud server can return the image of the data block requested within a timeout interval and the returned image matches with that locally computed by the mobile device, then the mobile user considers its data as having been encrypted properly. The timeout interval is the maximum amount of time needed for the cloud server to transmit the image of the requested block to the mobile user, which is much smaller than the time for performing encryption of the data block selected anew and generating an image out of the encrypted data block. The problem with this approach is that it may be difficult to define a proper timeout interval as many factors (e.g., limited wireless bandwidth) may affect the wireless transmission time. A mobile client also must ensure the application code running on the cloud is indeed the same application code it authorizes the cloud to run (called code integrity). There is little research work reported in the literature regarding code integrity. For computation/code offloading, code integrity is essential to ensure the correctness of application execution.

CONCLUSION

MCC allows the user to get benefitted by the services offered by the cloud. Through MCC user of the mobile device can access his/her data stored on the cloud at anytime, anywhere if there is an internet connection. Mobile cloud computing is one of mobile technology developments in the future since it combines the benefits of both mobile computing and cloud computing, by this means providing best services for mobile users. The necessity of mobility in cloud computing gave delivery to Mobile cloud computing. MCC provides more options for access facilities in appropriate manner. It is predictable that after some years a quantity of mobile users will go to usage cloud computing on their mobile devices. This paper has provided a summary of mobile cloud computing in which its definitions, security, issues and advantages have been presented. Users of the cloud are not aware of the physical location of their data on the cloud. As a result data security is the major concern of the cloud consumers. Customer does not want to lose their private information or do not want any change on their data without their permission as a result of malicious insiders in the cloud. So, data integrity is the most important issue related to security risks of cloud as well as MCC. Data stored on the cloud may suffer from any damage occurring during transition from cloud to mobile, while residing on the cloud, etc. So, it is very essential to ensure the integrity i.e. correctness of the data. In this chapter a scheme has been proposed to solve the problem of data security specially data integrity. The proposed scheme has been implemented and its performance has been analyzed. The proposed scheme has been compared with some of the existing schemes. The future work remains as improvement of the scheme in more realistic way and to analyze the performance of the proposed scheme in a large network.

REFERENCES

Yang, J. H., & Lin, P. Y. (2016). A Mobile Payment Mechanism with Anonymity for Cloud Computing. *Journal of Systems and Software, 116*(June), 69–74.

Afolabi, A. O. (2014). On Mobile Cloud Computing in a Mobile Learning System. *Journal of Information Engineering and Applications, 4*(5).

Chaturvedi, M., Malik, S., Aggarwal, P. & Bahl, S. (2011). Privacy & Security of Mobile Cloud Computing. *Ansal University, Sector, 55*.

Claudio, A., Ardagna, Mauro Conti, Mario Leone. (2014). An Anonymous End-to-End Communication Protocol for Mobile Cloud Environment. *IEEE Transactions on Services Computing, 7*(3).

Dinh, H. T., Lee, C., Niyato, D., & Wang, P. (2013). A Survey of Mobile Cloud Computing: Architecture, Applications and Approaches. *Wireless Communications and Mobile Computing, 13*(18), 1587–1611. doi:10.1002/wcm.1203

Huang, D., Zhou, Z., Xu, L., Xing, T., & Zhong, Y. (2011). Secure Data Processing Framework for Mobile Cloud Computing. In *Proceedings of IEEE Conference on Computer Communications Workshops (INFOCOM WKSHPS)*. (pp. 614-618). 10.1109/INFCOMW.2011.5928886

Kaur, R. P., & Kaur, A. (2014). Perspectives of Mobile Cloud Computing: Architecture, Applications and Issues. *International Journal of Computer Applications, 101*(3).

Kuo, W.-C., Wei, H.-J., & Cheng, J.-C. (2014). An efficient and secure anonymous mobility network authentication scheme. *Journal of Information Security and Applications, 19*(1), 18–24. doi:10.1016/j.jisa.2013.12.002

Mane, Y. D. & Devadkar, K. K. (2013). Protection Concern in Mobile Cloud Computing–A Survey. *IOSR Journal of Computer Engineering, 3*, 39-44.

Qi, H., & Gani, A. (2012). Research on Mobile Cloud Computing: Review, Trend and Perspectives. In *Proceedings of Second International Conference on Digital Information and Communication Technology and it's Applications (DICTAP)* (pp. 195-202). 10.1109/DICTAP.2012.6215350

Tsai, J.-L., & Lo, N.-W. (2015). A Privacy-Aware Authentication Scheme for Distributed Mobile Cloud Computing Services. *IEEE Systems Journal, 9*(3), 805–815. doi:10.1109/JSYST.2014.2322973

Youseff, L., Butrico, M., & Da Silva, D. (2008). Toward a Unified Ontology of Cloud Computing. In *Grid Computing Environments Workshop, GCE'08*. IEEE. 10.1109/GCE.2008.4738443

Zohreh, S., Saeid, A., Abdullah, G., & Buyya, R. (2013). Heterogeneity in Mobile Cloud Computing: Taxonomy and Open Challenges. *IEEE Communications Surveys and Tutorials*, (99): 1–24. doi:10.1109/SURV.2013.050113.00090

ADDITIONAL READING

Alizadeh, M., Abolfazli, S., Zamani, M., Baharun, S., & Sakurai, K. (2015). Authentication in Mobile Cloud Computing: A Survey. *Journal of Network and Computer Applications, 18*(October).

Alizadeh, M., Hassan, W. H., Behboodian, N., & Karamizadeh, S. (2013). A Brief Review of Mobile Cloud Computing Opportunities. *Research Notes in Information Science, 12*, 155–160.

Buyya, R., Yeo, C., & Venugopal, S. (2008). Market-Oriented Cloud Computing: Vision, Hype, and Reality for Delivering it Services as Computing Utilities. In *10th IEEE International Conference on High Performance Computing and Communications HPCC'08*. IEEE. 10.1109/HPCC.2008.172

Chandrasekaran, I. (2011). *Mobile Computing with Cloud*. In *Advances in Parallel Distributed Computing* (pp. 513–522). .

Chetan, S., Kumar, G., Dinesh, K., Mathew, K., & Abhimanyu, M. A. (2010). Cloud Computing for Mobile World. Retrieved from http://chetan.ueuo.com

Garg, P., & Sharma, V. (2013). Secure Data Storage in Mobile Cloud Computing. *International Journal of Scientific & Engineering Research*, *4*(4), 1154–1159.

Gupta, P., & Gupta, S. (2012). Mobile Cloud Computing: The Future of Cloud. *International Journal of Advanced Research in Electrical, Electronics and Instrumentation Engineering*, *1*(3), 134–145.

Gupta, V., & Rajput, I. (2013). Enhanced Data Security in Cloud Computing with Third Party Auditor. *International Journal of Advanced Research in Computer Science & Software Engineering*, *3*(2), 341–345.

Hewitt, C. (2008). Orgs for Scalable, Robust, Privacy-Friendly Client Cloud Computing. *IEEE Internet Computing*, *12*(5), 96–99. doi:10.1109/MIC.2008.107

Hsueh, S. C., Lin, J. Y., & Lin, M. Y. (2011). Secure Cloud Storage for Convenient Data Archive of Smart Phones. In *Proceedings of IEEE 15th International Symposium on Consumer Electronics (ISCE)* (pp. 156-161). 10.1109/ISCE.2011.5973804

Itani, W., Kayssi, A., & Chehab, A. (2010). Energy-Efficient Incremental Integrity for Securing Storage in Mobile Cloud Computing. In *Proceedings of International Conference on Energy Aware Computing (ICEAC)*. 10.1109/ICEAC.2010.5702296

Jia, W., Zhu, H., Cao, Z., Wei, L., & Lin, X. (2011). SDSM: A Secure Data Service Mechanism in Mobile Cloud Computing. In *Proceedings of IEEE Conference on Computer Communications Workshops (INFOCOM WKSHPS)* (pp. 1060-1065). 10.1109/INFCOMW.2011.5928784

Khan, A. N., Kiah, M. M., Khan, S. U., & Madani, S. A. (2013). Towards Secure Mobile Cloud Computing: A Survey. *Future Generation Computer Systems*, *29*(5), 1278–1299. doi:10.1016/j.future.2012.08.003

Ren, W., Yu, L., Gao, R., & Xiong, F. (2011). Lightweight and Compromise Resilient Storage Outsourcing with Distributed Secure Accessibility in Mobile Cloud Computing. *Tsinghua Science and Technology*, *16*(5), 520–528. doi:10.1016/S1007-0214(11)70070-0

Sareen, B., Sharma, S., & Arora, M. (2014). Mobile Cloud Computing Security as a Service using Android. *International Journal of Computer Applications, 99*(17).

Shamim, S. M., Sarker, A., Bahar, A. N., & Rahman, M. A. (2015). A Review on Mobile Cloud Computing. *International Journal of Computer Applications, 113*(16).

Chapter 7
Processing IoT Data:
From Cloud to Fog—It's Time to Be Down to Earth

Pijush Kanti Dutta Pramanik
National Institute of Technology Durgapur, India

Saurabh Pal
Bengal Institute of Technology, India

Aditya Brahmachari
National Institute of Technology Durgapur, India

Prasenjit Choudhury
National Institute of Technology Durgapur, India

ABSTRACT

This chapter describes how traditionally, Cloud Computing has been used for processing Internet of Things (IoT) data. This works fine for the analytical and batch processing jobs. But most of the IoT applications demand real-time response which cannot be achieved through Cloud Computing mainly because of inherent latency. Fog Computing solves this problem by offering cloud-like services at the edge of the network. The computationally powerful edge devices have enabled realising this idea. Witnessing the exponential rise of IoT applications, Fog Computing deserves an in-depth exploration. This chapter establishes the need for Fog Computing for processing IoT data. Readers will be able to gain a fair comprehension of the various aspects of Fog Computing. The benefits, challenges and applications of Fog Computing with respect to IoT have been mentioned elaboratively. An architecture for IoT data processing is presented. A thorough comparison between Cloud and Fog has been portrayed. Also, a detailed discussion has been depicted on how the IoT, Fog, and Cloud interact among them.

DOI: 10.4018/978-1-5225-4044-1.ch007

INTRODUCTION

Typically, IoT devices are attributed to very limited computation and storage capacity. To get over this limitation, Cloud Computing has been the most favoured platform for processing IoT data, which provides on-demand and scalable resources for computing and storage. The sensor data are transported to the Cloud data centre, where they are processed, and the outcome is sent to the subscribed applications. Furthermore, the data centres may store the IoT data, if necessary, for analysis to extract further knowledge which helps in business decision making. The Cloud platform has become popular for IoT data processing mainly because of economic reason. By opting Cloud Computing, organisations have freed themselves from the hassle of establishing their own computing setup and maintenance. But as we are heading towards the smart world for a smart living, uses of sensors and wireless networks locally has been on the rise, and the data generated locally is increasingly consumed locally (Chiang, 2015). In other words, instead of at the remote centralised Cloud data centre, the data gravity is shifting more and more towards the neighbouring to the data source or, formally what we call, the edge of the network. For these applications, it is extremely crucial to be facilitated by low and predictable communication latency for real-time interaction, location awareness, and support for mobility and large-scale networks (Milunovich, Passi, & Roy, 2014). The traditional Cloud Computing architecture lacks in these aspects. IoT requires a different computing architecture that enables distributed processing of IoT data with mobility support and quick response whenever and wherever wanted. Fog Computing perfectly befits this scenario. Fog Computing is particularly suited for applications that demand real-time response with predictable and minimal latency (Milunovich, Passi, & Roy, 2014). The edge devices such as set-top-boxes, access points, routers, switches, base stations etc. are becoming ever more powerful in terms of computing, storage and networking. Hence, they are being considered as capable candidates to perform computational jobs. Considering that, Fog Computing can play a big role in processing the huge amount of data generated from billions of distributed IoT sensors. Fog Computing is not to replace the Cloud Computing rather it augments Cloud Computing by extending its services to the edge of the network. Principally, both Cloud and Fog serve the end users by providing data, computing resource, storage, and application services. But Fog is differentiated from the Cloud with respect to its proximity to the source and sink, its distribution irrespective of the geography and last but not the least its support for mobility (Mora, 2014). In the case of Cloud-based IoT data processing, every single bit of data would have to be shipped to the data centre. When the size of data to be processed grows enormously (and that is the exact case of IoT), it becomes very expensive to move them around. Since in Fog Computing data are being processed locally, the burden of transporting these data is lessened. The processed data are sent to the Cloud only if they are to be stored for further analysis and historical purposes. Also, since the data are processed very close to the source, the end-user service becomes very prompt which is very crucial for maintaining QoS in real-time and machine-to-machine (M2M) applications. Handling services in the Fog provide better user experience and more efficient and effective applications of IoT data. In this chapter, we have advocated for employing Fog Computing for IoT applications while discussing and comparing it with Cloud Computing in several aspects.

The rest of the chapter is organized as follows. A brief review of IoT and Cloud Computing is presented in section 2. The section 3 discusses how IoT data is processed in the Cloud, along with the advantages and issues. In section 4, we shall discuss the basics of Fog Computing including its characteristics and architecture. We shall identify the differences between Cloud and Fog in section 5. Section 6 addresses the processing of IoT data in the Fog. An architecture has been laid out for this. This section also discusses how IoT, Fog, and Cloud interact with each other. The prevalent commercial Fog Computing solutions are also discussed briefly. Section 7 and 8 respectively mentions the applications and challenges of Fog Computing. And section 9 concludes the chapter.

A Brief Introduction to IoT and Cloud Computing

Internet of Things (IoT) is the network of physical things, connected together to share data among themselves and other computing devices. The 'things' may be sensors, automobile, kitchen appliances, electronic devices, building, elevator or other devices. These interconnected 'things' collect and exchange data to share their state information. With an application of intelligent middleware, 'things' will be transformed into intelligent entities thereby blending the physical and virtual world together making the machine and human interactions very personalized. According to IBM:

The IoT is expected to make the physical world every bit as easy to search, utilize, and engage with as the virtual world (Milunovich, Passi, & Roy, 2014).

The sole objective of IoT is automation and monitoring, automating every activity which involves digital interventions.

In terms of practical realization, IoT applications in real time produce huge data within a time lag of fraction of second as a constant stream. To process the data, further, it requires high-speed data processing in continuum for data analysis to find the valuable insights. This puts a lot of strain on traditional private data centres owns by individual businesses in terms of network load management, centralized high data storage, processing, scalability etc. To realize this feat the Cloud Computing came into picture which acts as mere enabler or catalyst (NxtraData, 2016). Cloud Computing often referred to as "Cloud", as defined by IBM "is the delivery of on-demand computing resource – everything from applications to data centres – over the Internet". The Cloud provides computing resources like software, platform and infrastructure as pay-and-use services. The key characteristics that have made Cloud Computing popular are (Rouse, 2017; What is Cloud Computing? A beginner's guide, 2017):

- **Self-Service Provision:** This feature enables to choose any type of computing resources as per the need.
- **Elasticity:** Computing resource is scaled up or down based on the need.
- **Pay Per Use:** Resources can be paid only for use.
- **Performance:** Cloud Computing runs over secure data centres which are regularly upgraded with fast and efficient computing hardware. The network latency is very low.
- **Reliability:** The data backup is taken at multiple sites.

The objective of Cloud Computing is to establish a high-performance scalable virtual system with enormous data capacity and virtually capable of serving all type of processing jobs. This environment gives facility to all business enterprises and start-ups in revolutionarily cost reduction for what being spent on putting up computing infrastructure like private data centres.

These two technologies are completely different, where IoT act a platform and Cloud as a service. Though these technologies are conceptually independent still they are complementary to each other. IoT generates huge data, where Cloud provides a way for these data to reach their destination (storage, processing – data analytics).

Even though Cloud-based IoT model is a suitable solution, the deployment of IoT application has many challenges originated from economic consideration, social concern, technical limitation and administrative issues. Cloud may not be suitable for deploying all kinds of IoT-based applications, for example, where the data generated by 'things' are useful in its very locality or other entities in local proximity.

IoT DATA PROCESSING IN THE CLOUD

Typically, IoT devices are attributed with very limited computation and storage capacity and as a reason, Cloud Computing is there as a choice of platform for processing IoT data for quite a long time.

IoT produces huge data and needs huge storage and real-time processing. Comprehending the current contextual situation of 'things' by analysing the present and past data is inherently complex. The current contextual information or the data insight may help in decision making to take current action and future predictions. In this perspective, Cloud Computing is a possible solution, offering IoT-based applications the advantage of huge data storage and computational power to process out the complex computation and other software services in dynamic, scalable and virtualized manner at a very low cost (Alamri et al., 2013).

The mechanism for IoT data processing through Cloud is straightforward. Cloud linked to wireless sensor node (WSN) through gateways (Cloud gateway and sensor gateway) incorporated at both ends of the link. These gateways would allow data collection, aggregation and flow management. The sensor gateway collects the huge data streamed from sensors, compresses it and sends it to Cloud gateway. Whereas the Cloud gateway further decompresses the sensor data and store it in large Cloud storage servers (Alamri et al., 2013).

Advantages

There are several advantages of Cloud-IoT model, which had earned this model reputation in all respects. The advantages are described as follows (Alamri et al., 2013):

- **Increased Data and Processing Power:** Cloud provides enormous storage facility and processing power. Organizations can keep IoT sensor data easily in the Cloud without the hassle of creating its own private data storage. The huge processing power helps to process big complex data for the large-scale application.
- **Scalability:** The large routing architecture of Cloud model allows the IoT-based application to scale up in the Cloud as the need for new computing resources and services arises. This enables existing IoT-based application to scale up to large sizes based on new requirements without having to invest heavily in the new resources added.

- **Collaboration:** Cloud enables huge IoT data stored in storage server to be shared among different IoT application and group of users.

- **Dynamic Provisioning of Services:** Cloud provides varying services which allows processing the relevant information dynamically whenever and wherever they are needed. The API available in Cloud for various services enables the IoT applications to communicate with the data source. Cloud maintains 99.99% uptime, making its services available practically to anywhere and anytime as long as the IoT's have Internet connection (Coles, 2017).

- **Multi-Tenancy:** The multi-tenancy attribute of Cloud allows instances of IoT applications to share the same service infrastructure of Cloud in a varying manner. Further, Cloud allows integrating several services (Infrastructure, platform and software) from different service providers available on Clouds and Internet to meet the tailor-made demand of the user.

- **Flexibility:** Cloud provides flexibility to support IoT applications to scale up based on the business requirement and IoT-based application development and other required services through Cloud's customizable software services. The Cloud flexibility can be realized in terms of scalability, storage option, control choice and security. Scalability allows Cloud to support dynamic workload of IoT. Whereas storage option gives flexibility of choice to store data based on business model into private, public or hybrid storage. Cloud gives the flexibility on how the IoT application get controlled by Cloud (Sauerwalt, 2017).

- **Agility of Services:** By accommodating changing business demands Cloud allows rapid application development, testing and deployment. In this perspective, IoT can gain access to more resources (expensive hardware and software/applications) very rapidly as well as relinquish them to Cloud when the task finishes. The Cloud agility thus efficiently allows IoT applications to adapt to the rapidly changing business need and policies in a very cost-effective manner (Kumari, 2015).

- **Resource Optimization:** IoT Cloud model enables resource optimization by enabling resources (infrastructure, platform and software) sharing among several numbers of application. This reduces the cost of operation and gains in the service quality. The IoT and Cloud model is benefited to all size of organization – small, medium or big by the concept of resource sharing based on requirement and pay for use scheme thus optimizes the resource use.

- **Analysis:** The huge scalable processing power of Cloud and other data processing services available make data analysis job easy. This makes Cloud very attractive for various kinds of data analysis jobs over the accumulated sensor data to get valuable data insight into the future decision making.

- **Visualization:** The Cloud provides tools (visualization API) that help to visualize sensor data pattern in terms of the diagram and allows applying statistics to predict the future data pattern.

Issues

Despite the increasing usage of Cloud, its application to IoT raises many challenges and is proved to be disadvantageous to IoT.

- **Network and Communication:** Cloud Computing is an Internet-based computing model, where Internet act as the backbone of the communication network. The Internet is a non-homogenous and loosely controlled structured, having numerous types and topologies, varying network speed and heterogeneous technologies. Internet communication paths are very dynamic and thus the data communication path often changes. The non-homogenous and loosely controlled nature raises many issues for Cloud-IoT model like network latencies and bandwidth constraints that badly affect Quality of Service (QoS) (Firdhous, Ghazali, & Hassan, 2014).

- **Latency Constraint:** Network latency caused by communication delay and delay jitters is one of the big issues in an Internet-based model. Any real-time applications which allow interaction in actual time are quite badly affected by network latency. IoT application in the industrial control system and other real-time systems like a vehicle to vehicle communication, a vehicle to signal system communication, Virtual Reality System, gaming and drone flight demands end to end device communication latency less than a millisecond. Since Cloud is distantly apart from the source of the event or the user it may cause a huge time delay in information communication. To meet the stringent time requirement of IoT-based application it is desirable that the data processing, analysis and decision making should be taken close to the data source or target user (Chiang & Zhang, 2016).

- **Network Bandwidth Constraint:** The huge number of connected 'things' produces data exponentially at high speed. Sending these enormous amounts of data to Cloud at high speed in the continuum is network constraining and bandwidth intensive which causes resource starvation. Catering the demand for very high bandwidth may not be possible, practically, in all IoT cases, as the devices are connected to Cloud through multi-hop and varying network structures where network devices have variable data transfer capacity (Chiang & Zhang, 2016).

- **Servicing Heterogeneous Devices:** IoT consists of heterogeneous devices of severely limited resources and each communicates with varying protocols. To fulfil their computation need, these devices rely on the Cloud. Interacting directly with all these devices is quite unrealistic and prohibitive for Cloud, as because each requires resource-intensive processing and handling complex or unknown protocols. For example, sending and receiving data from IoT device to and from Cloud requires data encryption and decryption. These processes carried at both ends need a sophisticated algorithm and are a resource and time-consuming process. Furthermore, IoT node ends require regular firmware updates from Cloud to handle sophisticated encryption and decryption techniques, which rather seems to be highly unrealistic (Chiang & Zhang, Fog and IoT: An Overview of Research Opportunities, 2016).

- **Security Challenges:** The IoT data, due to the considerable distance between the source and the Cloud, travel through multiple hops and complex network structures which makes it vulnerable to security issues. As the data travel through network edges, crossing multiple nodes, it becomes vulnerable to attack and corruption. Even though the data are encrypted, the more it goes away from user deep into the Internet, the more time it spends in transit, the higher the risk becomes (Firdhous, Ghazali, & Hassan, 2014).

INTRODUCTION TO FOG COMPUTING

We know that when Cloud descends to the ground, it is named as Fog. Similarly, when the computation has been shifted from remote Cloud to the system that is close to the data source is termed as Fog Computing. Fog Computing is the term used by Cisco for representing edge computing. In edge computing, the processing is done at the devices that reside at the edge of the network. The edge devices include routers, switches, Wi-Fi access points, set-top-boxes, base stations etc. These devices no longer are used merely for data transfer but they are incorporating significant capacity of computing and storage. So, the computing jobs, which otherwise had to be carried to some remote Cloud set-up, can be accomplished locally. This minimises the processing time and in turn the response time. This is beneficial especially for those applications that demand real-time response. And as services are hosted locally and close to the end-users, it caters the users better, thus improving the QoS significantly. Fog Computing relieves Cloud Computing by taking up most of its job, though in small scale. If every local data processing and the analytical job is to be sent to the Cloud, soon it will suffer from the issue of "Data Gravity". Fog Computing extends the services from Cloud Computing to the edge of the network. Like Cloud, Fog also provides computation, storage, and application services to end-users (Mora, 2014). By handling services at the edge, Fog enables more efficient data processing and effective application.

CHARACTERISTICS OF FOG COMPUTING

Some key characteristics of Fog Computing have been identified as follows (Bonomi, Milito, Zhu, & Addepalli, 2012):

- **Processing Close to the Source:** Because Fog devices are placed nearby to the IoT devices (within the same local network, in case of on-campus), the IoT data is processed close to the source.
- **Proximity to End-Users:** The Fog devices are not only close to the IoT devices, they are close to the end users as well.
- **Faster Response:** Since the data do not have to travel longer for processing and the effect is delivered to the nearby entities, rendering quick response is achievable.
- **Location Aware:** Since the Fog devices are deployed locally (close to the sensing devices) and in small scale, they are location aware.
- **Support for Mobility:** A majority of the IoT devices are mobile. Fog supports this mobility by having the Fog devices also mobile.
- **Massive in Size:** As the number of IoT devices, distributed over wide geospace, is growing enormously the Fog end-points also run in billions.
- **Predominantly Wireless Communication:** Wireless communication is predominant in connecting the IoT devices with the Fog nodes which makes the Fog architecture flexible and ubiquitous.
- **Support for Real-Time and Interactive Application:** Fog applications, generally, are intended for real-time interactions although batch processing applications can also be well carried by Fog.
- **Support for Online Data Analytic:** Fog not only can process real-time data, it can also have the capability for online data analytics.
- **Support for Heterogeneous Devices:** Ideally Fog architecture supports various heterogeneous IoT devices. Also, the Fog devices themselves are heterogeneous.

FOG COMPUTING ARCHITECTURE

The Fog architecture may either be centralised or distributed. Else, it can be a combination of both. In centralised architecture, every Fog node works under a central node. Managing a centralised Fog is easy but when the number of connected device increases it becomes a challenge. In a distributed architecture,

Fog devices interact in a P2P fashion. The processing loads are shared across multiple Fog devices. Each Fog node communicates to each other for several purposes (e.g. job distribution, self-organisation, peer discovery etc.). The Fog mediates three types of communication (Naranjo, et al.):

- **Machine-to-Machine:** Data generated from one 'thing' is consumed by another.
- **Machine-to-People:** Data generated from 'things' is consumed by human and vice versa.
- **People-to-People:** Data generated by a human is consumed by a human.

The duration of these interactions may span seconds to days. For example, interaction in real-time applications lasts for a few seconds to few minutes. Whereas the transactional analytics may take several days. Hence, Fog architecture can support different types of storages. For real-time interactions, it should have the transient memories and for the longer interactions, semi-permanent storages are required (Naranjo, et al.).

CLOUD VS. FOG

The major differences between Cloud Computing and Fog Computing are to provide services in real-time as compared to the delayed/offline services. The Cloud services are based upon the assumption that a centralized architecture is required to provide services and analytics on the data. The Fog architecture overcomes the drawback of the Cloud by processing and storing the IoT data nearby rather than sending to the Cloud.

To further elaborate the difference between the Cloud and Fog architectures we compare them with following perspectives:

- The Fog architecture allows the data to be stored nearer to the end user as compared to the remote data centres in the Cloud environment. This helps in reducing the roundabout time, which in case of the Cloud architecture will be huge.
- The Fog architecture also reduces the load on the network links as most of the communication happens near the user thus very few network links are engaged in the data/service in the Fog whereas in case of Cloud architecture the whole network can get involved in providing the service to the end user.
- The Fog architecture has an added advantage to the Cloud architecture is that on top of providing services to the end users it can also manage the network traffic as well as if needed can utilize resources of the Cloud when the processing of the data is out of its capacity. In Cloud architecture, the network management is done by the gateways, which are totally unrelated to the Cloud thus they are unable to prioritize the data/services requirement of the user (Chiang, Fog Networking, 2015).

Fog has more flexibility in terms of deployment as compared to Cloud as the Fog architecture enables edge devices to be local service providers thus allowing for the services to be provided in a distributed deployment (Bonomi, Milito, Zhu, & Addepalli, 2012). For example, on a highway, users can be provided with services related to the Cloud environment like constant monitoring of a diabetes patient on the highway and if anything goes wrong the system can immediately allow the GPS maps to direct the emergency services towards the vehicle or let the driver know the nearest hospitals.

The most basic issues of the Cloud that are still unresolved are unreliable latency, lack of mobility support and location awareness. The time taken by the service requested from the remote data centre to reach the end user cannot be precisely estimated (Yi, Li, & Li, 2015). The lack of mobility of the Cloud denies the availability of services ubiquitously. Also, since Cloud doesn't use location awareness algorithms, it cannot always locate the nearest service providing data centre which leads to unnecessary delay in service providing. Cloud Computing is more about centralization and it isolates end users from the computing resources. Fog architecture can address this by providing a flexible architecture which delivers computing solutions to the end user directly.

Fog architecture has many advantages over the Cloud architecture, but major drawbacks of the Fog architecture is that does not provide Global centralization, particularly for Big Data analytics. Cloud provides services with long temporal coverage which is a basic requirement for business intelligence (Bonomi, Milito, Zhu, & Addepalli, 2012).

The Cloud architecture has the key advantages over Fog architecture in domains like:

- **Archival Storage:** Here the Fog architecture fails as the devices involved don't have the capacity to store large amounts of data for a very long-time due to various physical limitations.
- **Heavy Duty Computation:** To compute a large amount of data is beyond the capacity of the Fog architecture due to the limited processing power of the IoT devices, thus making Fog unsuitable for services involving the heavy computing.
- **Global Coordination:** The architecture of the Cloud supports the global coordination as it is a centralized architecture where Cloud can even coordinate among various Fog devices across the globe.

The Fog architecture as compared to the Cloud architecture is more widely and densely spread across the geographic locations due to its use of different devices from all ranges like end-user devices, wireless access points, routers and switches. The Fog architecture enables a level of abstraction in these devices to deal with the diversity of Fog services (Milunovich, Passi, & Roy, 2014). This level of abstraction is not seen in Cloud architecture. On comparing the security parameters, Cloud infrastructure is vulnerable and more prone to sophisticated distributed intrusion attacks like DDOS (distribute denial of service) and XSS (cross-site scripting) (Alamri, et al., February 2013).

The Fog architecture was basically conceived with the idea that it'll help address the deficiencies of the applications and services in the Cloud paradigm. It includes:

- The Fog architecture supports endpoints by providing rich services at the network edges (Naranjo, et al.).
- The geographical distribution of the Fog architecture allows for it to create a centralized edge which can be widely distributed as compared to the Cloud's centralized backbone.
- Fog architecture can be used in a variety of real-life applications like the creation of sensor networks, where not only the Fog architecture provides the distributed computing paradigm but also data storage resources.

- Fog Computing architecture basically fulfils the inadequacies of the Cloud architecture in reliability, security, network bandwidth etc. like Fog supports Cloud architecture where applications require low latency, rapid movement or are widely distributed geographically (Naranjo, et al.).

The Fog and the Cloud are architecturally interdependent to each other. Cloud services may be used to manage the Fog. Fog devices can act as providers of cloud services to the endpoints, and also can collect cloud data and return it back to the cloud. Fog and Cloud are not two exclusively different paradigms, rather each complements the other by working on the areas where the other is weak, making a powerful tag team. They are mutually beneficial to each other by providing inter-dependent service continuum between the Cloud and the endpoints to make computation facility available possibly anywhere (Chiang & Zhang,2016). For example, in the Fog architecture, the surrounding edge devices such as a smartphone or traffic control post may provide the edge-based services to the mobile devices such as wearable devices, mobile phone and smart car. Therefore, Fog Computing is considered as the extension of Cloud.

PROCESSING IoT DATA IN THE FOG

Why IoT Need Fog Computing?

IoT-based applications and associated sensors produce huge data. For large-scale IoT application or the expanding ones, the increase in sensor numbers causes data blast. The increasing rate of data would consume a lot of Cloud storage space and may cost high to organizations. Besides, the overwhelming data relaying toward Cloud put tremendous pressure on the network. This led to network latency and thus delays.

Among all the data which IoT produces, some are useful and need storing while others not. A faulty sensor may produce wrong information or data and thus floods the network with it. This raises the question whether it is necessary to send all the data to Cloud, if not how to check the data before sending it?

To control and balance the data flow and address the intrinsic issues of IoT, a platform is needed in between 'things' and Cloud. The platform would retain the characteristics of Cloud-like flexibility and agility and provide a virtualized Cloud environment to 'things'. Local devices having the properties of high-speed processing and memory can be used to check the data flow that is needed to be sent to the Cloud (Naranjo, et al.). Cisco came up with a new technology called Fog Computing, where local devices have some of the data processing capacity which reduces the network latency by not sending everything to the Cloud. Fog Computing has been introduced as a practical and efficient solution to fulfil the need of IoT (Qaisar & Riaz, 2016).

The characteristic features of IoT which necessitate the use of Fog Computing are given below (Chiang & Zhang, 2016):

- **The Huge Volume of Data:** The magnitude of data produced by trillions of devices or 'things' connected to the Internet is astronomical. Managing and transferring this voluminous data to Cloud can incur issues like bandwidth consumption, network congestion and latency. In automation process, all the data need not necessarily be sent to the Cloud for processing but can be processed and analysed locally, near the source of the event with only relevant information is sent to the Cloud.

- **Geo-Distribution and Need of Cooperation:** IoT applications are evolving and its applications have been widespread globally across different domains like Industrial production, mining, traffic management, building and home automation, elevators, transportation and logistics, retails market etc. The rise of IoT applications has increased the use of sensors or IoT nodes globally in trillions. The sensor has limited resources need a platform which can manage and control the different IoT application and further maintaining consistency.

- **Latency Minimization:** As the distance between data/event source and processing platform widens, the network latency also increases. IoT applications based on real-time systems are stringent to network latency for less than a fraction of a millisecond. Increase in network latency may lose the instantaneous interaction requirement of the user or other applications. This issue can be eliminated by processing data at the network edge, removing the need of sending data to a distant location (Cloud). Processing data close or locally to the data source or user would eliminate network latency.

- **High-Mobility Applications:** Mobile IoT application requires sensing, processing, and analysing data on transit or move. For example, the driverless automatic car produces huge sensory data at the very high speed and demand instant decision making. Application of Cloud to wirelessly acquire and process the huge and high-velocity data is far beyond the effectiveness of Cloud. These types of mobile IoT applications demand virtual Cloud kind of service on the move which can process data and make a decision with or without Internet connectivity (in absence of Cloud).

- **Security Issues:** Security issues are the prevailing concerns for all Internet-based applications. The security vulnerability of data increases with multiple hops. As the data crosses multiple network nodes and goes away from the user, chances of data corruption, cyber-attack, etc. also increase. Thus, it is necessary that data processing should be carried out as close as possible to the user to prevent the chances of cyber-attack. Computing on the network edge close to the data source can evade most of the security vulnerabilities.

- **Scalability:** Another characteristic of IoT-based application is scalability. With changing and expanding business requirement, the number of devices or 'things' connected to the Internet may increase. With growing number of IoT application, the IoT network widens horizontally. The increasing sensors or 'things' demands software updates regularly to support data encryption/ decryption and communication protocols. It becomes quite unrealistic for Cloud to take care of each node and manage them. Thus, it is necessary for a new architecture which would locally and closely manage the scalability factor of IoT.

Driving Forces

In the last couple of decades, the price per unit memory and processing cycle has drastically fallen. The rapid advancement in memory and processing capacity reflects a huge improvement in performance. In comparison, networking technology lags in improvement in terms of computing and storage price-performance. Sensor, processors and storage memory are seeming to evolve very rapidly than the increase in network bandwidth (Milunovich, Passi, & Roy, 2014).

Today with IoT technology becoming a practical reality, billions of unlike devices including PCs, tabs, mobile devices, IP camera, elevator, cars, health devices, kitchen appliances, entertainment units, thermostat and others like building, industry and machinery, business sectors, etc. are all connected to the Internet to communicate and share data. Cisco estimated that by 2020, 50 billion devices will be connected to Internet (Cisco Delivers Vision of Fog Computing to Accelerate Value from Billions of Connected Devices, 2014). The increasing number of sensors and data processing units has escalated the data production and consumption rate exponentially. It is estimated that AT&T network communicates 200 petabytes a year in 2010, US smart grid produces 1000 petabytes of data each year, US Library of Congress generates about 2.4 petabytes of data a month and Google communicates about 1 petabyte each month (Chiang & Zhang, 2016). The estimated data consumed globally around a day is in hundreds of exabytes. Devices producing an overwhelming wave of data on Internet has outpaced the network bandwidth. The rate at which data produced incapacitate the network infrastructure and may lead to stall the network services.

In Cloud-IoT model, sensors produce huge data and consume most of the bandwidth causing significant network latency. The sense of automation which IoT brings based on real-time event detection, processing, and decision making may not be realized if the network latency is high. The data feed on sensor all the way to Cloud and then the processed output back to actuation can take a long-time due to heterogeneous and multi-hop network structure. This may loosen the actual necessity of real-time data processing. To fasten up the data processing Cisco believed that instead of sending all the data to Cloud at a far distance, it can analyse and processed near the source of data so that real-time effect can be gained (Milunovich, Passi, & Roy, 2014). Fog Computing is an extension to Cloud Computing which allows data processing and analyses locally at the edge of the network much closer to the source of data. It is not worth sending all the data to the Cloud but the delay tolerant ones to maintain the load balance over the network. Much of the IoT data computing need to be performed locally in real time in the areas of mining, disaster management, etc. which elevates the need for Fog.

To summarise, the critical technical factors which act as driving forces advocating Fog Computing for future IoT-based computing are (Milunovich, Passi, & Roy, 2014):

- Increasing use IoT device
- Production of Cumbersome volume of data
- Network Latency
- Reliable (zero downtime) network communication
- Localized data processing

Advantages of Fog Computing Over Cloud for IoT

Fog Computing, in comparison to its contemporary technologies, provides real advantages to what is a need for IoT to work effectively. The Fog Computing advantages are (Chiang & Zhang, 2016):

- Real-time processing.
- Homogeneous support to all varying kind and make of IoT device.
- Support rapid scalability.
- Secure IoT data while in transit from network edge to Cloud using sophisticated encryption algorithm.
- Rapid development and deploy of Fog applications.
- Fog Computing provides a pool of resources locally, near IoT.

- Fog Computing can balance the network load and computing by taking a decision where to best analyse the sensor data. Based on time sensitivity, privacy requirement and business policies, Fog Computing can decide whether sensor data need to be stored locally or on Cloud.
- Fog Computing automatically controls and manages IoT nodes dispersed geographically apart (Cisco, 2015).

IoT DATA PROCESSING ARCHITECTURE IN THE FOG

IoT produces an enormous amount of data. To maintain the quality regarding real-time data processing, probably Cloud is not the best solution for IoT. It is very clear that IoT needs a different kind of architecture which addresses the IoT's latency and mobility issues. In this regard, Fog Computing architecture typically suits IoT data processing.

Fog has extended Cloud Computing, bringing it closer to IoTs. The computing services which have been upheld by the Cloud will be carried out locally by numerous other computational devices near IoTs. Network devices like routers, switch, modem and other control devices have a good amount of processing speed and memory. These devices can act as data processing unit for IoT's, thereby offloading data processing burden from the Cloud. These Fog devices, capable of producing and processing IoT data, are termed as Fog nodes. The Fog nodes may include a range of devices having the processing and storage capacity like industrial controllers, set-top boxes, switches, routers, embedded servers and video surveillance cameras etc. These devices can be resource-poor machines such as set-top-boxes, access points, switches or resource-rich machine such as Cloudlet (Satyanarayanan, Bahl, Caceres, & Davies, 2009). Based on the business policies and application requirement (like real-time application) decisions are taken on where Fog nodes are to be deployed. In practice Fog nodes are kept on the network edges close to the 'things', to reduce latencies.

Even though Fog and Cloud are conceptually and technically different, Fog is merely an extension of Cloud in terms of data processing and control specificity. Fog is the virtualizations of Cloud making 'things' assume it as Cloud. Fog Computing incorporates virtualization to 'things' therefore introduces a new layer of abstraction to computing. This makes user/'things' concern-free, where the data is going and where it is stored. To the end-user, the abstraction blurs the distinction between the Fog and the Cloud. Fog Computing evolved from the research experience of many other similar computing paradigms, and do "balance" well the centralization and decentralization issues of IoT computing. In this view, the architecture on how IoT data is processed is significant.

Fog provides data service to IoT data, the data service includes (Figure 1):

- **Data Filtering:** Removing noisy data and other irrelevant data and thus separating the data of interest.
- **Segregation:** Since Fog allows a multi-tenancy model, multiple IoT application shares the same resources. Segregating involves distinctly identifying and separating which data belong to which application
- **Aggregation:** Aggregation involves collecting or gathering the same application data over a time span to get the data insight.
- **Data Encryption:** To maintain privacy and security parameters, plain raw data obtained from the sensor/'things' are encrypted.

Figure 1. Data processing architecture in the Fog

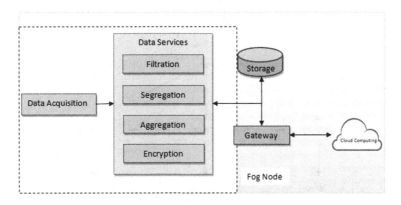

- **Caching:** Fog provides enough amount of storage space, this allows data to be stored near user rather at a remote/distance data centre.

Fog is a natural extension to the Cloud, where both are interdependent on each other. Fog connected to Cloud can take the advantage of the highly capable services and application tools of the Cloud. Fog collects and aggregates data for Cloud. Fog sent the relevant/critical information to the Cloud for further processing and storage. Fog pre-process the data before it is sent to Cloud.

INTERACTIONS AMONG THINGS, FOG, AND THE CLOUD

Fog is an extension of Cloud, prevailing data processing in a continuum ranging from network edges to core of the Internet. It basically bridges the gap between the Cloud and the 'things' bringing the services closer to the consumer. Since Fog resides on the edge of the network, it is advantageous to IoT in terms of locality-based computation, low bandwidth consumption and near-to-zero network latency, and flexible management and control of 'things'. Fog has its own limitation too, as a reason all the data are not analysed in Fog some is sent to Cloud for further analytics and storage. To get over the limitation of Fog, the assistance of Cloud services is taken into consideration. The selection of Cloud and Fog is not binary. These two technologies together make mutually beneficial and interdependent continuum. Fog devices over a network, for the same IoT application or different, may collaborate with each other for data intelligence and sharing resources like processing power and memory. The architecture of IoT application decides "who does what and what time scale" (Chiang, 2015). Basically, three kinds of interactions are found in an IoT-Fog-Cloud model (Figure 2):

1. **Fog-to-Thing Interaction:** Fog provides most of the services to 'things' in resource efficiency and secure way. Among the services include data filtration, segregation and aggregation. Besides this, it provides storage, analyses and decision making. The different tasks which Fog nodes perform for IoT application are:
   a. **Data Processing:** Data filtering, segregation, and aggregation.
   b. **Intelligence:** Data analysis and decision making.

Figure 2. Interaction between IoT, Fog, and Cloud

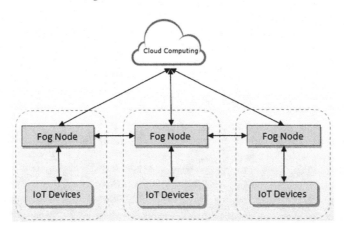

c. **Storage:** Fog allows data to be stored for a long or short time, depending upon the application requirement.

d. **Control and Management:** Fog communicates with different 'things' for data gathering, feeds and firmware update by using suitable protocols.

e. **Data Encryption and Decryption:** Data collected by 'things' are vulnerable to security threats and hence raise concerns for data protection. Fog node ensures data protection by encryption technology, data are encrypted before it is stored and relayed to other places.

2. **Fog-to-Fog Interaction:** Fog to Fog interaction leads to data sharing, data backup, a collaboration of software and computations among the Fog nodes. Fog nodes are often resourced poor with limitations seen in terms of processing power, software capabilities, and storage capacity. The Fog of Fog interaction, leading to Fog to Fog cooperation for resources (software and hardware), may help to overcome individual node's limitations. For example, the Fog nodes over the network edges for an IoT application may collaborate with each other to share the data storage and processing capabilities. Data gathered from a node with low memory is relayed to other nodes having high storage capacity. Similarly, nodes having high processing capacities collaborate with each other to provide an aggregated form of local data processing platform. Furthermore, while talking about the location-based application running over an IoT network, the data resources are often distributed or scattered. Collective data gathering for data analysis job will be accumulating data from scattered nodes. Fog of Fog interaction allows multiple Fog systems to share the data storage, software service and other computing tasks for one or multiple users or applications. Through the mutual collaboration, they serve as a backup for each other.

3. **Fog-to-Cloud Interaction:** Fog is a virtualized version of Cloud, sustaining all the features of Cloud. Fog is a kind of job handler of Cloud, with limitations of its own like resources and processing capabilities. It cannot substitute Cloud, as it has its own dependencies on Cloud in terms of software and Infrastructural support. Fog and Cloud exchange data with each other. The critical data gathered from 'things' are sent to Cloud and the then processed information is returned from Cloud. Cloud distributes and manages various services onto Fog; in a way Cloud services are availed to 'things' (end users) through Fog.

INDUSTRIAL INITIATIVES FOR FOG COMPUTING SOLUTIONS

Many Industrial developments have been made to up bring Fog Computing commercially. One of the pioneer development in delivering Fog Computing as distributed computing infrastructure is Cisco. Cisco has developed operating system and software for its network devices which would allow connecting billions of devices. Cisco IOX which is being developed for its routers, switches, and video cameras provide infrastructure for connecting IoT devices and running Fog Computing services (Cisco Delivers Vision of Fog Computing to Accelerate Value from Billions of Connected Devices, 2014). Currently, Cisco IOX works for Cisco routers only. Other product like Cisco DSX makes Fog application development easy. Cisco DSX which provides device abstraction by supporting various type of environment and programming languages thereby enabling Fog applications to run in multiple environments and communicate with multiple types of IoT devices (Cisco, 2015).

To virtualize the Cloud capability into Fog node, many amendments have been incorporated into the networking devices. Cisco routers and switches are coming with decent processing speed, storage and operating system. New improved software application stacked into devices provides good interfacing to 'things' and user. Software incorporated in these devices has the capability to efficiently control and manages the various IoT services, giving an ambience of virtual Cloud (Yi, Li, & Li, 2015).

Hewlett Packard Enterprise (HPE) a leading IoT solutions provider has come up with its own flavour of Fog Computing solutions with the aim of providing machine learning at the edge and also to support fraud prevention, automated maintenance support, and Augmented Reality (AR) technology. The HPE Converged Edge Systems provide data acquisition and high-performance computing facility at the edge. HPE Intelligent Gateway Systems provide sensor data aggregation facility with moderate compute capabilities for the IoT edge (HPE Edgeline Converged Edge Systems, 2017).

Dell Edge Gateways for brings analytics at the edge of the IoT network by aggregating and analyzing the inputs from different wired and wireless devices and systems. Only the filtered and required data are passed through the Gateway and sent to the cloud. The Edge Gateways are able to operate in and out the house with harsh conditions and also able to connect organisations' legacy systems (Dell Edge Gateways for IoT, 2017).

IoT APPLICATIONS WITH FOG COMPUTING

Fog Computing endeavour to fully realize IoT's potential has an open new horizon for real-life applications. Fog Computing is well suited for IoT applications which demand real-time action. The orchestration of Fog and IoT find its way in different areas like industrial automation, transportation, energy, mining, and oil & gas (Milunovich, Passi, & Roy, 2014). Some of the present and future applications are discussed below.

- **Environment Monitoring:** IoT applied for environmental monitoring will be helpful in early detection of natural disasters. The appliance of Fog Computing to IoT over a geographical region can detect events like volcanic explosion or earthquake by assessing the real-time data. Different sensors connected through a wireless network capable of measuring strain, temperature, light, image, sound, vibration, pressure, chemical changes etc. can be used detect environmental changes. Fog nodes process and analyses the real-time data produced by these IoT sensors, the exception in readings are calibrated and necessary alerts are raised (Alamri, et al., February 2013).

- **Transportation:** One of the biggest real-time application of IoT and Fog Computing would be intelligent transportation. In the forthcoming years, the number of vehicle on the road going to be high. The increase in vehicle count would bring new challenges in monitoring and control of transportation on road. The application of IoT and Fog Computing would help to ease of the situation.

Different types of sensor are available to monitor the traffic condition on roads and cities. These sensors are categorical of two types: Road sensors and vehicle sensors. The road sensors like a video camera, road tube, inductive loop, capacitive mats and the piezoelectric sensor would help to measure vehicle speed, type of vehicle and vehicle count. Whereas vehicle sensors like onboard camera, GPS, speedometer, proximity sensor etc. would enable to locate vehicle location, detect vehicles in near proximity and any road blockage. As the sensor continuously monitors the situation, they produce a huge amount of data. Furthermore, sensors are heterogeneous, producing a different type of data which need real-time analyses. Fog nodes alleviate this issue by providing a platform which uniformly aggregates data from different devices, storage space to keep past data and real-time analyses based on present and stored data.

Sensors communicate with the Fog nodes wirelessly. Fog nodes deployed at the roadside or in the smart vehicles gather data from the roadside sensors and the vehicle sensors. The Fog nodes at these different locations communicate and collaborate data with each other. Fog node analyses the data for the decision to be taken at the real time. Real-time service provided by Fog computer is like shortest distance between source and destination, alternative route search, energy efficient route and traffic density at a different location. Besides these, the other useful application of IoT and Fog model is in smart traffic signalling. Based on the vehicle's speed and traffic, Fog nodes take appropriate signalling decision, thus automating traffic controlling. This particular kind of information, in addition to the regular vehicle, would be helpful for other important and emergency services like a police car, ambulance, fire brigade, utility vehicle etc. Of course, the vehicle is fitted with onboard GPS, but they are not helpful for dynamic traffic condition when traffic condition changes rapidly like accident and road blockage, a sudden rush of vehicle etc. This situation demands continuous monitoring of traffic condition and instant decision taking locally as incorporated by Fog Computing.

- **Crowd Control:** Crowd control is one of the big challenges for police, volunteers and administration. Public functions, festivals, sports & game, concerts, parades, outdoor celebration welcomes a lot of crowds causing an outburst of the crowd in short time. The increase in the crowd may cause vandalism, accidents and mishap etc. Sensors can detect the rise of the crowd at certain places. In addition, the GPS in mobile devices allows for real-time tracking of individuals, their movement pattern and concentration in an area. It helps in resolving the contextual issues by taking a necessary decision like opening parking lots, closing and opening some roads or street and posting police in a critical area. Furthermore, crowd analyses may able to predict places of accidents, thus initiating new response methods including clearing routes, dispatch of emergency response vehicle etc.

- **Object Tracking:** Camera installed on road and street not only able to monitor traffic and mass movement but also tracks for objects. A large number of video surveillance camera deployed on roads, streets, building, airport, railway station and hospital. The camera produces a huge stream of data. Fog Computing provides enough storage and processing capabilities for processing real-time videos to look for objects captured in the video. The biggest security application is recognizing the object and tracking them. In crowded places, objects are often lost. Similarly, unoccupied objects in crowded places may be very dangerous and thus demand to identify and tracking them. Fog Computing process and analyses video frame in real time can track objects. Based on the relevancy it may raise alerts (Yi, Li, & Li, 2015).

- **Railway Security and Communication**: In many developing countries, railway maintenance and operations hasn't improved leading to accidents and poor operational management. Applications of IoT and Fog Computing in railways would provide an advanced way to monitor the operations. These technologies can able to address issues related to people negligence in maintenance and operations and thus would help in averting associated hazard. Sensors, being attached to different parts of the engine like wheels, brakes, hydraulics and other systems, can monitor their functionality and raise alert before any failure took place. Besides sensors attached on the railway tracks, railway crossing and at stations monitors the railway movements and subsequently notifies the operational centre for any anomaly found like a train travelling over speed limits, issues with signalling and trains in the same track etc. The other usage includes onboard video surveillance which continuously monitors for an anomaly in the train movement. To reduce the latency in video transmission and processing, the video streams are processed for summarization in the onboard Fog node. Continuous real-time information updates about the various systems of a moving train wirelessly through mobile and satellite communication to the operational centre are challenging. It causes latency in information transmission, processing, and further decision making for an applied action. In this direction, Fog nodes are quite useful in making communication localized and further aggregating the information as whole to be delivered to the operational centre. The Fog nodes in the train can communicate with the Fog nodes along the railway trackside through Wi-Fi to relay real-time information about the various systems of the train.

Besides Fog Computing imparting significant contribution to railway operational security, it can also be used as a mode of communication by passengers. Fog nodes attached onboard can communicate with other Fog nodes by the railway lines and in the stations to provide Internet to passenger through Wi-Fi (Cisco, 2015).

- **Smart Buildings:** Today's buildings like shopping malls, railway station, business enterprises, and hospitals have multi-functionality services such as cooling system, electricity, water, sewage and garbage system, elevator and escalators, fire system and others. These systems provide cyclically and, sometimes, on-demand operation. Failure of any of these systems may turn down the building operations. These services consume huge energy and resources; moreover, their steady operation demands high maintenance. Application of IoT would enable these services to function in an optimal manner and thus saving energy as well as resource consumption. Furthermore, real-time and regular monitoring of these services will be a utility for scheduled maintenance. Applications of IoT would bring a sense of automation, sensor attached to functional units may help to monitor, control and coordinate the services. Sensors can be used in for temperature regulation. Presence or absence of people in the room can switch on or off the light or AC. Tap fitted with the sensor can regulate the water flow based on requirement, thus saving wastage of water. Garbage can, fitted with a sensor, can notify if the can is filled.

In a multi-storeyed building, there can be thousands of IoT devices connected and produces enormous data to process (some in real time or near real-time). Moreover, these devices are heterogeneous and different vendor makes. Fog Computing that provides a virtual Cloud will be useful in low latency solution, a platform for integrating independent devices and flexibility in terms of computation and storage (Khan, 2015; Yi, Hao, Qin, & Li, 2015).

- **Health Data Management:** One of the pioneering issues in the personalized health system is how one's personal health data is gathered, managed and subsequently used for diagnosis. Leveraging IoT and Fog Computing model to the scenario could have a better solution. In a typical health monitoring and data management scenario, the sensors fitted or observing patient continuously stream the data to Fog nodes like smartphones or other devices. Fog nodes analyse the data and raise alert for any anomaly found. The summarized data are stored and outsourced when the patient seeking help in hospital, doctor or medical lab (Yi, Hao, Qin, & Li, 2015).

CHALLENGES IN FOG COMPUTING

For successful implementation of Fog Computing, we need to address the following challenges.

- **Network Management:** One of the key issues in the Fog architecture is to manage the network. The job entails connecting a number of 'things' to different Fog devices of heterogeneous nature and managing billions of connections (Vaquero & Rodero-Merino, 2014; Yi, Li, & Li, 2015). We must understand that the biggest challenge here is managing the virtualization of the devices involved in the Fog architecture, inter-connectivity of devices as well as the management of the resources of the network. These tasks are tedious and error-prone. The issue of handling virtualization is basically controlling the number of virtual machines running on a Fog device. This causes a problem with the management of IoT devices as well as distributed computing paradigms implemented in the Fog. The key challenge faced in network management in trying to manage the network using hardware is that there are too many devices and they are running billions of services, thus calling for the "Softwarisation" (Vaquero & Rodero-Merino, 2014). The automated scripts and virtual machines themselves make it easy to implement Fog on the heterogeneous devices homogeneously.
- **Resource Management:** Managing the resources of the Fog architecture including the level of virtualization, as well avoiding deadlocks in the system is a major challenge as demand for resources of the system will be high, therefore a proper resource management policy must be ensured.
- **Resource Discovery:** The IoT devices when requiring the Fog services must be easily able to seek out the resources required for processing and storing their data i.e. selecting a suitable node for a particular job i.e. the node must have the required bandwidth to perform the tasks at hand.

- **Resource Allocation:** Allocation of resources in the Fog architecture is a challenging issue because the devices involved in it are heterogeneous which are controlled using levels of virtualization, thus making it difficult to allocate specific resources. Thus, allocation of resources must be looked into as it can cause the whole system to stop.

- **Task Scheduling:** Scheduling of tasks is an essential part of any distributed system. It encourages the system to provide maximum throughput with minimum conflicts as a number of virtual machines are running over a distributed Fog architecture.

- **Job Offloading:** The Fog architecture supports the usage of the distributed computing architecture thus leading to the challenges of job offloading i.e. the architecture must be able to understand the workflow and support of reassigning the job to another Fog node in case of failure. It should also maintain proper replication of processes for fault tolerance.

- **Storage Issues:** Fog resources do not have very large storage. So, to tackle the continuous flow of streaming data, proper data backup (to Cloud or local data centres) policy is required.

Predictive caching at proxies as well as the installation of Sensor Cloud storage techniques will help solve these problems (Alamri, et al., February 2013).

- **Quality of Service:** Quality of Service (QoS) is a very important metric, as it gives insight into how well the architecture is working and what is its throughput under various conditions. The major part of QoS productivity is explained further.

- **Connectivity:** The connectivity of various devices of the Fog architecture is essential for ensuring good quality of service, as the services provided by the Fog architecture needs to be connected all the time to the end-user as well as among them. To ensure better productivity, clustering of nodes based on service/functionality, network segmentation and network relaying is used to ensure better connectivity and hence better deliverable service to the end user.

- **Fault-Tolerance and Reliability:** The Fog architecture must be robust and reliable to support all kinds of operations that it advertises. The major challenge here is that a failure of a virtual machine or the hardware device itself must not hamper the processing of the Fog architecture. Reliability can be increased by proper replication of the nodes providing services, but it should be balanced with the cost (Yi, Li, & Li, 2015). The Fault-tolerance of the system can be increased by applying techniques of the RAID (1 - 3) to improve the storage capacity, regarding services we need to have replicated the processes running on the faulty devices on the other devices which are correctly functioning. Fault Tolerance can never be achieved to 100% efficiency as the cost will be very high.

- **Delay:** The delay in providing any kind of services in the Fog architecture will have an adverse effect on the whole assumption on the development of the Fog. The delay in Fog must be minimized by using distributed architectures as well as inculcating the concepts of pipelining and parallel computing in providing the services to the end user thus reducing the delay in the provisioning of the service.

- **Security and Privacy:** Due to the inherent communication ability of these smart devices, the consideration of security and privacy of the exchange of data between the device and the controlling unit becomes paramount. Security attacks like data tampering, deactivation, and tag detaching can make the scenario really challenging for IoT systems along with usual networking threats such as spoofing, eavesdropping, denial of service etc. New approaches are required for maintaining and security of data.

The Fog architecture presents a completely new security challenges, as we know that Fog architecture has a very close relationship with the client, and most of the IoT devices of the clients are easily hackable thus making the Fog architecture also vulnerable. The architecture, due to its close proximity to the user, must provide some encryptions or provide contextual integrity and isolation of the user's private data and help in maintaining his privacy (Chiang, 2015). Fog architecture must maintain control over the data from the user as it is the first node most of the time to access the network. From the privacy point of view, Fog nodes generate and collect a lot of private information about the user. The privacy-preserving solutions of the earlier Cloud/distributed computing model need to be updated or a completely new set of solutions are required here (Miller, 2015).

The security scenario in Fog architecture is not good as most of the security measures have not yet been extended to the edges of the network. We must try to achieve holistic security systems which will help mitigate the system risk (Miller, 2015). Distributed Fog architecture is more vulnerable to the attacks than the centralized systems as centralized systems enjoy heavily protected facilities and even some devices may have an air gap with the outside network, the Fog devices operate in a vulnerable environment open for tampering due to user's requirements (Chiang & Zhang, 2016). Also, Fog nodes are significantly smaller than their Cloud counterparts, thus they lack resources for the proper protection. Fog, due to its proximity to the user, can also be helpful in protecting the end user from the security threats.

- **Standardisation:** Due to Fog being a pretty new architecture, there is still no specific standardization. Fog keeps local data close to the source, but that data needs to be integrated with other Fog architectures and Clouds for better processing (Miller, 2015). Various companies like Cisco is attempting to standardize by using its InterCloud approach. The standardisation will allow better handling of data and will also help in connecting the disconnected nodes or users.
- **Event Processing and Management:** Event processing and its management in Fog architecture are very difficult as it is a distributed architecture where several issues regarding management of events may occur. They can be:
  - Synchronizing events from different sources
  - Keeping in check the time delays in the network
  - Messaging among correlated events
  - Recognizing the context and its relevance

The above are some of the most common challenges in the event processing and management in the Fog architecture. In Fog architecture, efficient information dissemination mechanism is required to provide proper information about events to all the nodes, while maintaining the flexibility and scalability of the system (Alamri et al., 2013). Most of the applications need to be able to communicate with each other in real thus making it one of the primary requirements in the Fog architecture. The architecture must have the ability to deliver the raw inputs to the nodes and aggregate the data/events from them. The main challenge for Fog is to maintain the real-time event transfer as an event may need to be transferred from one node to the other for requisite action or for further processing. It is to be made sure that the user gets the desired service in time. We must always make sure that whatever aggregation or filtering we must always ensure that accuracy and optimality of the results are maintained.

- **Real-Time Analytics and Decision Making:** The main purpose of storage of data by IoT devices is to perform analytics on those devices. Fog architecture must perform these analytics in real time as they can be used to inform the end user about the various phenomenon. For example, a person is wearing a medical armband. The armband detects spike changes in blood pressure and other vitals. It sends that information to process with the Fog. The Fog architecture must respond almost immediately by diagnosing what has happened to that person and must simultaneously inform the emergency services. These real-time analytics, if delayed can cost lifes.

Fog architecture must analyse the data provided in real time and take a decision in real time about it. The major challenge here is that the Fog architecture cannot hold a huge amount of data as well as does not handle well the big data scenarios as it does not have huge computing powers. To solve this, additional hardware, as well as clustering of nodes, is required, thus increasing the cost.

- **Fog Infrastructure Management and Accounting:** The Fog architecture will be provided by the ISP (Internet Service Provider) or wireless carriers i.e. the bodies which can construct the necessary infrastructure to support it. End users may contribute to Fog Computing by lending their devices which will give them a scope to earn money/incentives as well. It reduces the cost of ownership significantly. The pricing issues for both service consumption and service offering should be resolved (Yi, Li, & Li, June 2015). The provision of dynamic pricing is to be introduced in the Fog architecture as people do not continuously need Fog services. Service pricing should be based on the usage of the architecture. The various issues associated with the pricing are (Alamri et al., 2013):
  - What price should be set as it cannot be as high as Cloud and not very low that it cannot support the infrastructure established?
  - Payment from the customers is also a challenge as a customer asked to pay every time he/she used the network is not a good strategy, one needs to figure out proper plans and price segments for whom they are targeted to.
  - The price that is quoted must be distributed unevenly based on various scales like storage, processing power, network devices etc. doing this is a challenge as each needs a different service to work with and maintaining it is difficult.

CONCLUSION

A number of IoT devices is increasing every day and if the latest estimations are to be believed this trend will continue to further shape the Internet. These devices generate a huge amount of data. Cloud

Computing is generally used to process, store, and analyse them. But most of the IoT applications are going to be real-time that are non-delay tolerant. This necessitates a new computing model that will compute that data close to the source, instead of sending to a remote data centre. Fog Computing has emerged as the solution which provides the Cloud like facility, in small scale, at the edge of the network. Fog Computing complements and extends the Cloud Computing thereby bringing the centralized Cloud Computing to a decentralized form near the IoT. As the data processing happens near IoT devices, the system has decreased the network latencies significantly. Fog Computing is essentially the better deal for real-time and time-constrained applications. The real-time applications can be experienced more quickly. The proliferation of Fog has abstracted the heavy weighted cloud, bringing powerful computing close to the user. The features like support for mobility, geographical distribution and locality aware-ness has supported much context-aware computing, which was otherwise would be very challenging in Cloud Computing. Even though Fog Computing has many challenges in terms of load distribution, supportability to heterogeneous devices, handling huge data and limitation to computing power and memory capacity, its advantages are overwhelming. In this spirit, many vendors like Cisco, Dell, HP, etc. are working hard to bring suitable solutions. Fog Computing would also be the other stepping stone in realizing Cognitive IoT, whereby physical world and the virtual world would blend together as one.

REFERENCES

Alamri, A., Ansari, W. S., Hassan, M. M., Hossain, M. S., Alelaiwi, A., & Hossain, M. A. (2013, February). A Survey on Sensor-Cloud: Architecture, Applications, and Approaches. *International Journal of Distributed Sensor Networks*, *2013*, 1–18.

Bonomi, F., Milito, R., Zhu, J., & Addepalli, S. (2012). Fog Computing and Its Role in the Internet of Things. In Proceedings of MCC'12, Helsinki, Finland.

Chiang, M. (2015). Fog Networking: An Overview on Research Opportunities. Retrieved from http://www.princeton.edu/~chiangm/FogResearchOverview.pdf

Chiang, M., & Zhang, T. (2016). Fog and IoT: An Overview of Research Opportunities. *IEEE Internet of Things Journal*, *3*(6), 854–864. doi:10.1109/JIOT.2016.2584538

Chiang, M., & Zhang, T. (2016). *Fog and IoT: An Overview of Research Opportunities*. IEEE Internet of Things Journal.

Cisco. (2014, January 29). *Cisco Delivers Vision of Fog Computing to Accelerate Value from Billions of Connected Devices*. Retrieved July 2017, from https://newsroom.cisco.com/press-release-content?articleId=1334100

Cisco. (2015). *Cisco Fog Computing Solutions: Unleash the Power of the Internet of Things*.

Coles, C. (2017). *11 Advantages of Cloud Computing and How Your Business Can Benefit From Them*. (SkyHigh) Retrieved from https://www.skyhighnetworks.com/cloud-security-blog/11-advantages-of-cloud-computing-and-how-your-business-can-benefit-from-them/

Dell Edge Gateways for IoT. (2017). (Dell) Retrieved November 6, 2017, from http://www.dell.com/us/business/p/edge-gateway

Firdhous, M., Ghazali, O., & Hassan, S. (2014). Fog Computing: Will it be the Future of Cloud Computing? In *International Conference on Informatics & Applications*, Kuala Terengganu, Malaysia.

Hewlett Packard Enterprise. (2017). *HPE Edgeline Converged Edge Systems*. Retrieved November 6, 2017, from https://www.hpe.com/in/en/servers/edgeline-iot-systems.html#header

Khan, N. N. (2015). Fog Computing: A Better Solution For IoT. *International Journal of Engineering and Technical Research*, *III*(2).

Kumari, S. (2015, December 28). *Agility on Cloud – A Vital Part of Cloud Computing*. (Sysfore Blog) Retrieved July 2017, from http://blog.sysfore.com/agility-on-cloud-a-vital-part-of-cloud-computing/

Microsoft. (2017). What is Cloud Computing? A beginner's guide. Retrieved July 2017, from https://azure.microsoft.com/en-in/overview/what-is-cloud-computing/

Miller, D. (2015, July 7). *Beware the Fog (Computing)*. Retrieved November 30, 2015, from http://www.cmswire.com/information-management/beware-the-fog-computing/

Milunovich, S., Passi, A., & Roy, J. (2014, December 4). After the Cloud Comes the Fog: Fog Computing to Enable the Internet of Things. *IT Hardware & Data Networking*.

Mora, R. D. (2014, January 29). *Cisco IOx: An Application Enablement Framework for the Internet of Things*. Retrieved November 8, 2016, from http://blogs.cisco.com/digital/cisco-iox-an-application-enablement-framework-for-the-internet-of-things

Naranjo, P. G., Shojafary, M., Vaca-Cardenasz, L., Canaliy, C., Lancellottiy, R., & Baccarelli, E. (n.d.). Big Data Over SmartGrid - A Fog Computing Perspective.

NxtraData. (2016, June 30). *Difference Between Clound & IOT*. (Nxtra Data) Retrieved July 2017, from http://nxtradata.com/blog/cloud-vs-iot.html

Qaisar, S., & Riaz, N. (2016). Fog Networking: An Enabler for Next Generation Internet of Things. *ICCSA 2016, Part II. LNCS*, *9787*, 353–365.

Rouse, M. (2017, July). Cloud Computing. *TechTarget*. Retrieved July 2017, from http://searchcloudcomputing.techtarget.com/definition/cloud-computing

Satyanarayanan, M., Bahl, P., Caceres, R., & Davies, N. (2009). *The case for vm-based cloudlets in mobile computing*. Pervasive Computing.

Sauerwalt, R. (2017). *Benefits of Cloud Computing*. IBM. Retrieved July 2017, from https://www.ibm.com/cloud-computing/learn-more/benefits-of-cloud-computing/

Vaquero, L. M., & Rodero-Merino, L. (2014). *Finding your Way in the Fog: Towards a Comprehensive Definition of Fog Computing*. HP Laboratories.

Yi, S., Hao, Z., Qin, Z., & Li, Q. (2015). Fog Computing: Platform and Applications. In *IEEE Workshop on Hot Topics in Web Systems and Technologies (HotWeb)*, Washington, DC. 10.1109/HotWeb.2015.22

Yi, S., Li, C., & Li, Q. (June 2015). A Survey of Fog Computing: Concepts, Applications and Issues. In *Workshop on Mobile Big Data (Mobidata '15)*, Hangzhou, China (pp. 37-42). ACM. 10.1145/2757384.2757397

Chapter 8
Data Classification and Prediction

Pudumalar S
Thiagarajar College of Engineering, India

Suriya K S
Thiagarajar College of Engineering, India

Rohini K
Thiagarajar College of Engineering, India

ABSTRACT

This chapter describes how we live in the era of data, where every event in and around us creates a massive amount of data. The greatest challenge in front of every data scientist is making this raw data, a meaningful one to solve a business problem. The process of extracting knowledge from the large database is called as Data mining. Data mining plays a wrestling role in all the application like Health care, education and Agriculture, etc. Data mining is classified predictive and descriptive model. The predictive model consists of classification, regression, prediction, time series analysis and the descriptive model consists of clustering, association rules, summarization and sequence discovery. Predictive modeling associates the important areas in the data mining called classification and prediction.

INTRODUCTION

The greatest challenge in front of every data scientist is making this raw data, a meaningful one to solve a business problem. Data is the beginning point of all data mining process. The raw data or the collected data cannot use directly to build the business models. Hence processing added value to the data called information. The information is the processed data which is stored and managed in the large database. The process of extracting knowledge from the large database is called as Data mining. Data mining software analyses relationships and patterns in stored transaction data based on open-ended user queries. In the data mining Major elements are listed follows 1) Extract, make over and load transaction data onto the data warehouse system. 2) Store and manage the data in a multidimensional database system. 3)

DOI: 10.4018/978-1-5225-4044-1.ch008

Provide data access to information technology professional and business analysts. 4) Analyze the data by application software. 5) Present the data in a useful format, such as a graph or table. Data mining is classified predictive and descriptive model. The predictive model consists of classification, prediction, regression, and time series analysis. The descriptive model is consist of clustering, summarization, association rules and sequence discovery. Predictive modeling associates the important areas in the data mining called classification and prediction. Applications of predictive modeling include customer retention management, cross-selling, direct marketing, and credit approval which are notable by the nature of the variable being predicted. "Why classification is important?" The classification problem attempts to learn the relationship between a set of feature variables and a target variable of interest. For example, the bank manager has massive customer's data, which consists of customer details and who all are applying for the loan. The manager will classify the customer data and easily identify the customers who all are in the risk and safe condition which is called as classification. The classified data are used to create a pattern to forecast the future condition of the customers, which is called as a prediction. Now a day's data classification and prediction holds promise in many fields to enhance efficiency and reduces the time complexity of the application. Classification and Prediction can be performed only when the data comes in the following steps, data pre-processing includes data cleaning, replace missing values, data relevance, data transformation, and data reduction. Most classification algorithms typically have two phases:

1. **Training Phase:** In this phase, a training model is constructed from the training instances. Intuitively, this can be understood as a summary mathematical model of the labeled groups in the training data set.
2. **Testing Phase:** In this phase, the training model is used to determine the class label (or group identifier) of one or more unseen test instances.

Classification predicts a certain outcome based on a given input. In order to predict the result, the algorithm processes a training set containing a set of attributes and the individual outcome, where usually called prediction attribute. The algorithm tries to determine relationships between the attributes that would make it possible to predict the conclusion. The inputs are analyzed by using data mining algorithms and produce a prediction. The prediction accuracy defines how "good" the algorithm is. Decision tree based, Rule-based, Instance-based learning, Bayesian Classification, Neural Networks, Ensemble methods, Support Vector are the most popular and powerful used in classification and prediction. A decision tree is a flow chart; similar to the data structure trees consists of decision node, leaf node, arc or edges, and path. Entropy is used to measure of homogeneity of the dataset. Information gain, Gain ratio, and Gini-index are the methods to select the attributes and generate the tree. Instance-based learning methods consist of K-nearest neighbor's algorithm, weighted regression, and case-based reasoning. The rule-based method is used to generate rules to classify the dataset which is consists of PRIMS and RIPPER. The Bayesian classification includes naïve Bayes and Bayesian belief network. Artificial Neural Network (ANN) of Neural Network is information -processing paradigm that is stimulated as the human brain's information processing mechanism. ANN has three different classes; these are single layer feed forward, multi-layer feeds forward and recurrent. Ensemble methods are used improve the accuracy of the classifiers which is achieved by bagging and boosting. Support vector machine is used for classification and regression methods which satisfying from theoretical points of view. SVM is used in many real-time applications such as text categorization, image classification, bioinformatics, and hand-written character recognitions.

Other classification methods are the genetic algorithm, rough set approach, and fuzzy set approach. Prediction models are continuous-valued functions which are used to predict unknown or missing values. It is supervised learning task where the data are used straightforwardly to predict the class value of a new instance. Education, healthcare, social media, supermarket, online shopping, and agriculture are the areas where prediction models are widely used. From the learned information, the future behavior and pattern will be predicted. It helps in making decisions and to increase the profit percentage of the particular field. A major matrix of predictive analysis is accurate. Prediction uses the classification algorithms and regression algorithms. Basic approaches: Instance-based (nearest neighbors), Statistical (naive Bayes), Bayesian networks, Regression (linear regression and nonlinear regression, logistic regression and poison regression.)The classification and prediction are compared and evaluated with the following measures 1) Accuracy 2) speed 3) robustness 4) scalability 5) interpretability. Visualization is most important in the data mining to represents the data and studies the results of various techniques. Visualization consists of plots, graphs representation such as pie chart, bar chart, histograms, and scatter plot.

A SURVEY ON PREDICTION AND CLASSIFICATION ALGORITHM

A survey on prediction and classification algorithms in data mining are discussed in Table 1.

Table 1. Survey on prediction and classification algorithm

S. No.	Title	Problem Addressed	Algorithms Used	Result
1	Comparison of models for the short-term prediction of rice stripe virus disease and its association with biological and meteorological factors (sun 2016).	Predict the RSV disease due to hot and humid environment condition.	Stepwise regression, a back propagation neural network, and support vector machines	The average prediction accuracies of support vector machines, back propagation neural network and stepwise regression were 98.95%, 93.75% and 77.35%
2	A mapping crop disease using survey data: The case of bacterial wilt in bananas in the East African highlands (Bouwmeestera 2016).	Mapping the crop (banana) diseases caused by bacteria at east Africa.	Regression analysis	Accuracy metrics that are computed from the comparison are the Mean Error and Root Mean Squared Error which are Mean Error is $9.6 \times 10-4$ for T0 and $8.7 \times 10-4$ and Root Mean Squared Error is namely $4.4 \times 10-11$ for T0 and $3.0 \times 10-15$.
3	Predicting instructor performance using data mining techniques in higher education (Agaoglu, 2016).	Predict the instructor performance based on students (satisfactory and not satisfactory).	Decision tree, support vector machine, artificial neural network, and discriminant anal1ysis	Seven different classifiers are used and the performance measure of all seven different classifiers are approximately give 90% accuracy and above in test dataset.
4	A Model to Predict Low Academic Performance a at a Specific Enrollment (Camilo 2015)	predict the academic attrition of student performance at University of Colombia	Decision tree and naïve bayes.	The prediction of the loss of academic status is improved by adding the academic data. Balanced accuracy ranged from 51 to 52% in the decision tree and between 54-57% in Naïve Bayes.
5	Heart Disease Prediction System (Purushottama 2016)	Efficient prediction of heart diseases.	Decision tree	The 10 fold methods is used for train and tests the system and find the accuracy of 86.3% in testing phase and 87.3% in training phase.
6	Smart beehive with preliminary decision tree analysis for agriculture and honey bee health monitoring (Murphy 2016).	Predict the internal condition and colony activity of beehive during all weather condition.	Decision tree	The beehive using sensor network data will gives a 95.38% accuracy

continued on following page

Table 1. Continued

S. No.	Title	Problem Addressed	Algorithms Used	Result
7	Climatic indicator for crop infection risk: Application to climate change impacts on five major foliar fungal diseases in Northern France (Launay 2014)	Predict the crop disease caused by fungus due to weather condition.	To develop two climatic indicators AIE and NID to quantify the potential effects of weather on the intensity and occurrences of pathogen infection.	The accuracy is not measured and mention in this paper. In the fungicide application decision support tools only used for the short term predictions. The conjunction with process-based epidemiological models, have an indicator which can be applied to large spatial scales and to various pathogens.
8	Prediction of climate change impacts on cotton yields in Greece under eight climatic models using the Aqua Crop crop simulation model and discriminant function analysis (Voloudakis 2014)	Predict the climatic impacts on cotton yields by designing a climatic model	stepwise discriminant function analysis	The Results indicate that keeping the present irrigation practices might have useful property on Cotton productivity for Western Greece.
9	A study on C.5 Decision Tree Classification Algorithm for Risk Predictions during Pregnancy (Lakshmi 2016)	predict the risk during the pregnancy using standardized and un standardized data	Decision tree	The accuracy percentage for standardized dataset and un-standardized dataset accounts to 71.3043%and 66.087% respectively and error percentages are 28.6957% and 33.913% respectively.
10	Predict the student's final GPA using decision tree (Mashael 2016).	Predict the student final GPA based on students grades.	Decision tree	It will generate largest rule for the entire subject. Don't using any metrics to measure the accuracy.
11	Analysis of crop yield prediction using data mining techniques (Ramesh 2016).	Predict the crop yield productivity.	Multiple Linear Regression (MLR) technique and Density based clustering technique	MLR technique which are ranging between -14% and +13% for 40 years interval. For the 6 cluster which has ranging between -13% and +8% by using Density-based clustering algorithm.
12	Decision trees and genetic algorithms for condition monitoring forecasting of aircraft air conditioning (Caubel 2014)	Condition monitoring forecasting of aircraft air conditioning, time series forecasting is major task to be done for the aircraft air conditioning.	Decision tree with genetic algorithm	The accuracy should be low due to the small dataset. The algorithm suited for the large dataset which will give a high accuracy.
13	Integrating genetic algorithm and decision tree learning for assistance in predicting in vitro fertilization outcomes (Guh 2011) .	Early prediction of the outcome of an In Vitro Fertilization (IVF) treatment which will important for both patients and physicians.	Decision tree with genetic algorithm	The accuracy of the algorithm is 73.2%.
14	A Fusion of Data Mining Techniques for Predicting Movement of Mobile Users (Duong 2015)	Proposed the fusion techniques to predict the future movements of mobile users in WLANs	sequential-pattern mining-based-clustering and clustering based-sequential-pattern-mining	The combinations of two techniques are improving the prediction accuracy.
15	Predictive Analysis in Agriculture to Improve the Crop Productivity using ZeroR algorithm (Rajasekaran 2016) (2016)	Based on the result, the farmer should invest the cost on the resources, pesticide and fertilizer. It will improve the profit for the farmer.	zeroR algorithm	WEKA tool is used to perform the zeroR algorithm. do not mention any accuracy in this paper.
16	Genetic algorithm based feature selection combined with dual classification for the automated detection of proliferative diabetic retinopathy (Welikala 2015)	GA used to select the feature and two SVM classification sre used to detect the proliferative diabetic retinopathy.	Dual SVM classifier	It gives 97% accuracy
17	Optimizing the number of trees in a decision forest to discover a sub forest with high ensemble accuracy using a genetic algorithm (Adnan 2016)	Reduce the no of trees using the ensemble methods and improve the accuracy.	Bagging and random forest	The results indicate that the proposed technique can select effective sub forests which are significantly smaller than original forests while achieving better (or comparable) accuracy than the original forests.

DATA CLASSIFICATION

Data Classification is the process of predicting the label or class for a given unlabelled object by designing a model. The derived model is based on the analysis of a training dataset (i.e., data objects whose class label is known). The goal of classification is to accurately predict the target class variable. For example, a classification model could be used to identify the crop yield as low, medium, high. Decision tree induction, frame-based or rule-based expert systems, hierarchical classification, neural networks, Bayesian network, and support vector machines are the several methods used to classify the data.

Tree Induction

Decision Tree

A decision tree is a tree like structure which includes root node, branches and leaf nodes. Each internal node is denoted by rectangles and leaf nodes are denoted by ovals. All internal nodes have two or more child nodes. All internal nodes undergo a test on an attribute, the outcome of a test is the branch and each leaf node holds a class label. Figure 1 shows the decision tree.

ID3 (Iterative Dichotomiser) is a simple decision tree learning algorithm. C4.5 algorithm is an improvedversionofID3usesgainratioassplitting criteria which became a benchmark for newer supervised learning algorithms are compared. The difference between ID3 and C4.5 algorithmisthatID3usesbinarysplits, whereas C4.5 algorithm uses multiway splits. SLIQ (Supervised Learning in Quest) is capable of handling large data sets with ease and lesser time complexity. SPRINT (Scalable Parallelizable Induction of Decision Tree algorithm) is also fast and highly scalable, and there is no storage constraint on larger data sets. Classification and Regression Trees (CART) is a nonparametric decision tree algorithm. It produces either classification or regression trees, based on whether the response variable is categorical or continuous. CHAID (chi-squared automatic interaction detector) focus on dividing a data set into exclusive and exhaustive segments that differ with respect to the response variable.

Figure 1. Decision tree

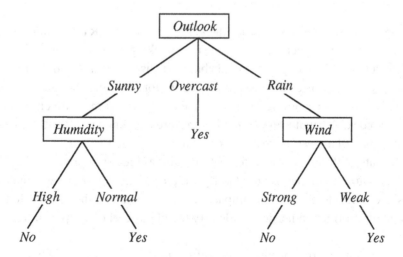

Algorithm: Generate decision tree.

The training tuples of data partition D is used to generate the decision tree.

Input: D is the Data partition, which is a set of training tuples and their associated class labels; attribute list, the set of candidate attributes; Attribute selection method, a method to decide the splitting measure that "most excellent" partitions the data tuples into individual classes.

This condition consists of a splitting attribute and, possibly, moreover a split point or splitting subset.

Output: A decision tree.

Method:

1. Create a node Nd;
2. If tuples in Dp are all of the same class, C then
3. Return Nd as a leaf node labeled with the class C;
4. If attribute list is empty then
5. Return Nd as a leaf node labeled with the majority class in Dp;// majority voting
6. Apply Attribute selection method (Dp, attribute list) to find the "most excellent" splitting criterion;
7. label node Nd with splitting criterion;
8. If splitting attribute is discrete-valued and multi way splits allowed then // not restricted to binary trees
9. Attribute list← attribute list−splitting attribute; // remove splitting attribute
10. for each outcome j of splitting criterion // partition the tuples and grow sub trees for each partition
11. Let Dpj be the set of data tuples in Dp satisfying outcome j; // a partition
12. If Dpj is empty then
13. Attach a leaf labeled with the majority class in Dp to node Nd;
14. Else attach the node returned by Generate decision tree (Dpj, attribute list) to node Nd; end for
15. return Nd;

The greedy approach are used to construct the C4.5, ID3 and CART decision trees in a top-down recursive divide-and-conquer manner and there is no backtracking method are used. The three parameters called by the algorithm are: D -data partition, attribute list- list of attributes describing the tuples, and attribute selection method specifies a heuristic procedure for selecting the "most excellent" attribute discriminates the given tuples according to class. Attribute selection measure employs either information gain or the gini index. Attribute selection measures are also known as splitting rules because they determine how the tuples at a given node are to be split.

To find the attribute with the highest information gain, a three step process is applied. In the first step we compute the information needed to classify a tuples in the dataset D. whereas step 2 considers attribute values since it tries to measure the impact of each attribute on the class. Info (D) or Entropy is the average amount of information needed to identify the class label of a tuples in D.

Step 1: to compute the information needed to classify a tuples in the dataset D by using equation 1

$$Info(D) = -\sum_{i=1}^{m} p_i \log_2 \left(p_i \right) \qquad (1)$$

Step 2: to find information needed to classify the dataset D. after using attributes X to split the dataset D into V partitions by using equation 2

$$Info_X(D) = -\sum_{j=1}^{v} \frac{|Dj|}{|D|} XI(Dj) \qquad (2)$$

Step 3: information gained by branching on attribute X can be obtained by subtracting the result of equation 2 form the result of equation 1.

$$Gain\ (X) = Info\ (D) - Info_X\ (D) \qquad (3)$$

Advantages

1. One big advantage of the decision tree model is its transparent nature.
2. Specificity
3. Comprehensive Nature
4. Ease of Use
5. Flexibility

Disadvantages

1. Unsuitability for estimation of tasks to predict values of a continuous attribute
2. Possibility of duplication with the same sub-tree on different paths
3. Limited to one output per attribute, and inability to represent tests that refer to two or more different objects

Probabilistic Classification

In the probabilistic classification, here two major algorithms are discussed which are naïve bayes and K Nearest Neighbor algorithm.

NAIVE BAYES ALGORITHM

The Bayesian Classification is a supervised learning method. This Naïve Bayes classifier is based on Bayes theorem. A Naïve Bayesian model is easy to build without any complication and mainly used for large datasets. Bayesian classifiers are the statistical classifiers. These Bayesian classifiers can predict the probability that a given tuple belongs to a particular class. It is robust to noise in input data.

Baye's theorem:

Baye's theorem is termed after the person named "Thomas Bayes". There are mainly two types of probabilities. They are,

1.   Posterior Probability:

[P(H/X)]

2.   Prior Probability:

[P(H)]

where
H = Hypothesis and
X = data tuple

Bayes theorem states that,

P(H/X) = P(X/H)P(H) / P(X)

Algorithm

1.   D: Set of tuples
2.   Each Tuple is an 'n' dimensional attribute vector
3.   X: (x1, x2, x3, …, xn)
4.   Let there be 'm' Classes: C1, C2, C3, …, Cm
5.   Naïve bayes classifier predicts X belongs to Class Ci if
6.   P(Ci/X)>P(Cj/X) for 1<=j<=m,j<>i
7.   Maximum Posteriori Hypothesis
8.   P(Ci/X) = P(X/Ci)P(Ci)/P(X)
9.   Maximize P(X/Ci)P(Ci) as P(X) is constant, With many attributes, P(X/Ci) is computationally expensive to evaluate.
10.   P(X/Ci) = P(x1/Ci)*P(x2/Ci)*…*P(xn/Ci)

BAYESIAN BELIEF NETWORK

It specifies joint conditional probability distributions. It is also called as Bayesian Network, Belief Network or Probabilistic Network. It allows class conditional independencies to be defined between subsets of variables. It provides a graphical model of relationship. A trained Bayesian network is used for classification.

There are two components to define Bayesian network. They are,

1.   Directed Acyclic graph
2.   A set of conditional probability tables.

Advantages

1. This algorithm affords fast, highly scalable model building and scoring.
2. Naïve bayes is scales linearly with the number of predictors and rows and it is a parallelized process.
3. Naïve Bayes can be used for both binary and multiclass classification problems.

Disadvantages

1. Naïve bayes classifier makes a very strong assumption on the shape of your data distribution, i.e. any two features are independent given the output classes.
2. Data scarcity
3. The other problem is continuous features. It is common to use a binning procedure to make them discrete. Another possibility is to use Gaussian distributions for the likelihoods.

K NEAREST NEIGHBOR (KNN) ALGORITHM

This is a non-parametric method used for classification and regression, which does not make any assumptions about the underlying joint probability density function. Instead, it directly uses the data sample to estimate the density, for example, using the density estimation methods. It is an instance based learning or lazy learning technique. It is an easiest machine learning algorithm.

Algorithm

1. Let "D" be a training dataset having "n" points $x_i \in R^d$, and let "D_i" denote the subset of points in D that are labeled with class "c_i", with $n_i = |D_i|$. Given a test point $x \in R^d$, and "K"- the number of neighbors, let "r" denote the distance from x to its K th nearest neighbor in D.
2. Consider the d-dimensional hyper ball of radius r around the test point x, defined as

$$Bd(x, r) = \{ x_i \in D \mid \delta(x, x_i) \le r \}$$

3. Here "$\delta(x, x_i)$" is the distance between x and x_i, which is assumed to be the Euclidean distance, i.e., $\delta(x, x_i) = kx - x_ik_2$. However, other distance metrics can also be used. We assume that $|Bd(x, r)| = K$.
4. Let "K_i" states the number of points among the K nearest neighbors of x that are labeled with class c_i, that is

$$K_i = \{ x_j \in Bd(x, r) \mid y_j = c_i \}$$

5. The class conditional probability density at x can be estimated as the fraction of points from class c_i that lie within the hyperball divided by its volume, that is

$$\hat{f}(x|c_i) = \frac{K_i/n_i}{V} = K_i/n_i V,$$

where $V = \text{vol}(B\text{d}\,(x, r))$ is the volume of the d-dimensional hyperball

6. The posterior probability P(ci |x) can be estimated a

$$P(ci\,|x) = \underline{f\char`^(x|ci)P\char`^\,(ci)}$$

$$\sum Pj=1\ f\char`^(x|cj)P\char`^(cj)$$

7. Because $P\char`^(ci) = ni/n$, we take

$$f\char`^(x|ci)P\char`^\,(ci) = Ki/niV * ni/n = Ki/nV$$

8. The posterior probability is given as,

$$P(ci\,|x)= \underline{Ki\,/\,nV} = Ki\,/\,K$$

$$\sum Kj\,/\,nV$$

9. Finally, the predicted class for "x" is

$$\char`^y = \text{argmax}_{ci}\,\{P(ci\,|\,x)\} = \text{argmax}_{ci}\{Ki\,/\,K\}= \text{argmax}_{ci}\,\{Ki\}$$

10. Because "*K*" is fixed, the KNN classifier predicts the class of x as the majority class among its *K* nearest neighbors.

Advantages

1. It is simple to implement.
2. It is flexible in nature.
3. It handles multi class classification.
4. Large dataset can be used.

Disadvantages

1. Large search problem exists to find nearest neighbors.
2. Storage of data is complex.
3. It must have knowledge of meaningful distance function.

Support Vector Machine (SVM)

It is a machine learning, supervised learning models that analyze data used for classification and regression analysis. An SVM training algorithm builds a model by making it a non-probabilistic binary linear classifier. The non-linear classifications are proficiently performed in this algorithm using the kernel trick. It will map their inputs into high dimensional feature spaces. The supervised learning is not possible, when data are not labeled and an unsupervised learning approach is required, which attempts to find natural clustering of the data to groups. Then map new data to these formed groups. The clustering algorithm which provides an improvement to the support vector machines is called support vector clustering.

MAXIMAL-MARGIN CLASSIFIER

It is a hypothetical classifier. It will show "How SVM works?". The numeric input variables "X" in our data form an n-dimensional space. The hyper-plane is a line that splits the input variable space. In 2D, we can visualize this as a line and we can assume that all of our input points can be completely separated by this line. Here for example we have an equation,

$$B0 + (B1 * X1) + (B2 * X2) = 0$$

Here the coefficients "B1 and B2" that finds the slope of the line and the intercept "B0" are found by the learning algorithm, and "X1 and X2 "are the two input variables.

Classifications can be done using this line. By adding input values into the line equation, we can find whether a new point is above or below the line.

1. If it is above the line, the equation returns a value greater than 0 and the point belongs to the first class (class 0).
2. If it is below the line, the equation returns a value less than 0 and the point belongs to the second class (class 1).
3. If a value is close to the line returns a value close to zero then it is difficult to classify.
4. If the magnitude of the value is large, there is more confidence in the prediction.

The distance between the line and the closest data points is defined as the margin. The optimal line that can separate the two classes is the line that as the largest margin. This is called the Maximal-Margin hyper-plane. The margin is calculated as the perpendicular distance from the line to only the closest points. These points are called as the support vectors. They support or define the hyper-plane. The hyper-plane is learned from training data using an optimization procedure that maximizes the margin.

Soft Margin Classifier

Maximizing the margin of the line that separates the classes must be relaxed. This is called as the soft margin classifier. This change allows some points in the training data to violate the separating line. An additional set of coefficients that yields the margin wiggle room in each dimension. These coefficients are called as slack variables. This increases the complexity of the model.

"C" - A tuning parameter that defines the magnitude. The "C" parameter defines the amount of violation of the margin allowed. no violation exists when C=0 and it is to the hard Maximal-Margin Classifier.

The larger the value of "C" the more violations of the hyper-plane are permitted. During learning, all training data that lie within the distance of the margin will affect the placement of the hyper-plane and are referred to as support vectors. The number of instances affected by the "C" that are allowed to fall within the margin; "C" influences the number of support vectors used.

1. The smaller the value of C, the algorithm is more sensitive (it has higher variance and lower bias).
2. The larger the value of C, the algorithm is less sensitive (it has lower variance and higher bias).

Support Vector Machines (Kernels)

The SVM algorithm can be implemented using a kernel. Linear SVM is done by transforming the problem using some linear algebra. Linear SVM can be done using the inner product of any two given observations. The inner product between two vectors is the sum of the multiplication of each pair of input values. Consider an example, here the inner product of the vectors [2, 3] and [5, 6] is 2*5 + 3*6 or 28. The equation for making a prediction between the input "x" and each support vector "xi" is found as follows:

f(x) = B0 + sum(ai * (x,xi))

This equation calculates the inner products of a new input vector "x" with all support vectors in training data. The coefficients "B0" and "ai" must be estimated from the training data by the learning algorithm.

Linear Kernel Svm

The dot-product is called the kernel and the equation can be re-written as follows:

K(x, xi) = sum(x * xi)

Here the kernel measures the distance between new data and the support vectors. The dot product is used to measure linear SVM. Other kernels can be used to transform the input space into higher dimensions such as a Polynomial Kernel and a Radial Kernel. This is called as the Kernel Trick. It is even more complex. These are more accurate classifiers.

Polynomial Kernel SVM

We can use a polynomial kernel. Assume that,

K(x,xi) = 1 + sum(x * xi)^d

Here the degree of the polynomial should be given. When d=1 it is the same as the linear kernel. The polynomial kernel which allows for curved lines in the input space.

Radial Kernel SVM

Complex radial kernel can also be used. Let's take an assumption that

$$K(x,xi) = exp(-gamma * sum((x - xi^2))$$

The default value for gamma is 0.1, where gamma is 0 < gamma < 1. The radial kernel is very local and can create complex regions within the feature space, like closed polygons in 2D space.

Advantages

1. It is efficient for usability.
2. This algorithm is more scalable.

Disadvantages

1. Best choice of kernel should be done.
2. Other problem is in usage of discrete data.
3. Becomes slow in test phase

Artificial Neural Network (ANN)

Neural network which is specifically "Artificial neural network" (ANN is a powerful data modeling tool based on the biological neural system. Artificial neurons are interconnected in groups and connectionist approach is used to process information .In learning phase, the system changes its structure based on external or internal information that flows through the network.

TOPOLOGIES

Feed Forward Neural Network

The Key features of Feed forward neural network are:

1. The information moves in only one direction, forward, from the input nodes, through the hidden nodes (if any) and to the output nodes
2. Network does not have any cycles or loops
3. The data processing can extend over multiple (layers of) units, but no feedback connections are present

Recurrent Network

The Key features of recurrent network are

1. It has feedback connections.
2. Bi-directional data flow

The nature of feed forward network is that it propagates data from input to output in a linear fashion, whereas RNs propagates data in reverse order.

Learning types in ANN are:

1. Associative learning or supervised learning in which the network is trained with input and its corresponding matching output patterns. These input-output pairs is supplied by an external teacher, or by the system which contains the neural network (self-supervised).
2. Unsupervised learning or Self-organization in which an (output) unit is trained to respond to clusters of pattern within the input.

Steps Involved in Data Mining Based on Neural Network

Data Preparation

Data preparation makes the data to fit for specific data mining method. It includes the following four processes:

1. Data cleaning,
2. Data Option,
3. Data Pre-processing,
4. Data Expression

Rule Extraction

The method of extracting fuzzy rules from recursive network is called Black Box method, the algorithm of binary input and output rules extracting (BIO-RE), partial rules extracting algorithm (Partial-RE) and full rules extracting algorithm (Full-RE) are various methods used for extracting rules.

Rules Assessment

1. Find the optimal sequence of extracting rules, making it obtains the best results in the given data set;
2. Test the accuracy of the rules extracted;
3. Detect how much knowledge in the neural network has been missed;
4. Detect the inconsistency between the extracted rules and the trained neural network.

Applications

Accounting

1. Identifying tax fraud
2. Enhancing auditing by finding irregularities

Finance

1. Signature and bank note verification
2. Customer credit scoring
3. Credit card approval and fraud detection
4. Loan approvals
5. Economic and financial forecasting

Marketing

1. Classification of consumer spending pattern
2. New product analysis
3. Sale forecasts

Advantages

1. ANNs have the ability of distributed information storage, parallel processing, reasoning, and self-organization.
2. Rapid fitting of nonlinear data, so it can solve many problems which are difficult for other method.
3. High Accuracy: Neural networks are able to approximate complex non-linear mappings
4. Independence from prior assumptions: Neural networks do not make a priori assumptions about the distribution of the data.

Disadvantages

1. ANN methods have not been popularly used in data mining tasks because how the classifications were made is not explicitly stated as symbolic rules that are suitable for verification or interpretation by human experts.

Other Classification Methods

In this section, we discuss about the other classification methods including genetic algorithm, rough set and fuzzy set which are less commonly used classifier in the data mining approach. Even though above algorithms are performed well in some application and it will have some strength to achieve the best results for the particular objective.

GENETIC ALGORITHM

Genetic algorithm is a searching technique which is used to search the best solution among the possible solution and it also called as an optimization algorithm. GA uses the evolutionary mechanisms such as initialization, selection, crossover and mutation. The genetic algorithm commonly used for the big problems for the example, in the data mining approach dataset is most important thing to process the classification. The large dataset is easily handled and processed by the genetic algorithm. GA has been used for classification as well as feature selection, optimization problem and evaluates the fitness of the algorithms. GA processes are as follow, we start with initialization process which will creates randomly generated rules. All the rules are coded by the string which is called as the chromosomes. The possible solutions are called as the individual and the group of all the individual is called as population. The fitness function is used to evaluate all the individuals in the population (e.g. ability to discriminate or classify). The selection method will contain many techniques like ranking selection, tournament section and roulette wheel selection. The crossover is used to combine the two individuals to create new individuals for possible solution for the next generation which is consists of three types. These are single point crossover, two point crossover and uniform crossover. Mostly the uniform crossover is used, because the mixing rations of the chromosomes are equal in this type of crossover. The chromosomes are interchanged and create the two new off springs. Mutation is the process of change the value of randomly selected genes and it implemented in 3 ways. These are flip bit (binary represented gene), boundary (integer and float represented gene) and uniform (integer and float represented gene). Mutation is the final step of the GA. The output of the mutation satisfies the conditions which are given by the user, it will stop. Otherwise, it will move on to the next new iteration with new set of rules. Figure 4 defines the process of the GA.

Rough Set Approach

Rough set approach can be used for classification to determine the structural relationship within noisy data and imprecise and the rough set analysis is induction of approximations of concepts. In the Classification, discrete and continuous valued attributes are used. Rough set approach applies in the discrete

Figure 2. GA process

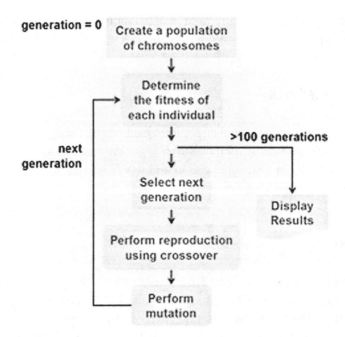

valued attributes and the continuous valued attributes are must therefore be discretized before its use. Rough set approach can be used for feature extraction, feature selection, data reduction, decision rule generation, and pattern extraction (templates, association rules), etc. and it is used to identify partial or total dependencies in data, eliminates redundant data, gives approach to missing data, null values, dynamic data and others. The Rough Set Theory is based on the concern of equivalence classes within the given training data. The tuples that forms the equivalence class are unclear. It means the samples are identical with respect to the attributes describing the data. There are some classes in the real-world data, which cannot be distinguished in terms of available attributes. The rough set definition is approximated by two sets as follows, by using the given class X. In the given Class X consists of all the data tuples that based on the information of the attributes in the lower approximation that are certain to belong to class X and the upper approximation of X consists of all the tuples, that based on the information of attributes, that cannot be described as not belonging to X. Figure 3 clearly explains the rough set approach approximation of given class X.

Fuzzy Set Approach

Fuzzy Logic is a superset of Boolean logic. The concept of partial truth is handle by the extended fuzzy logic, i.e. truth values between "completely true" and "completely false". It is multivalued logic and only allows the intermediate values to be defined between the conventional evaluation like yes/no, true/false, 1/0 etc. The set of user–supplied human language rules are generated and these rules are converted into their mathematical equivalent. It provides an easy way. The fuzzy classifier is one of the applications in the fuzzy logic. It can be expressed in a very natural way using linguistic variables, which are described by fuzzy sets. Consider two variables Entropy H and α-angle. These variables can be modeled as follows.

Figure 4 explains the classification model of the fuzzy approach. In fuzzy classification, a sample can have membership which will be in many different classes to different degrees. Usually, the membership values are constrained so that all of the membership values for a particular sample sum to 1. Now the professional knowledge for this variable can be formulated as a rule like IF Entropy *high* AND α *high* THEN Class = class 4. The above rules can be combined in a table, that the table is called as rule base. The example of fuzzy rule base as shown in Table 2.

Figure 3. Rough set approach

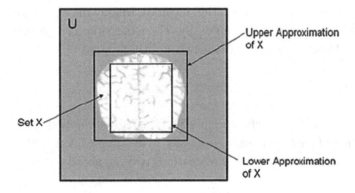

Figure 4. Fuzzy classification model

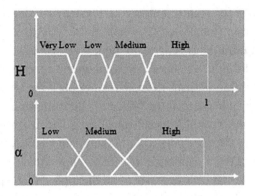

Table 2. Example for fuzzy rule base

Entropy	A	Class
Very low	Low	Class 1
Low	Medium	Class 2
Medium	High	Class 3
High	High	Class 4

The fuzzy approach might be useful for the complex problem and complex mathematical models. It will give the many different way of approach to the classification. Fuzzy logic requires a adequate expert knowledge for the formulation of the rule base, the combination of the sets and the defuzzification. It also called as optimization approach to enhance the performance of the classifiers.

Data Prediction

If you know something about A, this knowledge helps you predict something about B. Now a day, data prediction might be helpful for many applications which are predicting the pattern for the future. Prediction only used the continuous valued function. Initially the prediction model is constructed and the model is used to predict the unknown values. For the example, the crop diseases are predicted earlier and avoid the losses for the farmers by using the prediction methods. Mainly the regression methods are used for prediction, which will make the relationship easily. The regression methods are linear regression and non-linear regression. These are explained clearly below discussions

Regression Model

Regression model is one of the probabilistic models. The regression models are categorized into two types which are simple and multiple linear regressions. In the simple linear regression only one explanatory variable are used. In the multiple linear regressions two and above explanatory variables are used.

SIMPLE LINEAR REGRESSION

The simple linear regression is divided into two types. These are linear regression and nonlinear regression. First the simple linear regression is explained below:

The Relationship between the mean of the response variable and the level of the explanatory variable assumed to be approximately linear. Explanatory and Response Variables are Numeric. One variable is considered independent (=predictor) variable (X) and the other the dependent (=outcome) variable Y. The Figure 5 describes the linear regression line.

The equation of the linear relationship between the two variables as follows:

$$Y = \beta_0 + \beta_1$$

where,

y = dependent variable
x = independent variable
β_0 = y-intercept
β_1 = slope of the line

β_0 and β_1 are the regression coefficients which are solved by using least square method. It estimates the best-fitting straight line as the one that minimizes the error between the actual data and the estimate of the line. Consider D be a training set consisting of values of predictor variable, x and their associated values for response variable, y. The training set contains $|D|$ data points of the form $(x1, y1)$, $(x2, y2)$, ..., $(x|D|, y|D|)$

$$\beta_1 = \frac{\sum_{i=1}^{|D|}(x_i - \overline{x})(y_i - \overline{y})}{\sum_{i=1}^{|D|}(x_i - \overline{x})^2}$$

Figure 5. Regression line

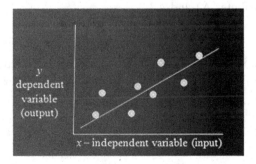

$$\beta_0 = \overline{y} - \beta_1 \overline{x}$$

where,

$\overline{x}$ = mean value of $x1, x2, ::::, xjDj$
$\overline{y}$ = mean value of $y1, y2, ::::, yjDj$

For example, if we have the month wise data of the employee experience and salary, then we predict the employee's future salary. The employee experience is the known variable X and the salary is the unknown variable Y. based on the known variable X we easily predict the unknown variable Y by using the least square method. Steps to perform the least square method as follows:

Step 1: Initially find the mean value of the x and y.
Step 2: Apply the mean values in the β_1 equation
Step 3: Calculate and find the β_1 value
Step 4: Substitute the β_1 value in the β_0 equation.
Step 5: By changing the values of x in the slope equation, predict the unknown variable y.

The equation of the least square is estimated by the line equation $y = \beta_0 + \beta_1 x$.

MULTIPLE LINEAR REGRESSION

The multiple linear regression is the extension of the simple linear regression. Here, more than one predictor variables (x1, x2...xn) are used to find the unknown variable (y). *A1, A2, …, An*, relating a tuples, *X*. Our training data set, *D*, contains data of the form (*X1, y1*), (*X2, y2*), …, (*X|D|, y|D|*), where the *Xi* are the *n*-dimensional training tuples with associated class labels, *yi*. An example of a multiple linear regression equation based on two predictor attributes or variables, *A1* and *A2*, is described below:

$$y = \beta_0 + \beta_1 x_1 + \beta_2 x_2$$

where,

Y= unknown variable
X1 and x2 = the values of attributes A1 and A2
$\beta_0, \beta_1, \beta_2$ = the co efficient of x

In the multi linear regression, the coefficient is estimated by using least square methods as same as above simple linear regression. Multiple regression problems are as a replacement for solved with the use of statistical software packages, such as SAS, SPSS, and S-Plus.

Performance Analysis

Accuracy and Error Measures

In the above section, how the prediction and classification algorithms are works, advantages and disadvantages of the algorithms are discussed. Now we discuss the performance evaluation of the algorithms. In the data mining, many methods are available to build the classification and prediction models. The efficient models are found out by the performance evaluations of the classifiers. For example, suppose you used data from previous patients to train a classifier to predict patient's diseases. You would like an estimate of how accurately the classifier can predict the patient's diseases, that is, future patient's data on which the classifier has not been trained. You may still have tried different methods to construct more than one classifier or predictor and now, to compare their accuracy. But some questions are a raised in our mind. 1. What is accuracy?, 2. How can we estimate it?, 3. Are there strategies for increasing the accuracy of a learned model? 4. These questions are explained in the following few sections.

Accuracy is to the ability of classifier which will predict the class label correctly. The accuracy of the predictor refers to how fit to the given predictor can estimate the value of predicted attribute for a fresh data. For example, if there were 95 rats and only 5 cats in the data set, the classifier could easily be biased into classifying all the samples as rats. The overall accuracy would be 95%, but in practice the classifier would have a 100% recognition rate for the rat class but a 0% recognition rate for the cat class.

The Confusion matrix is used to measure the accuracy of the classifier. The equation for the accuracy as shown below,

$$Accuracy = \left(number\ of\ correct\ prediction\right) / \left(total\ of\ all\ cases\ to\ be\ predicted\right)$$

Figure 6 clearly explains the confusion matrix. The error and misclassification rates are good complementary metrics to overcome this problem. Error classifying a record as belonging to one class when it belongs to another class is called as error and the percent of misclassified records out of the total records in the validation data is called as error rate. The error rate is measure by following formula,

$$Error\ rate = \left(number\ of\ wrong\ prediction\right) / \left(total\ of\ all\ cases\ to\ be\ predicted\right)$$

Figure 6. Confusion matrix

Confusion Matrix		Target			
		Positive	Negative		
Model	Positive	a	b	*Positive Predictive Value*	a/(a+b)
	Negative	c	d	*Negative Predictive Value*	d/(c+d)
		Sensitivity	*Specificity*	**Accuracy** = (a+d)/(a+b+c+d)	
		a/(a+c)	d/(b+d)		

The alternate methods are sensitivity, specificity, precision and recall.

1. True Positive recognition rate is called as sensitivity and it defined as follow,

Sensitivity = TP/P (positive)

2. The True Negative recognition rate is called as specificity and it defines as follow,

Specificity = TN/N(negative)

3. What percentage of tuples that the classifier labeled as positive are actually positives called as precision(exactness) and it defined as follow,

Precision=TP/TP+FP

4. What percentage of positive tuples did the classifier label as positive is called as recall (completeness) and it defines as follow,

Recall=TP/TP+FN

where,

TP (True Positive) = number of correct predictions that an instance is positive.
TN (True Negative) = number of correct predictions that an instance is negative
FP (False Positive) = number of incorrect predictions that an instance is positive
FN (False Negative) = number of incorrect of predictions that an instance negative
P=number of positive tuples
N=number of negative tuples

Evaluation of Classifier and Predictor Accuracy

In this section, the evaluations of the classifier and predictor accuracy measures techniques are discussed. Now the question is, "how can we use the above measures to obtain a reliable estimate of classifier accuracy (or predictor accuracy in terms of error)?" Partition or holdout, cross validation, and the bootstrap are common techniques for assessing accuracy based on randomly sampled partitions of the given data. To estimate accuracy increases the overall computation time by using such techniques and yet is useful for model selection.

PARTITION OR HOLDOUT

In this technique, the dataset is divided into two independent datasets. One is training dataset (2/3) and another is testing dataset (1/3). Random_sampling_is a variation of holdout Repeat holdout k times, accuracy = avg. of the accuracies obtained. These techniques are mainly used for the large dataset with large number of samples. If it is moderate dataset repeat the holdout. It will give different samples for each process.

CROSS-VALIDATION

In the cross-validation, initially the dataset is divided into k subsamples. Secondly use the k-1 subsamples as training dataset and one sub-sample as testing data. These processes are repeat k times. Cross-validation mainly used for the dataset with moderate size. frequently the subsets are stratified before the cross-validation is performed. The error estimates are averaged to yield an overall error estimate.

BOOTSTRAP

Bootstrap methods work well in the small dataset. It Samples the given training tuples uniformly with replacement. For example, each time a tuple is selected, it is equally likely to be selected again and re-added to the training set. Several bootstrap methods are used to evaluate the accuracy of the classifier, and a common one is .632 bootstrap. A data set with d tuples is sampled d times, with replacement and the resulting in a training set of d samples. The data tuples that did not make it into the training set end up forming the test set. About 63.2% of the original data end up in the bootstrap, and the remaining 36.8% forming the test set

REFERENCES

Adnan, N., & Islam, Z. (2016). Optimizing the number of trees in a decision forest to discover a sub forest with high ensemble accuracy using a genetic algorithm. *Knowledge-Based Systems*, *110*, 86–97. doi:10.1016/j.knosys.2016.07.016

Agaoglu, M. (2016). Predicting Instructor Performance Using Data Mining Techniques in Higher Education. *IEEE Access: Practical Innovations, Open Solutions*, *4*, 2379–2387. doi:10.1109/ACCESS.2016.2568756

Al-Barrak, M. A., & Al-Razgan, M. (2016). Predict the student's final GPA using decision tree. *International Journal of Information and Education Technology*, *6*(7), 528–533. doi:10.7763/IJIET.2016.V6.745

Arockiaraj, M.C. (2013, May). Applications of neural networks in data mining. *International Journal Of Engineering And Science*, *3*(1), 08-11.

Bouwmeestera, H., Heuvelink, G. B. M., & Stoorvogelc, J. J. (2016, March). Mapping crop diseases using survey data: The case of bacterial wilt in bananas in the East African highlands. *European Journal of Agronomy*, *74*, 173–184. doi:10.1016/j.eja.2015.12.013

Duong, T. V. T., & Tran, D. Q. (2015, December). A Fusion of Data Mining Techniques for Predicting Movement of Mobile Users. *Journal of Communications and Networks (Seoul)*, *17*(6), 568–581. doi:10.1109/JCN.2015.000104

Edwards-Murphy, F., Magno, M., Whelan, P. M., O'Halloran, J., & Popovici, E. M. (2016, June). Smart beehive with preliminary decision tree analysis for agriculture and honey bee health monitoring. *Computers and Electronics in Agriculture, 124*, 211–219. doi:10.1016/j.compag.2016.04.008

Gerdes, M. (2014). Decision trees and genetic algorithms for condition monitoring forecasting of aircraft air conditioning. *Computers and Electronics in Agriculture, 40*(12), 5021–5026.

Guh, R. S., Wu, T. C. J., & Weng, S. P. (2011). Integrating genetic algorithm and decision tree learning for assistance in predicting in vitro fertilization outcomes. *Expert Systems with Applications, 38*(4), 4437–4449. doi:10.1016/j.eswa.2010.09.112

Lakshmi, B. N., Indumathi, T. S., & Ravic, N. (2016). A study on C.5 Decision Tree Classification Algorithm for Risk Predictions during Pregnancy. *Procedia Technology, 24*, 1542–1549. doi:10.1016/j.protcy.2016.05.128

Launay, M., Caubel, J., Bourgeois, G., Huard, F., Garcia de Cortazar-Atauri, I., Bancal, M. O., & Brisson, N. (2014). Climatic indicators for crop infection risk: Application to climate change impacts on five major foliar fungal diseases in Northern France. *Agriculture, Ecosystems & Environment, 197*, 147–158. doi:10.1016/j.agee.2014.07.020

Lobella, D. B., & Burke, M. B. C. (2010). On the use of statistical models to predict crop yield responses to climate change. *Journal of Agricultural and Forest Meteorology, 150*(11), 1443–1452. doi:10.1016/j.agrformet.2010.07.008

López, C. E. G., Guzmán, E. L., & González, F. A. (2015, July). A Model to Model to Predict Low Academic Performance a at a Specific Enrollment Using Data Mining. *IEEE Revista Iberoamericana de Tecnologias del Aprendizaje, 10*(3), 119–125. doi:10.1109/RITA.2015.2452632

Pozos-Radilloa, B. E., de Lourdes Preciado-Serranoa, M., & Acosta-Fernándeza, M. (2014, June). Academic stress as a predictor of chronic stress in university students. *Psicología Educativa, 20*(1), 47–52. doi:10.1016/j.pse.2014.05.006

Purushottama, S. (2016). Efficient Heart Disease Prediction System. *Procedia Computer Science, 85*, 962–969. doi:10.1016/j.procs.2016.05.288

Ramesh, D., & Vardhan, B. V. (2016). Analysis of crop yield prediction using data mining techniques. *International Journal of Research in Engineering and Technology, 4*(1), 470–473.

Rosen, L., Carrier, L. M., Miller, A., Rokkum, J., & Ruiz, A. (2015). Sleeping with technology: Cognitive, affective, and technology usage predictors of sleep problems among college students. *Sleep Health, 2*(1), 49–56. doi:10.1016/j.sleh.2015.11.003 PMID:29073453

Sawale, G.J. (2013, April). Use of Artificial Neural Network in Data Mining For Weather Forecasting. *International Journal of Computer Science And Applications, 6*(2).

Singh, Y., & Chauhan, A. S. (2009). Neural Networks In Data Mining. *Journal of Theoretical and Applied Information Technology*. Retrieved from http://www.jatit.org/volumes/research-papers/Vol5No1/1Vol5No6.pdf

Sun, S., Bao, Y., Luc, M., Liu, W., Xie, X., Wang, C., & Liuc, W. (2016). A comparison of models for the short-term prediction of rice stripe virus disease and its association with biological and meteorological factors. *Acta Ecologica Sinica, 36*(3), 166–171. doi:10.1016/j.chnaes.2016.04.002

Voloudakis, D., Karamanos, A., Economou, G., Vahamidis, P., Kotoulas, V., Kapsomenakis, J., & Zerefos, C. (2014, September 22). Prediction of climate change impacts on cotton yields in Greece under eight climatic models using the AquaCrop crop simulation model and discriminant function analysis. *Journal of Agricultural Water Management, 147*, 116–128.

Welikala, R. A., Fraz, M. M., Dehmeshki, J., Hoppe, A., Tah, V., Mann, S., ... Barman, S. A. (2015, July). Genetic algorithm based feature selection combined with dual classification for the automated detection of proliferative diabetic retinopathy. *Computerized Medical Imaging and Graphics, 43*, 64–77. doi:10.1016/j.compmedimag.2015.03.003 PMID:25841182

Chapter 9
Ontology Based Feature Extraction From Text Documents

Abirami A.M
Thiagarajar College of Engineering, India

Askarunisa A.
KLN College of Information Technology, India

Shiva Shankari R A
Thiagarajar College of Engineering, India

Revathy R.
Thiagarajar College of Engineering, India

ABSTRACT

This article describes how semantic annotation is the most important need for the categorization of labeled or unlabeled textual documents. Accuracy of document categorization can be greatly improved if documents are indexed or modeled using the semantics rather than the traditional term-frequency model. This annotation has its own challenges like synonymy and polysemy in the document categorization problem. The model proposes to build domain ontology for the textual content so that the problems like synonymy and polysemy in text analysis are resolved to greater extent. Latent Dirichlet Allocation (LDA), the topic modeling technique has been used for feature extraction from the documents. Using the domain knowledge on the concept and the features grouped by LDA, the domain ontology is built in the hierarchical fashion. Empirical results show that LDA is the better feature extraction technique for text documents than TF or TF-IDF indexing technique. Also, the proposed model shows improvement in the accuracy of document categorization when domain ontology built using LDA has been used for document indexing.

DOI: 10.4018/978-1-5225-4044-1.ch009

INTRODUCTION

Necessity of annotating the text documents has become increased for analyzing the large amount of documents existing in the World Wide Web. But most of the documents are in unstructured format and the machines cannot simply process them. People who buy/sell the products give their comments, feedback, additional features needed, etc., in the form of text which is mostly unstructured. It becomes necessary to categorize these voluminous texts to make business intelligent solutions. The huge data available in the internet has to be modeled, analyzed and then the decision has to be taken. Retrieving the information from the unstructured text is the difficult task. Document annotation with added semantics enables the information or knowledge extraction from the repository in an intelligent way.

Feature extraction is the process which starts from an initial set of measured data and builds features intended to be informative and non-redundant. It involves reducing the amount of resources required to represent a large set of data. Many algorithms are used for identifying the features from the textual data that requires grouping or classifying the entities based on their similar property.

Some of the problems faced with feature extraction by traditional methods are: (i) existing techniques aren't compatible with the current Web size and growth rate and hence automated techniques are essential if practical and scalable solutions are to be obtained (ii) absence of semantic relations between concepts in feature search processes (iii) imperfections in classifying the feature reviews into more degrees of polarity terms and (iv) misinterpretation of textual features due to lack of prior knowledge.

Ontology is a set of concepts and categories in a subject area or domain that shows their properties and the relations between them. Domain specific Ontology represents the particular meanings of terms as they apply to that domain. The semantic web technologies can be used to model the textual data to represent domain vocabularies and their relationships through Ontologies, RDF, etc. The analysis has to be done in such a way that the context has to be matched both between the writer and the reader. All these challenges can be well handled by representing the different vocabularies for the domain, and their relationship between the concepts. Ontology-based information extraction is the use of ontologies and their specifications to "drive" or inform the information extraction process. The terms and concepts in the source Ontology form the basis for term matching when tagging text documents. Difficulties in feature extraction problems can be overcome if the text document can be modeled using the Ontology representation along with the use of topic modeling techniques. The objective of this proposed work is set to build domain Ontology for the set of documents with relevant features extracted from the text documents.

BACKGROUND

Use of Ontology in Information Extraction

Ontology is an explicit description of a domain. It defines a concept by describing its properties, attributes, and constraints. It defines a common vocabulary and it gives a shared understanding. UML diagrams are used to identify and classify biological entities and interactions between proteins and genes using Ontology (Rindfleisch, 2000). Ontology provides a formal conceptualization of a particular domain that is shared by a group of people. In the context of the Semantic Web, Ontology describes domain theories for the explicit representation of the semantics of the data (Maedeche, 2003). Ontology-based information extraction enables named entity identification and hotel/movie review classification using rule based systems and deeper level analysis (Maynard, 2003; Castells, 2007; Larissa, 2013). Knowledge management of web documents is enabled by extracting the semantic data like named entities using the document annotations and rules (Ciravegna, 2001; Bontcheva, 2003; Alani, 2003). Semantic web technologies like Ontology learning, RDF repositories enable the building of Knowledge and Information Management extraction framework for automatic annotation, and retrieval of documents (Popov, 2004). Lexicon-based dictionaries and Ontology like WordNet are in place to identify lexicons, their relationship and to extract sentiments for sentiment classification (Kamps, 2004; Taboada, 2006).

Information Extraction (IE) needs Ontology as part of the understanding process for extracting the relevant information. Its domain specificity reduces the complexity. IE is used for populating and enhancing the Ontology. Texts are useful sources of knowledge to design and enrich Ontology (Nédellec, 2005). SentiWordNet enables the building of sentiment dictionary using document vectors and SVM classification for positive and negative categorization (Verma, 2008). Lu (2010) recommended conditional entropy-based method for opinion extraction and developed structured Ontology for two different datasets like US President and Digital Camera. Using the hierarchical learning algorithm, Wei (2010) developed sentiment ontology tree (HL-SOT) to build hierarchical classification for products and their attributes, which helped in sentiment classification of products and their features.

Semantic Approach for Text Analysis

Knowledge base is the dictionary for the concepts of a certain restricted domain. Ontology is the semantic knowledge dictionary for the instances of concepts. The semantic approach is used to extract the meaning of the documents using concepts instead of terms present in the documents. Synonymy and polysemy issues in text analysis cannot be resolved if terms are used as indexes. However, semantic-based approach like LSI (Guo, 2009) and LDA (Colace, 2016) techniques are used for extracting and categorizing the related terms and build relationship among the index terms. Unsupervised learning techniques had been used (Guo, 2009) to extract product features from the review documents and Latent Semantic Association (LaSA) model was built to group words belonged to the same concept. Product quality is measured and it is ranked by using text analysis from multiple websites and statistical techniques (McGlohon, 2010).

Somprasertsri (2010) developed an Ontology-based opinion model for mining features of product from customer reviews. Ma (2012) classified Chinese research proposals into disciplines and cluster them based on similarity measures and Genetic Algorithms using Ontology. Saif (2012) implemented a new set of semantic features for training a model for sentiment analysis of tweets. Baldoni (2012) presented application software ArsEmotica to extract the predominant emotions from the social media platform. Ontology learning was used to derive sentiment lexicons of emotional categories. Ontology learning along with lexicon-based approach was applied on twitter posts of mobile products (Kontopoulos, 2013). Penalver-Martinez (2014) used Ontology for feature selection by deploying an existing Ontology and a new vector analysis based method for sentiment analysis for movie reviews. Thakor (2015) developed Ontology-based sentiment analysis model for negative tweets collected about postal services of United States and Canada using the rule based classification. Colace (2016) used domain-based Ontology and probabilistic Latent Dirichlet Allocation (LDA) model for developing sentiment grabber model by annotating semantics in text. Ali (2016) proposed a method to automate online review classification for hotels using Support Vector Machine (SVM) on fuzzy domain ontology. The Appendix details the related work in these research areas.

From the literature review conducted on the use of Ontology for indexing the text documents, only very few research have been focused in this area (Verma, 2008; Ma, 2012; Kontopoulos, 2013; Thakor, 2015; Colace, 2016; Ali, 2016). Because most of the methods are keyword based and they do not represent the contextual relationship between the terms present in the text. LSI-based information extraction resulted in 60% precision and 20% recall for Medline document classification (Paralic, 2003). However, Ontology-based approach resulted in 75% precision and 40% recall (Paralic, 2003), and recall value 82% for mobile product review classification (Kontopoulos, 2013). The Ontology enabled IE when combined with lexicon or machine learning techniques give average accuracy greater than 80%. The machine learning techniques for sentiment classification (Kang, 2012; Ali, 2016) and the lexicon based Senticircle algorithm (Saif, 2016) on twitter data resulted in 81% accuracy. The hybrid approach based on Ontology and Genetic Algorithm for automatic clustering of 900 Chinese proposals into 60 topics resulted in 91% F-measure value (Ma, 2012). It is noticed that when IE process is combined with Ontology for data modeling, it reduces the human intervention, enables automatic machine processing, saves time and effort for querying the documents. The intention of this research is to propose a new domain-based indexing technique for online reviews of product or service written by the users in the social media platform. The method proposes to develop a domain knowledge base using Ontology by integrating it with the topic modeling technique like LDA. The proposed model is generic and it is suitable for any domain.

METHODOLOGY

Feature extraction is one of the major tasks in text analysis. Applications like document classification, document clustering and sentiment analysis majorly depend on the technique that has been used for the feature extraction. The issues as stated in Section 1 can be overcome if the text documents are modeled using the ontology representation along with the topic modeling techniques. The problem statement is stated as follows: Given a set of text documents, the proposed model extracts features by using topic modeling techniques and the domain specific ontology to achieve improved accuracy in feature extraction process by deploying ontology learning techniques. Ontology based learning enables to achieve better accuracy in feature extraction. This section describes the methodology involved in the feature extraction, ontology development and ontology learning. Figure 1 shows the overall framework of the proposed method. Feature extraction is done using Latent Dirichlet Allocation (LDA) technique and domain ontology is built incorporating these features in the training phase. This ontology is used for further feature extraction in the testing phase.

DATASET PREPARATION

The dataset consists of about 400 plain text reviews on mobile phones collected from amazon.com. The dataset speaks about different features of mobile products. The reviews span from Jan-Dec 2015 and 2016. Preprocessing is required to facilitate efficient processing of the algorithm by elimination unwanted noise text from the original data. It comprises of the following steps:

- Convert all text to lowercase
- Remove stop words like articles, prepositions, and so on

Figure 1. Proposed framework of feature-based text analysis

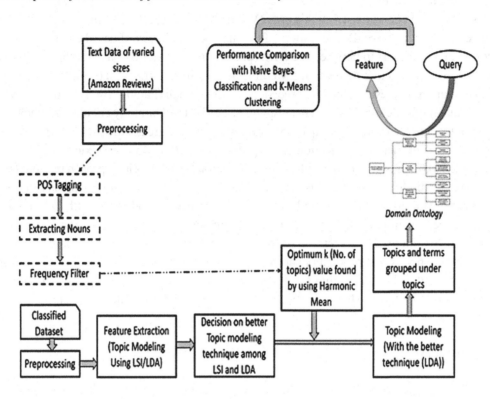

- Remove punctuations
- Remove numbers and extra white spaces

Feature Extraction

PartOfSpeech (PoS) Tagging

Part-of-speech tagging (POS tagging or POST), is the process of marking up a word in a text corpus as corresponding to a particular part of speech, based on both its definition and its context (i.e.), its relationship with adjacent and related words in a phrase, sentence, or paragraph. Tagset is the set of tags from which the tagger is supposed to choose to attach to the relevant word. Every tagger will be given a standard tagset. The tagset may be coarse such as N (Noun), V (Verb), ADJ (Adjective), ADV (Adverb), PREP (Preposition), CONJ (Conjunction) or fine-grained such as NNOM (Noun-Nominative), NSOC (Noun-Sociative), VFIN (Verb Finite), VNFIN (Verb Nonfinite) and so on.

Feature-opinion pairs are extracted from review documents using Partof-Speech (PoS) tagging. In this step, the sentences in the data set collection are tokenized using the PoS tag function written in R. During this process, a Part of Speech (PoS) such as noun, verb, adverb, adjective, conjunctions, negations and the like are assigned to every word in the sentences, and is shown in Table 1.

Usually, a topic in a text is represented by a noun word. Hence nouns alone are extracted and used for text data modeling. Because a word that is an opinion may not indicate any topic, so these words are excluded from word counting.

Table 1. PoS tags and description

Tag Name	Descriptions	
NN	Noun, Singular	Feature Word
NNS	Noun, Plural	
VBN	Verb	Opinion Word
RB	Adverb	
JJ	Adjective, Numeral, Ordinal	

Nouns Extraction

A product attribute is usually a noun phrase, and that people generally talked about a small set of common attributes of the product. The approach for extracting features is based on the intuition that product features are usually nouns or noun phrases.Using the POS associated with words during the data generation phase, BagOfWords (BoW) is created for each document. The words chosen to represent a sentence were those that were marked as nouns (NN/NNS).

Frequency Filters

This arranges every term according to its frequency. Terms with higher frequencies are more likely to appear in the results as compared ones with low frequency. The low frequency terms are essentially weak features of the Corpus, hence it is a good practice to get rid of all those weak features. An exploratory analysis of terms and their frequency can help to decide what frequency value should be considered as the threshold.

Data Modeling

Based on the above feature processing and extraction techniques, three types of data models were built to analyze the performance of LDA in each case and to choose the better one among those models for further processing. The three types of data models are: (i) modeling without PoS tagging (ii) modeling with PoS tagging and (iii) modeling with PoS tagging and frequency filters

Model Without POS Tagging

This model uses the data after preprocessing as such for feature extraction. Since there will be a combination of every part of speech, there will be more number of weak features making the model inefficient and complex.

Model With POS Tagging

This model enforces POS Tagging on the data after preprocessing and extracts nouns from the data. It uses only these nouns for feature extraction and topic modeling. Since only nouns are used, the number of weak features gets reduced and the model becomes less complex.

Model With POS Tagging and Frequency Filter

This model extracts nouns from the preprocessed data and puts on a frequency filter thereby removing weak features from the data. This may sound more efficient, but it suits only for a very large dataset because the frequency filter on a smaller dataset may remove the necessary features making the data sparse for computation.

The above three data models are analyzed and compared for their efficiency. The best one among the three is selected for implementation of the proposed methodology.

Topic Modeling

A topic is always known as the main idea of the entire document. Topic modeling is a form of text mining, that is used for identifying patterns that helps in classifying the given text document to a particular category. This topic modeling provides a suite of algorithms to discover hidden thematic structure in large collections of texts. The results of topic modeling algorithms can be used to summarize, visualize and explore about a corpus. Topic modeling is done using Latent Semantic Indexing (LSI) and Latent Dirichlet Allocation (LDA) and the results are compared to select one of them for the implementation of feature extraction.

Latent Semantic Indexing

Latent Semantic Indexing (LSI) is a technique in distributional semantics, of analyzing relationships between a set of documents and the terms they contain by producing a set of concepts related to the documents and terms. LSI includes two major steps:

1. A document-term matrix *M* is constructed from a given text base of *n* documents containing *m* terms.
2. Apply Latent Semantic Analysis on M to obtain a similarity/distance matrix. It includes the following steps:

Singular Value Decomposition (SVD)

The matrix M of the size m*n is decomposed via SVD into: the Term vector matrix T (left singular vectors), the Document vector matrix D (right singular vectors) being both orthonormal, and the diagonal matrix S (singular values).

$$M = TSD^T$$

These matrices are then reduced to the given number of dimensions *k* to result into truncated matrices T_k, S_k and D_k— the latent semantic space.

$$M_k = \sum t_i .s_i .d_i^T \text{ where } i = 1...n$$

If these matrices T_k, S_k, D_k were multiplied, they would give a new matrix M_k (of the same format as M, i.e., rows are the same terms, columns are the same documents), which is the least-squares best fit approximation of M with k singular values.

In the case of folding-in, i.e., multiplying new documents into a given latent semantic space, the matrices T_k and S_k remain unchanged and an additional D_k is created (without replacing the old one).

All three are multiplied together to return a new document-term matrix M_{new} in the term-order of M.

Computation of Correlation Matrix/Cosine Similarity Matrix

After obtaining the M_{new} matrix via Singular Value Decomposition, a n*n similarity matrix of cosine values, comparing all n column vectors against each of M_{new} computed. This matrix might be document-term matrix, so columns would be expected to be documents and rows to be terms. The cosine measure is nearly identical with the Pearson correlation coefficient (besides a constant factor)

1. By using the resultant matrix as a distance measure, do K-Means clustering until convergence.
2. Plot the clusters and compute accuracy

Latent Dirichlet Allocation

Latent Dirichlet Allocation (LDA) is a generative probabilistic model for collections of discrete data such as text corpora. It is a three-level hierarchical Bayesian model, in which each item of a collection is modeled as a finite mixture over an underlying set of topics. LDA assumes mixture of topics produces documents. These topics then generate terms based on their probability distribution. Given a set of documents, LDA recursively tries and figures out what topics would create those documents in the first place. It includes the following processing steps:

1. LDA is a matrix factorization technique. In vector space, any corpus (collection of documents) can be represented as a Term-Document matrix. The matrix represents a corpus of M documents D_1, D_2, D_3, …, D_m and vocabulary size of N words W_1, W_2, …, Wn. The value of cell $_{i,j}$ gives the frequency of wordWj in Document Di.
2. LDA converts this Term-Document matrix into two lower dimensional matrices – M1 and M2. M1 is a document-topics matrix and M2 is a topic-terms matrix with dimensions (M, K) and (K, N) respectively, where M is the number of documents, K is the number of topics and N is the vocabulary size.
3. These two matrices provide topic-term and document-topic distributions. However, these distributions need to be improved, which is the main objective of LDA. It makes use of sampling techniques like Gibbs sampling in order to improve these matrices. It iterates through each word (or term) "w" for each document "d" and tries to adjust the current topic–term assignment with a new assignment. A new topic "k" is assigned to word "w" with a probability P which is a product of two probabilities p1 and p2.
4. For every topic, two probabilities p1 and p2 are calculated.
    a. **P1:** p(topic t / document d) = the proportion of words in document d that are currently assigned to topic t.

    b.   **P2:** p(word w / topic t) = the proportion of assignments to topic t over all documents that come from this word w.

5.   The current topic–term assignment is updated with a new topic with the probability, product of p1 and p2. In this step, the model assumes that all the existing topic-term assignments except the current word are correct. This is the probability that topic t generated word w, and the current word's topic is adjusted with new probability.

6.   A steady state is achieved after a number of iterations, where the document topic and topic term distributions are fairly good. This is the convergence point of LDA.

Plate Notation of LDA

With plate notation, as shown in Figure 2, the dependencies among different variables are captured concisely. The boxes are "plates" representing replicates. The outer plate represents documents, while the inner plate exhibits the repeated choice of topics and terms within a document. M denotes the number of documents, N the number of terms in a document andK denotes the number of topics. The terms w_{ij} are the only observable variables, and the other variables are latent variables.

Generative Process

The generative process is as follows. Documents are represented as random mixtures over hidden topics, where each topic is characterized by a distribution over terms. LDA assumes the following generative process for a corpus D consisting of M documents each of length Ni:

1.   Choose $\theta_i \sim Dir(\alpha)$, where $i \in \{1,...,M\}$ and $Dir(\alpha)$ is a Dirichlet distribution with a symmetric parameter α which typically is sparse $(\alpha<1)$

2.   Choose $\varphi_k \sim Dir(\beta)$, where $k \in \{1,...,K\}$ and β typically is sparse

3.   For each of the word positions i, j where $j \in \{1,...,N_i\}$, and $i \in \{1,...,M\}$

    a.   Choose a topic $z_{i,j} \sim Multinomial(\theta_i)$

    b.   Choose a word $w_{i,j} \sim Multinomial(\varphi z_{i,j})$

Figure 2. Plate notation of LDA
where,
α is the parameter of the Dirichlet prior on the per-document topic distributions
β is the parameter of the Dirichlet prior on the per-topic word distribution
θ_m is the topic distribution for document m
φ_k is the word distribution for topic k
z_{mn} is the topic for the nth word in document m
w_{mn} is the specific word

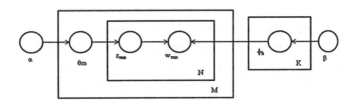

Parameters of LDA

- **Alpha and Beta Hyper Parameters:** Alpha represents document-topicdensity and beta represents topic-term density. If alpha is higher, it means that the documents are composed of more topics and vice versa. On the other hand, if beta is higher, it means that the topics are composed of a large number of terms in the corpus, and vice versa.
- **Number of Topics:** Number of topics to be identified from the corpus
- **Number of Topic Terms:** Number of terms grouped under a single topic. Number of topics could be higher, if the requirement is to extract topics from the corpus. On the other hand, lesser number of topics is recommended if the requirement is to extract terms.
- **Number of Iteration:** Maximum number of iterations needed by LDA for convergence.

LDA Model Estimation Using Harmonic Mean

Harmonic mean method can be used to determine the optimum number of topics k.For every word w in the corpus, the likelihood $p(w \mid K)$ is computed where K is the number of topics. The all possible assignments of the words to topics z[i.e., $p(w \mid K) = \int p(w \mid z, K) p(z) \, dz$] is computed. The value of p ($w \mid K$) is approximated by taking the Harmonic mean of a set of values of $p(w \mid z, K)$ when z is sampled from the posterior $p(z \mid w, K)$.

Training and Testing

The Latent Dirichlet Allocation algorithm is executed on the dataset with the optimum number of topics (k). It results in a topic model which assigns topics to the document based on the probability values and also provides words under each topic and their corresponding probability with respect to the topic. It is the LDA score, the probability of a word to occur in a given topic. These results are supplied as the input for Ontology creation. The training phase involves the creation of the ontology from the results of LDA and the testing phase involves querying the ontology to extract features, as shown in Figure 3.

ONTOLOGY DEVELOPMENT

From the results of Latent Dirichlet Allocation, domain ontology is built using the Protégé tool. The Ontology consists of terms along with their corresponding LDA scores in the last level which are associated to their topics in the above level. The topics are associated to the domain in the parent level. Figure 4 shows the sample ontology developed for mobile product reviews.

RESULTS AND DISCUSSION

We have initiated our experiments with the labeled datasets. It is just done to study the performance measure of two different techniques like Latent Semantic Indexing (LSI) and Latent Dirichlet Allocation (LDA). Nearly 510 documents are tested for 51 topics classification. Table 2 shows the results of both LSI and LDA techniques. LDA has been selected for feature extraction and categorization rather than LSI.

Figure 3. Training and testing phase

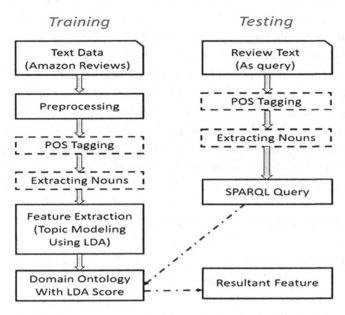

Figure 4. Sample mobile ontology

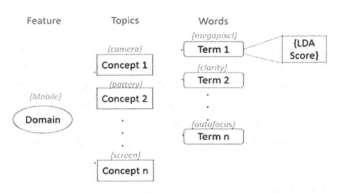

Table 2. Performance of LSI and LDA

Measures	LSI	LDA
No. of documents correctly modeled	389	456
Accuracy	76.3%	89.4%

Mobile product online reviews are used in our experiments. The dataset for training consists of 200 plain text reviews on mobile phones collected from the website amazon.com. The data is loaded into the R environment and preprocessed using the tm package. The preprocessed data is tagged, and nouns are extracted for further processing. Table 3 shows the description of data set used in the experiments.

Table 3. Data set description

Description	Training Dataset	Testing Dataset
No. of reviews	200	200
No. of features	10	10
Average number of terms per review	8	7
No. of terms before preprocessing	1608	1523
No. of terms after preprocessing	1138	1041
No. of nouns	503	459

Table 4 shows the three types of data models and their performance when used with LDA topic modeling. Results show that the model with POS tagging is comparatively better and it is selected for further implementation.

The Optimum number of topics present in the test dataset is identified by using the Harmonic mean. Figure 5 (a, b, c, and d) shows the number of topics identified by LDA for varying number of product review documents. It is interpreted that as the data size increases the optimum number of topics and the efficiency of the model increases.

Figure 6 shows the top 20 terms generated by LDA topic modeling for the number of topics 10. Features extracted from the results of LDA topic modeling are given to ontology builder, the Protégé tool and its plugin Cellfie, to develop domain ontology.

The Ontology consists of terms along with their corresponding LDA scores in the last level which are associated to their topics in the above level. The topics are associated to the domain in the parent level. Figure 7 shows the snapshot of Cellfie plugin for ontology creation.

Ontology is built in hierarchical fashion such that topic forms the root node and the words under that topic form its children. LDA score of each word is stored in ontology which further improves the query processing time and accuracy. Ontology is visualized using the ontograf plugin. The spring view and the custom view are shown in Figures 8 and 9.

Querying the Ontology

The Ontology built from the training dataset is tested with 200 reviews on mobiles products from amazon. com. Every review is transformed into a query into the ontology and the resultant features are tested for correctness. Feature or topic extraction is done as queries into the ontology using the ontoCAT package in R. Four types of queries are addressed using the query model, as shown in Figure 10.

Table 4. Comparison of data models

Type of Model	Without POS Tagging	With POS Tagging	With POS Tagging and Frequency Filter
Number of terms	1138	503	328
Number of unnecessary terms during topic modeling	718	36	3
Search Performance	More time, Less accuracy	Less time, more accuracy	Less time, moderate accuracy

Figure 5. Optimal number of topics for varying data sizes

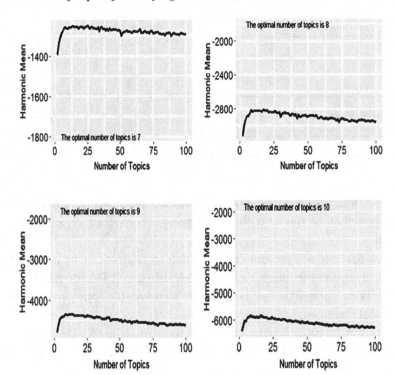

Figure 6. Term Topics of LDA for number of topics 10

	CAMERA	BATTERY	SCREEN	HEAT	PERFORMANCE	PRICE	SOFTWARE	STORAGE	WARRANTY	HARDWARE
1 camera	battery	screen	heating	performance	price	os	storage	warranty	screen
2 megapixels	backup	capacitive	hot	speed	money	android	memory	year	weight
3 aperture	charge	resolution	phone	processor	cheap	kitkat	internal	damage	size
4 picture	life	touch	charge	life	overpriced	3g	card	replacement	display
5 autofocus	capacity	hd	hour	hang	range	storage	gigabytes	proof	battery
6 lens	charger	cm	battery	fast	compare	software	capacity	mobile	fingerprint
7 selfie	turbo	pixel	burst	load	less	speed	shared	screen	built
8 flash	cell	look	soon	series	economic	upgradable	external	feauture	damage
9 video	voltage	soft	issue	backup	value	internal	expandable	quality	processor
10 hdr	discharge	display	usage	apps	cost	usage	low	model	camera
11 quality	drain	inches	compare	storage	low	4g	system	service	usage
12 photo	problem	brightness	flickering	camera	amazing	apps	picture	waterproof	software
13 backup	removable	panel	time	weight	model	battery	apps	long	well
14 secondary	power	size	damage	handling	average	sim	size	note	storage
15 shutter	mAh	flicker	metal	features	concern	features	cool	software	cell
16 clarity	speed	aspect	problem	model	pricerange	fast	feauture	bonus	sim
17 front	current	ratio	low	price	high	gsm	range	concern	slot
18 primary	pressure	clarity	hang	specs	correct	ui	great	brand	brand
19 professional	capacitive	feel	surface	great	happy	notification	gb	phone	replacement
20 pixels	design	design	cell	satisfy	mobile	experience	proof	cover	concern

Figure 7. Snapshot of Protégé tool for Mobile Ontology Development

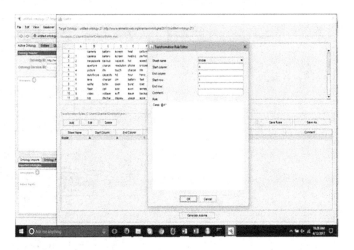

Figure 8. Spring view of Mobile Ontology for topics and terms

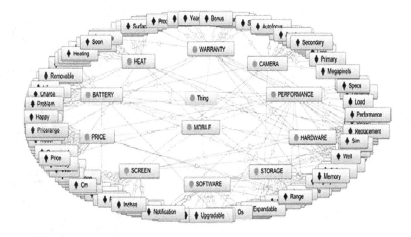

Type 1: Terms Under Only One Feature

In this case the terms are matched into the ontology and the corresponding feature is returned as the result. For example, "The battery power is consistent" is considered for Type 1 query. Here, the nouns battery and power are extracted. Both these words come under the topic *"BATTERY"* and it is returned as the feature.

Type 2: Terms Under Multiple Features, Each Term Under Only One Feature

In this case, the cumulative LDA score is computed for each feature and the feature(s) with stronger LDA score is returned as the result. Cumulative LDA score of a feature is determined by the sum of LDA scores of terms of the corresponding feature. For example, "Discharge of the battery is high while

Figure 9. Custom view of Mobile Ontology for topics and terms

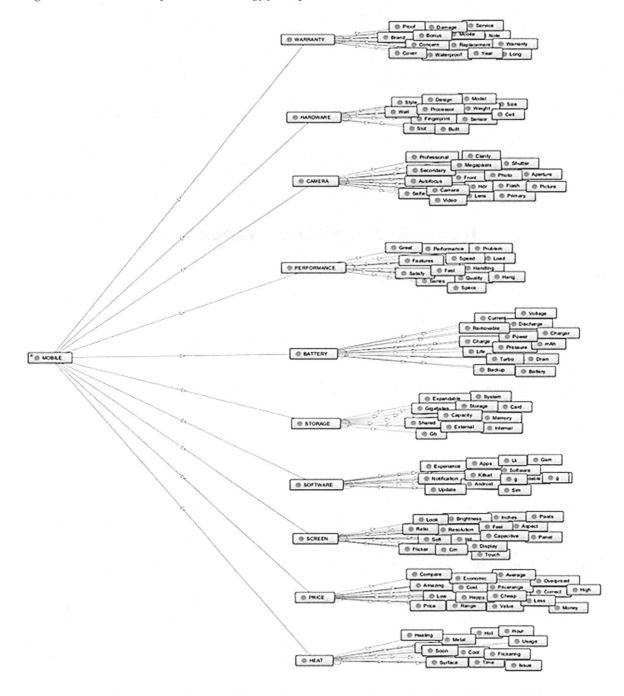

taking videos" is considered for Type 2 query. Here, the nouns discharge, battery and video are extracted. The terms discharge and battery come under the topic "battery" while the term video comes under the topic "camera". Suppose if LDAscore(*discharge*, BATTERY)= 0.05, LDAscore(*battery*, BATTERY) = 0.26 and LDAscore(*video*, CAMERA) = 0.26. Computing the cumulative LDA scores for each feature:

Figure 10. Query processing in Ontology data model

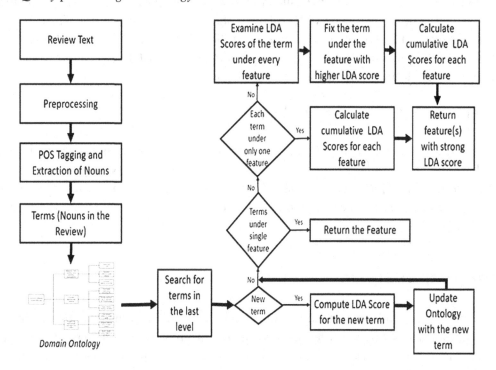

```
CumulativeLDAscore(BATTERY)=
LDAscore(discharge, BATTERY) + LDAscore(battery, BATTERY), which is 0.31.
CumulativeLDAscore(CAMERA) =
LDAscore(video,CAMERA), which is 0.26
```

Comparing the cumulative LDA scores for the different features, the difference between them is 0.05. Since the different is less than 0.5, the threshold value which is fixed, both the features "BATTERY" and "CAMERA" are returned for the query. If the difference between the cumulative scores is greater than 0.5, the feature with the higher cumulative score is returned as the feature.

Type 3: Terms Under Multiple Features, One Term Under More Than One Feature

In this case the term is associated to a feature by comparing the LDA score under each feature. The cumulative score for each feature is calculated and the resultant strong feature(s) is returned as the result. For example, *"the external storage is not sufficient to support many apps"* is considered for Type 3 query. Here, the terms *external, storage, and apps* are extracted as nouns. The term *storage* comes under both the topics "performance" and "storage" and the term *apps* comes under the topic "software". First fix the term *storage* under a single topic (either *performance* or *storage*). To do this, calculate the cumulative scores of the topics under which the term occurs. We do this by examining the nearby words present in the query document under those topics. Suppose, LDAscore(*storage*, PERFOR-MANCE) = 0.17, LDAscore(*storage*, STORAGE) = 0.38, and LDAscore(*external*, STORAGE) = 0.26. CumulativeLDAscore(PERFORMANCE) is 0.17, and the CumulativeLDAscore(STORAGE) is 0.64. Since 0.64 > 0.17, the term *storage* is assigned the feature as STORAGE. Repeat the same process as in Type 2 to return the feature(s) for the input query document.

Type 4: Term Not Present in the Ontology

In this case the LDA score is computed for the new term and the ontology is updated with the new term. For example, *"The Android nougat update is good"* is considered for Type 4 query. Here, the nouns like *android, nougat, and update* are extracted. The term *nougat* is a new term and not present in the ontology. LDA modeling is repeated and the ontology is updated. Further querying is done as one of the above three types.

PERFORMANCE ANALYSIS

The performance of the proposed method is compared with two different methodologies namely Naïve Bayes classification and K-Means clustering techniques. 200 online reviews are used for testing. Naïve Bayes classification is a supervised learning method and it requires prior knowledge of data. So, the training data is manually labeled and a Naïve Bayes model is created. The topics are given as the class labels and the testing phase is carried out on the model. It is implemented using the packages e1071, sparseM and tm in R.

K-Means clustering groups documents into a distinct number of clusters (k) by computing the distance between the documents i.e., the similarities. Here the number of clusters is the number of topics. K-Means

Figure 11. K-Means clustering plot for documents

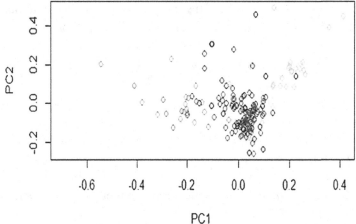

clustering is done in R using the tm package with Euclidean distance as the distance measure. Figure 11 shows the k-means clustering plot, where PC1 and PC2 are Euclidean distance between two documents.

Table 5 shows the performance comparison supervised and unsupervised learning techniques for document categorization. The results show that the proposed method using LDA topic modeling and ontology for feature extraction performs better than Naïve Bayes classification and K-Means clustering.

Figure 12 shows the average precision and recall values when the proposed Ontology-based LDA modeling technique is applied on the datasets for different number of query documents like 50, 75, 100, 125, 150, 175 and 200. It shows that recall improves continues for the varying number of query documents. When the document size is 200, the Ontology-based LDA modeling technique gives precision 0.54, recall 0.58 and F-measure 0.56 values.

CONCLUSION

An unsupervised topic model for feature extraction was used to build an ontology that serves as the knowledge base for feature extraction. Latent Dirichlet Allocation (LDA) performed better when compared with Latent Semantic Indexing (LSI) as a topic model for feature extraction. Also, LDA gave better results when the nouns from the data alone were supplied for topic modeling. It can also be interpreted that LDA performed better with increasing size of the data. The ontology built from the results of LDA was used for feature extraction. This resulted in the accuracy of 90.5% and it was better when compared with Naïve Bayes classification and K-Means clustering techniques.

Table 5. Performance analysis of categorization of documents

Description	Naïve Bayes	k-MEANS	LDA + Ontology
Number of documents whose features were correctly identified	159	168	181
Recall value	31%	35%	45%
Accuracy	79.5%	84%	90%

Figure 12. Precision vs. recall curve

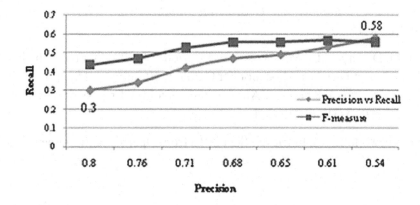

FUTURE RESEARCH DIRECTIONS

Ontology can be used in the automatic feature extraction process. Fuzzy techniques can be applied in the query modeling phase to overcome the assignment of particular term to a feature, if there are more than one discrepancies exist. Further decision-making algorithms can be used on the categorized data set to build business intelligence in the product or service.

REFERENCES

Alani, H., Kim, S., Millard, D. E., Weal, M. J., Hall, W., Lewis, P. H., & Shadbolt, N. R. (2003). Automatic ontology-based knowledge extraction from web documents. *IEEE Intelligent Systems*, *18*(1), 14–21. doi:10.1109/MIS.2003.1179189

Ali, F., Kwak, K. S., & Kim, Y. G. (2016). Opinion mining based on fuzzy domain ontology and Support Vector Machine: A proposal to automate online review classification. *Applied Soft Computing*, *47*(3), 235–250. doi:10.1016/j.asoc.2016.06.003

Baldoni, M., Baroglio, C., Patti, V., & Rena, P. (2012). From Tags to Emotions: Ontology-driven Sentiment Analysis in the Social Semantic Web. *IntelligenzaArtificiale*, *6*(1), 41–54.

Castells, P., Ferna'ndez, M., & Vallet, D. (2007). An Adaptation of the Vector-Space Model for Ontology-Based Information Retrieval. *IEEE Transactions on Knowledge Engineering*, *19*(2), 261–271. doi:10.1109/TKDE.2007.22

Chen, M., Ebert, D., Hagen, H., Laramee, R. S., van Liere, R., Ma, K.-L., ... Silver, D. (2009). Data, Information, and Knowledge in Visualization. *Journal IEEE Computer Graphics and Applications*, *29*(1), 12–19. doi:10.1109/MCG.2009.6 PMID:19363954

Ciravegna, F. (2001). Adaptive information extraction from text by rule induction and generalization. In *Proceedings of Seventeenth International Joint Conference on Artificial Intelligence IJCAI*, Seattle, WA (Vol. 2, pp. 1251-1256).

Ciravegna, F., Dingli, A., Petrelli, D., & Wilks, Y. (2002). User-System Cooperation in Document Annotation based on Information Extraction. In *International Conference on Knowledge Engineering and Knowledge Management: Ontologies and the Semantic Web EKAW02, LNCS* (Vol. 2473, pp. 122-137). 10.1007/3-540-45810-7_15

Colace, F., Santo, M. D., Greco, L., Moscato, V., & Picariello, A. (2016). Probabilistic Approaches for Sentiment Analysis: Latent Dirichlet Allocation for Ontology Building and Sentiment Extraction. In W. Pedrycz, & S.-M. Chen, (Eds.), Sentiment Analysis and Ontology Engineering (Vol. 639, pp. 75-91). Springer. doi:10.1007/978-3-319-30319-2_4

Open Semantic Framework. (n.d.). Retrieved Sept 2016 from Opensemanticframework.org

Freitas, L. A., & Vieira, R. (2013). Ontology based Feature Level Opinion Mining for Portuguese Reviews. In *WWW'13 Companion Proceedings of the 22nd International Conference on World Wide Web*, Rio de Janeiro, Brazil (pp. 367-370). 10.1145/2487788.2487944

Guo, H., Zhu, H., Guo, Z., & Su, Z. (2009). Product feature categorization with multilevel latent semantic association. In *Proceedings of the Eighteenth ACM Conference on Information and Knowledge Management CIKM '09*, Hong Kong, China (pp. 1087-1096). 10.1145/1645953.1646091

Kamps, M. M., Mokken, R. J., & De Rijke, M. (2004). Using wordnet to measure semantic orientation of adjectives. In *Proceedings of 4th International Conference on Language Resources and Evaluation*, Lisbon, Portugal (pp. 1115- 1118).

Kontopoulos, E., Berberidis, C., Dergiades, T., & Bassiliades, N. (2013). Ontology-based sentiment analysis of twitter posts. *Expert Systems with Applications*, *40*(10), 4065–4074. doi:10.1016/j.eswa.2013.01.001

Lu, Y., Duan, H., Wang, H., & Zhai, C. X. (2010). Exploiting Structured Ontology to Organize Scattered Online Opinions. In *Proceedings of the Twenty Third International Conference on Computational Linguistics*, Beijing, China (pp. 734–742).

Ma, J., Xu, W., Sun, Y., Turban, E., Wang, S., & Liu, O. (2012). An Ontology-Based Text-Mining Method to Cluster Proposals for Research Project Selection. *IEEE Transactions on Systems, Man, and Cybernetics. Part A, Systems and Humans*, *42*(3), 784–790. doi:10.1109/TSMCA.2011.2172205

Maedche, A., Pekar, V., & Staab, S. (2003). Ontology Learning Part One - On Discovering Taxonomic Relations from the Web. In N. Zhong (Ed.), Web Intelligence (pp. 301-320). Springer. doi:10.1007/978-3-662-05320-1_14

Maynard, D., Bontcheva, K., & Cunninham, H. (2003). *Towards a semantic extraction of named entities*. Bulgaria: Recent Advances in Natural Language Processing.

Nedellec, C., & Nazarenko, A. (2005). *Ontology and Information Extraction: A Necessary Symbiosis*. In P. Buitelaar, P. Cimiano, & B. Magnini (Eds.), *Ontology Learning from Text: Methods, Evaluation and Applications* (pp. 3–14). Amsterdam, The Netherlands: IOS Press Publications.

Paralic, J., & Kostial, I. (2003). A Document Retrieval Method based on Ontology Associations. *Journal of Information and Organizational Sciences*, *27*(2), 93–99.

Penalver-Martinez, I., Garcia-Sanchez, F., Valencia-Garcia, R., Rodríguez-García, M. Á., Moreno, V., Fraga, A., & Sánchez-Cervantes, J. L. (2014). Feature-based opinion mining through ontologies. *Expert Systems with Applications*, *41*(13), 5995–6008. doi:10.1016/j.eswa.2014.03.022

Popov, B., Kiryakov, A., Ognyanoff, D., Manov, D., & Kirilov, A. (2004). KIM – a semantic platform for information extraction. *Journal Natural Language Engineering*, *10*(3-4), 375–392. doi:10.1017/S135132490400347X

Rindflesch, T. C., Tanabe, L., Weinstein, J. N., & Hunter, L. (2000). EDGAR: Extraction of Drugs, Genes and Relations from the Biomedical Literature. In *Proceedings of Pacific Symposium on Biocomputing* (pp. 517–528).

Saif, H., He, Y., & Alani, H. (2012). Semantic Sentiment Analysis of Twitter. In *International Semantic Web Conference ISWC 2012* (pp. 508-524). 10.1007/978-3-642-35176-1_32

Stanford Center for Biomedical Informatics Research. (2016). Retrieved September 2016 from www. protege.stanford.edu

Taboada, M., Anthony, C., & Voll, K. (2006). Methods for creating semantic orientation dictionaries. In roceedings of the Fifth International Conference on Language Resources and Evaluation LREC'06, Genoa, Italy, pp. 427-432.

Taboada, M., Brooke, J., Tofiloski, M., Voll, K., & Stede, M. (2011). Lexicon-based methods for sentiment analysis. Computational linguistics, 37(2), 267–307. doi:10.1162/COLI_a_00049

Verma, S., & Bhattacharyya, P. (2008). Incorporating Semantic Knowledge for Sentiment Analysis. In *Proceedings of ICON-2008: 6th International Conference on Natural Language Processing.*

Vidhya, A. (2018). Beginners Guide to Topic Modeling in Python. Retrieved March 2017 from https://www.analyticsvidhya.com/blog/2016/08/beginners-guide-to-topic-modeling-in-python/

Wei, W., & Gulla, J. A. (2010). Sentiment Learning on Product Reviews via Sentiment Ontology Tree. In *Proceedings of the 48th Annual Meeting of the Association for Computational Linguistics ACL '10*, Uppsala, Sweden (pp. 404–413).

APPENDIX

Table 6.

Year	Paper Title/Journal	Approach	Technique Used	Feature Selection	Data Scope	Data Source	Accuracy
2016	Opinion mining based on fuzzy domain ontology and Support Vector Machine: A proposal to automate online review classification	Fuzzy ontology	Fuzzy and Machine learning techniques	SVM & Fuzzy Domain Ontology	Hotel Reviews	tripadvisor.com, hotel.com, booking.com	83%
2015	INESC-ID: A Regression Model for Large Scale Twitter Sentiment Lexicon Induction	Lexicon based	Regression	-	Labeled tweets	Twitter	67%
2014	Feature-based opinion mining through ontologies	Ontology	Semantic web and sentiment analysis techniques	Domain ontologies	Movie reviews	Spanish Documents	89%
2014	Combining classification and clustering for tweet sentiment analysis	Supervised and Unsupervised learning	SVM and K-medoids	-	Healthcare, Sanders, Stanford Corpus	HCR, Sentiment Corpus	81%
2014	Topic Classification using Latent Dirichlet Allocation at Multiple Levels	Supervised Learning	NB, SVM	BagOfWords, LDA	Social media data, Newsgroup	FriendFeed, Reuters 21578	80%
2013	Text Classification based on Feature Selection and LDA Model	Supervised learning	Information Retrieval techniques	Chi-square value and LDA	Car, Health, Finance, Art documents	Sogou Corpus	96%
2013	Ontology-based Sentiment Analysis of Twitter Posts	Domain ontology, Sentiment analysis	OpenDover tool for sentiment analysis	Domain ontology	Mobile reviews	Twitter	82%
2013	Ontology-based Feature Level Opinion Mining for Portuguese Reviews	Lexicon and Ontology based	Dictionary based	Domain ontology - Hontology	Hotel reviews	TripAdvisor.com, Booking.com	58%, 62%
2012	Senti-lexicon and improved Naïve Bayes algorithms for sentiment analysis of restaurant reviews	Lexicon and supervised learning	Senti-Lexicon and Naïve bayes	unigrams and bigrams	Restaurant reviews	Restaurant search sites	81%
2012	An Ontology-Based Text-Mining Method to Cluster Proposals for Research Project Selection	Research ontology, and Neural network	Self-organizing Map	TF-IDF and LSI	Research proposals (English, Chinese)		91%
2012	Semantic sentiment analysis of twitter	Supervised Learning	Naïve Bayes Classification	Unigrams, PoS Tagging	Healthcare, Stanford Docs	HCR, OMD, STS	75%
2011	A neural network based approach for sentiment classification in the blogosphere	Neural Network	BPN algorithm	PMI and LSA	Blogs on products, movies,	Livejournal.com, ReviewCentre.com	77%
2011	Mining Millions of Reviews: A Technique to Rank Products Based on Importance of Reviews	Supervised learning	SVM, Linear Regression	Human annotation and WordNet	SLR Camera and TV	Amazon.com	78%
2011	lustering Product Features for Opinion Mining	Semi-supervised Learning	Augmented EM algorithm	Topic modeling	Product reviews	Company websites	NA
2011	Multi-class text categorization based on LDA and SVM	Supervised Learning	SVM	Latent Dirichlet Allocation (LDA)	University text Documents	Fudan University China	91%
2011	A comparative study of TF_IDF, LSI and multi-words for text classification	Indexing	TF-IDF, LSI	TermWeighting	News groups and Academic Journals	Reuters-21578 and TanCorpV1.0	87% for LSI
2010	Star Quality: Aggregating Reviews to Rank Products and Merchants	Statistical and heuristics	Average rating, Reweighting	-	Product and Merchant reviews	Epinions.com	70%
2010	Improving customer decisions using product reviews: CROM - Car Review Opinion Miner	Lexicon based	WordNet and Sentiment Analysis	Human annotation	Car Reviews	whatcar.com	83%
2010	Lexicon-Based Methods for Sentiment Analysis	Lexicon based	Semantic Orientation Calculator	Dictionaries	Reviews of books, cars, music, etc	Epinions.com	78%
2010	Sentiment Learning on Product Reviews via Sentiment Ontology Tree	Ontology	Hierarchical Sentiment Ontology	Human annotation and sentiment ontology tree	Digital Cameras	Customer Reviews	NA
2008	Leveraging Sentiment Analysis for Topic Detection	Lexicon based	Dictionary and SA techniques	TF, PMI	Vegemite DB Australia, Insurance Dataset		60%

Chapter 10
Location–Based Advertising Using Location–Aware Data Mining

Wen-Chen Hu
University of North Dakota, USA

Naima Kaabouch
University of North Dakota, USA

Hongyu Guo
University of Houston – Victoria, USA

AbdElRahman Ahmed ElSaid
University of North Dakota, USA

ABSTRACT

This chapter describes how mobile advertisements are critical for both mobile users and businesses as people spend more time on mobile devices than on PCs. However, how to send relevant advertisements and avoid unnecessary ones to specific mobile users is always a challenge. For example, a concert-goer may like to visit restaurants or parks before the concert and may not like the advertisements of grocery stores or farmers' markets. This research tries to overcome the challenge by using the methods of location-aware data mining. Furthermore, privacy is always a great concern for location-based advertising (LBA) users because their location information has to be shared in order to receive the services. This chapter also takes the concern into serious consideration, so the user privacy will not be compromised. Preliminary experiment results show the proposed methods are effective and user-privacy is rigorously preserved.

INTRODUCTION

Advertisements are a double-edged sword. They are a lifeline for businesses and a great service for many people, but at the same time the customers may receive a negative impression of the businesses if they are not used appropriately. For example, concert goers would appreciate the advertisements of restaurants or souvenir stores, which will make more profit because of the advertisements. On the other

DOI: 10.4018/978-1-5225-4044-1.ch010

hand, the same people may not appreciate the advertisements of farmers' markets or hardware stores. However, sending the advertisements based on the people's locations may not solve the problems completely. Another example is the advertisements of rental cars and hotels, but not the ones of grocery stores or car dealers, will be sent to the mobile users when they show up at an airport. Nevertheless, the users may be airport workers like flight attendants or they go to the airports to pick up someone. Most of the mobile advertising methods are based on one or two features of human travel behavior such as the current locations or popular destinations. This research tries to send more relevant advertisements to mobile users based on the current and past travel patterns of the users and others. It is based on several, not just one or two, features of travelers' behavior and expect to receive better results. At the same time, one major concern for this research or most location-based services (LBSs) is user privacy preservation. Most LBSs require the users' current locations and many users are reluctant to share their locations and identities. The proposed method not only successfully produces accurate advertisements, but also rigorously protects users' privacy.

This research is to send more relevant advertisements to mobile users and protect the users' privacy at the same time. It works as follows. The mobile user keeps sending his/her locations to the server. Based on the previous stored data and the locations it receives, the server sends appropriate advertisements back to the user. For example, when the user visits a landmark or a store, two incremental mining methods, incremental location-aware association-rule and sequential-pattern mining, start kicking in. The association-rule mining is used to find related advertisements. For example, if the user stops by a rest stop, then advertisements of motels will be displayed. After visiting the site, the sequential-pattern mining is used to discover the next sites. For example, after checking into a motel, advertisements of restaurants will be shown. At the same time, user privacy is rigorously enforced by sending dummy locations along with the user locations to the server, so the server is not able to tell the correct user locations among the locations it receives. The server then tries to send related advertisements back to the client (user). This research is useful and popular and involved a couple of subjects such as mobile computing, security and privacy, location-based services, data mining, augmented reality, and human behavior recognition. The proposed research gives researchers a new way of thinking about tackling the location-based and user-privacy problems.

Chapter Organization

The rest of this article is organized as follows. Section 2 gives the background information of this chapter including three themes: (i) association rule mining, (ii) sequential pattern mining, and (iii) LBS (location-based service) privacy preservation. Section 3 introduces the proposed system and Section 4 gives details of the proposed method. Experiment results are shown in Section 5. The last section summarizes this research.

BACKGROUND AND RELATED LITERATURE

Three themes related to this research, (i) association rule mining, (ii) sequential pattern mining, and (iii) privacy preservation of location-based services, are discussed in this section. The data mining methods used in this research are revised to include the consideration of user locations and travel behavior. They are incremental data mining, which is to incrementally maintain the ongoing discovered patterns in large dynamic data sets.

Association Rule Mining

Association Rule Mining Association rule mining is a computational process for discovering frequent patterns (associations) from large data sets such as relational databases. The patterns (associations) could be used to predict an event about to take place based on other events happened before in the transaction. For example, if a grocery-store customer purchases milk, then most likely he/she will buy bread too. A classical association-rule mining paper can be found from Agrawal & Srikant (1994). This research tries to enhance the association rule mining to an incremental one to meet our requirement, the high mobility of mobile users. It is defined as incrementally maintaining the ongoing discovered association rules in dynamic large data sets where new data is added and obsolete data is discarded as time advances. Many methods have been dedicated to the development of incremental association-rule mining. Among them, Tsai, Lee, & Chen (1999) propose a method to reduce the cost of processing an updated database by storing the potential large itemsets that may become large itemsets after updating the database. Surveys of incremental association-rule mining can be found from Nath, Bhattacharyya, & Ghosh (2013) and Tend & Chen (2005).

Sequential Pattern Mining

Sequential pattern mining is a computational process for discovering frequent sequences of relevant events in large data sets. The sequences could be used to predict an event about to take place after other events happened before in the transaction. For example, if a student takes a pre-calculus course, then most likely he/she will take a calculus course next. A classical sequential-pattern mining paper can be found from Agrawal & Srikant (1995). This research also tries to enhance the sequential pattern mining to an incremental one, which is similar to an incremental association rule mining, but the associate rules are replaced by sequential patterns. Several methods have been dedicated to the development of incremental sequential-pattern mining. Among them, Masseglia, Poncelet, & Teisseire (2013) present an algorithm for mining frequent sequences that uses information collected during an earlier mining process to cut down the cost of finding new sequential patterns in the updated database. IncSpan by Cheng, Yan, & Han (2004) exploits the technique of buffering semi-frequent patterns for incremental mining of sequential patterns. IncSpan outperforms the non-incremental method and a previously proposed incremental mining algorithm ISM by a wide margin. Brief review of incremental sequential pattern mining is given by Zhao and Bhowmick (2003).

Privacy Preservation of Location-Based Services

Various methods of user privacy preservation of location-based services have been proposed (Chow & Mokbel, 2011), but most of them do not meet our need, consistent user identities. There are two methods, spatial cloaking and dummy locations/paths, has the feature of consistent user identities and are introduced in this subsection. Two related privacy preservation methods include space encoding/transformation and private information retrieval. The former method transforms the location data and location-dependent queries from one space into another space. In order to answer the queries correctly, the transformation has to maintain the spatial relationship among the data and queries. The latter method, private information retrieval (PIR), allows a location-dependent query to retrieve an item from a database located at a server without it knowing which item is retrieved. For example, one simple way to achieve this is for the server to send an entire copy of the database to the user. Other privacy preservation methods can be found in the articles (Ardagna, Livraga, & Samarati, 2012; Dewri, Ray, Ray, & Whitley, 2010; Nergiz, Atzori, Saygin, & Guc, 2009; Gruteser & Liu, 2004).

Location Obfuscation

It is a method used to hide the users' true locations in a location-based service by lightly obscuring their locations. Several techniques could be used for this method. For example, one of the techniques is spatial cloaking, which obscures a user's true location into a cloaked area, so there is low possibility of associating users to locations. Chow, Mokbel, & Liu (2011) propose a spatial cloaking algorithm for the mobile P2P environment. A spatial cloaking algorithm includes the feature that when a mobile user wants to obtain services from an LBS provider, he/she collaborates with other peers via multi-hop communication to blur her location into a cloaked area. Additionally, their method includes three key features: Reducing communication overhead, overcoming the network partition problem, and guaranteeing that their spatial cloaking algorithm is free from a "center-of-cloaked-area" privacy attack. Pan, Meng, & Xu (2009) propose a δ_p-privacy model and a δ_q-distortion model to balance the tradeoff between user privacy and QoS (quality of service). Furthermore, two incremental utility-based cloaking algorithms—bottom-up cloaking and hybrid cloaking, are proposed to anonymize continuous queries. Related research can be found in the articles (Deutsch, Hull, Vyas, & Zhao, 2010; Xu & Cai, 2007).

Dummy/Fake Locations/Paths

Users send their true location data along with several dummy/false location data to the service providers. User location privacy is preserved because service providers cannot distinguish the true location data from the dummies. Though this approach is effective, it is also simple, so not many articles focus on this approach. Pingley, Zhang, Fu, Choi, Subramaniam, & Zhao (2011) develop a user-centric technique for query privacy protection which operates solely on the user side and does not require any trusted third party. The key idea is to confuse the adversary by issuing multiple counterfeit queries with varying service attributes but the same (real) location, henceforth referred to as dummy queries, along with each real query issued by the user. Lu, Jensen, & Yiu (2008) propose an approach that is capable of offering privacy-region guarantees. It uses dummy locations that are deliberately generated according to either a virtual grid/circle. These cover a user's actual location, and their spatial extents are controlled by the generation algorithms. Related articles can be found from You, Peng, & Lee (2007) and Kido, Yanagisawa, & Satoh (2005).

THE PROPOSED SYSTEM

Location-based advertising (LBA) receives great attention these days because of its effectiveness and popularity. Mobile users need its services to enhance their life experience, whereas companies require mobile advertising to promote their products. However, mobile advertising is not without its own problems such as user privacy and advertisement accuracy and effectiveness. This research tries to mitigate the problems by proposing a privacy-preserving, location-based advertising using location-aware mining and based on the current and past user locations and travel paths and behavior. This section introduces the proposed system by discussing its two major components: server-side LBA and client-side LBA, where the former component generates mobile advertisements by using location-aware mining and the latter component collects user locations and travel paths and displays the appropriate, generated advertisements to users.

Server-Side LBA (Location-Based Advertising)

Figure 1 shows the system structure of the server-side LBA, which includes two phases: training and testing, where the training phase is used to fill up the LBA Database with path data, whereas the testing phase is used by the application to produce advertisements, which will be detailed in the next section, Section IV. It includes the following components:

- **LBA Manager:** A 2D path matrix is used to represent a path, a sequence of locations, whereas a 3D path matrix is built by superimposing 2D path matrices (Hu, Kaabouch, & Yang, 2016). The LBA Manager receives the user's 3D path matrix including the current path along with several dummy paths. It then restores the paths and relays them to the LBA Database, which sends the related location and path information to the rest components based on the paths it receives.
- **LBA Database:** It is a tiny geographical database including three tables: Events, Transactions, and Sequences, whose schema and sample values are given in Figure 2. The Events table stores a small set of events such as restaurants, motels, and entertainment events like theaters and concerts. The Transactions and Sequences are used for data mining discussed in the next section, Section

Figure 1. Structure of the server-side LBA

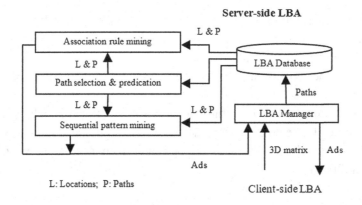

IV. Each transaction or sequence consists of a list of events. The difference between a transaction and a sequence is the events of the former are unordered, whereas the ones of the latter are ordered. In addition, each item of a sequence is an event, instead of a set of events.

- **Path Selection and Prediction:** This component performs the following steps: (i) selecting related, stored paths from the LBA Database, (ii) matching the stored paths to the current path, (iii) superimposing the result matrices after the matching, (iv) the superimposed matrix containing a weighted tree and the trunk of the tree being treated as the predicted path, and (v) the predicted paths are then used by the association rule and sequential pattern mining.
- **Association Rule and Sequential Pattern Mining:** The revised mining methods will be discussed in the next section, Section IV.

Client-Side LBA (Location-Based Advertising)

Past user travel paths provide useful information about user travel behavior. For example, a popular path may suggest a likely destination. Other than the location-aware mining methods, this research also uses the path information to create location-based advertisements. The client-side subsystem collects user locations, builds a user travel path along with several dummy paths, and sends a 3D path matrix encoding the travel paths to the server-side LBA. It also displays the correct advertisements sent from the server-side LBA. Figure 3 shows the structure of the client-side subsystem, which includes the following components:

Figure 2. Schemas and sample values of the tables events, transactions, and sequences

Events			
EID	**Type**	**Name**	**Location**
E01	Restaurant	Gourmet Café	47° 55' 31" N, 97° 01' 57" W
E02	Motel	Best Motel	47° 55' 37" N, 97° 01' 63" W
E03	Theater	AMC	47° 55' 28" N, 97° 01' 59" W
E04	Restaurant	Pasta House	47° 55' 38" N, 97° 01' 84" W
...	...	...	...

Transactions	
T#	**EID**
T05	E12
T02	E03
T05	E26
T24	E18
...	...

Sequences		
S#	**EID**	**Next**
S01	E03	S04
S02	E12	S10
S03	E38	S54
S01	E27	—
...	...	...

Figure 3. Structure of the client-side LBA

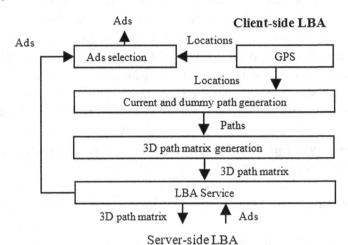

- **LBA Service:** It send a 3D path matrix, encoding the current path along with several dummy locations, to the server. On the other hand, it receives several advertisements from the server and presents the correct ones to the users based on the current paths and locations.

- **Path Matrix Generation:** Since matrices are a well-known mathematical subject and plenty of tools are available for them, user travel paths are represented by using a path matrix representation to facilitate the path processing (Hu, Kaabouch, & Yang, 2016). Equation 1 shows a generic matrix notation for the path p:

$$T_p = \begin{bmatrix} t_{1,1} & t_{1,2} & \cdots & t_{1,n} \\ t_{2,1} & t_{2,2} & \cdots & t_{2,n} \\ \cdots & \cdots & \cdots & \cdots \\ t_{m,1} & t_{m,2} & \cdots & t_{m,n} \end{bmatrix}, \text{ where } t_{i,j} = w_{i,j,p} \tag{1}$$

where $w_{i,j,p}$ is the weight of the path p on the map. By using this representation, path processing then becomes matrix processing, which is much easier compared to list-of-locations processing.

- **3D Path Matrix Generation:** This research requires transmissions of a set of paths between the clients and server. A 3D matrix representation is therefore used to facilitate the path storage, transmission, and processing (Hu, Kaabouch, & Yang, 2016). A generic 3D path matrix notation is given as follows:

$$D = \begin{bmatrix} d_{1,1} & d_{1,2} & \cdots & d_{1,n} \\ d_{2,1} & d_{2,2} & \cdots & d_{2,n} \\ \cdots & \cdots & \cdots & \cdots \\ d_{m,1} & d_{m,2} & \cdots & d_{m,n} \end{bmatrix},, \text{ where } d_{i,j} = \left[d_{i,j,1}, d_{i,j,2}, \ldots, d_{i,j,h} \right] \text{ and } d_{i,j,p} = w_{i,j,p} \tag{2}$$

where each entry $d_{i,j}$ is an array of weights of the paths, h is the number of paths, and $w_{i,j,p}$ is the weight of the path p on the map. Each 3D matrix encodes several paths, so the server is not able to associate paths to the user and privacy is preserved.

PRIVACY-PRESERVING LOCATION-BASED ADVERTISING (LBA)

This research proposes a method for privacy-preserving location-based advertising by using location-aware mining, as well as based on travelers' behavior because a generalization of the past user behavior usually indicates a use trend. A discussion of the proposed algorithm is given in this subsection.

The Proposed Method

Two representations of the proposed method are given in this section. Figure 4 gives the algorithm of the proposed privacy-preserving location-based advertising and Figure 5 shows the corresponding flowchart. Path storage, transmission, indexing, searching, and matching could be very complicated and are required in this research. To facilitate path processing, a 3D path matrix representation is used in this research. In addition, the target advertisements are retrieved from several advertisements sent by the server on the client side, so it is not possible to associate paths and advertisements to the user other than the user himself/herself.

Location-Aware Data Mining

Two revised methods of association rule mining (Agrawal & Srikant, 1994) and sequential pattern mining (Agrawal & Srikant, 1995) with a consideration of user travel paths are used in this research to find relevant advertisements. For example, if users stop by a hotel, advertisements of nearby restaurants could be sent to them, knowing that the users probably would not cook themselves. However, this approach may not be accurate because the users might just shop around a hotel before settling down. If that is the case, advertisements of nearby hotels should be sent instead. This research uses a version of association

Figure 4. Algorithm of the privacy-preserving location-base advertising

Privacy-Preserving Location-Based Advertising
1. *(Client) Send a 3D path matrix encoding the current path along with several dummy paths to the LBA Server.*
2. *(Server) Restore paths from the 3D path matrix.*
3. *(Server) For each of the restored paths, perform the Steps 4-8.*
4. *(Server) Save the stored paths if they meet the traveler's behavior.*
5. *(Server) Generate a weighted matrix after match the restored path to the saved paths.*
6. *(Server) Superimpose the matching result matrices.*
7. *(Server) Find the trunk of the tree, the predicted path, in the superimposed matrix.*
8. *(Server) Generate ads using either association rules or sequential patterns.*
9. *(Client) Select and display the relevant ads according to its locations.*

Figure 5. Flowchart of the privacy-preserving location-based advertising

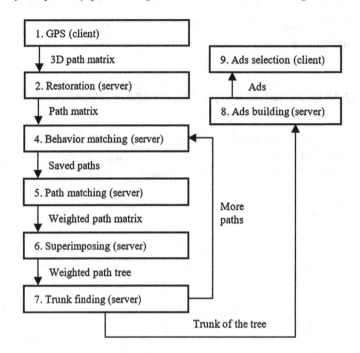

rule mining with a consideration of current locations to produce more relevant advertisements. Only the advertisements of relevant events within a certain radius will be used after applying the association-rule mining. Figure 6 shows an example of this method.

In addition, this research tries to deliver more relevant advertisements based on user paths (a set of locations) instead of individual locations. The location-based sequential-pattern mining is used to find the subsequent events nearby the projected path. For example, if the user visits a hotel the first time, the advertisements of restaurants and shopping malls within a certain radius and in the predicted paths will be sent. Figure 7 shows an example of this method.

Figure 6. Ads of relvant events from association-rule mining

Figure 7. Ads of related events from sequential-pattern mining

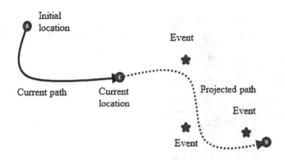

EXPERIMENT RESULTS

This research proposes a method of location-based advertising by using location-aware mining, as well as based on current and previous travel paths because a generalization of the past traffic flows usually indicates a travel trend.

System Setup

It is not simple to draw travel paths by using Google Maps Android API. Therefore, old versions of Android are used because they are more stable compared to the newer ones. The proposed system is implemented in the environment including:

- Android Studio IDE 2.0,
- Android 6.0 (Marshmallow) Platform (API 23),
- Android Virtual Device (AVD) (API 23 and 3.2" GVGA), and
- Google Play Services 8.4.0, which includes Google Maps Android API.

Since the system is still in its early stage of development, most data are entered via simulation, instead of road tests. The simulation sends a location (including longitude and latitude) to the app via the DDMS (Dalvik Debug Monitor Service) of Android Studio.

App Launched and Path Drawn

Figure 8a shows the proposed app displayed on the Android launcher window. Before the app starts working, a training phase, including path data collection and pattern discovery, has been carried out in the background for some time, so other apps like phone calls and texting can still work without being interrupted. While the app is working, the current travel path could be drawn when requested as shown in Figure 8.b, where the markers are beginning and current locations. The path is not smooth compared to the one drawn by Google Directions API because it is drawn according to the visited locations.

Figure 8. (a) The app on an Android launcher and (b) a current travel path shown

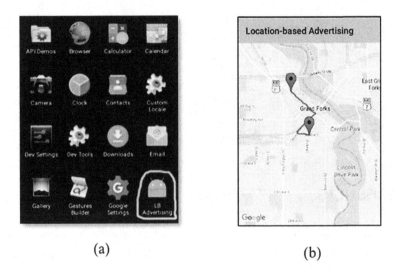

(a)   (b)

Location-Aware Association Rule Data Mining for Advertising

Two location-aware mining methods, association rules and sequential patterns, are applied in this research. Figure 9.a shows the advertisements by using location-aware association rule mining, where the red markers are initial and current locations, the current path is with a red color, and the yellow markers are the locations that dispatch the advertisements. According to the association rules, advertisements

Figure 9. (a) Relevant locations marked from association rule mining and (b) ads shown by clicking a yellow marker

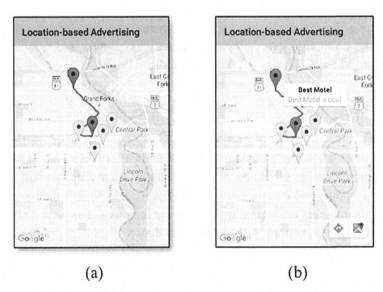

(a)   (b)

For a more accurate representation see the electronic version.

of nearby interesting locations are displayed based on the past and current locations. For example, if motels are visited now or before, nearby motels are marked, so users could have more choices. Figure 9.b shows the advertisement when the user clicks the yellow marker.

Location-Aware Sequential Data Mining for Advertising

Figure 10.a shows the relevant locations by using location-aware sequential pattern mining and path prediction, where the red markers are initial, current, and projected locations, the yellow markers are the locations that dispatch the advertisements, the current path is with a red color, and the projected path is with a green color. For example, if the current location is a motel, advertisements of nearby restaurants or gas stations will be shown. Figure 10.b shows the advertisement when the user clicks the yellow marker.

CONCLUSION

Traditional advertisements are normally displayed on the Internet, TVs, newspapers, or magazines. Since smartphones became the most popular communication tools, companies have to adapt to the new trend. Smartphones have the features such as high mobility, small screens, short battery life, and limited Internet connection, which are not found in the traditional media. This provides new opportunities, but it also creates new challenges at the same time. For example, mobile users can conveniently locate local events like concerts and farmers' markets, which might be difficult to find in the past. However, how to send relevant advertisements to interested mobile users is a challenge too; e.g., sending the advertise-

Figure 10. (a) Relevant locations from sequential pattern mining and a projected path and (b) ads shown by clicking a yellow marker

(a)   (b)

*For a more accurate representation see the electronic version.

ments of farmers' markets to tourists may not be appealing. Better methods have to be found for the new opportunities and to tackle the new challenges, so relevant advertisements can be effectively sent to mobile users. This research proposes an innovative but effective method for location-based advertising. Many contributions have been made by this project. Four of the major contributions are given as follows:

- More accurate and effective mobile advertisements are created by using our method, which includes the features of user locations and paths and behavior patterns.
- User travel paths, lists of locations, are normally difficult to manage. Paths in this research are represented by an innovative matrix representation, the path matrices, which facilitate path storage, indexing, transmission, and processing.
- The proposed method makes user privacy preservation simple and robust by sending the target path with several dummy (false) paths. Therefore, the server is not able to associate the paths with users.
- Human travel behavior is useful and has been applied in many applications such as city and street design and planning. This research studies various issues related to human travel behavior; e.g., what are the frequent paths from location A to location B?

Experiment results show this method is effective and secure for building location-based advertisements, which is based on the features of human travel behavior. This research also uses a novel matrix representation for path processing. The ideas appear effective and secure, but have not yet been formally validated. For example, the system has no problem generating ads, but how satisfied are users with the results? Theoretically, the system is secure, but how secure is it? Experiments and solid proofs need to be carried out to prove the effectiveness and robustness of the proposed system and method. The ideas and system will be further improved or revised based on users' feedbacks and testing data.

REFERENCES

Agrawal, R., & Srikant, R. (1994, September 12-15). Fast algorithms for mining association rules. In *Proceedings of the 20th VLDB (Very Large Data Bases) Conference*, Santiago, Chile.

Agrawal, R., & Srikant, R. (1995, March 6-10). Mining sequential patterns. In *Proceedings of the 11th International Conference on Data Engineering*, Taipei, Taiwan.

Ardagna, C. A., Livraga, G., & Samarati, P. (2012, December 5-7). Protecting privacy of user information in continuous location-based services. In *Proceedings of the 15th IEEE International Conference on Computational Science and Engineering (CSE 2012)*, Paphos, Cyprus. 10.1109/ICCSE.2012.31

Cheng, H., Yan, X., & Han, J. (2004). IncSpan: incremental mining of sequential patterns in large database. In *Proceedings of the 10th International 113 Conference on Knowledge Discovery in Databases*, (pp. 527-532). 10.1145/1014052.1014114

Chow, C.-F., Mokbel, M. F., & Liu, X. (2011). Spatial cloaking for anonymous location-based services in mobile peer-to-peer environments. *GeoInformatica*, *15*(2), 351–380. doi:10.100710707-009-0099-y

Chow, C.-Y., & Mokbel, M. F. (2011). Privacy of spatial trajectories. In Y. Zheng & X. Zhou (Eds.), *Computing with Spatial Trajectories* (pp. 109–141). New York: Springer. doi:10.1007/978-1-4614-1629-6_4

Deutsch, A., Hull, R., Vyas, A., & Zhao, K. K. (2010, March 1-6). Policy aware sender anonymity in location based services. In *Proceedings of the 26th International Conference Data Engineering (ICDE 2010)*, Long Beach, CA. 10.1109/ICDE.2010.5447823

Dewri, R., Ray, I., Ray, I., & Whitley, D. (2010, March 23-26). Query m-invariance: preventing query disclosures in continuous location-based services. In *Proceedings of the 11th International Conference on Mobile Data Management (MDM 2010)*, Kansas City, MS (pp. 95-104). 10.1109/MDM.2010.52

Gruteser, M., & Liu, X. (2004, March/April). Protecting privacy in continuous location-tracking applications. *IEEE Security and Privacy*, 2(2), 28–34. doi:10.1109/MSECP.2004.1281242

Hu, W.-C., Kaabouch, N., & Yang, H.-J. (2016, May 19-21). Secure spatial trajectory prediction based on traffic flows. In *Proceedings of the 2016 IEEE International Electro/Information Technology Conference (EIT 2016)*, Grand Forks, ND. 10.1109/EIT.2016.7535328

Kido, H., Yanagisawa, Y., & Satoh, T. (2005). An anonymous communication technique using dummies for location-based services. In *Proceedings of IEEE International Conference on Pervasive Services (ICPS'05)*, Santorini, Greece (pp. 88-97). 10.1109/PERSER.2005.1506394

Lu, H., Jensen, C. S., & Liu, M. L. (2008, June 13). PAD: Privacy-area aware, dummy-based location privacy in mobile devices. In *Proceedings of the 7th ACM International Workshop on Data Engineering for Wireless and Mobile Access (Mobide 2008)*, Vancouver, Canada. 10.1145/1626536.1626540

Masseglia, F., Poncelet, P., & Teisseire, M. (2013, July). Incremental mining of sequential patterns in large databases. *Journal of Data and Knowledge Engineering*, 46(1), 97–121. doi:10.1016/S0169-023X(02)00209-4

Nath, B., Bhattacharyya, D. K., & Ghosh, A. (2013, May). Incremental association rule mining: A survey. *Wiley Interdisciplinary Reviews. Data Mining and Knowledge Discovery*, 3(3). doi:10.1002/widm.1086

Nergiz, M. E., Atzori, M., Saygin, Y., & Guc, B. (2009). Towards trajectory anonymization: A generalization-based approach. *Transactions on Data Privacy*, 2, 47–75.

Pan, X., Meng, X., & Xu, J. (2009, November 4-6). Distortion-based anonymity for continuous queries in location-based mobile services. In *Proceedings of the 17th ACM SIGSPATIAL International Conference on Advances in Geographic Information Systems (ACM SIGSPATIAL GIS 2009)*, Seattle, WA (pp. 256-265). 10.1145/1653771.1653808

Pingley, A., Zhang, N., Fu, X., Choi, H.-A., Subramaniam, S., & Zhao, W. (2011, April 10-15). Protection of query privacy for continuous location based services. In *Proceedings of the 30th IEEE International Conference on Computer Communications (INFOCOM 2011)*, Shanghai, China (pp. 1710-1718). 10.1109/INFCOM.2011.5934968

Teng, W.-G., & Chen, M.-S. (2005). Incremental mining on association rules. In *Foundations and Advances in Data Mining* (pp. 125–162). Springer. doi:10.1007/11362197_6

Tsai, P. S. M., Lee, C.-C., & Chen, A. L. P. (1999, April 26-28). An efficient approach for incremental association rule mining. In *Proceedings of the 3rd Pacific-Asia Conference on Methodologies for Knowledge Discovery and Data Mining (PAKDD '99)*, Beijing, China (pp. 74-83). 10.1007/3-540-48912-6_10

Xu, T., & Cai, Y. (2007, November 7-9). Location anonymity in continuous location-based services. In *Proceedings of the 15th ACM SIGSPATIAL International Conference on Advances in Geographic Information Systems (ACM SIGSPATIAL GIS 2007)*, Seattle, WA.

You, T. H., Peng, W. C., & Lee, W. C. (2007, May 11). Protecting moving trajectories with dummies. In *Proceedings of the International Workshop on Privacy-Aware Location-Based Mobile Services (PALMS)*, Mannheim, Germany.

Zhao, Q., & Bhowmick, S. S. (2003). Sequential pattern mining: a survey (technical report). CAIS, Nanyang Technological University, Singapore.

ADDITIONAL READING

Brata, K. C., Liang, D., & Pramono, S. H. (2015, February). Location-based augmented reality information for bus route planning system. *Iranian Journal of Electrical and Computer Engineering*, 5(1), 142–149.

Dang, H., & Chang, E.-C. (2015, November 3-6). PrAd: enabling privacy-aware location based advertising. In *Proceedings of the 2nd Workshop on Privacy in Geographic Information Collection and Analysis (GeoPrivacy 2015)*, Seattle, WA.

Deng, K., Xie, K., Zheng, K., & Zhou, X. (2011). Trajectory indexing and retrieval. In Y. Zheng & X. Zhou (Eds.), *Computing with Spatial Trajectories* (pp. 35–59). New York: Springer. doi:10.1007/978-1-4614-1629-6_2

Hardt, M., & Nath, S. (2012, October 16-18). Privacy-aware personalization for mobile advertising. In *Proceedings of the 2012 ACM Conference on Computer and Communications Security (CCS 2012)*, Raleigh, NC.

Khoshgozaran, A., Shirani-Mehr, H., & Shahabi, C. (2013). Blind evaluation of location based queries using space transformation to preserve location privacy. *GeoInformatica*, 17(4), 599–634. doi:10.100710707-012-0172-9

Liou, S.-C., & Huang, Y.-M. (2005). Trajectory predictions in mobile networks. *International Journal of Information Technology*, 11(11), 109–122.

Shang, S., Ding, R., Yuan, B., Xie, K., Zheng, K., & Kalnis, P. (2012, March 26-30). Users oriented trajectory search for trip recommendation. In *Proceedings of the 15th International Conference on Extending Database Technology (EDBT 2012)*, Berlin, Germany. 10.1145/2247596.2247616

Wei, L.-Y., Peng, W.-C., & Lee, W.-C. (2013, June). Exploring pattern-aware travel routes for trajectory search. *ACM Transactions on Intelligent Systems and Technology*, 4(3), 48. doi:10.1145/2483669.2483681

KEY TERMS AND DEFINITIONS

Android Studio: Since 2014, Android Studio became the primary IDE (Integrated Development Environment) for native Android application development. It is free software under the Apache License 2.0 developed by Google. It includes the following features: (i) intelligent code editor, (ii) code templates and GitHub integration, (iii) multi-screen app development, (iv) virtual devices for all shapes and sizes, and (v) Android builds evolved, with Gradle.

Apps: A mobile app (or application) is a kind of software designed to run on mobile handheld devices such as smartphones. Examples of apps are calendars, video games, and short message services (SMS).

Association Rule Mining: A computational process for discovering frequent patterns (associations) from large data sets such as relational databases. The patterns (associations) could be used to predict an event about to take place based on other events happened before in the transaction. For example, if a grocery-store customer buys milk, then most likely he/she will buy bread too.

Data Mining: Data mining is to discover patterns in large data sets and transform the patterns into a comprehensible structure for further applications.

Location-Aware Data Mining: The data mining method that takes the locations of data into consideration when discovers knowledge.

Location-Based Advertising: To promote or sell a product by sending relevant audio or visual information or data to mobile users based on their locations.

Mobile User Privacy: The ability of mobile users to conceal information about themselves like IDs and locations. The information will be revealed only with their permission.

Sequential Pattern Mining: A computational process for discovering frequent sequences of relevant events in large data sets. The sequences could be used to predict an event about to take place after other events happened before in the transaction. For example, if a student takes a pre-calculus course, then most likely he/she will take a calculus course next.

Chapter 11
Amelioration of Big Data Analytics by Employing Big Data Tools and Techniques

Stephen Dass
Vellore Institute of Technology, India

Prabhu J.
Vellore Institute of Technology, India

ABSTRACT

This chapter describes how in the digital data era, a large volume of data became accessible to data science engineers. With the reckless growth in networking, communication, storage, and data collection capability, the Big Data science is quickly growing in each engineering and science domain. This paper aims to study many numbers of the various analytics ways and tools which might be practiced to Big Data. The important deportment in this paper is step by step process to handle the large volume and variety of data expeditiously. The rapidly evolving big data tools and Platforms have given rise to numerous technologies to influence completely different Big Data portfolio.In this paper, we debate in an elaborate manner about analyzing tools, processing tools and querying tools for Big datahese tools used for data analysis Big Data tools utilize numerous tasks, like Data capture, storage, classification, sharing, analysis, transfer, search, image, and deciding which might also apply to Big data.

INTRODUCTION

Current advancement in the field digital information improves the data which are exceptional to both software and hardware. About 70% unstructured data deals with multimedia data, in that 60% of them are from internet traffic (Boyd & Crawford, 2012; Hartmann et al., 2014; Jagadish et al., 2014; Katal, Wazid, & Goudar, 2013; Purcell, 2013). Unexpectedly huge data creates stints multi-media data semantic definitions searched by conventional methods are difficult to any set of forms. Unsorted raw data are complicated to deal directly so few easy and machine processing forms are made to design semantic data. This type of data works on content-based retrieval methods from which data are restored. This phenomenon is known as Feature Extraction (Katal, Wazid, & Goudar, 2013). Miloslavaskaya and Tolstoy

DOI: 10.4018/978-1-5225-4044-1.ch011

(2014) state "...big data concept are the datasets of such size and structure that exceed the capabilities of traditional programming tools (databases, software, etc.) for data collection, storage and processing in a reasonable time and a-fortiori exceed the capacity of their perception by a human..."

In General, Big Data is exported as data wealth peculiarize as high volume, velocity, and variety to get particular technology and analytical methods to change to value. Since from the invention of the internet in the early 1990s, the growth of the data has been increasing steadily. In Past Decade data generation growth is massively high which become a great challenge in storing, managing and process of data. This set a path to the new concept of Big Data, a concept that concerns with all generated data that are analyzed and processed in the day to day tools (Fayyad, Piatetsky-Shapiro, & Smyth, 1996). Jeong and Shin (2016) posted a security management scheme that allows users to easily access Big Data from different network environments. For implementing security management using key management, they added furthermore as future research as to Design and operate a model that can integrate and manage the stratified properties of the security awareness information sent and received between users and servers (Bakshi, 2012).

RELATED WORK

Literature Survey

Liu et al. (2014) proposed a mining system with Big Graph analysis by performing in bulk synchronous parallel (BSP) naming it as BSP based Graph Mining (BSPGM). This System inferred is compared with Hadoop Map-Reduce concept in processing Massive Data and it is developed based on Cloud platform. The drawback of this system often it restricts the graph data in the processing phase.

Meng et al. (2014) suggested keyword-Aware service recommendation method using Hadoop when customer service is growing rapidly with online information generation is difficult to use traditional service recommendation system for large scale data. This lacks scalability and inefficiency in processing the massive data. Usually recommending system uses same rating and ranking of service but here the author uses frequently used keyword for search of particular word and they are analysed. The author uses MapReduce framework.

Chen, Mao, and Liu (2014) put forth system as privacy aware cross cloud service for Big Data application using MapReduce. This paper uses medical data as dataset in large scale for analysis the data. They propose Hiresome-II (History record based service optimization method). Cloud uses QaS for history records. Complexity of the cloud system is resolved using Hiresome-II.

Jamshidi et al. (2015) discuss how Big Data and system of service (SoS) works together. Big Data analytics tools used in this paper are Principal Component analysis (PCA), fuzzy logic clustering and K means. These tools of Big Data help in handling (a) Extract information. (b) Build acknowledge from derived data. (c) Develop model for Big Data.

Elgendy and Elragal (2014) explain the Large data graph analyzing by Big Data. Graph processing is implemented using the shortest path of the data. Map Reduce is used to determine the graph processing.

Boyd and Crawford (2012) discuss the question raised by various different field of technology where huge data are generated, processed and handled. The author discusses the varies tools from which Big Data are processed and studied. Furthermore, author an intimate user who uses Big Data and its provocation about its mystery.

Alexander Boicen et al. (2013) present the difference between SQL and NoSQL database management system and explains about the feature, architecture, restriction and integrity of both oracle and MongoDB. He concluded in context with database management system as if we need fast and flexible, MongoDB is the best option. Otherwise Oracle is the best for its rapidness and tables collection and relation with classic solution.

Vithal Yenkar and Mahip Bartere (2014) explain the major domain of Data Mining with Big Data. How Big data analysis is implemented in data Mining. Author explains the tough issues in Big Data and data driven model. They elaborate as heterogeneous mixture learning technology implementing in Big Data analysis.

Demchek et al. (2014) discussed all about big data used in technology, industries with defining an architecture and operational models such as Big Data management and security, Big Data infrastructure (BDI), Big Data Architecture Framework (BDAF), Big Data lifecycle management (BDLM)and Big Data Cloud based Infrastructure. The author initiates to discuss about the Big Data Tools more intensively.

COMPARATIVE ANALYSIS

Based on the functionality Big Data is classified into three categories such as Big Data Storage management, Big Data Processing and Big Data Streaming.

Big Data Storage Usage

Big Data nowadays usually deals with very large unstructured data sets, and relies on fast analytics, with answers provided in seconds. For instance, Facebook, Google or Amazon analyse users' statuses or search terms to trigger targeted advertising on user pages. However big data analytics aren't restricted to those internet giants. All type of organisations, and not essentially large ones, will take pleasure in finance houses inquisitive about analysing stock exchange behaviour, to police departments getting to analyse and predict crime trends. In this section we compare Big Data Storage tools MongoDB, CouchDB and Big Table and traditional database Structure Query Language like MySql, Oracle and SQL server. Table 1 elaborately describes the Storage management. MongoDB and MySql Database System.

Limitations of RDBMS Over Big Data

First, the data size has accumulated hugely to the vary of petabytes—one petabyte = 1,024 terabytes. RDBMS finds it difficult to handle such immense data volumes. to deal with this, RDBMS extra more central processing units (or CPUs) or more memory to the direction system to rescale vertically. Second, the bulk of the data comes in an exceedingly semi-structured or unstructured format from social media, audio, video, texts, and emails. However, the second drawback concerning unstructured data is outside the view of RDBMS as a result of relational databases simply can't reason unstructured data. They're designed and structured to accommodate structured information love weblog device and money information. Also, "big data" is generated at a really high speed. RDBMS lacks in high velocity as a result of it's designed for steady data retention instead of rapid climb. Even if RDBMS is employed to handle and store "big data," & nbsp; it'll prove to be terribly dear. As a result, the lack of relational databases to handle "big data" led to the emergence of latest technologies.

Table 1. Comparative analysis of MongoDB and MySql

Name	MongoDB	MySql
Description	Most popular document store	Used in relational database base
Primary Database model	Document store	Relational RDBMS
Initial release	2009	1995
Implementation language	C++	C and C++
Server operating System	Linux, OS X, Soloris, Windows	Free BSD, Linux, Windows
Data Scheme	Scheme free	Yes
SQL	No	Yes
Server-side Scripts	Java Script	YES
Map Reduce	YES	NO
Consistency concepts	Eventual consistency and Immediate consistency	Immediate consistency
Advantage	1. Non-Relational means table-less 2. Less expensive and open source 3. Easier scalability in order to support for Map Reduce 4. No detailed database model is required	1. derives with standard schema 2. Support is instantly available whenever is required 3. developed according to Industry Standard
Disadvantage	1. Community not as well defined 2. Lack of standardization	1. Mysql Suffers From Relatively Poor Performance Scaling 2. Development Is Not Community Driven – and Hence Has Lagged 3. Its Functionality Tends To Be Heavily Dependent On Add-ons 4. Developers May Find Some Of Its Limitations To Be Frustrating

DATA ANALYSIS

All data associated with big data is generated every second by second and are available from completely different sources; it's exactly the good diversity of data varieties what complicates the storage and analysis as a result of the combination of data with different structures because it has been mentioned (Liu et al., 2014). As a result of this, big data classified in 3 main operations: storage, analytics, and integration, through that solutions are display so in an efficient manner the size of this tool is often scaled. There are totally different techniques for big data Analysis; some of these tools are.

Need for Big Data Analytics

Big data Analysis resolved many issues related to a real-time application which is shown in a different structure such as graphical structure (Meng et al., 2014). They set an example in optimizing the railway paths, disease prediction, and analysis related to social media network, genome constraint analysis, Information network and semantic analysis etc.

Figure 1. Need for Big Data analytics

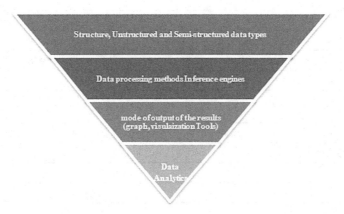

Big Data Processing

Big data are processed in two ways

1. Integrated processing
2. Distributed processing

Integrated Processing

Data is collected and stored in one integrated location where storage and processing are done on the single machine. This integrated processing machine is computed by the very high processor, storage has high configuration. This type of processing structure is defined too small organization where storage and processing are done on the single machine. It promotes to be as Supercomputing system.

Distributed Processing

The collection, storage, and processing are done in the different architecture of distributed processing. Peer to peer architecture and clustering architecture are a prominent example of distributed processing.

BIG DATA ANALYSIS STEP

Big data uses a very large data set which cannot be processed by classical tools and techniques (Sánchez et al, 2008). Steps involved in making our material into a finite data are as follows:

1. **Data Collection:** Data collection is gathering the raw data from real time generating data resources then stored in storage device. Data collection process is done in high concern from which it fails leads to inaccurate and inappropriate results. Tools used for data collections are Chekwa, WebCrawler, pig, and flume.

Figure 2. Big Data processing

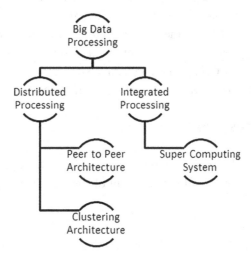

2. **Data Partition:** Since large data are difficult to process there comes different partition techniques such as data tagging classification and clustering approaches.to reduce the complexity of processing a huge volume data, many clustering approaches are designed they are classified into algorithms like text mining, data mining, Mahout, scalable nearest neighbor algorithm and pattern processing.

3. **Data Coordination:** Coordination denotes the data move towards any data warehouse or any other Big data database technique. In common, it is denoted as the exchange of data from one format to another big data technique. Sqoop is a Big data technology used to exchange data from the relational database. Flume is the technology used in big data defined to hold and manage the huge amount of data from one system network to another efficiently. Zookeeper provides data synchronization which is used the configuration information programming language like java, python, was used in data coordination.

4. **Data Transformation:** Converting one data format from sources to another format refers to data transformation. Data migration tools help to convert the relational database to Hadoop repository.

5. **Data Storage:** In laymen terms, Big Data is defined to storage of data and how voluminous data are stored in the storage management. Data storage must perform retrieval, manipulation and data collection efficiently. Handling different types of data also plays a role in data storage. Tools used are HBase, NoSQL, cluster HDFS and GFS.

6. **Data Processing:** Till now, there is no defining and devise a tool for processing Big Data. Hadoop, NoSQL and apache-spark etc. helps in processing structured and unstructured data in various formats. QlikView is a perfect instance of in-memory data processing for big data which gives advanced reporting. Infinispan is scalable and available grid platform data processing.

7. **Extract Data:** Extracting required files or data from the database and resulted in output preferred in different result reports such as visualization, integration, and reporting. Two methods used in data extract. Data query tools-using query language like Hive helps in fetching the data. Big Data search – using parallel or distributing processing with clustering fetching data.

8. **Data Analysis:** Data Analysis is defined as checking, investigating or analyzing and inspecting the data and then modeling according to the goal set by the client's expectation by making useful

data. Rapid Miner is open sources software where the text is mining for using the data for predictive analysis. Pentaho- is business intelligence software where video; data OLAP, Service, ETL are used. Talend and Spago BI- are the tools which are used in many managerial organizations. Weka- is machine learning tool where data mining algorithm is implemented for data analysis.

9. **Data Visualisation:** DIVE & Orange are Big data Visualisation tools used for formatting the huge data to structure format are inadequate. It works in order to solve the inadequate issue.

Big Data Analytics Processing

For analytics processing of Big Data, four critical requirements are suggested (Bakshi, 2012): 1. Fast data loading 2. Fast query processing, 3. High efficient utilization of storage space 4. Strong adaptivity to high dynamic workload.

Hadoop

MapReduce

MapReduce is a processing model used in Hadoop. The word "MapReduce" itself denotes, "Map" and then "Reduce". These type of processing is suitable for Big Data. It performs both analytics and processing function (Chen, Mao, Liu, 2014). MapReduce is a process by which, it adds additional system or resources rather than increasing the storage space of individuals systems. The main idea of MapReduce is breaking the job into many phases and executing each phrases parallel in which it reduces the processing time and completes the job before its scheduled time.

Two jobs are performed in MapReduce. They are

1. Map-job
2. Reduce Job

Map job is setting Map input value to the output value. This Map function computes huge jobs into little jobs and issue a required set of input keys to map output keys. Reduced function is implemented to collect and combine all key values, which are shared, to get the final computation. When MapReduce and Hadoop meet, they perform two different nodes. First, Job Tracker takes care of distributing Map and Reduce function and monitor them. It schedules the work for the execution of Map job. Second, Task tracker runs related to jobs and get backs the result of the task monitor and the work of the reduce functions. We explain MapReduce functions in four steps

Step 1: Data collection in massive volume including log files, sensors data etc.

Step 2: Job tracker defines and executes the MApjobs and reduce job and send the both

Step 3: Job Tracker allows jobs to task tracker it runs mapper provide output then it is stored in HDF file system.

Step 4: Data are mapped, and it reduces jobs to get the result.

Principal Component Analysis

Principal Component Analysis (PCA) is a statistical system to identify a pattern in the dataset in order to find the similarities and dissimilarities which are reduced to a set of value according to the client desire. It highlights the specific attributes accordingly to client's choice (Hinton, Osindero, & Teh, 2006). It helps in compressing the data PCA is implemented and solved by both numerical and also image data. It eliminates the unrelated set of value. The simple steps to perform PCA is as follows steps

Step 1: Fetch a data set
Step 2: Find the mean value and the then eliminate each data value
Step 3: Covariance matrix is calculated
Step 4: Finding Eigen values and Eigen vectors for covariance matrix
Step 5: Forms feature vector.

This Eigen values & Eigenvectors values are necessarily useful for Big Data concepts which become a little disadvantage to PCA in analytics of Big Data.

Fuzzy Logic

The concept of fuzzy logic was initially developed by Zadeh in 1965. Fuzzy logic mainly focuses on two terms fuzzy sets and fuzzy system. It is a problem-solving system which consists of methodology to lead and implement network embedded system or work station based on data acquisition and control system. *Fuzzy set*-It deals with knowing and probability in truth table and it's analyzing like human reasoning. Two problems are developed in fuzzy logic is fuzzy set theory finds the vacuum in semantic. Fuzzy measure theory evaluating the nature which has many sets of analyzing points. *The fuzzy system is* reasoning methods based on the almost accurate collection. Fuzzy consist of fuzzy mathematics, fuzzy operating, fuzzy clustering are few examples of fuzzy systems. Fuzzy systems are eliminated because of it low tolerance and experience in nature. The fuzzy system is implemented using if-then conditional operator methods. Each and every parameter in fuzzy logic have definite and individual operations and context.

Fuzzy C- Mean Clustering

Fuzzy clustering is an unsupervised learning method implemented in many other domains such that machine learning, bioinformatics, data mining and pattern recognition. Fuzzy clustering is used in application-oriented domains such as processing medical imaging and Image partition. Clustering analysis is defined as a grouping similar type of feature attributes (Elgendy & Elragal, 2016). Fuzzy c means clustering algorithms is denoted in the following function.

$$F_m = \sum_{a=1}^{N} \sum_{b=1}^{c} U_{ab}^{m} \left\| x_a - C_b \right\| 2, 1 < M < \infty$$

where

U_{ab} = degree of ownership of x_a in the cluster b
x_a = the pa[th] of the d dimensional meaning data
C_b = the d- dimensional center of cluster
$\|*\|$ = the norm expressing the similarity between measured data and the center

Ownership of U_{ab} and cluster centers C_b is denoted as

$$U_{ab} = \cfrac{1}{\sum_{k=1}^{C} \cfrac{\left\| x_{i-c_j} \right\|}{\left\| x_i - c_k \right\|} \Big/ {}^{2}\!\!\big/ m - 1}$$

where

$$C_b = \frac{\sum_{i=1}^{N} U_{ab}^m x_a}{\sum_{i=1}^{N} U_{ab}^m}$$

Traditional Artifical Neutral Network

The idea of the artificial neural network is initially incorporated from computation model of human brains of the human neuron. This traditional artificial neural network is data formulating system which carries a certain set of data in it. Signals are generated by neurons from other neurons or outside layer that is interlinked. The important concept Multilayer perception (MLP) comprises of three layers:

1. One input layer
2. Hidden layer
3. Output layer

   Functions are manipulated in a hidden layer so hidden layers are also greater in number than Input layer which gives high threshold. From this MLP we learn layered feedforward network trained with back propagation method. This type of network has static pattern classification. The main advantage of MLP is that learn to use and mapping of input and output approximation is popular.the main disadvantage is when the data are one in process of training it takes much time to train data. The acceleration of learning decreases when a lot of training data are in processing so, the traditional artificial neural network will not much applicable to big data and deep architecture. But they are in the field of information technology for more than 30 yrs (Hinton, Osindero, The, 2006). From this point the algorithms yet to be established to prove the best of knowledge discovery

Traditional Genetic Algorithm

Genetic algorithms are the very voluminous class of data processing method called evolutionary computations. GA is inquisitive search method which imitates the technique of natural selection and survival of fittest. This GA adds with genetic programming concept from which text data, symbolic representation is improved with evolutionary computations (Ho Chi Minh City University of Technology, n.d.). After many generations, inheritance, mutation, and selection are obtained. In GA, population is initiated in initial stage as such denoted by 0 and 1 bits. Each and every pair of the chromosome is exchanged and modified after the process of selection. When a new population is obtained, they are commended withhold chromosome and compared for the survival of the chromosome. The life cycle of Genetic Algorithm is shown in Figure 3.

Tools Used for Data Analytics: From Storage Management Perspective

The complying dividing put forth the several numbers of tools which are presently in use of storage, management, and analysis of data which tends to form Big Data.

- **Hadoop (HDFS):** Stands for distributed file system projected to be performed by the commodity hardware (Gilbert, Lynch, 2012; Kamat, Singh, 2013).
- **Hardware:** Hadoop is interconnected with several hundreds of cluster of nodes which store and perform user's job. Failure occurrence in the commodity hardware is high, therefore if the only Master node fails in its task which leads to failure of whole clusters failure. Moreover, the Hadoop platform unremittingly has an assertive percentage of inactivity (Jagadish et al., 2014; Gilbert, Lynch, 2012).
- **Transmission:** The data performed by Hadoop are not in general for usage since the set of data is processed by the user without any connection.
- **Data:** Generally, applications performed during this kind of tool are of huge in size; Hadoop incorporate in supporting it with a handsome variety of nodes that distributed for data. This handling brings as a profit the rapid growth in the information measured is obtainable in many nodes, A fair performance within the access to data and its continuous presentation (streaming).

Figure 3. Life cycle of Genetic Algorithm

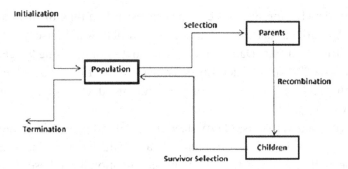

- **Computation:** One of the advantages of Hadoop when comparing with other tools is that both storage and processing of data done in the same system from which, data transmission, collision is avoided in the network.
- **Portability:** Many of Open Source application is developed with easy of diaspora with different platforms. Hadoop is also designed in such a way.
- **Accessibility:** Java programming merges with web sources to give an access and browsing structure of the data in which its data nodes are carried out.

MongoDB

MongoDB is a NoSQL database from which data manager of a documental sort of non-relational database. Exchange of data is performed by means of BSON. For a text file, data structuring and Mapping are implemented using binary representation (Yenkar, Bartere, 2014). NoSQL data manager is written in C++ programming. Characteristics structures are as follows:

- Lithe Data Storage is supported by JSON and does not need any priority scheme
- Many numbers of indexes are initiated in order to use it however, it is not essential to use or define MapReduce or parallel processes
- MongoDB performs the replication and scalability for highly efficient processing. this property is continued when there is an increasing number of the machine.
- In query conceptive, they have high performance with updating and processing. The query is based on documents.

Big Data Analytics Tools and Methods

Big- Data, Analytics, and Decision (B-DAD) are supported by big data tools and methods in the decision-making process. This framework is categories big data into few such as Storage, management and processing tools which help the methods to visualize and evaluate in different levels of decision making. These methods have three main levels such as Big Data Storage and architecture, Data and analytics processing, Big data analysis Kamat, Singh, 2013). These levels incorporate from knowledge discovery where a still lot of research is needed in finding suitable tools in developing the big data tools.

BIG DATA STORAGE AND MANAGEMENT

When dealing with big data the foremost time in the process is handling the data to be placed in correct storage or acquired. A relational database, data marts, and data warehouse are traditional methods to store and retrieve the structured data. Data admitted in big data storage using the general phenomenon of Extract, Transform, Load (ETL) or Extract, Load, Transform (ELT) data are added from the resources. This is done in order to clean and then been fatigued before the data mining and online analytical functions (Katal, Wazid, Goudar, 2013).

Traditional enterprise data warehouse (TDW) have a lot of disadvantage in admitting new data sources of different forms (unstructured and semi-structured data) so Big data introduces Magnetic, Agile, Deep (MAD) analysis to clear all disadvantage to the traditional relational database. This resource attracts by all data sources by its storage quantity and requires the agile database to help in data evolution. Massive Parallel Processing (MPP) database gives a solution to distributing system where it provides rapid query performance with respect to the velocity of the data transferred. To solve this type of issues with semi-structured and unstructured data, NoSQL (Not only SQL) is developed in storing the different types of data. The main aim is to store massive data, with scaling, flexibility in data models.

Big Data Storage Concepts

The most important concepts in Big Data tools is Big data storage. When there is a massive generation of data, leads to a large volume of data storage, so here come the Big Data storage concepts. Some key concepts involved in Big Data storage are Data Models, Data partitioning, Data Replication, and Data Persistence.

1. **Data Models:** For accessing and manipulation of data in Big Data technology uses various data models such as Relational model, NoSQL database model, Graph based model and Schema based model. Relational model (Chen, Mao, Liu, 2014) is ancient and widely used model proposed in 1960 by Edgar F Codd. He suggested in the model as represented in terms of tuples (or records), group (table) connected with a specific key, database combined with relational model lead to outcome and usage of Structured Query Language (SQL) to define and access data. Consequently, Big Data technologies support database model which does not relate to the relational model. They are defined as NoSQL database. They pertain attribute key, key based model support to all data type (integer, character, byte). Another important data model supporting Big Data Technologies is graph data model. They are denoted by nodes and links or edges. Graph data model solves many different problems like computing line is, getting cycle like a relationship supporting the connection etc. Graph model has much application used in real life Use cases when we compare to other models. Some of the real-life applications are customer network, social media, and payment transaction networks etc.

Big Data Technologies are developed on a new concept known as 'Schema and Read' which is based on run time models definition. When data are available in the data store, they moved into data models getting into reading mode. This concept is best game changer when we compared with traditional DB Technologies reading a data to be well defined.

2. **Data Partitioning:** All data in the data store cannot be stored in the single system so partition concept can be implemented. In Big Data technologies, some approaches methods to partition the data are implemented across various nodes. Accessing and data modeled are done by value/ or key for partition by key. The following table explains the various type of scheme in Data partition.

Data partition in data node is typically identifying in following approaches such as the First Approach- writing on the node which is local to the client program. This approach is used by Block partition. Second Approach- Identifying the key node. This approach is applicable to hash partition, Round Robin partition, and random partition. The third Approach- they are used by Range Partition, List partition, Tag partition. The fourth Approach- data is allocated with selected data with the same node based on reference key/Foreign key.

Table 2. Types of data partitioning

S. No.	Types	Description
1	Range Partition	Partition based on range of an attribute key
2	Hash Partition	Hash function applied to one or more attribute
3	Random Partition	Assigning keys in a random manner
4	Round Robin Partition	Assigning keys to node in round robin mechanism
5	Tag based partition	Based on tag or data, keys are grouped in logical partition
6	Block based Partition	Data stored and accessed in bulk without any predefined schema.

3. **Data Replication:** Data replication is a common characteristic of all methods in Big Data Technologies. Replication gradually increased the data availability and provides redundancy when it is different, and many copies of data are stored in nodes. This helps in increasing the availability and locality of data in query processing in distributed systems. There are three types of replica that take care of most of the failure in data replication. The first replica is defined putting in a rack from one replica into another same partition. Second replica- data required in emergency and recovery put into the different data center.

4. **Data Compression:** The basic problem arises in Big Data are storing and processing of large volume of data, thus compression technique has been considered even before the data are in large. Many different ways are introduced to data compression techniques initially it reduces the volume/size of the data. This denotes low storage needs lower time to read and write the data from disk. Secondly, use of network bandwidth which large data process needs to move from one to other. Compression which is also defined as split and define ability in reading and writing the data. Traditionally compression technology has lot of limitation when Big Data Technology is processing by the compression Technique (Kamat, Singh, 2013).

5. **Data Persistence:** Data persistence is one of the substantial features of Big Data Technologies as for network involving the system for high performance and processing and also for disk input and output data in accessing large data. Data Persistence is implemented in two dominant ways. First Approach Data persistence is used to store the data in the local hard disk of each data node. The second Approach holds Distributed Filesystem APIs for implementing the generic set of distributed files and also ensure all product/ vendor in Quality of service. This approach gives vital solution for Big data. Implementation is done in two types for Distribution file system. In a traditional database system, data are stored in a shared local disk of the data node.

OTHER BIG DATA PROCESSING TOOLS AND METHODS

Apache Group established Apache Software Foundation (ASF) in June 1999 held in Delaware, U.S. ASF is an open source form for software developers. They started developing in terms of Apache Free license providing distribution open source (Apache Software Foundation, n.d.). Projects of Apache are characterized by consumer-based development, collaborative and an open and pragmatic software license. Apache Software Foundation is denoted as a second generation open source organization providing security working without any risk to the platform. Each and every project in ASF is organized by a team of experts with good sound of knowledge. There are some volunteers who dedicatedly working in Apache project who contribute in large number.

The quick time stamp of Apache software foundation in related with Apache HTTP server which is established in early 1993. A small group of eight developers working to strengthen NCSA HTTP Daemon are the ones who designed Apache group on March 25, 1999. Early a members of Apache Software Foundation (ASF) projects are Behlendorf, KenCoar, Mignel Gonzales, Mark Cox, Lars Eilebrecht, Ben Hyde, Ralf S. Engelschall, Roy T. Fielding, Dean Gaudet, Ben Hyde, Jim Jagielski, Alexi Kosut, Martin Kraemer, Sameer parekh, Cliff Skolnick, Marc Slemko, William Stoddord, Paul Sutton, Randy Terbush and Dirk-Willen Van Gulik. They conducted a first official meeting on April 13, 1999. Later after a serial of the meeting, the elected board members formed a legal board committee as Apache Software Foundation as a corporation on June 1, 1999. The name "Apache" is selected from an American native people who were well known for greater skills in the strategy of wars and endurance (Apache Airvata, n.d.). ASF started releasing so many softwares and started calling themselves as Apache Group.

Table 3 shows a list of Apache Software tools developed for Dealing with Big Data Technologies.

PROGRAMMING FOR BIG DATA

There are various programs helpful for big data processing the foremost distinguished and powerful languages are R, Python, Java, Storm, etc. Python is extremely helpful to programmers for doing statistics and economic manipulation of applied mathematics data. This includes usually vectors, lists, and data frames that represent data sets organized in rows and columns, Whereas R, outshines in the range of applied mathematics libraries it compromises. Most applied mathematics tests/methods area unit a part of associate degree R library. It's terribly straightforward to be told language with an enormous quantity of inherent methods. NumPy library in Python encompasses homogenized, a two-dimensional array that gives numerous ways for information manipulation. it's many functions for activity advanced arithmetic and statistics Java and Storm additionally play a major role in massive information programming.

RESEARCH GAP

The research gap in of big data Tools and Platforms is ever-changing speedily. It's not solely obtaining oil-fired by the innovations happening within the open supply world however additionally having support from the licensed product world in maturing those innovations for the mainstream use. The prevailing technologies are becoming richer in terms of options and stability quarterly. At the same time, the frequent emergence of latest tools and frameworks fostering different paradigms in big data computation is creating the prevailing ones stale. In NoSQL database gap technologies like Foundation dB and cockroach DB are to be watched for. The support for acid and multiple data models will create Foundation dB selection for numerous use cases. On the opposite hand cockroach, dB is double-geared to resolve real distributed transaction issues alongside different NoSQL options.

Table 3. Detailed description about Apache software developed for Big Data

S. No.	Apache Tools	Short Description	Category	Data File	Programming Language	Release Year	Latest Version
1	Airavata (Apache Airvata, n.d.)	Airavata is a software framework, mini- service architecture used to implement and manage the flow of work and reckoning job. They use distributed computing resources.	Cloud, Big data and network-server	DOAP RDF (json)	Java	2014	V 0.11
2	Ambari (Apache Ambari, 2015)	Software Framework to process Hadoop cluster and other data processing domains.	Big data	DOAP RDF (json)	Java, Python and JavaScript	2014	V 1.5.0
3	Apex (Apache Apex, n.d.)	Batch processing Search engine	Big-Data	DOAP RDF (json)	Java	2016	V 3.7.0
4	Avro (Apache Avro, 2015)	Data Serialization System	Library, Big-Data	DOAP RDF (json)	C, C++, C#, Java, PHP, Python, Ruby	2012	V 1.7.2
5	Beam (Apache Beam, n.d.)	Programming model runs with data processing pipelines	Big-Data	DOAP RDF (JSON)	Java, Python	2014	V 2.0.0
6	Bigtop (Apache BigTop, n.d.)	Community- driven BigData management platform	Big-Data	DOAP RDF (json)	Java	2016	V 1.2.0
7	BookKeeper (Apache BookKeeper, n.d.)	Authentic Log service	Big-data	DOAP RDF (json)	Java	2014	V 4.3.0
8	Calcite (Apache Calcite, n.d.)	Dynamic data Management Framework	Big-Data, Hadoop, SQL	DOAP RDF (JSON)	Java	2013	V1.13.0
9	Couch DB (Apache Couch DB, n.d.)	NoSQL- Database using JSON and MapReduce and HTTP	Database, Big-data	DOAP RDF (json)	JavaScript, Erlang, C++,C	2014	V 1.6.1
10	Crunch (Apache Crunch, n.d.)	The framework used to implement writing, testing and running MapReduce pipelines.	Big-Data Library	DOAP RDF (json)	Java and Scala	2011	V 0.5.0
11	DataFu (Apache DataFu, n.d.)	Consist of two library- pig and hourglass. This works for data mining and statistics	Big-Data Incubating	DOAP RDF (JSON)	Java	2015	V 1.3.0
12	Drill (Apache Drill, 2015)	Query language as distributed SQL MPP with Hadoop and NoSQL	Big- data	DOAP RDF (json)	Java	2014	V 0.7.0
13	Edgent (Apache Edgent, n.d.)	It is programming model used for streaming process to execute analytics	Big-Data, Library, Mobile network client	DOAP RDF (JSON)	Java, JavaScript	2016	V 1.0.0
14	Falcon (Apache Falcon, 2015)	Platform for Data management and processing	Big-Data Incubating	DOAP RDF (json)	Java	2014	V 0.7.0
15	Flink (Apache Flink, 2015)	Rapid and trustworthy for voluminous scale data processing	Big-Data	DOAP RDF (JSON)	Java and Scala	2017	V 1.2.7
16	Flume (Apache Flume, 2015)	Flume is trustworthy, distributed, efficient, aggregation to store data in a centralized manner	Big-Data	DOAP RDF (JSON)	Java	2014	V 1.5.0
17	Giraph (Apache Giraph, 2015)	Giraph is developed to high scalability and iterative graph processing	Big-Data	DOAP RDF (JSON)	Java	2016	V 1.2.0
18	Hama (Apache Hama, n.d.)	Hama consist of BSP computing engine	Big-data	DOAP RDF (json)	Java	2014	V 0.6.4
19	Helix (Appache Helix, n.d.)	Framework uses clustering analysis for data partition and replication data resources	Big-Data	DOAP RDF (JSON)	Java	2016	V 0.6.8
20	Ignite (Apache Ignite, 2015)	Ignite is In-Memory Data providing processing, querying components	Big-Data, SQL, Cloud, OSGi IoT	DOAP RDF (JSON)	Java, C#, C++, SQL, JDBC, and ODBC	2015	V 1.5.0
21	Kafka (Apache Kafka, 2015)	Open source programming provides distributed fault tolerance	Big-Data	DOAP RDF (JSON)	Scala, Java	2011	V 0.10.2.1
22	Knox (Apache Knox, n.d.)	API gateway to Hadoop service	Big-Data, Hadoop	DOAP RDF (JSON)	Java	2014	V 0.4.0
23	Lens (Apache Lens, n.d.)	Provides Unified Analytics interface	Big-Data	DOAP RDF (JSON)	Java	2015	V 2.6.1

continued on following page

Table 1. Continued

S. No.	Apache Tools	Short Description	Category	Data File	Programming Language	Release Year	Latest Version
24	MetaModal (Apache MetaModal, n.d.)	Put forth uniform connector, query API to various Datastore Types	Database, Big-Data library	DOAP RDF (JSON)	Java	2014	V 4.3.1
25	Oozie (Apache Oozie, 2015)	Workflow scheduler to access Hadoop jobs	Big-Data	DOAP RDF (JSON)	Java, JavaScript	2014	V 4.3.0
26	ORC (Apache ORC, n.d.)	Columnar File format for Hadoop jobs	Big-Data, Database, Hadoop library	DOAP RDF (json)	Java, C++	2016	V 1.2.1
27	Phoenix (Apache Phoenix, 2015)	Provides OLTP and operational analytics for Sql	Big-Data, Database	DOAP RDF (json)	Java, SQL	2016	V 4.7.0
28	REEF (Apache REEF, n.d.)	Retainable Evaluator Execution framework(REEF) is Framework to control for scheduling and coordination	Big-Data	DOAP RDF (json)	Java, C#, C++	2016	V 0.15.0
29	Parquet (Apache Parquet, 2015)	Parquet is a columnar storage format	Big-Data	DOAP RDF (json)	Java	2015	V 1.6.0
30	Samza (Apache Samza, n.d.)	Samza executes Stream processing task.	Big-Data	DOAP RDF (json)	SCALA	2014	V 0.8.0
31	Spark (Apache Spark Streaming, 2015)	Spark is rapid speed and efficient in handling data stream processing for large-scale data	Big-Data	DOAP RDF (JSON)	Java. Scala, Python	2014	V 2.1.1
32	Sqoop (Apache Sqoop, 2015)	Sqoop is tools which help to process and transfer a massive amount of data in Hadoop and relational database.	Big-Data	DOAP RDF (json)	Java	2014	V 1.4.5
33	Storm (Apache Storm, n.d.)	The storm is framework used for doing distributed real-time computation system through batch processing.	Big-Data	DOAP RDF (json)	Java	2015	V 0.9.5
34	Tajo (Apache Tajo, n.d.)	It is an open source big data Warehouse system	Big-Data, Database	DOAP RDF (JSON)	Java	2013	V0.11.3
35	Tez (Apache Tez, 2015)	Framework to develop generic application to process Direct Acyclic Graph (DAG)	Big-Data	DOAP RDF (JSON)	Java	2014	V 0.8.5
36	VXQuery (Appache VXQuery, n.d.)	VXQuery is XML query processor to evaluate massive data collection	Big data, XML	DOAP RDF (json)	Java	2015	V 0.6
37	Zeppelin (Zeppelin, 2015)	Zeppelin is visualization tool for data analytics to exploration of data	Big data	DOAP RDF (JSON)	Java, JavaScript, and Scala	2015	V 0.7.1
38	Chukwa (Apache Chukwa, n.d.)	Chukwa is an open source programming framework for surveillance the large dataset	Hadoop	DOAP RDF (JSON)	Java, JavaScript	2012	V 0.5.0
39	Pig (Apache Pig, 2015)	Pig is framework to evaluate large data set on Hadoop	Database	DOAP RDF (json)	Java	2008	V0.16.0
40	Accumulo (Apache Accumulo, n.d.)	Accumulo is based in Google Big Table which stores distributed key values at various data management system	Database	DOAP RDF (json)	Java	2011	V 1.8.1
41	Cassandra (Apache Cassandra, 2015)	Cassandra helps in scalability, high availability without any adjustment.	Database	DOAP RDF (json)	Java	2008	V 3.10
42	ZooKeeper (Apache ZooKeeper, n.d.)	ZooKeeper is framework used for data coordination	Database	DOAP RDF (json)	Java	2015	V3.4.10
43	Curator (Apache Curator, n.d.)	Java libraries additional to ZooKeeper in executing	Database	DOAP RDF (json)	Java	2016	V 3.5.0
44	Gora (Apache Gora, n.d.)	Gora supports column based support and helps in In-memory data model	Database	DOAP RDF (JSON)	Java	2014	V 0.5
45	Hbase (Apache Hbase, 2015)	HBase is a Hadoop Database for big data storage processing	Big-Data Database	DOAP RDF (JSON)	Java	2010	V 1.2.6
46	Hive (Apache Hive, n.d.)	Hive is a framework to process querying and maintain the large datasets in distributed system.	Big-Data, Database	DOAP RDF (json)	Java	2013	V 2.1.1

On the opposite hand, the Spark from Berkeley Data Analytics Stack is rising out as a robust contestant to varied Distributed processing components (and corresponding Application Components) in the Hadoop system. At identical time industry has also seen Flink, the contestant to Spark. Flink is still less matured compared to Spark and only time can say which one is going to win during this area. Tachyon is another promising technology happening in Berkeley Data Analytics Stack.

CONCLUSION

A modified paradigm of contemporary business and are advancement in communication and technology has given a brand-new face to the analytics. Just like the light-weight fastening in computers, currently people would like super-fast deciding and it's attainable with big data analytics. Advancement in tools and technologies created it attainable. Best practices have emerged to assist huge data processing. a stimulating truth is that a lot of those practices are the new empowered, versatile extensions of the old one. the biggest issue behind the recognition of big data analysis is that it helps a company to require corrective actions and helpful choices while not a lot of data processing latency. Thus, big data allows call capability, nearly in run time setting.

REFERENCES

Apache O.R.C. (n.d.). the smallest, fastest columnar storage for Hadoop workloads. Retrieved from https://orc.apache.org/

Apache REEF. (n.d.). Apache REEF™ - a stdlib for Big Data. Retrieved from http://reef.apache.org/

Apache Accumulo. (n.d.). Apache Accumulo. Retrieved from https://accumulo.apache.org/

Apache Airavata. (n.d.). Apache Airavata. Retrieved from https://airavata.apache.org/

Apache Ambari. (2015, August). Apache Ambari. Retrieved from https://ambari.apache.org

Apache Apex. (n.d.). Apache Apex. Retrieved from https://apex.apache.org/

Apache Avro. (2015, August 6). Welcome to Avro. Retrieved from http://avro.apache.org/docs/1.3.0/

Apache Beam. (n.d.). Apache Beam: An advanced unified programming model. Retrieved from https://beam.apache.org/

Apache BigTop. (n.d.). Apache Bigtop. Retrieved from http://bigtop.apache.org/

Apache BookKeeper. (n.d.). Apache BookKeeper. Retrieved from http://bookkeeper.apache.org/

Apache Calcite. (n.d.). The foundation for your next high-performance database. Retrieved from https://calcite.apache.org/

Apache Cassandra. (2015, August 6). Manage massive amounts of data, fast, without losing sleep. Retrieved from: http://cassandra.apache.org/

Apache Chukwa, (n.d.). Overview. Retrieved from: https://chukwa.apache.org/docs/r0.8.0/

Apache Couch DB. (n.d.). Data Where You Need It. Retrieved from http://couchdb.apache.org/

Apache Crunch. (n.d.). Getting Started. Retrieved from https://crunch.apache.org/getting-started.html

Apache Curator. (n.d.). Welcome to Apache Curator. Retrieved from: http://curator.apache.org/

Apache DataFu. (n.d.). Apache DataFu. Retrieved from https://datafu.incubator.apache.org/

Apache Drill. (2015, August 6). Apache Drill. Retrieved from http://drill.apache.org/

Apache Edgent. (n.d.). Apache Edgent a Community for Accelerating Analytics at the Edge. Retrieved from http://edgent.apache.org/

Apache Falcon. (2015, August 6). Falcon - Feed management and data processing platform. Retrieved from http://falcon.apache.org/index.html

Apache Flink. (2015, August 6). Introduction to Apache Flink. Retrieved from https://flink.apache.org/

Apache Flume. (2015, August 6). Welcome to Apache Flume. Retrieved from https://flume.apache.org/

Apache Giraph. (2015, August 6). Welcome to Apache Giraph. Retrieved from http://giraph.apache.org/

Apache Gora, (n.d.). Welcome to the Apache Gora project. Retrieved from: https://gora.apache.org/

Apache Hama, (n.d.). Apache Hama. Retrieved from https://hama.apache.org/

Apache Hbase. (2015, August 6). Welcome to Apache HBase. Retrieved from: http://hbase.apache.org/

Apache Helix, (n.d.). Helix A cluster management framework for partitioned and replicated distributed sources. Retrieved from http://helix.apache.org/

Apache Hive, (n.d.). Home. Retrieved from: https://cwiki.apache.org/confluence/display/Hive/Home

Apache Ignite. (2015, August 6). Database and Caching Platform. Retrieved from https://ignite.incubator.apache.org/

Apache Kafka. (2015, August 6). Documentation. Retrieved from http://kafka.apache.org/documentation.html

Apache Knox, (n.d.). REST API and Application Gateway for the Apache Hadoop Ecosystem. Retrieved from https://knox.apache.org/

Apache Lens, (n.d.). Welcome to Lens. Retrieved from https://lens.apache.org/

Apache Metamodal, (n.d.). Apache MetaModel. Retrieved from http://metamodel.apache.org/

Apache Oozie. (2015, August 6). Apache Oozie Workflow Scheduler for Hadoop. Retrieved from http://oozie.apache.org/

Apache Parquet. (2015, August 6). Parquet. Retrieved from http://parquet.apache.org/

Apache Phoenix. (2015, August 6). Overview. Retrieved from http://phoenix.apache.org/

Apache Pig. (2015, August 6). Welcome to Apache Pig. Retrieved from: https://pig.apache.org/

Apache Samza, (n.d.). What is Samza? Retrieved from http://samza.apache.org/

Apache Software Foundation. (n.d.). Apache Software Foundation. Retrieved from http://en.wikipedia.org/wiki/Apache_Software_Foundation

Apache Spark Streaming. (2015, August 6). Apache Spark Streaming. Retrieved from https://spark.apache.org/streaming/

Apache Sqoop. (2015, August 6). Apache Sqoop. Retrieved from http://sqoop.apache.org/

Apache Storm. (n.d.). Storm Distributed and Fault-Tolerant Realtime Computation. Retrieved from: http://storm-project.net/

Apache Tajo. (n.d.). Apache Tajo: A big data warehouse system on Hadoop. Retrieved from http://tajo.apache.org/

Apache Tez. (2015, August 6). Introduction. Retrieved from http://tez.apache.org/

Apache VXQuery. (n.d.). Apache VXQuery. Retrieved from: https://vxquery.apache.org/

Apache Zeppelin. (2015, August 6). Apache Zeppelin. Retrieved from: https://zeppelin.incubator.apache.org/

Apache ZooKeeper. (n.d.). General Information. Retrieved from: https://cwiki.apache.org/confluence/display/ZOOKEEPER/Index

Bakshi, K. (2012, March). Considerations for big data: Architecture and approach. In *Proceedings of 2012 IEEE Aerospace Conference*. IEEE. 10.1109/AERO.2012.6187357

Borthakur, D. (2007). The hadoop distributed file system: Architecture and design. *Hadoop Project Website*, *11*, 21.

Boyd, D., & Crawford, K. (2012). Critical questions for big data: Provocations for a cultural, technological, and scholarly phenomenon. *Information Communication and Society*, *15*(5), 662–679. doi:10.1080/1369118X.2012.678878

Chen, M., Mao, S., & Liu, Y. (2014). Big data: A survey. *Mobile Networks and Applications*, *19*(2), 171–209. doi:10.100711036-013-0489-0

Demchenko, Y., Ngo, C., de Laat, C., Membrey, P., & Gordijenko, D. (2013, August). Big security for big data: Addressing security challenges for the big data infrastructure. In *Workshop on Secure Data Management* (pp. 76-94). Springer.

Dou, W., Zhang, X., Liu, J., & Chen, J. (2015). HireSome-II: Towards privacy-aware cross-cloud service composition for big data applications. *IEEE Transactions on Parallel and Distributed Systems*, *26*(2), 455–466. doi:10.1109/TPDS.2013.246

Elgendy, N., & Elragal, A. (2014, July). Big data analytics: a literature review paper. In *Industrial Conference on Data Mining* (pp. 214-227). Springer, Cham. 10.1007/978-3-319-08976-8_16

Elgendy, N., & Elragal, A. (2016). Big Data Analytics in Support of the Decision Making Process. *Procedia Computer Science*, *100*, 1071–1084. doi:10.1016/j.procs.2016.09.251

Fayyad, U., Piatetsky-Shapiro, G., & Smyth, P. (1996). From data mining to knowledge discovery in databases. *AI Magazine*, *17*(3), 37.

Gilbert, S., & Lynch, N. (2012). Perspectives on the CAP Theorem. *Computer*, *45*(2), 30–36. doi:10.1109/MC.2011.389

Hartmann, P. M., Zaki, M., Feldmann, N., & Neely, A. (2014, March 27). Big data for big business? A taxonomy of data-driven business models used by start-up firms. *A Taxonomy of Data-Driven Business Models Used by Start-Up Firms*.

Hinton, G. E., Osindero, S., & Teh, Y. W. (2006). A fast learning algorithm for deep belief nets. *Neural Computation*, *18*(7), 1527–1554. doi:10.1162/neco.2006.18.7.1527

Jagadish, H. V., Gehrke, J., Labrinidis, A., Papakonstantinou, Y., Patel, J. M., Ramakrishnan, R., & Shahabi, C. (2014). Big data and its technical challenges. *Communications of the ACM*, *57*(7), 86–94. doi:10.1145/2611567

Jamshidi, M., Tannahill, B., Yetis, Y., & Kaplan, H. (2015). Big data analytic via soft computing paradigms. In *Frontiers of higher order fuzzy sets* (pp. 229–258). Springer New York. doi:10.1007/978-1-4614-3442-9_12

Jeong, Y. S., & Shin, S. S. (2016). An Efficient Authentication Scheme to Protect User Privacy in Seamless Big Data Services. *Wireless Personal Communications*, *86*(1), 7–19. Retrieved from http://web.a.ebscohost.com/abstract?direct=true&profile=ehost&scope=site&authtype=crawler&jrnl=09296212&AN=111455684&h=7IFKiKh0Lg%2fy2FHp%2b55gtkcsVzZJxAEGRQ15KxUutmue2vo481ON7i1qe1jDHwu%2fkZg0y%2b7wVoBerrtIukr5PQ%3d%3d&crl=c&resultNs=AdminWebAuth&resultLocal=ErrCrlNotAuth&crlhashurl=login.aspx%3fdirect%3dtrue%26profile%3dehost%26scope%3dsite%26authtype%3dcrawler%26jrnl%3d09296212%26AN%3d111455684 doi:10.100711277-015-2990-1

Kamat, G., & Singh, S. (2013). Comparisons of compression. In: Hadoop Summit 2013. Retrieved from http://www.slideshare.net/Hadoop_Summit/kamat-singh-june27425pmroom210cv2

Katal, A., Wazid, M., & Goudar, R. H. (2013, August). Big data: issues, challenges, tools and good practices. In *2013 Sixth International Conference on Contemporary Computing (IC3)* (pp. 404-409). IEEE. 10.1109/IC3.2013.6612229

Liu, Y., Wu, B., Wang, H., & Ma, P. (2014). Bpgm: A big graph mining tool. *Tsinghua Science and Technology*, *19*(1), 33–38. doi:10.1109/TST.2014.6733206

Mazumder, S. (2016). Big Data Tools and Platforms. In Big Data Concepts, Theories, and Applications (pp. 29-128). Springer International Publishing. doi:10.1007/978-3-319-27763-9_2

Meng, S., Dou, W., Zhang, X., & Chen, J. (2014). KASR: A keyword-aware service recommendation method on mapreduce for big data applications. *IEEE Transactions on Parallel and Distributed Systems*, *25*(12), 3221–3231. doi:10.1109/TPDS.2013.2297117

Miller, J. A., Ramaswamy, L., Kochut, K. J., & Fard, A. (2015, June). Research directions for big data graph analytics. In *2015 IEEE International Congress on Big Data (BigData Congress)* (pp. 785-794). IEEE. 10.1109/BigDataCongress.2015.132

Miloslavskaya, N., & Tolstoy, A. (2016). Big Data, Fast Data and Data Lake Concepts. *Procedia Computer Science*, *88*, 300–305. Retrieved from https://ac.els-cdn.com/S1877050916316957/1-s2.0-S1877050916316957-main.pdf?_tid=4d5629d4-ff7f-11e7-bdfe-00000aab0f6c&acdnat=1516630968_7bf0960c12ee94bb5d00caa036126bfc doi:10.1016/j.procs.2016.07.439

Purcell, B. (2013). The emergence of" big data" technology and analytics. *Journal of technology research, 4*, 1.

Sánchez, D., Martín-Bautista, M. J., Blanco, I., & de la Torre, C. J. (2008, December). Text knowledge mining: an alternative to text data mining. In *IEEE International Conference on Data Mining Workshops ICDMW '08* (pp. 664-672). IEEE. 10.1109/ICDMW.2008.57

Sánchez, D., Martín-Bautista, M. J., Blanco, I., & de la Torre, C. J. (2008, December). Text knowledge mining: an alternative to text data mining. In *IEEE International Conference on Data Mining Workshops ICDMW '08* (pp. 664-672). IEEE.

Smith, L. I. (2002). A tutorial on principal components analysis. *Cornell University, 51*(52), 65.

Tannahill, B. K. (2014). Big Data Analytic Techniques: Predicting Renewable Energy Capacity to Facilitate the Optimization of Power Plant Energy Trading and Control Algorithms.

Yenkar, V., & Bartere, M. (2014). Review on "Data Mining with Big Data". *International Journal of Computer Science and Mobile Computing, 3*(4), 97–102.

Chapter 12
Recent Development in Big Data Analytics:
Research Perspective

M. Sandeep Kumar
Vellore Institute of Technology, India

Prabhu J.
Vellore Institute of Technology, India

ABSTRACT

This chapter describes how big data consist of an extreme volume of data, velocity, and more complex variable data that demands current technology changes in capturing, storage, distribution, management, analysis data. Business facing more struggles in identifying the pragmatic approach in capturing the data about customer, products, and services. Usage of big data mainly with the analytical method, but it specifically compares with features of an analytical method based on unstructured data contributed around 95% of big data. The analytical approach depends on heterogeneous data and unstructured data's like text, audio, video format. It demands new effective tool for predictive analysis for big data with the unstructured format. This chapter describes explanation of big data and characteristics of big data compress of Volume, Velocity, Variety, Variability, and Value. Recent trends in the development of big data that applies in real time application perspectives like health care agriculture, education etc.

INTRODUCTION

Big data is a current trend and future research area in today's scenario. Savitz and Gartner (2012) point out some ten strategic technologies and in 2013 describe the next five years of critical technologies in big data. Big data is revolutionary in most domains like Businesses, specific research, Public, and Management. The standard definition of big data compresses from 3Vs to 4Vs. Doug Laney, (2001) describes only 3Vs such as Volume, Velocity, and Variety it provides some dynamic characteristics of

DOI: 10.4018/978-1-5225-4044-1.ch012

big data. The term Volume refers to more datasets, Velocity specific in and out about speed of data, and Variety relates to types of data sources. Zikopoulos & Eaton (2011) enhance the characteristics of big data with 4vs: Value, Variability and Virtual. More Commonly, big Data refers to large datasets with various types, which are difficult to process in a traditional data processing infrastructure. Garter et al. (2012) acquired and analyzed the data in more detail, explaining that big data has these characteristics: large volume, high velocity, and wide variety.

Common datasets are called big data when it can perform in capturing, curation, and visualization with current technologies. Modern use of intelligent data analysis techniques combined with existing domains, such as Artificial intelligence (AI) and Machine Learning (ML), offer the capability to process a significant amount of unstructured data that is generated day by day to extract valuable, actionable knowledge. It also provides more opportunity for many researchers to make use of this data for improving their valuable expertise and insights (Hilbert 2013). As such, big data development is essential in accessing and gaining data related to the user; it provides more exclusive data from the government in the form of a document. Moreover, there has been new growth in something called open access or open data, which consists of both public and private data. In public data, shared data from different public entries need to be converted to a machine-readable format or structure to further big data development. As stated in Chatterjee & Finger's (2014) current report analysis by Mckinsey Global Institute, open data calculates up to $3 trillion. The Report analysis is an essential part of public data with several specific fields: education, health, consumer product, transportation, electricity, oil, gas, and consumer finance.

The primary goal of this chapter is to answers the necessary questions: what is the use of big data technology in the emerging, developing world? Specifically, analysis of the application of big data techniques helps to improve and point out even the most delicate improvement areas that offer the advantage of using big data technologies. Doshi et al. (2013), Mayer-Schönberger, & Cukier (2013) mostly depend on consistency given the tremendous influence of big data with some other facts in current society. Big data is the sizeable essential domain of human improvement. We ask some questions like: A) How can we use complete data that can explain and allow most companies and organizations to improve? B) What are the specific fields that can benefit from big data? C) What are some well-known techniques used in big data analytics that can further develop and improve big data?

BIG DATA DEVELOPMENT AREAS

This section describes the primary development field to which big data applies. We describe the role of big data for development and explored with natural disasters and political crises. Additionally, humanitarians show how big data is used in fields like agriculture, healthcare, education, etc. We also examine the tabulation for determining big data projects with various development areas.

Humanitarian Emergencies

In this section, we use a case study to present the potential role of big data concerning emergencies and natural disasters. We also describe various issues with the acquisition, storage, and sharing of the essential data for emergency situations.

Figure 1. Big Data development areas

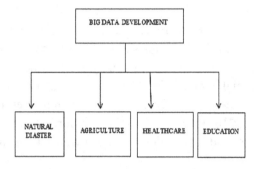

Natural Disasters

Meier (2015) specifies the necessary and vital role in using big data for natural disasters affect in part of the world. When an earthquake occurred in Haiti in 2010, most of the online community played a role in helping to fight the disasters by spreading information about the disaster and the ways people could help. They did this by crowdsourcing, using real-world imaging, and criticism mapping. Big data techniques, both AI (Artificial intelligence) and ML (Machine learning), were deployed for identifying the substance of vast and quick alternation in online data comprising of tweets and SMS. This mainly generates after the disasters occurr. Meier (2015) calls member of the humanitarian community in for making the disaster digitalized. It describes the importance of big data criticism; nature does not vary from the usual concept of big data except when it assembles the time and duration of the crisis or disaster. By using the analytical approach with ML tools and methods, needed action information will be extracted from those data, and provide an overview of the essential challenges and harms that were used big data criticism. Most necessary among that, there is the credibility of data. Connecting with proliferated digital devices and current trends can be easily generated or accessed. Finally, we describe the effect of using the both AI and ML approaches in verifying the data.

Agriculture

Kshetri (2014) analyzes the factors that contribute to the usage of big data techniques in development along with the inhibitor for processing. The necessity of a modern data source, like that of social media and getting data from mobile devices is also defined. Skill is a capacity that provides data in a given culture and industrializes the processes for using the modern technology; it results with non-uniform diffusion for making innovative technology and creates new trends in the process. We describe an agricultural case study and its challenges. The opportunity deployed in big data technology for making farmer in the development process. Most developing countries farmers are rarely without information about the content of the soil, changes in weather pattern, growth, and access to markets. Most of the data is collected by using sensors and satellite imagery with the help of field expertise in analyzing and predicting the growth of crops. The predictive model used for farming and obtaining necessary information is sent through the network to every farmer.

Healthcare

Big data analytics in healthcare provides more culture modifications in the way of a traditional operation method for diagnosis and treatment. Diagnosis is an evaluation of big data and integrates with data collections from different medical histories and also analyze real-time covering sensors for diagnosing the patient's history. It offers initial warning signs when diagnosis patients are in critical condition. By assisting in making preventive measures for diagnosing and treating potentially harmful diseases in their initial stages. Crowcroft et al. (2016) treats more efficiently for individuals by using a smartphone to access medical service providers and applications for healthcare; it gets a faster response and doesn't inconvenience individuals.

It is important for those in healthcare to embrace these modern, technology-driven trends because they combine medical science and data science to more effectively and efficiently treat patients. In the present scenario, most of the patients' data is stored in electronic form in various databases of different medical service providers. Nowadays, challenges for healthcare lie in the collection of data from the electronic forms, which place the information in multiple locations by representing types of fragments and offers incomplete images to similar medical care providers. Elhauge (2010) further explain that the challenging issues are integrated, then the fragments will be resolved and also have the democratization of prospective health information, by which analyzing diseases of growth is mixed with both medicine and data science. Integration can be more enhanced in analyses of the entire country for implementing the learning health system (LHS). Lohr (2015) offers faculties like policy-making and medical care. Both engineering and technology combined for analyzing the diseases quickly to provide accurately. This framework is essential in creating the surroundings of the research because clinical practices are not analyzed separately. Instead, in this new study, the report displays everything for patients in real-time. By enhancing this concept by covering the entire world, it offers valuable data about the current state of health in every country. It will also help to assess initial warning signs and access critical outbreaks. Using this enhancement will help to ensure that people receive appropriate medical assistance in the process of immunization vaccinations and other preventive measures are taken. Most of the existing system, the practical framework, develops the uses of big data technology for constructing the initial warning sign to the essential epidemic outbreak.

Education

Sullivan et al. (2014) describes the education field that made the transition for digital era by replacing physical textbooks with the digital versions and providing digitalized studying materials. Education is one of fields that will most benefit from the critical advantages of big data analytics. Conventional practices of students' learning, habits, and entire education frameworks are being developed and are always in search of more beneficial practices.

In specific, the practice of both online and blended learning is getting more popular. The conventional pedagogical approach/technique combined online teachings with blended learning and assessments.

There are two essential correlation of big data development in an educational framework. Picciano (2012) presents that those two things are: learning analytics and education data mining. In learning agile analytics development of a cross-disciplinary domain, it mixed data analytics and learning. Hence, it brings most of the researchers together from different fields of computer science, data science, and social science. In this area, most of the research is quantified for a different purpose that includes, but is not restricted to, predictive analysis, social network, and sentiment analysis, personalized learning and improved curriculum development. Educational data mining (EDM) is similar to LA (Learning analysis), it has new trends that are related to the educational domain. In EDM, both data mining and machine learning techniques are performed for data representing interaction with student contact and an online education framework, which could easily store the substantial online course called (MOOCs). Siemens, (2012, April) shows the online test that shows the student how they learn best. In the proliferation of digital services, it consumes more internet and social media. Most of internet users leave a data trail, which learns, records, and mines the interactions the user has online. With the student learning framework, it also assists in operating the experience of student learning systems. Crowcroft et al. (2016) creates data-driven products for educators on a user-friendly platform to connect the research outcome with real practices. International education data mining society offers the interface for the researcher to publish and implement the possible techniques and needs a solution based on data mining to efficiently learn and teach.

Moreover, LA and EDM have made changes to the traditional teaching and learning method. Various data-driven products are accessible for teachers to construct tests for students that are closely related based on student behavior and stages of understanding in collecting. The various aspects are analyzed and described at the end of the assessment process only. We get data similar to the student answers to multiple questions: how long a student will look at particular questions, how many times students used other links to understand the numerous issues that are gathered and finalized, and the visual analytical document will be given to the teachers. Teachers quickly find out which of the students excel with specific kinds of content and questions. Individual help can be provided to the student to enhance their performance and find where their issues lie. In a similar fashion, data from the various teachers are determined together.

BIG DATA TECHNIQUES

Collobert & Weston (2008, July) present advanced datasets called big data that varies with traditional datasets consisting of 3V's: Volume, Velocity, and Variety. Nowadays, a large volume of data is generated with more velocity and enormous data source are offer more variety in it. Entire data mainly rely on the information age. Actionable information is collected from data and performs an intelligent process in analytics. The technique, particularly related to machine learning, is associated with receiving, storing, processing, and analyzing the significant data. We also discuss with a various example namely, the "concept of Humanitarian development." The primary goal of this section is to briefly examine and relate the work used with a similar technique to help them understand the concept of applications and describe how they can aid in humanitarian development.

Machine Learning

Machine learning is part of artificial intelligence (AI) and its primary goal is to perform the computational framework to study data and how to determine the desired duty automatically. Machine learning

Table 1. Big data projects used in various development fields and tools used in big data analytics

Projects	Description	Type	Open Data
Humanitarian Growth			
Ushahidi	Crowdsourcing infrastructure is combined with different source for different humanitarian growth	Online Service	×
Digital Humanitarian Network	IT volunteers leverage technology fight with human crisis happen in network	Online Service	×
Trace the face	Crowdsource online infrastructure used to identify split migrants	Non-Profit	×
GNU coop	A network of IT professional to distribute information and interact technology for development.	Online Service	×
Open Street Map	For natural mapping crisis in region of service in real –time, crowdsourced and online	Non-Profit	×
Pakistan Body Count	Make use of user available data to plot causes of the suicide bomb and drone attacks.	Online Analysis	×
Services Advisor(UNHCR)	Real-time, interactive map services for integrated to identify aid agencies. Quickly to locate and operate.	Web App	
Health Care			
Personal Genome Project (PGP)	Due to research usage sharing of genomic data to the public.	Non-Profit	√
1000 Genomes project	It related to phenotypes and genotype in study of human genomes sequencing	Non-Profit	√
Google Flu trends	Currently inactive, but it offers data about flu and dengue affect regions.	Non-Profit	√
Data.gov	Open health data tools and its application in healthcare domain.	Governmental	√
UNGP(Health Projects)	Case study for education over the regions in world	Non-Profit	×
Health Data (The world bank)	Publicly available data from various research and studies.	Non-Profit	√
Individual Health Initiative(JHU)	Integrating and analysis different patient data from various resources from healthcare domain.	Academic	×
Human Connectome Project	Correct mapping of human connectome.	Non-Profit	√
Education			
PSLC Data Shop	Open data tools used for storing and learning data in mining education.	Non-Profit	√
Education Data Mining	R&D based on learning data mining of various education data.	Non-Profit	√
Data.Gov(Education)	Free data, tool, an app that related to education at all stages of US government.	Governmental	√
Education data	Case study related to education	Non-Profit	√
All tuition	Make use best educations for students and financial benefits offer for students.	Online Service	N/A
Simple Tuition	It offers similar to various financial opportunities given by educational institutes	Online Service	N/A
Mastery connect	Tools offer teacher for real-time processing and understanding each student.	Service Provider	N/A
Knowlton	Adaptive for managing both teaching and learning the individuals	Service Provider	N/A
Think CERCA	Personal online tool teaching tool, it used for teachers to describe and teach based on standards	Service Provider	N/A
UNGP (Education projects)		Non-Profit	
Miscellaneous			
Billion Prices Project	Data from many online retailers are needed to be analyzed for real-time research.	Academic	√
Predictify.me	Understanding of business growth and marketing based on data collection and predictive analytics.	Service Provider	×
Data-driven	Developing a product from various Organizations based on data.	Service Provider	×
First Mile Geo	Data collection, Visualization, and analysis are some platform utilized.	Service Provider	√
Data.gov	Offers open data for a various domain like health, education, and agriculture.	Governmental	√
UNGP	Provide for deploy technology and specifically for big data development	Non-Profit	
The World Bank(Data)	Offers open data from various studies and projects for different domain	Non-Profit	√
Weka	Deploy machine learning algorithm for analyzing large data.	Open Source Tool	N/A
Elastic Mao reduce(Amazon)	Data processing service for large datasets	Processing Tool	N/A

Figure 2. Big Data techniques

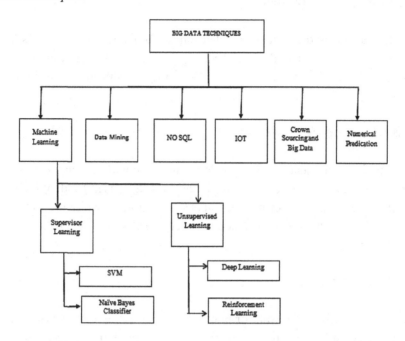

offers many applications like decision-making, forecasting, and predicting, which are some of the key technologies in deploying the data mining and big data techniques in various domains like healthcare, business, and finance. Mainly, machine learning is categorized into two important types.

Supervised Learning

In this class of machine learning, learning duty is assigned using a training set and labeling it "Supervisor," w consists of information regarding the class. For example, predictions can be made based on recent trends and data. When the output is assigned to continuous values and have issues in classification, we describe some classification and few approaches.

Naïve Bayes Classifiers

Knight (2015) depends on Bayes' theorem by assuming that independent features that allowed in class. Azuaje (2006) used internet traffic classification with an example of the naïve Bayesian classification in internet traffic.

Decision Trees (DT)

Decision Trees are mainly used for an intuitive approach that makes use of both learnings and predicting the features of the quantitative target's attributes and the nominal target's attributes. Moreover, DT will not perform adequately. The main advantages of intuitive interpretation are crucial when network operators are examined and interpret with classification methods and their outcomes.

Support Vector Machines (SVM)

SVM techniques are mostly used as supervised learning techniques because it has both practical and theoretical functions which are frequently used. SVM approach is rooted in a domain of statistical learning theory and systematic theory. For example, it offers unique result by concern with optimization of a concave relation.

Unsupervised Learning Techniques

It is mainly based on clustering, learning assigned to categorize without any need of a labeled dataset. An example of this is the cluster based on similarity aspects. It is used to identify the group of inputs that have similar characteristics. Clustering is unsupervised learning, while the supervised learning assumes the availability of a most excellent labeled data set; the unsupervised task is used to find out the right structure of the input.

Reinforcement Learning

Reinforcement learning is based on reward or punishment and it mainly consists of the ML technique. It finds the input received and runs with some actions, that are essential and pertain to its surrounding, then will be reward or punish. The primary goal of a learner is to describe the mapping from its effects in getting rewards or punishments. It is maximized based on the average long-term rewards.

Deep Learning

Smyth et al. (1996) & Leavitt (2010) describe deep learning as similar to machine learning, both compressed of the deep and more complex structure. The structure consists of more than one process layer; each of these as its ability to generate non-linear responses according to the input data. Layers consist of different small processors that perform in parallel with data processing offered, processors are also called neutrons. It gives efficient pattern recognition, image, and natural processing (Crowcroft, 2016). Deep learning identifies applications with broad spectrum applications ranging from healthcare to industry. Most of the critical technology in deploying the deep learning techniques are applied in making intelligent products for Google, IBM, Facebook, etc.

Association Rule Learning

Association rule learning describes fascinating relations between variables in the vast database. We know about the association between features at present with examples. Supervised learning is more strictly represented as a class of links combined with different variables, Db is associated with being part of rule learning. We illustrate this with a sample of weather data sets. Usual classification issues present themselves with weather and feature attributes used in a dataset like a temperature, outlook, and weather condition. Moreover, we consider association rule learning with various rules among the different features and variables used for consideration. For example, rule estimates the outlook is shiny and the game starts playing, then day processes with non-windy conditions. These types of learning techniques are especially important to a farmer in planning their activities with most exceptional possible crop manufacturing.

Numeric Prediction

Numeric prediction pertains to the numeric quantity data related to the example. For instance, we consider weather datasets that go with the association rule learning and find the issues of classification. Instead of predicting weather depending on some potential features that are played, it cannot be numerically quantified. In a similar scenario, we can focus on the necessity of rainfall for the farmer. In this example, there is numeric amount in time, in which we can predict how much rainfall a specific region is supposed to receive in a given amount of time.

Data Mining, Knowledge Discovery, and Data Science

Data mining is mostly classified in automated pattern discovery and make predictions from large data using machine learning techniques (Vogels, 2007). Data mining used for performing the OLAP (Online analytical processing) or SQL queries are called decision support queries. It may difficult to use because the complex questions take more time due to the considerable volume of data. It is a process of extracting needed information or knowledge gained by structured and unstructured data in DB using both mining and machine learning techniques; it is known as Knowledge discovery in databases. Knowledge may briefly describe, in the form of a visual report, predictive values or models for a large data generation framework (Crowcroft, 2016). Data science is a more interdisciplinary domain in which various KDD techniques and processes are analyzed. Finally, presented in the current trends in non-relational databases, a store of unstructured data examined by giving an introduction to predictive analysis that assists in knowledge discovery from a significant amount of data (i.e. structured and unstructured).

New Trends in Database Technology: NoSQL

The recent advance of big data and Web 2.0 are based on the significant amount of unstructured data, like word documents, emails, blogs, social and multimedia data. Unstructured data varies from structured data because it cannot be stored in an organized manner for the conventional relational database. For storing and accessing the unstructured data, different approaches and techniques are needed. Scoglio et al. (2016) & González-López (2016) examine NoSQL databases for the same reason. Most companies like Amazon, dynamo, Google, Big table, etc. use NoSQL databases because it makes the data more easily scalable and flexible compared to some relational counterparts. One essential thing in using NoSQL databases is that it does not usually or inherently assist with ACID property and it also assists by using relational databases. The functionality of NoSQL database is needed to program in DB manually.

Predictive Analytics

It is similar to technology; the primary goal is to offer the potential advantage in predicting some future aspects or action using data mining and machine learning techniques that depend on previous performance in the form of gathering data. It compresses the data science, machine learning, predictive and statistical modeling, results, mainly prediction based on the input given in empirical data (Miettinen.M. (2012). Predicate premise depends on previous experiences and only analyze the inevitable necessity. Without understanding the objectives of prior knowledge, we a cannot be able to analyze and predict the future. In most cases, we need to enhance the decision-making with proper reasoning about predicting future results by taking into consideration the "black swan" (as it may be performed unexpectedly as wait for our prediction). Predictive analytics identifies the application in different humanitarian development domains ranging from healthcare to education.

Crowdsourcing and Big Data

Frias-Martinez (2011) describes crowdsourcing, which is different from outsourcing. In crowdsourcing, the significance of the task or job is outsourced, but it constructs the organization and is publicized in the form of an open call. Crowdsourcing is a technique or method that will be deployed in collecting data from a differing source like a text message, social media updates, and blogs. Data may be harmonized and determined by using mapping disaster placed regions and enhance the point of the search operation. Eagle & Pentland (2006) present an approach that was used in 2010 for the Haiti earthquake. Moreover, crowdsourcing based on social media and is presented based on opportunities offered by disaster relief and challenges faced in this process.

IOT (Internet of Things)

IOT is the current trend in the hype of big data; it arises from network science, some common population like digital communication devices and access to the internet (Chen & Zhang, 2014). Thiagarajan (2016) shows how Mckinsey Global Institute consists of IOT terms in economic values. Based on a study conducted, when entire challenges are overcome, IOT can build 3-11$ trillion USD worth of profit value. In IOT, various sensors and actuators are linked with the network to different computing frameworks that offer data for achieving knowledge. In this way, IOT, big data, network science all are intimately combined. Interoperability harmony of data is from one framework to another with essential challenges of IoT enhancement. IOT identify its application with healthcare monitoring framework. Data on wearable body sensor devices and hospital health care dB, when it could make interoperable, to assist the doctor in making more efficient decisions for diagnosis and to monitor chronic diseases. Moreover, with the assist of machine learning and predictive analytics, data is circulated in real time to a computing framework using sensors and actuators. It is mainly utilized for making revolutions in task managing and the industries with a potential reduction in a fall-down of substance and framework downtimes.

BIG DATA TOOLS

We require big data tools when getting a sense of big data. Recent big data tools listen on three classes: batch processing tools, stream processing tools, interactive analysis tools. Many batch processing tools depend on Apache Hadoop platforms like Mahout and dryad. Further, we come to know real-time necessities/requirements of stream data applications. One of the most excellent examples of large-scale stream data platform infrastructures is Storm, S4, which is needed in these cases. Interactive analysis process of data will interact with the platform; it affords user to take information by own analysis. User straight link with a computer and it will interact with real-time also. In the active process, we can review the data, analysis and make a comparison in both tabular format and graphical format at some duration. Big Data platform /infrastructure in the interactive report based on Google 'S Dremel and Apache Drill.

Apache Mahout

Liu (2016) describes Apache Mahout: it mainly concentrates on offering the scalable and machine learning techniques used in huge scale and data analysis application. Google, Amazon, Yahoo! IBM, Twitter, and Facebook are some companies using machine learning for their projects. Apache mahout offers tools for solving big data challenges and issues. Clustering, classification, pattern mining, regression, dimension reduction, and collaborative filtering are some of Mahout's core algorithms that run on top of Hadoop infrastructure with map-reduce framework (Greer et al., 2012). Libraries of that algorithm are well constructed for performing with useful abilities. The main aim of mahout is to develop the essential use case. The business requires the user to purchase an Apache software license for Mahout.

Sky Tree Server

Koshy (2012) presents sky tree Servers that offer standard usage of machine learning and modern analytical frameworks, which ensure accuracy in performing huge datasets with more speeds. It provides n number of sophisticated machine learning algorithms. It is simple to use for a user with correct command in the command lines. Outlier identification, predictive analysis, clustering, and segmentation using market are five particular use case recommend framework. It mainly concentrates on real-time analytics, and it optimizes for building N sophisticated ma-congeneric infrastructures. It deals with both structured and unstructured data get from relational databases like HDFS, Flat files, general statistical packages and libraries of machine learning.

Tableau

It mainly consists of three essential parts of processing the vast dataset like Tableau desktop, server, public (Jones, 2012). Tableau desktop based on visualization tools it makes use for data visualization and to overview in various intuitive manner. The tool provides optimization for the entire user of column data sets and the user can combine them. A Tableau server is based on the business intelligence framework that offers browser-based analytics. Finally, the Tableau public is used to build the interactive visuals. Tableau also combines/embed with Hadoop platform. It performs with a hive to make structure queries and cache data for the in-memory analytics. Caching assist in reducing the latency of Hadoop clusters. Moreover, it offers the interactive process between big data application and users.

Karmasphere Studio and Analyst

Kesari (2010) presents Hadoop-based big data infrastructure that performs in Business data analysis. It offers the new innovative approach to self-accessing service and presenting big data quickly and efficiently in a collaborative manner. Karmasphere developed for Hadoop infrastructure; it provides users with integration and user-friendly space for implementing the big data applications and also represents the workflow. From overviewing the performance, it can display the business insight from a significant amount of data like data ingestion, iterative analysis, reporting, and visualization. It constructs set up like pluggable at the top of eclipse. It built for development surrounding; the user can quickly perform both write and development Hadoop job platform. Karmasphere analyst called as big data tool is used for creating the Karmasphere to escalate the analytical process in Hadoop cluster. Moreover, additional criteria to employ the hive project for analysis both structured and unstructured data in Hadoop cluster. Experimental studies of Hadoop can be done in graphical platforms like a technical analyst, SQL programmer and database administrator. Enterprise-class of big data platforms makes it easy to perform Karmasphere analyst.

Talend Open Studio

Greer (2012) describes open source software used in big data applications and offers the graphical platform to link in visual analysis. It is implemented from Apache Hadoop and process involved in HDFS, Pig, HBase, Sqoop, and Hive. The user can solve the issues of big data platform without any requirement of the write operation in Java code; it will not avoid in Hadoop. By performing the Talend Open studio, users can develop the own assign duty by dragging and dropping the variation of icons on canvas. Stringing together as block visually make it easy after users come to know the need of component actually what will do or not do. Visual programming is similar to Superordinate; it aims the icon will never describe mechanism having need details, make sure need to understand deeply.

Big Data Tool in Stream Processing

Many big data tools depend on stream processing. Most of the important platforms or infrastructures in Stream processing are Storm and some other like S4 (Samson, 2012), SQL Stream (Koshy, 2012), SAP Hana (Vassilakis, 2010), Splunk (Kelly, 2013), and Apache Kafka (Simonite, 2013).

Storm

Storm is distributed and is able to perform real-time processing. Storm is open source and users are able to remold it. Storm is particularly built for real-time performing in contrast to Hadoop for making batch processing. It is simple to make and determine and guarantees complete data for processing. It offers competitive performance in both scalable and Fault Tolerance. It is more efficient in producing benchmarks for measuring more than millions of tuple performances per second and node. Real-time analytics, Interactive operation framework, online machine learning, distributed RPC and ETL are some of the applications. Storm clusters are the same as Hadoop clusters; the user determines the various topologies for various storm duties. Moreover, Hadoop infrastructure built in map reduce jobs related to the application. They have more variation in map reduce job and topologies. The essential thing that map-reduce complete job but topology process message entire time or it user get terminate.

Construction of real-time performance in the storm is that users need to assemble the various topologies. Topology is based on graph computation and assembly, submitted with any programming languages. The topology consists of two kinds of nodes such as spouts and bolts. Representation of topology based on graph transformation in the stream and each node in topology run in parallel (Zhang, 2014).

S4

Ted Samson (2012) describes the usage of standard purpose like distributed, fault tolerance, pluggable computing infrastructure for making continuous unbound data streaming. At the starting stage, it was introduced by Yahoo in 2010, which became the Apache incubator project subsequently in 2011. It

Table 2. Batch processing tool used in big data

Batch Processing	Description	Advantages	Disadvantage
Hadoop	To determine the processing of data-intensive app.	• Distributed data processing • Independent task • Easy to deals with partial failures • A Linear scale for ideal scenario • Simple programming model	• Protective programming model • Combine with multiple datasets to produce as tricky and low • Difficult cluster management • Single master node • Unapparent configuration of nodes
Sky tree	Process of large datasets at high speed	• Quick processing of large datasets with accuracy way • Advanced analysis • High-performance machine learning	More complexity
Talend open studio	It offers a graphical platform to connect analysis for big data applications.	• High component sets • Code conversion • Connectivity with entire databases • High-level design	• The system turns slower after Talend open studio installation. • Small parallelism
Jasper soft	To make a report from database columns.	• Less cost • Very easy to install • Good functionality and efficiency	• Jasper soft affirms documentation errors and has issues in extending its functionality
Dryad	To increase both parallel and distributed programs and scaling up the ability to process small nodes to large nodes.	• Simple programming • Permits various inputs and outputs • By comparing with map reduce it offers more flexibility	• Not suitable for iterative and nesting program • Conversion of random computing data flow graph is more difficult
Pentaho	To create a report from large structured and unstructured data.	• Easy to access and control data • Quick reporting due to in-memory caching techniques • Detailed visualization • Seamless integration	The inconsistent way of working and less advance analytics as compared to the tableau
Tableau	To determine large datasets.	• Data visualization • For upgrading less cost requires • Excellent mobile support	• Lacking in predictive ability • Modifying management issues • Risky security
Karmasphere	In performing with business analysis.	• Quick pattern representation • Self-service • Parallel collaboration	More complexity

permits the programmer to be pure in implementing the application and processing various essential properties used such as robustness, decentralization, scalability, managing clusters, and enhancement. Important core platform or infrastructure is implemented using Java. Development of S4 job is built to get modular and utilized for pluggable and dynamic processing for substantial stream data. It employed with a zookeeper in maintaining it cluster like storm run. S4 is made use of production framework in yahoo And perform thousands of query search and most exceptional performance view with other applications.

SQL Streams Server

Eynon (2013) describe SQL stream server is other big data infrastructure that constructs for processing massive data stream in a real scenario. It mainly concentrates on intelligent and automatic operation in streaming big data. SQL stream is particular describe a pattern for substantial unstructured log files, sensor, network, and the machine produces data. Newly introduced SQL stream s-Server 3.0 for performing in real-time data gathering, sharing and transformation in favor of the real scenario of big data management and big data analytics. Standard SQL language still needs to acquire in lying the applications. It works more quickly in using the memory processing like "NO Database technology.' Storing of data will not be in disk form, instead attain of data as stream and process in memory by streaming SQL queries. Streaming SQL introduced from standard SQL by getting advantages from multi-core programming and success tremendous in parallel streaming data processing.

SAP Hana

Scoglio (2016) describes SAP Hana that consists of in-memory analytics infrastructure that offers the real-time analysis in performing or determines business, predictive analysis, and sentiment analysis in processing data. It is an essential part of the real-time infrastructure in SAP HANA database. It may have few variations with another database framework. They are three HANA particular in real time analytics. It runs with broad access to an application, whether it not from SAP like demographics and social media content.

Figure 3. Big Data tools

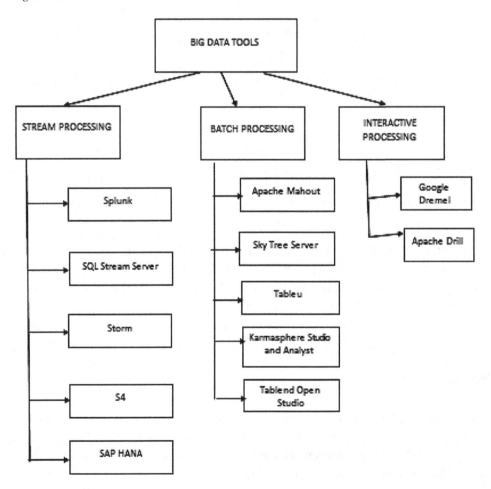

Splunk

On real-time intelligence of big data infrastructure that applying information from machine produce big data. Amazon, Senthub, Heroku are some famous companies that employed Splunk. Splunk gathers entire moments of cloud technology and big data; it helps in making use of search, manage, analyze the machine produce data from the web interface. It demonstrates the result in many ways like Graph, document, and report. It constructed to offer the metrics from most of the application, diagnose issues for the framework and IT platform also offers some intelligence in making business operations. Splunk Storm it is cloud version of Spunks in big data analytics.

Splunk varies from other stream processing tools it includes like indexing structures or unstructured machine produce data in real time processing and documenting the result and dashboard. Moreover, a significant application is Log files.

Apache Kafka

Simonite (2013) describes more throughput messaging framework that built by LinkedIn. It runs as a tool to maintain streaming, performing data with memory analytical technique for getting the decision making. Persistent with o (1) disk shape, more throughput, assist in distributed processing and parallel loading of data inside Hadoop. Data pipelines and messaging tools are some the used widely in many companies. Now a day essential role of extracting the features of websites based on activity and operational data. Page content, copy content, checklist, searching keyword are some of the activity data used for the record the human actions. Valuable to log that activity into the file for performing the subsequent analysis. Knowledge discovery of operational data is used entirely for making real-time operations. It gathers both online and offline process by offering the two type of data like production and most excellent solution.

Interactive Analysis Tools Based on Big Data

Nowadays, the open source of big data framework is new growing thing for addressing the requires not only for scalable batch processing and batch processing it also in interactive analysis processing. It represents the data into interactive surrounding; it permits with a real scenario. The data will be reviewed, compare, and determine /analysis in the form of tabular or graphical type and some time it occurred both as well.

Google's Dremel

Google introduced interactive analysis framework called Dremel in 2010 (Schintler & Kulkarni, 2014). It has scalable processing for nested data. It is distinct architecture compare with other design like Apache Hadoop it performs more successful in Map/reduce computation. It can play the aggregation queries above trillions of row tables in per sec by gathering multi-level execution trees and columnar data design. The framework is scalable with thousands of CPU and petabytes of data for users in google.

Apache Drill

Apache drill distributed framework for the interactive analysis of big data. It is same as Google's Dremel. It offers more flexibility to afford with different in various query languages, data format, and source. Like Dremel Drill is a particular implementation of getting efficient in performing/ run nested data. Primary goal to scale up to 10,000 servers to complete the process of data in petabyte and trillions of record run in second.

Both drill and Dremel have experience in scaling the data queries. It mainly used in storage for HDFS and Perform batch analysis in map reduce. Searching/ collecting data from storage column form or distributed file system, it has potential to scan above petabytes of data in seconds, providing hoc queries. We can look out open source version for Dremel, and Google offers Dremel –as-a-service on big data query providers. It mainly focuses on big data platform, it constructed for batch processing and efficiently used for real-time analytics. Big data platform used primarily for functionality with an example like statistical analysis, machine learning and stream processing. We also describe pros and cons in performing the real-time process, and it runs in response time from left to right and also deals batch processing is more from low to high.

CHALLENGES, OPEN ISSUES AND FUTURE PERSPECTIVES OF BIG DATA FOR DEVELOPMENT

Today's age is similar to big data it benefits potential and necessary required for shifting the paradigm in the conventional human development process in daily day life. Moreover, it does not cure the entire data kept with many significant challenges. In this section, we briefly examine the challenges of big data development in two perspectives Technical and Ethical.

Technical Challenges

They are many challenges lies in technical aspects of developing big data for development. For example, now the day is daily producing more amounts of data in processing and storing ability in scaling quantity.

Crowdsourcing

We determined the potential of crowdsourcing while analyzing the Migrant crisis. The rich source of Crowdsourcing data is Social media sites, and most of the agencies depend on collecting data from those sites. Moreover, it has not still established system when organizations are collaborating mainly combined with each other with identity and efforts. It provides issues of second response. When two agencies offer the same action in same matters when coordinate between two of one of the organizations will be in operating with different problems or addictive work for the same problems.

Table 3. Big data tool for Stream processing

Stream-Based Processing	Description	Advantages	Disadvantage
Storm	To determine real-time processing with large datasets.	• Very simple to use • It can work with any programming languages. • Scalable and fault –tolerant.	Reliability, performance, efficiency, and manageability are some of the disadvantages of the storm.
Splunk	It captures both indexing and correlated real-time data to achieve in accelerating report, alert and visualization from the storage.	More benefits from security to business analytics to monitoring infrastructure.	High complexity and setup cost regarding money
S4	In processing unbounded data streams efficiently.	• Scalable • Fault –tolerant • Pluggable environment.	Lack of support for dynamic load balancing.
SAP Hana	It offers real-time analysis of business processing.	• High-performance analytics. • Quick processing. • In-memory processing.	• High cost and challenging to manage SAP Hana database. • Lack of affirming for entire ERP products.
SQL stream s-Server	To determine a vast number of services and log file data in real time.	• Low cost and latency. • Scalability offers more volume and velocity data.	High complexity
Apache Kafka	To maintain a significant stream of data by using in-memory analytics for decision-making.	• High throughput and efficiency. • Stable • Scalable • Fault –tolerant.	High –level API

Bias and Polarization

Personal content predicate based on algorithm previously used by the user for making polarization. It means two various users will get a completely different searching result for the same content. Moreover, Advance in-depth learning approach, it will not entirely depend on previous data, and content aware computing and Issues are the address of from algorithms. For example, Facebook applies research group with the name of face book's AI Group. A critical task in that category and goal to complete in identify the user post it will not entirely depend on a keyword search. Cognitive computing is based on in-depth learning and brain encourages neural algorithm approach; it provides in getting the construction of Watson, a context-aware AI based Computing Framework.

Data Supply Chain

With entire benefit, analysis policy used by big data is an uneasy task. Most of essential challenges and perils entail this process. Privacy is a most critical aspect and hugely debated in collecting data from users. During the process of collecting data (big data supply chain), the context and semantics of data sources will be unerect to sophisticated and spatial restraints because of disparity in worldwide technology development, result in statistical bias, it turns result with inefficient policy (Bilal, 2014).

Technology Usage

Content primarily based on online data gathering from students, it is essential for considering in LA. Issues arise when tracking the data trail left by student online, most of the student will have different behaviors towards the usage of technology. Both social network and sentimental analysis perform based on care of each student, analysis usage of internet loss, as compared with another student, it will not be any penalized in analyzing the data.

Spatial Issues

Most of the user updates the status with the data similar to crisis sitting, collecting together, in various geographical sites. Most of the challenges lie in crisis the data it provides at first place, data collecting from real ground depends on the survey, and aerial imagery needs to combine with effective action in a fight with critical time.

The Vulnerability of Connectivity

Most of the scientist work on trust management or maintenance framework for verifying the data collected from the proper action. Fraudulent information and entities still infiltrated with network data. Information will be taken care of standard data and essential to diffuse and infect with other connected objects of network data. The vulnerability is main causes for connecting with nature information in taking and getting the entities, Vulnerability of connectivity and error cascading failure briefly explained in Barabasi book.

Interoperability

Big data analytics will provide in collecting data and combining the unstructured data with a variety of data types. For example Record of call detail from the mobile factory, data getting from the satellite image, face to face review of data that are collaborated each other for getting improved and less biased analysis. Combining and harmonizing in analyzing data is the primary potential for Interoperability. Forgetting the data analytics required framework, it makes data streams with various essential formats inhomogenous.

Fragmentation

Challenges of fragmentation consider based on impediment for extreme scale in the deployment of big data analytics. For example, the patient may view various specialists for different medical issues. Then specialist will describe multiple tests in examining the various kinds of results. Moreover, some protocol or framework need to develop the integrate of those fragments each other and also perform analysis based on gathering; then it clears the broad picture of patient's current situation will be extracted. When the problem of fragmentation resolved, then it not only with speed up in the process of diagnosis and also in capability in giving the personalized treatment mostly it will be suitable for the patient for consideration.

Technology Scaling

In recent days, both software-defined network (SDN) and Cloud computing technology verified in need of efficient for constructing big data solutions, by moving forward with more work are required to ensure that both computing and network facilities in scaling for improving scalable data (Crowcroft, 2016).

Ethical

Apart from entire technology are similar to challenges describe above is imperative in considering the ethical difficulties in performing the Big data for development. It describes benefits and essential challenges in deploying the big data for development usage. Privacy is a significant concern with big data analytics; some of the most great difficulties of confidentiality called as fragmentation it impediment for massive scale in deploying the big data analytics. Some well-known issues in ethical challenges, listing out some challenges facing with perspective of ethics in handling the big data for development

Figure 4. Challenges of Big Data

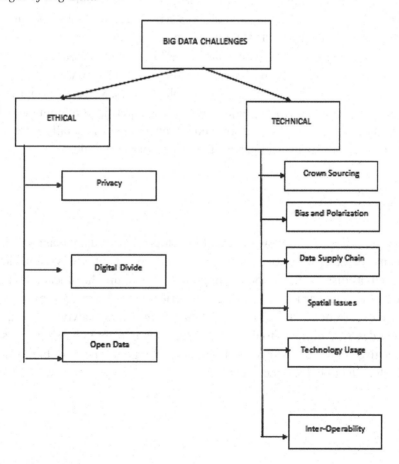

Privacy

It is crucial challenges in the event of big data analytics. For example with an extreme amount of data gathered from individuals, most important that such information will not be abused for financial gains purpose.

Digital Divide

It will be easy for non-uniform diffusion technology for expertise and modern throughout the worldwide. The result is split based on harm nations with the absence of infrastructure, feasibility, affordability, and data saving facilities. It divides well-known issues called privacy that can be controlled and monitor the entities for exploiting data among some need challenge that hidden in worldwide for scaling the development of big data techniques.

Open Data

Many possible problems in open data, it is more transparency and more desirable with government/development data for open access. Moreover, it also describes need to think about the right to perform, use, links and usage of open data (It tells flexibility are a need for different misuse and privacy). The recent rise in the usage of big data in humanitarian, the effort of government need to focus on ensuring the sensitive data like humanitarian locations of actors and internally displaces the person(IDPs) will not provide open, due to maliciously in exploited the malevolent actors. Moreover, finally, the evaluation of data science is more challenging due field required/ need an expert in combining people with different domain and fields. The interdisciplinary effort needs to encourage financially incentive with big data for determining the analysis with correct perspective and in place of ethics.

CONCLUSION

In this chapter, we describe an overview of recent development big data analytics. The Main goal of this chapter to point out the specification of big data for development with various domain setups like Humanitarian growth as disaster and critics of migrants, agriculture, healthcare, and education. Some of the big data techniques like Machine learning categories into supervised learning and unsupervised learning, data mining, current trends in NoSQL database, predictive analytics, IOT and crowdsourcing and big data. Then describe big data tools which categories into three batch processing, stream processing, and interactive analysis. It points out different challenging aspects of big data for development sub-coordinate with both ethical and technical.

REFERENCES

Ali, A., Qadir, J., Rasool, R., Sathiaseelan, A., Zwitter, A., & Crowcroft, J. (2016). Big data for development: Applications and techniques. *Big Data Analytics*, *1*(1), 2. doi:10.118641044-016-0002-4

Armstrong, T. G., Ponnekanti, V., Borthakur, D., & Callaghan, M. (2013, June). LinkBench: a database benchmark based on the Facebook social graph. In *Proceedings of the 2013 ACM SIGMOD International Conference on Management of Data* (pp. 1185-1196). ACM. 10.1145/2463676.2465296

Auradkar, A., Botev, C., Das, S., De Maagd, D., Feinberg, A., Ganti, P., & Koshy, J. (2012, April). Data infrastructure at LinkedIn. In 2012 IEEE 28th International Conference on Data Engineering (ICDE), (pp. 1370-1381). IEEE. 10.1109/ICDE.2012.147

Auradkar, A., Botev, C., Das, S., De Maagd, D., Feinberg, A., Ganti, P., & Koshy, J. (2012, April). Data infrastructure at LinkedIn. In *2012 IEEE 28th International Conference on Data Engineering (ICDE)* (pp. 1370-1381). IEEE. 10.1109/ICDE.2012.147

Azuaje, F. (2006). Witten IH, Frank E: Data Mining: Practical Machine Learning Tools and Techniques (2nd ed.).

Chatterjee, P., & Finger, M. (2014). *The earth brokers: power, politics and world development*. Routledge.

Chen, C. P., & Zhang, C. Y. (2014). Data-intensive applications, challenges, techniques, and technologies: A survey on Big Data. *Information Sciences*, *275*, 314–347. doi:10.1016/j.ins.2014.01.015

DeCandia, G., Hastorun, D., Jampani, M., Kakulapati, G., Lakshman, A., Pilchin, A., & Vogels, W. (2007). Dynamo: Amazon's highly available key-value store. *Operating Systems Review*, *41*(6), 205–220. doi:10.1145/1323293.1294281

Digital Humanitarian Network. (n.d.). Retrieved October 4, 2015 from http://digitalhumanitarians.com/

1000. Durbin, R. M., Altshuler, D. L., Durbin, R. M., Abecasis, G. R., Bentley, D. R., Chakravarti, A., ... McVean, G. A.Genomes Project Consortium. (2010). A map of human genome variation from population-scale sequencing. *Nature*, *467*(7319), 1061–1073. doi:10.1038/nature09534

Eagle, N., & Pentland, A. S. (2006). Reality mining: Sensing complex social systems. *Personal and Ubiquitous Computing*, *10*(4), 255–268. doi:10.100700779-005-0046-3

Elhauge, E. (2010). *The fragmentation of US health care: causes and solutions*. Oxford University Press on Demand.

Eynon, R. (2013). The rise of Big Data: what does it mean for education, technology, and media research?

Fayyad, U., Piatetsky-Shapiro, G., & Smyth, P. (1996). From data mining to knowledge discovery in databases. *AI Magazine*, *17*(3), 37.

Fraga-Lamas, P., Fernández-Caramés, T. M., Suárez-Albela, M., Castedo, L., & González-López, M. (2016). A review on the internet of things for defense and public safety. *Sensors (Basel)*, *16*(10), 1644. doi:10.339016101644

Frias-Martinez, E., Williamson, G., & Frias-Martinez, V. (2011, October). An agent-based model of epidemic spread using human mobility and social network information. In *2011 IEEE Third International Conference on Privacy, Security, Risk and Trust (PASSAT) and 2011 IEEE Third International Conference on Social Computing (SocialCom)* (pp. 57-64). IEEE. 10.1109/PASSAT/SocialCom.2011.142

Friedman, C., Rubin, J., Brown, J., Buntin, M., Corn, M., Etheredge, L., & Sullivan, K. (2014). Toward a science of learning systems: a research agenda for the high-functioning Learning Health System. *Journal of the American Medical Informatics Association*.

1000. Genomes. (2016). IGSR and the 1000 Genomes Project. Retrieved October 2, 2015 from http://www.1000genomes.org/

Hadoop. (2014). What Is Apache Hadoop? Retrieved from https://hadoop.apache.org/

Hilbert, M. (2013). Big data for development: From information-to knowledge societies.

Humanitarian Open Street Map Team. (n.d.). Ongoing Projects. Retrieved from. http://hotosm.org/projects/ongoing

Katal, A., Wazid, M., & Goudar, R. H. (2013, August). Big data: issues, challenges, tools and good practices. In *2013 Sixth International Conference on Contemporary Computing (IC3)* (pp. 404-409). IEEE 10.1109/IC3.2013.6612229

Kelly, J. (2013). Apache drill brings SQL-like, ad-hoc query capabilities to big data.

Knight, W. (2015). *Deep learning catches on in new industries, from fashion to finance*. MIT Technol. Rev.

Kraft, S., Casale, G., Jula, A., Kilpatrick, P., & Greer, D. (2012, June). Wiq: work-intensive query scheduling for in-memory database systems. In *2012 IEEE 5th International Conference on Cloud Computing (CLOUD)* (pp. 33-40). IEEE. 10.1109/CLOUD.2012.120

Kraft, S., Casale, G., Jula, A., Kilpatrick, P., & Greer, D. (2012, June). Wiq: work-intensive query scheduling for in-memory database systems. In *2012 IEEE 5th International Conference on Cloud Computing (CLOUD)* (pp. 33-40). IEEE. 10.1109/CLOUD.2012.120

Kshetri, N. (2014). The emerging role of Big Data in key development issues: Opportunities, challenges, and concerns. *Big Data & Society*, *1*(2). doi:10.1177/2053951714564227

Laney, D. (2001). 3D data management: Controlling data volume, velocity, and variety. *META Group Research Note*, *6*, 70.

Laurila, J. K., Gatica-Perez, D., Aad, I., Bornet, O., Do, T. M. T., Dousse, O., & Miettinen, M. (2012). The mobile data challenge: Big data for mobile computing research. In Pervasive Computing.

Leavitt, N. (2010). Will NoSQL databases live up to their promise? *Computer*, *43*(2), 12–14. doi:10.1109/MC.2010.58

Lohr, S. (2015). Using patient data to democratize medical discovery. *New York Times, Bits Blog*.

Manyika, J., Chui, M., Groves, P., Farrell, D., Van Kuiken, S., & Doshi, E. A. (2013). Open data: Unlocking innovation and performance with liquid information. McKinsey Global Institute.

Mayer-Schönberger, V., & Cukier, K. (2013). *Big data: A revolution that will transform how we live, work, and think*. Houghton Mifflin Harcourt.

Meier, P. (2015). *Digital humanitarians: how big data is changing the face of humanitarian response*. CRC Press. doi:10.1201/b18023

Melnik, S., Gubarev, A., Long, J. J., Romer, G., Shivakumar, S., Tolton, M., & Vassilakis, T. (2010). Dremel: Interactive analysis of web-scale datasets. *Proceedings of the VLDB Endowment International Conference on Very Large Data Bases*, *3*(1-2), 330–339. doi:10.14778/1920841.1920886

Modha, D. S., Ananthanarayanan, R., Esser, S. K., Ndirango, A., Sherbondy, A. J., & Singh, R. (2011). Cognitive computing. *Communications of the ACM*, *54*(8), 62–71. doi:10.1145/1978542.1978559

Moore, A. W., & Zuev, D. (2005, June). Internet traffic classification using Bayesian analysis techniques. *Performance Evaluation Review*, *33*(1), 50–60. doi:10.1145/1071690.1064220

Neumeyer, L., Robbins, B., Nair, A., & Kesari, A. (2010, December). S4: Distributed stream computing platform. In *2010 IEEE International Conference on Data Mining Workshops (ICDMW)* (pp. 170-177). IEEE.

Patil, S., Polte, M., Ren, K., Tantisiriroj, W., Xiao, L., López, J., & Rinaldi, B. (2011, October). YCSB++: benchmarking and performance debugging advanced features in scalable table stores. In *Proceedings of the 2nd ACM Symposium on Cloud Computing* (p. 9). ACM. 10.1145/2038916.2038925

Picciano, A. G. (2012). The Evolution of Big Data and Learning Analytics in American Higher Education. *Journal of Asynchronous Learning Networks*, *16*(3), 9–20.

T.A. Press. (2015). Research it: 5 Things to Know About Apple's Medical Apps. Retrieved from http://www.nytimes.com/aponline/2015/03/11/technology/ap-us-tec-apple-researchkit.html

PSLC Data Shop. (2017). Welcome to DataShop, the world's largest repository of learning interaction data. Retrieved from https://pslcdatashop.web.cmu.edu/

Pulse, G. (2015). United Nations Global Pulse Information Sheet.

Qadir, J., Ahad, N., Mushtaq, E., & Bilal, M. (2014, December). SDNs, clouds, and big data: new opportunities. In *2014 12th International Conference on Frontiers of Information Technology (FIT)* (pp. 28-33). IEEE. 10.1109/FIT.2014.14

Rish, I. (2001, August). An empirical study of the naive Bayes classifier. In IJCAI 2001 workshop on empirical methods in artificial intelligence (Vol. 3, No. 22, pp. 41-46). IBM New York.

Samson, T. (2012). Splunk Storm Brings Log Management to the Cloud. Retrieved from https://www.infoworld.com/article/2615403/managed-services/splunk-storm-brings-log-management-to-the-cloud.html

Savitz, E. (2012). Gartner: 10 critical tech trends for the next five years. *Forbes.* http://www.Forbes.Com/sites/ericsavitz/2012/10/22/gartner-10-critical-tech-trends-for-the-next-five-years

Savitz, E. (2012). Gartner: Top 10 strategic technology trends for 2013. URL http://www. forbes.Com/sites/ericsavitz/2012/10/22/gartner-10-critical-tech-trends-for-the-next-five-years

Schintler, L. A., & Kulkarni, R. (2014). Big data for policy analysis: The good, the bad, and the ugly. *The Review of Policy Research, 31*(4), 343–348. doi:10.1111/ropr.12079

Shakeri, H., Poggi-Corradini, P., Albin, N., & Scoglio, C. (2016). Modulus of families of loops with applications in network analysis. arXiv preprint arXiv:1609.00461

Shakeri, H., Poggi-Corradini, P., Albin, N., & Scoglio, C. (2016). Modulus of families of loops with applications in network analysis. arXiv preprint arXiv: 1609.00461

Siegel, E. (2013). *Predictive analytics: The power to predict who will click, buy, lie, or die.* John Wiley & Sons.

Siemens, G. (2012, April). Learning analytics: envisioning a research discipline and a domain of practice. In *Proceedings of the 2nd international conference on learning analytics and knowledge* (pp. 4-8). ACM.

Simonite, T. (2013). Facebook launches advanced AI effort to find meaning in your posts. *Tech. Review.* http://www.technologyreview.com/news/519411/facebook-launches-advanced-ai-effort-to-find-meaning-in-your-posts

SimpleTuition. (n.d.). Retrieved October 2, 2015 from http://www.simpletuition.com/

The World Bank (Education Data). (n.d.). Education. Retrieved October 4, 2015 from http://data.worldbank.org/topic/education

Thinkcerca. (n.d.). Teach Critical Thinking Through Argumentative Writing. Retrieved September 2, 2015 from http://www.thinkcerca.com/

Tim Jones, M. (2013). Process Real-Time Big Data with Twitter Storm. Retrieved from https://www.ibm.com/developerworks/library/os-twitterstorm/

Trace the Face. (n.d.). Restoring Family Links. Retrieved September 29, 2015 from http://familylinks. icrc.org/europe/en/Pages/Home.aspx

Ushahidi. (n.d.). Retrieved October 4, 2015 from http://www.ushahidi.com/

Wang, H., Xu, Z., Fujita, H., & Liu, S. (2016). Towards felicitous decision making: An overview on challenges and trends of Big Data. *Information Sciences, 367*, 747–765. doi:10.1016/j.ins.2016.07.007

Yaqoob, I., Hashem, I. A. T., Gani, A., Mokhtar, S., Ahmed, E., Anuar, N. B., & Vasilakos, A. V. (2016). Big data: From beginning to future. *International Journal of Information Management, 36*(6), 1231–1247. doi:10.1016/j.ijinfomgt.2016.07.009

Zikopoulos, P., & Eaton, C. (2011). *Understanding big data: Analytics for enterprise-class Hadoop and streaming data*. McGraw-Hill Osborne Media.

Compilation of References

(2011). Stave 2011. *Communications in Computer and Information Science, 187*, 190–197.

1000. Durbin, R. M., Altshuler, D. L., Durbin, R. M., Abecasis, G. R., Bentley, D. R., Chakravarti, A., ... McVean, G. A.Genomes Project Consortium. (2010). A map of human genome variation from population-scale sequencing. *Nature, 467*(7319), 1061–1073. doi:10.1038/nature09534

1000. Genomes. (2016). IGSR and the 1000 Genomes Project. Retrieved October 2, 2015 from http://www.1000genomes.org/

Abolfazli, S., Sanaei, Z., Ahmed, E., Gani, A., & Buyya, R. (2014). Cloud-based augmentation for mobile devices: Motivation, taxonomies, and open challenges. *IEEE Communications Surveys and Tutorials, 16*(1), 337–368. doi:10.1109/SURV.2013.070813.00285

Adnan, N., & Islam, Z. (2016). Optimizing the number of trees in a decision forest to discover a sub forest with high ensemble accuracy using a genetic algorithm. *Knowledge-Based Systems, 110*, 86–97. doi:10.1016/j.knosys.2016.07.016

Afolabi, A. O. (2014). On Mobile Cloud Computing in a Mobile Learning System. *Journal of Information Engineering and Applications, 4*(5).

Agaoglu, M. (2016). Predicting Instructor Performance Using Data Mining Techniques in Higher Education. *IEEE Access: Practical Innovations, Open Solutions, 4*, 2379–2387. doi:10.1109/ACCESS.2016.2568756

Agrawal, R., & Srikant, R. (1994, September 12-15). Fast algorithms for mining association rules. In *Proceedings of the 20th VLDB (Very Large Data Bases) Conference*, Santiago, Chile.

Agrawal, R., & Srikant, R. (1995, March 6-10). Mining sequential patterns. In *Proceedings of the 11th International Conference on Data Engineering*, Taipei, Taiwan.

Agudo, I., Nuñez, D., Giammatteo, G., Rizomiliotis, P., & Lambrinoudakis, C. (2011, June). Cryptography goes to the cloud. In *FTRA International Conference on Secure and Trust Computing, Data Management, and Application* (pp. 190-197). Springer, Berlin, Heidelberg.

Ahuja, S. P., & Muthiah, K. (2017). Advances in Green Cloud Computing. In Green Computing Strategies for Competitive Advantage and Business Sustainability. Hershey, PA: IGI-Global.

Alamri, A., Ansari, W. S., Hassan, M. M., Hossain, M. S., Alelaiwi, A., & Hossain, M. A. (2013, February). A Survey on Sensor-Cloud: Architecture, Applications, and Approaches. *International Journal of Distributed Sensor Networks*, *2013*, 1–18.

Alani, H., Kim, S., Millard, D. E., Weal, M. J., Hall, W., Lewis, P. H., & Shadbolt, N. R. (2003). Automatic ontology-based knowledge extraction from web documents. *IEEE Intelligent Systems*, *18*(1), 14–21. doi:10.1109/MIS.2003.1179189

Al-Barrak, M. A., & Al-Razgan, M. (2016). Predict the student's final GPA using decision tree. *International Journal of Information and Education Technology*, *6*(7), 528–533. doi:10.7763/IJIET.2016.V6.745

Albers, S. (2010). Energy-efficient algorithms. *Communications of the ACM*, *53*(5), 86–96. doi:10.1145/1735223.1735245

Ali, A., Qadir, J., Rasool, R., Sathiaseelan, A., Zwitter, A., & Crowcroft, J. (2016). Big data for development: Applications and techniques. *Big Data Analytics*, *1*(1), 2. doi:10.118641044-016-0002-4

Ali, F., Kwak, K. S., & Kim, Y. G. (2016). Opinion mining based on fuzzy domain ontology and Support Vector Machine: A proposal to automate online review classification. *Applied Soft Computing*, *47*(3), 235–250. doi:10.1016/j.asoc.2016.06.003

Allison, B., Hawley, R., Borr, A., Muhlestein, M., & Hitz, D. (1998). File System Security: Secure Network Data Sharing for NT and UNIX. *Network Appliance, 16.*

Al-Muhtadi, J., Ranganathan, A., Campbell, R., & Mickunas, M. (2002). A flexible, privacy-preserving authentication framework for ubiquitous computing environments. In *International Conference on Distributed Computing Systems Workshops* (pp. 771-776). 10.1109/ICDCSW.2002.1030861

Altamimi, M., Palit, R., Naik, K., & Nayak, A. (2012). Energy-as-a-service (EaaS): On the efficacy of multimedia cloud computing to save smartphone energy. In *IEEE 5th International Conference on Cloud Computing* (pp. 764–771). 10.1109/CLOUD.2012.72

Ananthanarayanan, G., Douglas, C., Ramakrishnan, R., Rao, S., & Stoica, I. (2012). True elasticity in multi-tenant data-intensive compute clusters. In *ACM Symposium on Cloud Computing*. 10.1145/2391229.2391253

Anderson, B. D. O., & Vongpanitlerd, S. (1973). *Network Analysis and synthesis*. Prentice-Hall.

Apache Accumulo. (n.d.). Apache Accumulo. Retrieved from https://accumulo.apache.org/

Apache Airavata. (n.d.). Apache Airavata. Retrieved from https://airavata.apache.org/

Apache Ambari. (2015, August). Apache Ambari. Retrieved from https://ambari.apache.org

Apache Apex. (n.d.). Apache Apex. Retrieved from https://apex.apache.org/

Apache Avro. (2015, August 6). Welcome to Avro. Retrieved from http://avro.apache.org/docs/1.3.0/

Apache Beam. (n.d.). Apache Beam: An advanced unified programming model. Retrieved from https://beam.apache.org/

Apache BigTop. (n.d.). Apache Bigtop. Retrieved from http://bigtop.apache.org/

Apache BookKeeper. (n.d.). Apache BookKeeper. Retrieved from http://bookkeeper.apache.org/

Apache Calcite. (n.d.). The foundation for your next high-performance database. Retrieved from https://calcite.apache.org/

Apache Cassandra. (2015, August 6). Manage massive amounts of data, fast, without losing sleep. Retrieved from: http://cassandra.apache.org/

Apache Chukwa, (n.d.). Overview. Retrieved from: https://chukwa.apache.org/docs/r0.8.0/

Apache Couch DB. (n.d.). Data Where You Need It. Retrieved from http://couchdb.apache.org/

Apache Crunch. (n.d.). Getting Started. Retrieved from https://crunch.apache.org/getting-started.html

Apache Curator. (n.d.). Welcome to Apache Curator. Retrieved from: http://curator.apache.org/

Apache DataFu. (n.d.). Apache DataFu. Retrieved from https://datafu.incubator.apache.org/

Apache Drill. (2015, August 6). Apache Drill. Retrieved from http://drill.apache.org/

Apache Edgent. (n.d.). Apache Edgent a Community for Accelerating Analytics at the Edge. Retrieved from http://edgent.apache.org/

Apache Falcon. (2015, August 6). Falcon - Feed management and data processing platform. Retrieved from http://falcon.apache.org/index.html

Apache Flink. (2015, August 6). Introduction to Apache Flink. Retrieved from https://flink.apache.org/

Apache Flume. (2015, August 6). Welcome to Apache Flume. Retrieved from https://flume.apache.org/

Apache Giraph. (2015, August 6). Welcome to Apache Giraph. Retrieved from http://giraph.apache.org/

Apache Gora, (n.d.). Welcome to the Apache Gora project. Retrieved from: https://gora.apache.org/

Apache Hama, (n.d.). Apache Hama. Retrieved from https://hama.apache.org/

Apache Hbase. (2015, August 6). Welcome to Apache HBase. Retrieved from: http://hbase.apache.org/

Apache Helix, (n.d.). Helix A cluster management framework for partitioned and replicated distributed sources. Retrieved from http://helix.apache.org/

Apache Hive, (n.d.). Home. Retrieved from: https://cwiki.apache.org/confluence/display/Hive/Home

Apache Ignite. (2015, August 6). Database and Caching Platform. Retrieved from https://ignite.incubator.apache.org/

Apache Kafka. (2015, August 6). Documentation. Retrieved from http://kafka.apache.org/documentation.html

Apache Knox, (n.d.). REST API and Application Gateway for the Apache Hadoop Ecosystem. Retrieved from https://knox.apache.org/

Apache Lens, (n.d.). Welcome to Lens. Retrieved from https://lens.apache.org/

Apache Metamodal, (n.d.). Apache MetaModel. Retrieved from http://metamodel.apache.org/

Apache O.R.C. (n.d.). the smallest, fastest columnar storage for Hadoop workloads. Retrieved from https://orc.apache.org/

Apache Oozie. (2015, August 6). Apache Oozie Workflow Scheduler for Hadoop. Retrieved from http://oozie.apache.org/

Apache Parquet. (2015, August 6). Parquet. Retrieved from http://parquet.apache.org/

Apache Phoenix. (2015, August 6). Overview. Retrieved from http://phoenix.apache.org/

Apache Pig. (2015, August 6). Welcome to Apache Pig. Retrieved from: https://pig.apache.org/

Apache REEF. (n.d.). Apache REEF™ - a stdlib for Big Data. Retrieved from http://reef.apache.org/

Apache Samza, (n.d.). What is Samza? Retrieved from http://samza.apache.org/

Apache Software Foundation. (n.d.). Apache Software Foundation. Retrieved from http://en.wikipedia.org/wiki/Apache_Software_Foundation

Apache Spark Streaming. (2015, August 6). Apache Spark Streaming. Retrieved from https://spark.apache.org/streaming/

Apache Sqoop. (2015, August 6). Apache Sqoop. Retrieved from http://sqoop.apache.org/

Apache Storm. (n.d.). Storm Distributed and Fault-Tolerant Realtime Computation. Retrieved from: http://storm-project.net/

Apache Tajo. (n.d.). Apache Tajo: A big data warehouse system on Hadoop. Retrieved from http://tajo.apache.org/

Apache Tez. (2015, August 6). Introduction. Retrieved from http://tez.apache.org/

Apache VXQuery. (n.d.). Apache VXQuery. Retrieved from: https://vxquery.apache.org/

Apache Zeppelin. (2015, August 6). Apache Zeppelin. Retrieved from: https://zeppelin.incubator.apache.org/

Apache ZooKeeper. (n.d.). General Information. Retrieved from: https://cwiki.apache.org/confluence/display/ZOOKEEPER/Index

Ardagna, C. A., Livraga, G., & Samarati, P. (2012, December 5-7). Protecting privacy of user information in continuous location-based services. In *Proceedings of the 15th IEEE International Conference on Computational Science and Engineering (CSE 2012)*, Paphos, Cyprus. 10.1109/ICCSE.2012.31

Armbrust, M., Fox, A., Griffith, R., Joseph, A. D., Katz, R., Konwinski, A., ... Zaharia, M. (2010). A view of cloud computing. *Communications of the ACM*, *53*(4), 50–58.

Armstrong, T. G., Ponnekanti, V., Borthakur, D., & Callaghan, M. (2013, June). LinkBench: a database benchmark based on the Facebook social graph. In *Proceedings of the 2013 ACM SIGMOD International Conference on Management of Data* (pp. 1185-1196). ACM. 10.1145/2463676.2465296

Arockiaraj, M.C. (2013, May). Applications of neural networks in data mining. *International Journal Of Engineering And Science*, *3*(1), 08-11.

Auradkar, A., Botev, C., Das, S., De Maagd, D., Feinberg, A., Ganti, P., & Koshy, J. (2012, April). Data infrastructure at LinkedIn. In *2012 IEEE 28th International Conference on Data Engineering (ICDE)*, (pp. 1370-1381). IEEE. 10.1109/ICDE.2012.147

Avcibas, I., Memon, N., & Sankur, B. (2003). Steganalysis using Image Quality Metrics. *IEEE Transactions on Image Processing*, *12*(2), 221–229. doi:10.1109/TIP.2002.807363 PMID:18237902

Azuaje, F. (2006). Witten IH, Frank E: Data Mining: Practical Machine Learning Tools and Techniques (2nd ed.).

Bakshi, K. (2012, March). Considerations for big data: Architecture and approach. In *Proceedings of 2012 IEEE Aerospace Conference*. IEEE. 10.1109/AERO.2012.6187357

Baldoni, M., Baroglio, C., Patti, V., & Rena, P. (2012). From Tags to Emotions: Ontology-driven Sentiment Analysis in the Social Semantic Web. *IntelligenzaArtificiale*, *6*(1), 41–54.

Battikh, D., El Assad, S., Bakhache, B., Deforges, O., & Khalil, M. (2014). Steganalysis of a chaos-based steganographic method. In *Proceedings: of 10ᵗʰ International Conference on Communications (COMM)*, Bucharest, Romania. 10.1109/ICComm.2014.6866665

Bent, L., Rabinovich, M., Voelker, G. M., & Xiao, Z. (2006). Characterization of a large web site population with implications for content delivery. *World Wide Web (Bussum)*, *9*(4), 505–536. doi:10.100711280-006-0224-x

Berg, G., Davidson, I., Duan, M., & Paul, G. (2003). Searching For Hidden Messages: Automatic Detection of Steganography. In *Proceedings of the Fifteenth Conference on Innovative Applications of Artificial Intelligence*, Acapulco, Mexico, August 12-14.

Bo, X., Wang, J., Liu, X., & Zhe, Z. (2007). Passive steganalysis using image quality metrics and multi-class support vector machine. In *Proceedings of IEEE third international conference on natural computation* (pp. 215–220).

Bobroff, N., Kochut, A., & Beaty, K. (2007, May). Dynamic placement of virtual machines for managing sla violations. In *10th IFIP/IEEE International Symposium on Integrated Network Management IM'07* (pp. 119-128). IEEE. 10.1109/INM.2007.374776

Bohme, R., & Kerb, A. D. (2006). *A Two-Factor Error Model for Quantitative Steganalysis. In proceedings of: SPIE 2006: Security, Steganography, and Watermarking of Multimedia Contents VIII.*

Bohrer, P., Elnozahy, E. N., Keller, T., Kistler, M., Lefurgy, C., McDowell, C., & Rajamony, R. (2002). The case for power management in web servers. In Power aware computing (pp. 261-289). Springer US. doi:10.1007/978-1-4757-6217-4_14

Bonneau, J., Herley, C., van Oorschot, P., & Stajano, F. (2012). The quest to replace passwords: A framework for comparative evaluation of web 25 authentication schemes. In *IEEE Symposium on Security and Privacy* (pp. 553–567). 10.1109/SP.2012.44

Bonomi, F., Milito, R., Zhu, J., & Addepalli, S. (2012). Fog Computing and Its Role in the Internet of Things. In Proceedings of MCC'12, Helsinki, Finland.

Borthakur, D. (2007). The hadoop distributed file system: Architecture and design. *Hadoop Project Website*, *11*, 21.

Bouwmeestera, H., Heuvelink, G. B. M., & Stoorvogelc, J. J. (2016, March). Mapping crop diseases using survey data: The case of bacterial wilt in bananas in the East African highlands. *European Journal of Agronomy*, *74*, 173–184. doi:10.1016/j.eja.2015.12.013

Boyd, D., & Crawford, K. (2012). Critical questions for big data: Provocations for a cultural, technological, and scholarly phenomenon. *Information Communication and Society*, *15*(5), 662–679. doi:10.1080/1369118X.2012.678878

Brooks, D., & Martonosi, M. (2001). Dynamic thermal management for high-performance microprocessors. In *The Seventh International Symposium on High-Performance Computer Architecture, HPCA '01* (pp. 171-182). IEEE. 10.1109/HPCA.2001.903261

Byres, E. J. (2012). *Defense in Depth. InTech Magazine*. Nov-Dec.

Campbell, A., Eisenman, S., Lane, N., Miluzzo, E., Peterson, R., Lu, H., ... Ahn, G. (2008). The rise of people centric sensing. *IEEE Internet Computing*, *12*(4), 12–21. doi:10.1109/MIC.2008.90

Candes, E. J., & Donoho, D. L. (2004). New tight frames of curvelets and optimal representations of objects with C2 singularities. *Communications on Pure and Applied Mathematics*, *57*(2), 219–266. doi:10.1002/cpa.10116

Castells, P., Ferna'ndez, M., & Vallet, D. (2007). An Adaptation of the Vector-Space Model for Ontology-Based Information Retrieval. *IEEE Transactions on Knowledge Engineering*, *19*(2), 261–271. doi:10.1109/TKDE.2007.22

Celik, M. U., Sharma, G., & Tekalp, A. M. (2004). Universal Image Steganalysis Using rate- distortion curves. In Proceedings of SPIE: Security, Steganography, and Watermarking of Multimedia Contents VI, San Jose, CA (pp. 19-22).

Chakraborty, R., & Reddy, S. (2010, March). The Information Assurance Practices of Cloud Computing Vendors. *IT Professional*, *12*(4), 29–37. doi:10.1109/MITP.2010.44

Chang, V., Kuo, Y. H., & Ramachandran, M. (2016). Cloud computing adoption framework: A security framework for business clouds. *Future Generation Computer Systems*, *57*, 24–41.

Chari, S., Jutla, C. S., & Roy, A. (2011). Universally Composable Security Analysis of OAuth v2. 0. *IACR Cryptology EPrint Archive*.

Chase, J. S., Anderson, D. C., Thakar, P. N., Vahdat, A. M., & Doyle, R. P. (2001). Managing energy and server resources in hosting centers. *Operating Systems Review*, *35*(5), 103–116. doi:10.1145/502059.502045

Chatterjee, P., & Finger, M. (2014). *The earth brokers: power, politics and world development*. Routledge.

Chaturvedi, M., Malik, S., Aggarwal, P. & Bahl, S. (2011). Privacy & Security of Mobile Cloud Computing. *Ansal University, Sector, 55*.

Chen, C. P., & Zhang, C. Y. (2014). Data-intensive applications, challenges, techniques, and technologies: A survey on Big Data. *Information Sciences*, *275*, 314–347. doi:10.1016/j.ins.2014.01.015

Chen, D., & Zhao, H. (2012). Data Security and Privacy Protection issues in Cloud Computing. In *International Conference on Computer Science and Electronics Engineering*. 10.1109/ICCSEE.2012.193

Cheng, H., Sun, F., Buthpitiya, S., & Griss, M. (2012). *Sensorchestra: Collaborative sensing for symbolic location recognition. In Mobile Computing, Applications, and Services* (pp. 195–210). .

Cheng, H., Yan, X., & Han, J. (2004). IncSpan: incremental mining of sequential patterns in large database. In *Proceedings of the 10th International 113 Conference on Knowledge Discovery in Databases*, (pp. 527-532). 10.1145/1014052.1014114

Chen, I., & Wang, Y. (2012, October). Reliability analysis of wireless sensor networks with distributed code attestation. *IEEE Communications Letters*, *16*(10), 1640–1643. doi:10.1109/LCOMM.2012.091212.121454

Chen, M., Ebert, D., Hagen, H., Laramee, R. S., van Liere, R., Ma, K.-L., ... Silver, D. (2009). Data, Information, and Knowledge in Visualization. *Journal IEEE Computer Graphics and Applications*, *29*(1), 12–19. doi:10.1109/MCG.2009.6 PMID:19363954

Chen, M., Mao, S., & Liu, Y. (2014). Big data: A survey. *Mobile Networks and Applications*, *19*(2), 171–209. doi:10.100711036-013-0489-0

Chhikara, R. R., Sharma, P., & Singh, L.(2016). An improved dynamic discrete firefly algorithm for blind image steganalysis. *International Journal of Machine Learning and Cybernetics*.

Chhikara, R. R., Sharma, P., & Singh, L. (2016). A hybrid feature selection approach based on improved PSO and filter approaches for image steganalysis. *International Journal of Machine Learning and Cybernetics*, *7*(6), 1195–1206. doi:10.100713042-015-0448-0

Chiang, M. (2015). Fog Networking: An Overview on Research Opportunities. Retrieved from http://www.princeton.edu/~chiangm/FogResearchOverview.pdf

Chiang, M., & Zhang, T. (2016). Fog and IoT: An Overview of Research Opportunities. *IEEE Internet of Things Journal*, *3*(6), 854–864. doi:10.1109/JIOT.2016.2584538

Chiang, M., & Zhang, T. (2016). *Fog and IoT: An Overview of Research Opportunities*. IEEE Internet of Things Journal.

Cho, E., Myers, S. A., & Leskovec, J. (2011, August). Friendship and mobility: user movement in location-based social networks. In *Proceedings of the 17th ACM SIGKDD international conference on Knowledge discovery and data mining* (pp. 1082-1090). ACM.

Chow, C.-F., Mokbel, M. F., & Liu, X. (2011). Spatial cloaking for anonymous location-based services in mobile peer-to-peer environments. *GeoInformatica*, *15*(2), 351–380. doi:10.100710707-009-0099-y

Chow, C.-Y., & Mokbel, M. F. (2011). Privacy of spatial trajectories. In Y. Zheng & X. Zhou (Eds.), *Computing with Spatial Trajectories* (pp. 109–141). New York: Springer. doi:10.1007/978-1-4614-1629-6_4

Christensen, J. H. 2009. Using RESTful web-services and cloud computing to create next generation mobile applications. In *Proceedings of the 24th ACM SIGPLAN conference companion on Object oriented programming systems languages and applications* (pp. 627-634). ACM. 10.1145/1639950.1639958

Chun, B. G., Ihm, S., Maniatis, P., Naik, M., & Patti, A. (2011). Clone Cloud: Elastic execution between mobile device and cloud. In *Proceedings of EuroSys* 2011.

Chun, B.-G., Ihm, S., Maniatis, P., Naik, M., & Patti, A. (2011). Clone Cloud: elastic execution between mobile device and cloud. In *ACM Conference on Computer systems* (pp. 301–314).

Chutani, S., & Goyal, A. (2017). Improved universal quantitative steganalysis in spatial domain using ELM ensemble. *Multimedia Tools and Applications*. doi:10.100711042-017-4656-3

Cimler, R., Matyska, J., & Sobeslav, V. (2014). Cloud based solution for mobile health care application. In *ACM 18th International Database Engineering and Applications Symposium*.

Ciravegna, F. (2001). Adaptive information extraction from text by rule induction and generalization. In *Proceedings of Seventeenth International Joint Conference on Artificial Intelligence IJCAI*, Seattle, WA (Vol. 2, pp. 1251-1256).

Ciravegna, F., Dingli, A., Petrelli, D., & Wilks, Y. (2002). User-System Cooperation in Document Annotation based on Information Extraction. In *International Conference on Knowledge Engineering and Knowledge Management: Ontologies and the Semantic Web EKAW02, LNCS* (Vol. 2473, pp. 122-137). 10.1007/3-540-45810-7_15

Cisco. (2014, January 29). *Cisco Delivers Vision of Fog Computing to Accelerate Value from Billions of Connected Devices*. Retrieved July 2017, from https://newsroom.cisco.com/press-release-content?articleId=1334100

Cisco. (2015). *Cisco Fog Computing Solutions: Unleash the Power of the Internet of Things*.

Clark, D., Hunt, S., & Malacaria, P. (2002). Quantitative Analysis of the leakage of Confidential Data. Elsevier Electronic Notes in Theoretical Computer Science, 59(3), 238-251.

Claudio, A., Ardagna, Mauro Conti, Mario Leone. (2014). An Anonymous End-to-End Communication Protocol for Mobile Cloud Environment. *IEEE Transactions on Services Computing*, *7*(3).

Colace, F., Santo, M. D., Greco, L., Moscato, V., & Picariello, A. (2016). Probabilistic Approaches for Sentiment Analysis: Latent Dirichlet Allocation for Ontology Building and Sentiment Extraction. In W. Pedrycz, & S.-M. Chen, (Eds.), Sentiment Analysis and Ontology Engineering (Vol. 639, pp. 75-91). Springer. doi:10.1007/978-3-319-30319-2_4

Coles, C. (2017). *11 Advantages of Cloud Computing and How Your Business Can Benefit From Them.* (SkyHigh) Retrieved from https://www.skyhighnetworks.com/cloud-security-blog/11-advantages-of-cloud-computing-and-how-your-business-can-benefit-from-them/

Consolvo, S., McDonald, D. W., Toscos, T., Chen, M. Y., Froehlich, J., Harrison, B., ... Smith, I. (2008, April). Activity sensing in the wild: a field trial of ubifit garden. In *Proceedings of the SIGCHI Conference on Human Factors in Computing Systems* (pp. 1797-1806). ACM.

Cooper, E., Lindley, S., Wadler, P., & Yallop, J. (2007). *Links: Web programming without tiers. In Formal Methods for Components and Objects* (pp. 266–296). Springer. doi:10.1007/978-3-540-74792-5_12

Coppersmith, D. (1994). The Data Encryption Standard (DES) and its strength against attacks. IBM journal of research and development, 38(3), 243-250. doi:10.1147/rd.383.0243

Cuervo, E., Balasubramanian, A., Cho, D. K., Wolman, A., Saroiu, S., Chandra, R., & Bahl, P. (2010). Maui: Making smartphones last longer with code offload. In AMC international conference on Mobile systems, applications, and services (pp. 49-62).

Damasevicius, R., Ziberkas, G., Stuikys, V., & Toldinas, J. (2012). Energy consumption of hash functions. *Elektronika ir Elektrotechnika*, *18*(10), 81–84. doi:10.5755/j01.eee.18.10.3069

Damgård, I. (1990). A design principle for hash functions. In Advances in Cryptology—CRYPTO'89 Proceedings (pp. 416-427). Springer Berlin/Heidelberg. doi:10.1007/0-387-34805-0_39

DeCandia, G., Hastorun, D., Jampani, M., Kakulapati, G., Lakshman, A., Pilchin, A., & Vogels, W. (2007). Dynamo: Amazon's highly available key-value store. *Operating Systems Review*, *41*(6), 205–220. doi:10.1145/1323293.1294281

Dell Edge Gateways for IoT. (2017). (Dell) Retrieved November 6, 2017, from http://www.dell.com/us/business/p/edge-gateway

Demchenko, Y., Ngo, C., de Laat, C., Membrey, P., & Gordijenko, D. (2013, August). Big security for big data: Addressing security challenges for the big data infrastructure. In *Workshop on Secure Data Management* (pp. 76-94). Springer.

Denemark, T., Sedighi, V., Holub, V., Cogranne, R., & Fridrich, J. (2014). Selection-channel-aware rich model for steganalysis of digital images. In *Proceedings of IEEE International Workshop on Information Forensics and Security (WIFS)* (pp. 48–53).

Deutsch, A., Hull, R., Vyas, A., & Zhao, K. K. (2010, March 1-6). Policy aware sender anonymity in location based services. In *Proceedings of the 26th International Conference Data Engineering (ICDE 2010)*, Long Beach, CA. 10.1109/ICDE.2010.5447823

Dewri, R., Ray, I., Ray, I., & Whitley, D. (2010, March 23-26). Query m-invariance: preventing query disclosures in continuous location-based services. In *Proceedings of the 11th International Conference on Mobile Data Management (MDM 2010)*, Kansas City, MS (pp. 95-104). 10.1109/MDM.2010.52

Digital Humanitarian Network. (n.d.). Retrieved October 4, 2015 from http://digitalhumanitarians.com/

Dinesha, H. A., & Agrawal, V. K. (2012, February). Multi-level authentication technique for accessing cloud services. In *2012 International Conference on Computing, Communication and Applications (ICCCA)*. IEEE. doi:10.1109/ICCCA.2012.6179130

Dinh, H. T., Lee, C., Niyato, D., & Wang, P. (2013). A Survey of Mobile Cloud Computing: Architecture, Applications and Approaches. *Wireless Communications and Mobile Computing*, *13*(18), 1587–1611. doi:10.1002/wcm.1203

Dou, W., Zhang, X., Liu, J., & Chen, J. (2015). HireSome-II: Towards privacy-aware cross-cloud service composition for big data applications. *IEEE Transactions on Parallel and Distributed Systems*, *26*(2), 455–466. doi:10.1109/TPDS.2013.246

Duong, T. V. T., & Tran, D. Q. (2015, December). A Fusion of Data Mining Techniques for Predicting Movement of Mobile Users. *Journal of Communications and Networks (Seoul)*, *17*(6), 568–581. doi:10.1109/JCN.2015.000104

Eagle, N., & Pentland, A. S. (2006). Reality mining: Sensing complex social systems. *Personal and Ubiquitous Computing*, *10*(4), 255–268. doi:10.100700779-005-0046-3

Edwards-Murphy, F., Magno, M., Whelan, P. M., O'Halloran, J., & Popovici, E. M. (2016, June). Smart beehive with preliminary decision tree analysis for agriculture and honey bee health monitoring. *Computers and Electronics in Agriculture*, *124*, 211–219. doi:10.1016/j.compag.2016.04.008

Elgendy, N., & Elragal, A. (2014, July). Big data analytics: a literature review paper. In *Industrial Conference on Data Mining* (pp. 214-227). Springer, Cham. 10.1007/978-3-319-08976-8_16

Elgendy, N., & Elragal, A. (2016). Big Data Analytics in Support of the Decision Making Process. *Procedia Computer Science*, *100*, 1071–1084. doi:10.1016/j.procs.2016.09.251

Elhauge, E. (2010). *The fragmentation of US health care: causes and solutions*. Oxford University Press on Demand.

Elminaam, D. S. A., Abdual-Kader, H. M., & Hadhoud, M. M. (2010). Evaluating the performance of symmetric encryption algorithms. *International Journal of Network Security*, *10*(3), 216–222.

Eynon, R. (2013). The rise of Big Data: what does it mean for education, technology, and media research?

Farid, H. (2002). Detecting hidden messages using higher-order statistical models. In *Proceedings of International Conference on Image Processing*, Rochester, NY (pp. 905–908). 10.1109/ICIP.2002.1040098

Fayyad, U., Piatetsky-Shapiro, G., & Smyth, P. (1996). From data mining to knowledge discovery in databases. *AI Magazine*, *17*(3), 37.

Felter, W., Rajamani, K., Keller, T., & Rusu, C. (2005, June). A performance-conserving approach for reducing peak power consumption in server systems. In *Proceedings of the 19th annual international conference on Supercomputing* (pp. 293-302). ACM. 10.1145/1088149.1088188

Femal, M. E., & Freeh, V. W. (2004, December). Safe overprovisioning: Using power limits to increase aggregate throughput. In PACS (pp. 150-164).

Ferretti, S., Ghini, V., Panzieri, F., & Turrini, E. (2010). Seamless support of multimedia distributed applications through a cloud. In *IEEE 3rd International Conference on Cloud Computing* (pp. 548–549). 10.1109/CLOUD.2010.16

Firdhous, M., Ghazali, O., & Hassan, S. (2014). Fog Computing: Will it be the Future of Cloud Computing? In *International Conference on Informatics & Applications*, Kuala Terengganu, Malaysia.

Fraga-Lamas, P., Fernández-Caramés, T. M., Suárez-Albela, M., Castedo, L., & González-López, M. (2016). A review on the internet of things for defense and public safety. *Sensors (Basel)*, *16*(10), 1644. doi:10.339016101644

Freitas, L. A., & Vieira, R. (2013). Ontology based Feature Level Opinion Mining for Portuguese Reviews. In *WWW'13 Companion Proceedings of the 22nd International Conference on World Wide Web*, Rio de Janeiro, Brazil (pp. 367-370). 10.1145/2487788.2487944

Frias-Martinez, E., Williamson, G., & Frias-Martinez, V. (2011, October). An agent-based model of epidemic spread using human mobility and social network information. In *2011 IEEE Third International Conference on Privacy, Security, Risk and Trust (PASSAT) and 2011 IEEE Third International Conference on Social Computing (SocialCom)* (pp. 57-64). IEEE. 10.1109/PASSAT/SocialCom.2011.142

Fridrich, J., Goljan, M., Hogea, D., & Soukal, D. (2003). Quantitative Steganalysis of Digital Images estimating the Secret Message Length. *ACM Multimedia Systems*, *9*(3), 288-302.

Fridrich, J., & Goljan, M. (2002). Practical steganalysis of digital images-state of the art. In *Proc. SPIE Photonics West, Electronic Imaging, Security and Watermarking of Multimedia Contents*, San Jose, CA.

Friedman, C., Rubin, J., Brown, J., Buntin, M., Corn, M., Etheredge, L., & Sullivan, K. (2014). Toward a science of learning systems: a research agenda for the high-functioning Learning Health System. *Journal of the American Medical Informatics Association*.

Geetha, S., Sindhu, S. S. S., & Kamaraj, N. (2008). StegoBreaker: Defeating the steganographic systems through genetic Xmeans approach using image quality metrics. In *Proceedings: of the 16th IEEE International Conference on Advanced Computing and Communication* (pp. 382–391).

Geetha, S., Sivatha Sindhu, S. S., & Kamaraj, N. (2009). Blind image steganalysis based on content independent statistical measures maximizing the specificity and sensitivity of the system. *Computers & Security*, *28*(7), 683–697. doi:10.1016/j.cose.2009.03.006

Gerdes, M. (2014). Decision trees and genetic algorithms for condition monitoring forecasting of aircraft air conditioning. *Computers and Electronics in Agriculture*, *40*(12), 5021–5026.

Gilbert, S., & Lynch, N. (2012). Perspectives on the CAP Theorem. *Computer, 45*(2), 30–36. doi:10.1109/MC.2011.389

Giurgiu, I., Riva, O., Juric, D., Krivulev, I., & Alonso, G. (2009). Calling the cloud: Enabling mobile phones as interfaces to cloud applications. *Middleware, 2009*, 83–102.

Gmach, D., Rolia, J., Cherkasova, L., & Kemper, A. (2007, September). Workload analysis and demand prediction of enterprise data center applications. In *IEEE 10th International Symposium on Workload Characterization IISWC '07* (pp. 171-180). IEEE. 10.1109/IISWC.2007.4362193

Gordon, L. A., & Loeb, M. P. (2002). The economics of information security investment. *ACM Transactions on Information and System Security, 5*(4), 438–457.

Gruteser, M., & Liu, X. (2004, March/April). Protecting privacy in continuous location-tracking applications. *IEEE Security and Privacy, 2*(2), 28–34. doi:10.1109/MSECP.2004.1281242

Guan, Q., Dong, J., & Tan, T. (2010). Blind Quantitative steganalysis Based on Feature Fusion and gradient boosting. In *Proceeding of Digital Watermarking: 9th International Workshop, IWDW.*

Guh, R. S., Wu, T. C. J., & Weng, S. P. (2011). Integrating genetic algorithm and decision tree learning for assistance in predicting in vitro fertilization outcomes. *Expert Systems with Applications, 38*(4), 4437–4449. doi:10.1016/j.eswa.2010.09.112

Guo, H., Zhu, H., Guo, Z., & Su, Z. (2009). Product feature categorization with multilevel latent semantic association. In *Proceedings of the Eighteenth ACM Conference on Information and Knowledge Management CIKM '09*, Hong Kong, China (pp. 1087-1096). 10.1145/1645953.1646091

Guo, T., Yan, Z., & Aberer, K. (2012). An adaptive approach for online segmentation of multi-dimensional mobile data. In *ACM International Workshop on Data Engineering for Wireless and Mobile Access.* 10.1145/2258056.2258059

Gupta, S., Goyal, A., & Bhushan, B. (2012). Information Hiding Using Least Significant Bit Steganography and Cryptography. *International Journal of Modern Education and Computer Science, 4*(6), 27.

Hadoop. (2014). What Is Apache Hadoop? Retrieved from https://hadoop.apache.org/

Hamid, N., Yahya, A. R., Ahmad, B., & Al-Qershi, O. M. (2012). *Image Steganography Techniques: An Overview. International Journal of Computer Science and Security, 6*(3).

Hammer-Lahav, E. (2010). *The OAuth 1.0 Protocol.* Internet Engineering Task Force.

Hao, F., Lakshman, T. V., Mukherjee, S., & Song, H. (2009, August). Enhancing dynamic cloud-based services using network virtualization. In *Proceedings of the 1st ACM workshop on Virtualized infrastructure systems and architectures* (pp. 37-44). ACM.

Harbitter, A. & Menasc´e, D.A. (2001). The performance of public key enabled Kerberos authentication in mobile computing applications. In *ACM conference on Computer and Communications Security* (pp. 78–85).

Harmsen, J. J. (2003). Steganalysis of Additive Noise Modelable Information Hiding [Master dissertation]. Rensselaer Polytechnic Institute, Troy, NY.

Hartmann, P. M., Zaki, M., Feldmann, N., & Neely, A. (2014, March 27). Big data for big business? A taxonomy of data-driven business models used by start-up firms. *A Taxonomy of Data-Driven Business Models Used by Start-Up Firms.*

Herring, R., Hofleitner, A., Amin, S., Nasr, T., Khalek, A., Abbeel, P., & Bayen, A. (2009). *Using mobile phones to forecast arterial traffic through statistical learning.* Transportation Research Board.

Hewlett Packard Enterprise. (2017). *HPE Edgeline Converged Edge Systems.* Retrieved November 6, 2017, from https://www.hpe.com/in/en/servers/edgeline-iot-systems.html#header

He, Y., Elnikety, S., Larus, J., & Yan, C. (2012). Zeta: scheduling interactive services with partial execution. In *ACM Symposium on Cloud Computing.* 10.1145/2391229.2391241

Hilbert, M. (2013). Big data for development: From information-to knowledge societies.

Hinton, G. E., Osindero, S., & Teh, Y. W. (2006). A fast learning algorithm for deep belief nets. *Neural Computation, 18*(7), 1527–1554. doi:10.1162/neco.2006.18.7.1527

Holotyak, T., Fridrich, J., & Voloshynovskiy, S. (2005). *Blind statistical steganalysis of additive steganography using wavelet higher order statistics.* doi:10.1007/11552055_31

Holub, V., & Fridrich, J. (2015). Phase-aware projection model for steganalysis of JPEG images. In *Proceedings of Media Watermarking, Security, and Forensics 2015*, San Francisco, CA, February 9-11.

Holub, V., & Fridrich, J.(2013). Random Projections of Residuals for Digital Image Steganalysis. *IEEE Transactions on Information Forensics and Security, 8*(12), 1996-2006.

Holub, V., & Fridrich, J. (2015). Low Complexity Features for JPEG Steganalysis Using Undecimated DCT. *IEEE Transactions on Information Forensics and Security, 10*(2), 219–228. doi:10.1109/TIFS.2014.2364918

Holub, V., Fridrich, J., & Denemark, T. (2013). Random Projections of Residuals as an Alternative to Co-occurrence in Steganalysis. In *Proceedings of SPIE, Electronic Imaging, Media Watermarking, Security and forensics XV*, San Francisco, CA. 10.1117/12.1000330

Houle, K. J., & Weaver, G. M. (2001). *Trends in Denial of Service Attack Technology (v1.0).* Carnegie Mellon University.

Huang, D., Zhou, Z., Xu, L., Xing, T., & Zhong, Y. (2011). Secure Data Processing Framework for Mobile Cloud Computing. In *Proceedings of IEEE Conference on Computer Communications Workshops (INFOCOM WKSHPS).* (pp. 614-618). 10.1109/INFCOMW.2011.5928886

Hueniverse. (n.d.). Oauth 2.0 (without signatures) is bad for the web. Retrieved from http://hueniverse.com/2010/09/oauth-2-0-without-signatures-isbad- for-the-web/

Huerta-Canepa, G., & Lee, D. (2010). A Virtual Cloud Computing Provider for Mobile Devices. In *ACM Workshop on Mobile Cloud Computing & Services: Social Networks and Beyond. MCS'10.* 10.1145/1810931.1810937

Humanitarian Open Street Map Team. (n.d.). Ongoing Projects. Retrieved from. http://hotosm.org/projects/ongoing

Hunt, G., & Scott, M. (1998). The coign automatic distributed partitioning system. ACM Operating systems review, 33, 187–200.

Hunter, T., Moldovan, T., Zaharia, M., Merzgui, S., Ma, J., Franklin, M., ... Bayen, A. (2011). Scaling the mobile millennium system in the cloud. In *ACM Symposium on Cloud Computing 2011* (p. 28). 10.1145/2038916.2038944

Hussain, M., and Hussain M. (2013). A Survey of Image Steganography Techniques. *International Journal of Advanced Science and Technology, 54.*

Hu, W.-C., Kaabouch, N., & Yang, H.-J. (2016, May 19-21). Secure spatial trajectory prediction based on traffic flows. In *Proceedings of the 2016 IEEE International Electro/Information Technology Conference (EIT 2016)*, Grand Forks, ND. 10.1109/EIT.2016.7535328

IEEE. (2009). Cloud computing drives mobile data growth. Retrieved from http://spectrum.ieee.org/telecom/wireless/cloudcomputing-drives-mobile-data-growth

Immagic. (n.d.). Compromising twitter's oauth security system. Retrieved from http://www.immagic.com/eLibrary/ARCHIVES/GENERAL/GENPRESS/A090903P.pdf

Intel. (2012). Int. cloud services platform beta location-based services. Retrieved from http://software.intel.com/enus/articles/cloud-services-location-based-api-overview

Irani, S., Shukla, S., & Gupta, R. (2003). Online strategies for dynamic power management in systems with multiple power-saving states. *ACM Transactions on Embedded Computing Systems, 2*(3), 325–346. doi:10.1145/860176.860180

Isci, C., Contreras, G., & Martonosi, M. (2006, December). Live, runtime phase monitoring and prediction on real systems with application to dynamic power management. In *Proceedings of the 39th Annual IEEE/ACM International Symposium on Microarchitecture* (pp. 359-370). IEEE Computer Society. 10.1109/MICRO.2006.30

Iyengar, A. K., Squillante, M. S., & Zhang, L. (1999). Analysis and characterization of large-scale Web server access patterns and performance. *World Wide Web (Bussum), 2*(1), 85–100. doi:10.1023/A:1019244621570

Jagadish, H. V., Gehrke, J., Labrinidis, A., Papakonstantinou, Y., Patel, J. M., Ramakrishnan, R., & Shahabi, C. (2014). Big data and its technical challenges. *Communications of the ACM, 57*(7), 86–94. doi:10.1145/2611567

Jamshidi, M., Tannahill, B., Yetis, Y., & Kaplan, H. (2015). Big data analytic via soft computing paradigms. In *Frontiers of higher order fuzzy sets* (pp. 229–258). Springer New York. doi:10.1007/978-1-4614-3442-9_12

Jasim, O. K., Abbas, S., El-Horbaty, E. S. M., & Salem, A. B. M. (2013). Cloud Computing Cryptography. World Academy of Science, Engineering and Technology, International Journal of Computer, Electrical, Automation. *Control and Information Engineering*, 7(8), 1161–1164.

Jeong, Y. S., & Shin, S. S. (2016). An Efficient Authentication Scheme to Protect User Privacy in Seamless Big Data Services. *Wireless Personal Communications*, 86(1), 7–19. Retrieved from http://web.a.ebscohost.com/abstract?direct=true&profile=ehost&scope=site&authtype=crawler&jrnl=09296212&AN=111455684&h=7IFKiKh0Lg%2fy2FHp%2b55gtkcsVzZJxAEGRQ15KxUutmue2vo481ON7i1qe1jDHwu%2fkZg0y%2b7wVoBerrtIukr5PQ%3d%3d&crl=c&resultNs=AdminWebAuth&resultLocal=ErrCrlNotAuth&crlhashurl=login.aspx%3fdirect%3dtrue%26profile%3dehost%26scope%3dsite%26authtype%3dcrawler%26jrnl%3d09296212%26AN%3d111455684 doi:10.100711277-015-2990-1

Jessica Fridrich, J. Kodovsky. (2012). Rich Models for Steganalysis of Digital Images. IEEE Transactions on Information Forensics and Security, 7(3).

Juneja, M., & Sandhu, P. S. (2013). An Improved LSB Based Steganography Technique for RGB Color Images. *International Journal of Computer and Communication Engineering*, 2(4).

Kamat, G., & Singh, S. (2013). Comparisons of compression. In: Hadoop Summit 2013. Retrieved from http://www.slideshare.net/Hadoop_Summit/kamat-singh-june27425pmroom210cv2

Kamps, M. M., Mokken, R. J., & De Rijke, M. (2004). Using wordnet to measure semantic orientation of adjectives. In *Proceedings of 4th International Conference on Language Resources and Evaluation*, Lisbon, Portugal (pp. 1115- 1118).

Kandukuri, B. R., & Rakshit, A. (2009, September). Cloud security issues. In *IEEE International Conference on Services Computing SCC '09* (pp. 517-520). IEEE. doi:10.1109/SCC.2009.84

Kangas, K., & Röning, J. (1999, August). Using code mobility to create ubiquitous and active augmented reality in mobile computing. In *Proceedings of the 5th annual ACM/IEEE international conference on Mobile computing and networking* (pp. 48-58). ACM.

Kaps, J. P., & Sunar, B. (2006, August). Energy comparison of AES and SHA-1 for ubiquitous computing. In *International Conference on Embedded and Ubiquitous Computing* (pp. 372-381). Springer Berlin Heidelberg. 10.1007/11807964_38

Karlin, A. R., Manasse, M. S., McGeoch, L. A., & Owicki, S. (1994). Competitive randomized algorithms for nonuniform problems. *Algorithmica*, 11(6), 542–571. doi:10.1007/BF01189993

Katal, A., Wazid, M., & Goudar, R. H. (2013, August). Big data: issues, challenges, tools and good practices. In *2013 Sixth International Conference on Contemporary Computing (IC3)* (pp. 404-409). IEEE. 10.1109/IC3.2013.6612229

Kaur, R. P., & Kaur, A. (2014). Perspectives of Mobile Cloud Computing: Architecture, Applications and Issues. *International Journal of Computer Applications, 101*(3).

Kelly, J. (2013). Apache drill brings SQL-like, ad-hoc query capabilities to big data.

Kemp, R., Palmer, N., Kielmann, T., & Bal, H. (2012). Cuckoo: A computation offloading framework for smartphones. In *Mobile Computing, Applications, and Services, LNICSSITE* (Vol. *76*, pp. 59–79) . *Springer.*

Ker, A. D. (2014). *Implementing the projected spatial rich features on a GPU. SPIE 9028.* Media Watermarking Security, and Forensics.

Khalid, O., Khan, M., Khan, S., & Zomaya, A. (2014). Omni Suggest: A Ubiquitous Cloud based Context Aware Recommendation System for MobileSocial Networks. *IEEE Transactions on Services Computing, 7*(3), 401–414. doi:10.1109/TSC.2013.53

Khan, N. N. (2015). Fog Computing: A Better Solution For IoT. *International Journal of Engineering and Technical Research, III*(2).

Khorshed, M. T., Ali, A. S., & Wasimi, S. A. (2012). A survey on gaps, threat remediation challenges and some thoughts for proactive attack detection in cloud computing. *Future Generation Computer Systems, 28*(6), 833–851.

Kido, H., Yanagisawa, Y., & Satoh, T. (2005). An anonymous communication technique using dummies for location-based services. In *Proceedings of IEEE International Conference on Pervasive Services (ICPS'05)*, Santorini, Greece (pp. 88-97). 10.1109/PERSER.2005.1506394

Knight, W. (2015). *Deep learning catches on in new industries, from fashion to finance.* MIT Technol. Rev.

Kodovsky, J. Jessica Fridrich. (2012). Steganalysis of JPEG images Using rich Models. In *Proceedings of SPIE, Electronic Imaging, Media Watermarking, Security, and Forensics XIV.*

Kodovsky, J., & Fridrich, J. (2010). Quantitative steganalysis of LSB embedding in JPEG domain. In *MM&Sec '10 Proceedings of the 12th ACM workshop on Multimedia and security* (pp. 187-198). 10.1145/1854229.1854265

Kodovský, J., & Fridrich, J. (2013). Quantitative Steganalysis Using Rich Models. In *Media Watermarking, Security, and Forensics XV*, San Francisco, CA, February 3-7.

Kodovsky, J., Fridrich, J., & Holub, V. (2011). On dangers of overtraining steganography to incomplete cover model. In *Proceedings of 13th ACM Multimedia and security workshop*, Niagara Falls, New York (pp. 69-76). 10.1145/2037252.2037266

Kodovsky, J., Fridrich, J., & Holub, V. (2012). Ensemble classifiers for steganalysis of digital media. *IEEE Transactions on Information Forensics and Security, 7*(2), 432–444. doi:10.1109/TIFS.2011.2175919

Kontopoulos, E., Berberidis, C., Dergiades, T., & Bassiliades, N. (2013). Ontology-based sentiment analysis of twitter posts. *Expert Systems with Applications, 40*(10), 4065–4074. doi:10.1016/j.eswa.2013.01.001

Kosta, S., Aucinas, A., Hui, P., Mortier, R., & Zhang, X. (2012, March). Think Air: Dynamic resource allocation and parallel execution in the cloud for mobile code offloading. In IEEE INFOCOM (pp. 945-953).

Kotla, R., Ghiasi, S., Keller, T., & Rawson, F. (2005, April). Scheduling processor voltage and frequency in server and cluster systems. In *Proceedings. 19th IEEE International Parallel and Distributed Processing Symposium*. IEEE. 10.1109/IPDPS.2005.392

Kovachev, D., Renzel, D., Klamma, R., & Cao, Y. (2010). Mobile Community Cloud Computing: Emerges and Evolves. In *Proceedings of the First International Workshop on Mobile Cloud Computing (MCC)*, Kansas City, MO. 10.1109/MDM.2010.78

Kowsigan, M., & Balasubramanie, P. (2016). An Improved Job Scheduling in Cloud Environment using Auto-Associative-Memory Network. *Asian Journal of Research in Social Sciences and Humanities*, *6*(12), 390–410.

Kowsigan, M., Kalicharan, S., Karthik, P., Manikandan, A., & Manikandan, R. M. (2017). An Enhanced Job Scheduling in Cloud Environment Using Probability Distribution. *IACSIT International Journal of Engineering and Technology*, *9*(2), 1374–1381.

Kowsigan, M., Rajkumar, S., Seenivasan, P., & Kumar, C. V. (2017). An Enhanced Job Scheduling in Cloud Environment using Improved Metaheuristic Approach. *International Journal of Engineering Research and Technology*, *6*(2), 184–188.

Kowsigan, M., Rubasri, M., Sujithra, R., & Banu, H. S. (2017). Data Security and Data Dissemination of Distributed Data in Wireless Sensor Networks. *International Journal of Engineering Research and Applications*, *7*(3 part 4), 26–31.

KPMG. (2014). Cybercrime Survey Report 2014. Retrieved from https://cyberlawin.files.wordpress.com/2014/09/kpmg_cyber_crime_survey_report_2014.pdf

Kraft, S., Casale, G., Jula, A., Kilpatrick, P., & Greer, D. (2012, June). Wiq: work-intensive query scheduling for in-memory database systems. In *2012 IEEE 5th International Conference on Cloud Computing (CLOUD)* (pp. 33-40). IEEE. 10.1109/CLOUD.2012.120

Krutz, R. L., & Vines, R. D. (2010). Cloud security: A comprehensive guide to secure cloud computing. Wiley Publishing.

Krutz, R. L., & Vines, R. D. (2010). *Cloud security: A comprehensive guide to secure cloud computing*. Wiley Publishing.

Kshetri, N. (2014). The emerging role of Big Data in key development issues: Opportunities, challenges, and concerns. *Big Data & Society*, *1*(2). doi:10.1177/2053951714564227

Kumar, A., & Pooja, K.M. (2010). Steganography: A Data Hiding Technique. *International Journal of Computer Applications*, *9*(7).

274

Kumari, S. (2015, December 28). *Agility on Cloud – A Vital Part of Cloud Computing*. (Sysfore Blog) Retrieved July 2017, from http://blog.sysfore.com/agility-on-cloud-a-vital-part-of-cloud-computing/

Kuo, W.-C., Wei, H.-J., & Cheng, J.-C. (2014). An efficient and secure anonymous mobility network authentication scheme. *Journal of Information Security and Applications*, *19*(1), 18–24. doi:10.1016/j.jisa.2013.12.002

Kutter, M., & Petitcolas, F. A. P. (1999). A fair benchmark for image watermarking systems. In E. J. Delp, & P. W. Wong (Eds.), *Proceedings SPIE, Electronic Imaging, Security and Watermarking of Multimedia Contents I*, San Jose, CA (pp. 226–239). 10.1117/12.344672

La, H., & Kim, S. (2010). A conceptual framework for provisioning context aware mobile cloud services. In *IEEE 3rd International Conference on Cloud Computing* (pp. 466–473). 10.1109/CLOUD.2010.78

Laimeche, L., & Merouani, H. F. & Mazouzi, S. (2017). A new feature extraction scheme in wavelet transform for stego image classification. Evolving Systems.

Lakshmi, B. N., Indumathi, T. S., & Ravic, N. (2016). A study on C.5 Decision Tree Classification Algorithm for Risk Predictions during Pregnancy. *Procedia Technology*, *24*, 1542–1549. doi:10.1016/j.protcy.2016.05.128

Lampe, U., Siebenhaar, M., Papageorgiou, A., Schuller, D., & Steinmetz, R. (n.d.). Maximizing cloud provider profit from equilibrium price auctions [pre-print].

Lane, N., Miluzzo, E., Lu, H., Peebles, D., Choudhury, T., & Campbell, A. (2010). A survey of mobile phone sensing. *IEEE Communications Magazine*, *48*(9), 140–150. doi:10.1109/MCOM.2010.5560598

Laney, D. (2001). 3D data management: Controlling data volume, velocity, and variety. *META Group Research Note*, *6*, 70.

Lau, F., Rubin, S. H., Smith, M. H., & Trajkovic, L. (2000). Distributed denial of service attacks. In 2000 IEEE International Conference on Systems, Man, and Cybernetics (Vol. 3, pp. 2275-2280). IEEE. doi:10.1109/ICSMC.2000.886455

Launay, M., Caubel, J., Bourgeois, G., Huard, F., Garcia de Cortazar-Atauri, I., Bancal, M. O., & Brisson, N. (2014). Climatic indicators for crop infection risk: Application to climate change impacts on five major foliar fungal diseases in Northern France. *Agriculture, Ecosystems & Environment*, *197*, 147–158. doi:10.1016/j.agee.2014.07.020

Laurila, J. K., Gatica-Perez, D., Aad, I., Bornet, O., Do, T. M. T., Dousse, O., & Miettinen, M. (2012). The mobile data challenge: Big data for mobile computing research. In Pervasive Computing.

Lawton, S. (2015) Cloud Encryption: Using Data Encryption In The Cloud, tomsitpro.com. Available at: http://www.tomsitpro.com/articles/cloud-data-encryption,2-913.html

Leavitt, N. (2010). Will NoSQL databases live up to their promise? *Computer*, *43*(2), 12–14. doi:10.1109/MC.2010.58

Ledesma, S., Aviña, G., & Sanchez, R. (2008). Practical considerations for simulated annealing implementation. In *Simulated Annealing*. InTech.

Li, H., Cher, C. Y., Vijaykumar, T. N., & Roy, K. (2003, December). VSV: L2-miss-driven variable supply-voltage scaling for low power. In *Proceedings. 36th Annual IEEE/ACM International Symposium on Microarchitecture MICRO-36* (pp. 19-28). IEEE.

Li, J., Wang, Q., Wang, C., Cao, N., Ren, K., & Lou, W. (2010, March). Fuzzy keyword search over encrypted data in cloud computing. In INFOCOM, 2010 Proceedings IEEE. IEEE. doi:10.1109/INFCOM.2010.5462196

Li, H., & Li, H. (2011). A research of resource provider-oriented pricing mechanism based on game theory in cloud bank model. In *IEEE International Conference on Cloud and Service Computing* (pp. 126–130). 10.1109/CSC.2011.6138509

Li, M., Yu, S., Zheng, Y., Ren, K., & Lou, W. (2013). Scalable and secure sharing of personal health records in cloud computing using attribute-based encryption. *IEEE Transactions on Parallel and Distributed Systems*, 24(1), 131–143. doi:10.1109/TPDS.2012.97

Liu, L., Moulic, R., & Shea, D. 2010. Cloud service portal for mobile device management. In *2010 IEEE 7th International Conference on e-Business Engineering (ICEBE)* (pp. 474-478). IEEE. 10.1109/ICEBE.2010.102

Liu, F., Shu, P., Jin, H., Ding, L., Yu, J., Niu, D., & Li, B. (2013). Gearing resource-poor mobile devices with powerful clouds: Architectures, challenges, and applications. *Wireless Communications, IEEE*, 20(3), 14–22. doi:10.1109/MWC.2013.6549279

Liu, Y., Wu, B., Wang, H., & Ma, P. (2014). Bpgm: A big graph mining tool. *Tsinghua Science and Technology*, 19(1), 33–38. doi:10.1109/TST.2014.6733206

Li, W., Zhang, T., Wang, R., & Zhang, Y. (2014, February 18). Quantitative steganalysis of least significant bit matching revisited for consecutive pixels. *Journal of Electronic Imaging*, 23(1), 013025. doi:10.1117/1.JEI.23.1.013025

Lobella, D. B., & Burke, M. B. C. (2010). On the use of statistical models to predict crop yield responses to climate change. *Journal of Agricultural and Forest Meteorology*, 150(11), 1443–1452. doi:10.1016/j.agrformet.2010.07.008

Lohr, S. (2015). Using patient data to democratize medical discovery. *New York Times, Bits Blog*.

López, C. E. G., Guzmán, E. L., & González, F. A. (2015, July). A Model to Model to Predict Low Academic Performance a at a Specific Enrollment Using Data Mining. *IEEE Revista Iberoamericana de Tecnologias del Aprendizaje*, 10(3), 119–125. doi:10.1109/RITA.2015.2452632

Lord, N. (2017). Cryptography in the Cloud: Securing Cloud Data with Encryption. *digitalguardian.com*. Retrieved from https://digitalguardian.com/blog/cryptography-cloud-securing-cloud-data-encryption

Lu, H. K. (2014). U.S. Patent Application No. 13/729,070.

Lu, Y., Duan, H., Wang, H., & Zhai, C. X. (2010). Exploiting Structured Ontology to Organize Scattered Online Opinions. In *Proceedings of the Twenty Third International Conference on Computational Linguistics*, Beijing, China (pp. 734–742).

Lu, H., Jensen, C. S., & Liu, M. L. (2008, June 13). PAD: Privacy-area aware, dummy-based location privacy in mobile devices. In *Proceedings of the 7th ACM International Workshop on Data Engineering for Wireless and Mobile Access (Mobide 2008)*, Vancouver, Canada. 10.1145/1626536.1626540

Lu, H., Pan, W., Lane, N., Choudhury, T., & Campbell, A. (2009). Sound sense: scalable sound sensing for people-centric applications on mobile phones. In *International conference on Mobile systems, applications, and services* (pp. 165–178).

Luo, X. (2009, July). From augmented reality to augmented computing: A look at cloud-mobile convergence. In *International Symposium on Ubiquitous Virtual Reality* (pp. 29–32). 10.1109/ISUVR.2009.13

Madhavi B. Desai, S. V. Patel, Bhumi Prajapati. (2016). ANOVA and Fisher Criterion based Feature Selection for Lower Dimensional Universal Image Steganalysis. *International Journal of Image Processing*, *10*(3), 145- 160.

Maedche, A., Pekar, V., & Staab, S. (2003). Ontology Learning Part One - On Discovering Taxonomic Relations from the Web. In N. Zhong (Ed.), Web Intelligence (pp. 301-320). Springer. doi:10.1007/978-3-662-05320-1_14

Ma, J., Xu, W., Sun, Y., Turban, E., Wang, S., & Liu, O. (2012). An Ontology-Based Text-Mining Method to Cluster Proposals for Research Project Selection. *IEEE Transactions on Systems, Man, and Cybernetics. Part A, Systems and Humans*, *42*(3), 784–790. doi:10.1109/TSMCA.2011.2172205

Mane, Y. D. & Devadkar, K. K. (2013). Protection Concern in Mobile Cloud Computing–A Survey. *IOSR Journal of Computer Engineering*, *3*, 39-44.

Manyika, J., Chui, M., Groves, P., Farrell, D., Van Kuiken, S., & Doshi, E. A. (2013). Open data: Unlocking innovation and performance with liquid information. McKinsey Global Institute.

Ma, R. K. K., & Wang, C.-L. (2012). Lightweight Application level Task Migration for Mobile Cloud Computing. In *Proceedings of 26th IEEE International Conference on Advanced Information Networking and Applications*. 10.1109/AINA.2012.124

Masseglia, F., Poncelet, P., & Teisseire, M. (2013, July). Incremental mining of sequential patterns in large databases. *Journal of Data and Knowledge Engineering*, *46*(1), 97–121. doi:10.1016/S0169-023X(02)00209-4

Mayer-Schönberger, V., & Cukier, K. (2013). *Big data: A revolution that will transform how we live, work, and think*. Houghton Mifflin Harcourt.

Maynard, D., Bontcheva, K., & Cunninham, H. (2003). *Towards a semantic extraction of named entities*. Bulgaria: Recent Advances in Natural Language Processing.

Mazumder, S. (2016). Big Data Tools and Platforms. In Big Data Concepts, Theories, and Applications (pp. 29-128). Springer International Publishing. doi:10.1007/978-3-319-27763-9_2

Meier, P. (2015). *Digital humanitarians: how big data is changing the face of humanitarian response.* CRC Press. doi:10.1201/b18023

Melnik, S., Gubarev, A., Long, J. J., Romer, G., Shivakumar, S., Tolton, M., & Vassilakis, T. (2010). Dremel: Interactive analysis of web-scale datasets. *Proceedings of the VLDB Endowment International Conference on Very Large Data Bases, 3*(1-2), 330–339. doi:10.14778/1920841.1920886

Meng, S., Dou, W., Zhang, X., & Chen, J. (2014). KASR: A keyword-aware service recommendation method on mapreduce for big data applications. *IEEE Transactions on Parallel and Distributed Systems, 25*(12), 3221–3231. doi:10.1109/TPDS.2013.2297117

Merkle, R. (1990). A certified digital signature. In Advances in Cryptology—CRYPTO'89 Proceedings (pp. 218-238). Springer Berlin/Heidelberg. doi:10.1007/0-387-34805-0_21

Merkle, R. C., & Charles, R. (1979). Secrecy, authentication, and public key systems.

Microsoft. (2017). What is Cloud Computing? A beginner's guide. Retrieved July 2017, from https://azure.microsoft.com/en-in/overview/what-is-cloud-computing/

Miculan, M. & Urban, C. (2011). Formal analysis of Facebook connects single sign-on authentication protocol. *SOFSEM, 11,* 22–28.

Miller, D. (2015, July 7). *Beware the Fog (Computing).* Retrieved November 30, 2015, from http://www.cmswire.com/information-management/beware-the-fog-computing/

Miller, J. A., Ramaswamy, L., Kochut, K. J., & Fard, A. (2015, June). Research directions for big data graph analytics. In *2015 IEEE International Congress on Big Data (BigData Congress)* (pp. 785-794). IEEE. 10.1109/BigDataCongress.2015.132

Miloslavskaya, N., & Tolstoy, A. (2016). Big Data, Fast Data and Data Lake Concepts. *Procedia Computer Science, 88,* 300–305. Retrieved from https://ac.els-cdn.com/S1877050916316957/1-s2.0-S1877050916316957-main.pdf?_tid=4d5629d4-ff7f-11e7-bdfe-00000aab0f6c&acdnat=1516630968_7bf0960c12ee94bb5d00caa036126bfc doi:10.1016/j.procs.2016.07.439

Milunovich, S., Passi, A., & Roy, J. (2014, December 4). After the Cloud Comes the Fog: Fog Computing to Enable the Internet of Things. *IT Hardware & Data Networking.*

Miluzzo, E., Lane, N. D., Fodor, K., Peterson, R., Lu, H., Musolesi, M., . . . Campbell, A. T. (2008). Sensing meets mobile social networks: the design, implementation and evaluation of the cenceme application. In ACM conference on Embedded network sensor systems (pp. 337-350).

Min, L., Ming, L., Xue, Y., Yu, Y., & Mian, W. (2016). Improvement of Universal Steganalysis Based on SPAM and Feature Optimization. In *Proceedings Second International conference ICCCS,* Nanjing, China.

Mobilecommercedaily. (2011). AT&T to launch cloud-based lbs mobility data offering. Retrieved from http://www.mobilecommercedaily.com/attto-launch-cloud-based-lbs-mobility-data-offering

Modha, D. S., Ananthanarayanan, R., Esser, S. K., Ndirango, A., Sherbondy, A. J., & Singh, R. (2011). Cognitive computing. *Communications of the ACM*, *54*(8), 62–71. doi:10.1145/1978542.1978559

Moerland, T. (2003). Steganography and Steganalysis. *Leiden Institute of Advanced Computing Science*. Retrieved from http://www.liacs.nl/home/tmoerl/privtech.pdf

Moore, A. W., & Zuev, D. (2005, June). Internet traffic classification using Bayesian analysis techniques. *Performance Evaluation Review*, *33*(1), 50–60. doi:10.1145/1071690.1064220

Mora, R. D. (2014, January 29). *Cisco IOx: An Application Enablement Framework for the Internet of Things.* Retrieved November 8, 2016, from http://blogs.cisco.com/digital/cisco-iox-an-application-enablement-framework-for-the-internet-of-things

Mosca, P., Zhang, Y., Xiao, Z., & Wang, Y. (2014). Cloud Security: Services, Risks, and a Case Study on Amazon Cloud Services. *International Journal of Communications. Network and System Sciences*, *7*(12), 529.

Mun, M., Reddy, S., Shilton, K., Yau, N., Burke, J., Estrin, D., . . . Boda, P. (2009). Peir, the personal environmental impact report, as a platform for participatory sensing systems research. In ACM international conference on Mobile systems, applications, and services (pp. 55-68).

Muñoz, C., Rocci, L., Solana, E., & Leone, P. (2016). Performance Evaluation of Searchable Symmetric Encryption in Wireless Sensor Networks. In *Internet of Things. IoT Infrastructures: Second International Summit, IoT 360° 2015*, Rome, Italy, October 27-29, 2015. Revised Selected Papers, Part I (pp. 40-51). Springer International Publishing.

Nan, X., He, Y., & Guan, L. (2011). Optimal resource allocation for multimedia cloud based on queuing model. In *IEEE 13th International Workshop on Multimedia Signal Processing*. 10.1109/MMSP.2011.6093813

Naranjo, P. G., Shojafary, M., Vaca-Cardenasz, L., Canaliy, C., Lancellottiy, R., & Baccarelli, E. (n.d.). Big Data Over SmartGrid - A Fog Computing Perspective.

Nath, B., Bhattacharyya, D. K., & Ghosh, A. (2013, May). Incremental association rule mining: A survey. *Wiley Interdisciplinary Reviews. Data Mining and Knowledge Discovery*, *3*(3). doi:10.1002/widm.1086

Nathuji, R., & Schwan, K. (2007, October). Virtualpower: Coordinated power management in virtualized enterprise systems. *Operating Systems Review*, *41*(6), 265–278. doi:10.1145/1323293.1294287

Nedellec, C., & Nazarenko, A. (2005). *Ontology and Information Extraction: A Necessary Symbiosis.* In P. Buitelaar, P. Cimiano, & B. Magnini (Eds.), *Ontology Learning from Text: Methods, Evaluation and Applications* (pp. 3–14). Amsterdam, The Netherlands: IOS Press Publications.

Nergiz, M. E., Atzori, M., Saygin, Y., & Guc, B. (2009). Towards trajectory anonymization: A generalization-based approach. *Transactions on Data Privacy*, *2*, 47–75.

Neuman, B. C., & Ts'o, T. (1994, September). Kerberos: An authentication service for computer networks. *IEEE Communications Magazine*, *32*(9), 33–38. doi:10.1109/35.312841

Neumeyer, L., Robbins, B., Nair, A., & Kesari, A. (2010, December). S4: Distributed stream computing platform. In *2010 IEEE International Conference on Data Mining Workshops (ICDMW)* (pp. 170-177). IEEE.

Newhouse, T., & Pasquale, J. (2004). Resource-controlled remote execution to enhance wireless network applications. In *Workshop on Applications and Services in Wireless Networks* (pp. 30-38). 10.1109/ASWN.2004.185152

Nie, T., Song, C., & Zhi, X. (2010, April). Performance evaluation of DES and Blowfish algorithms. In *2010 International Conference on Biomedical Engineering and Computer Science (ICBECS)*. IEEE. 10.1109/ICBECS.2010.5462398

Noubir, G. (n.d.). Fundamentals of Cryptography: Algorithms, and Security Services. Retrieved from http://www.ccs.neu.edu/home/noubir/Courses/CSU610/S06/cryptography.pdf

NxtraData. (2016, June 30). *Difference Between Clound & IOT*. (Nxtra Data) Retrieved July 2017, from http://nxtradata.com/blog/cloud-vs-iot.html

Oauth2.0. (n.d.). Retrieved from http://oauth.net/2/

Open Semantic Framework. (n.d.). Retrieved Sept 2016 from Opensemanticframework.org

Outguess – Universal Steganography. (n.d.). Retrieved from http://www.outguess.org

Pai, S., Sharma, Y., Kumar, S., Pai, R., & Singh, S. (2011). Formal verification of oauth 2.0 using alloy framework. In *IEEE International Conference on Communication Systems and Network Technologies* (pp. 655–659). 10.1109/CSNT.2011.141

Pan, X., Meng, X., & Xu, J. (2009, November 4-6). Distortion-based anonymity for continuous queries in location-based mobile services. In *Proceedings of the 17th ACM SIGSPATIAL International Conference on Advances in Geographic Information Systems (ACM SIGSPATIAL GIS 2009)*, Seattle, WA (pp. 256-265). 10.1145/1653771.1653808

Paper, W. (2010). *Mobile Cloud Computing Solution Brief*. AEPONA.

Paralic, J., & Kostial, I. (2003). A Document Retrieval Method based on Ontology Associations. *Journal of Information and Organizational Sciences*, 27(2), 93–99.

Parno, B., Kuo, C., & Perrig, A. (2006). *Pool proof phishing prevention*. In *Financial Cryptography and Data Security*.

Patil, S., Polte, M., Ren, K., Tantisiriroj, W., Xiao, L., López, J., & Rinaldi, B. (2011, October). YCSB++: benchmarking and performance debugging advanced features in scalable table stores. In *Proceedings of the 2nd ACM Symposium on Cloud Computing* (p. 9). ACM. 10.1145/2038916.2038925

Pearson, S., & Benameur, A. (2010). Privacy, Security and Trust Issues Arising from Cloud Computing. In *IEEE Second International Conference on Computer Science and Technology*. 10.1109/CloudCom.2010.66

Penalver-Martinez, I., Garcia-Sanchez, F., Valencia-Garcia, R., Rodríguez-García, M. Á., Moreno, V., Fraga, A., & Sánchez-Cervantes, J. L. (2014). Feature-based opinion mining through ontologies. *Expert Systems with Applications*, *41*(13), 5995–6008. doi:10.1016/j.eswa.2014.03.022

Perez, S. (2009, August 4). Why cloud computing is the future of mobile. *Readwriteweb*. Retrieved February 2015 from http://www.readwriteweb.com/archives/why_cloud_com.puting_is_the_future_of_mobile.php

Pevny, T., & Jessica Fridrich, A. D. Ker. (2009). From Blind to Quantitative Steganalysis. In *Proc. SPIE, Electronic Imaging, Media Forensics and Security XI*, San Jose, CA, January 18-22.

Pevny, T., Bas, P., & Fridrich, J. (2010). Steganalysis by Subtractive Pixel Adjacency Matrix. *IEEE Transactions on Information Forensics and Security*, *5*(2), 215–224. doi:10.1109/TIFS.2010.2045842

Picciano, A. G. (2012). The Evolution of Big Data and Learning Analytics in American Higher Education. *Journal of Asynchronous Learning Networks*, *16*(3), 9–20.

Pingley, A., Zhang, N., Fu, X., Choi, H.-A., Subramaniam, S., & Zhao, W. (2011, April 10-15). Protection of query privacy for continuous location based services. In *Proceedings of the 30th IEEE International Conference on Computer Communications (INFOCOM 2011)*, Shanghai, China (pp. 1710-1718). 10.1109/INFCOM.2011.5934968

Popov, B., Kiryakov, A., Ognyanoff, D., Manov, D., & Kirilov, A. (2004). KIM – a semantic platform for information extraction. *Journal Natural Language Engineering*, *10*(3-4), 375–392. doi:10.1017/S135132490400347X

Potlapally, N. R., Ravi, S., Raghunathan, A., & Jha, N. K. (2003, August). Analyzing the energy consumption of security protocols. In *Proceedings of the 2003 international symposium on Low power electronics and design* (pp. 30-35). ACM. 10.1145/871506.871518

Potlapally, N. R., Ravi, S., Raghunathan, A., & Jha, N. K. (2006). A study of the energy consumption characteristics of cryptographic algorithms and security protocols. *IEEE Transactions on Mobile Computing*, *5*(2), 128–143. doi:10.1109/TMC.2006.16

Pozos-Radilloa, B. E., de Lourdes Preciado-Serranoa, M., & Acosta-Fernándeza, M. (2014, June). Academic stress as a predictor of chronic stress in university students. *Psicología Educativa*, *20*(1), 47–52. doi:10.1016/j.pse.2014.05.006

Prasithsangaree, P., & Krishnamurthy, P. (2003, December). Analysis of energy consumption of RC4 and AES algorithms in wireless LANs. In *Global Telecommunications Conference GLOBECOM'03* (Vol. 3, pp. 1445-1449). IEEE. 10.1109/GLOCOM.2003.1258477

Pritesh Pathak, S. (2014). Blind Image Steganalysis of JPEG images using feature extraction through the process of dilation. *Digital Investigation*, *11*(1), 67–77. doi:10.1016/j.diin.2013.12.002

PSLC Data Shop. (2017). Welcome to DataShop, the world's largest repository of learning interaction data. Retrieved from https://pslcdatashop.web.cmu.edu/

Pulse, G. (2015). United Nations Global Pulse Information Sheet.

Purcell, B. (2013). The emergence of" big data" technology and analytics. *Journal of technology research, 4*, 1.

Purushottama, S. (2016). Efficient Heart Disease Prediction System. *Procedia Computer Science, 85*, 962–969. doi:10.1016/j.procs.2016.05.288

Qadir, J., Ahad, N., Mushtaq, E., & Bilal, M. (2014, December). SDNs, clouds, and big data: new opportunities. In *2014 12th International Conference on Frontiers of Information Technology (FIT)* (pp. 28-33). IEEE. 10.1109/FIT.2014.14

Qaisar, S., & Riaz, N. (2016). Fog Networking: An Enabler for Next Generation Internet of Things. *ICCSA 2016, Part II. LNCS, 9787*, 353–365.

Qi, H., & Gani, A. (2012). Research on Mobile Cloud Computing: Review, Trend and Perspectives. In *Proceedings of Second International Conference on Digital Information and Communication Technology and it's Applications (DICTAP)* (pp. 195-202). 10.1109/DICTAP.2012.6215350

Rai, A., Bhagwan, R., & Guha, S. (2012). Generalized resource allocation for the cloud. In *ACM Symposium on Cloud Computing*.

Rajeshkumar, J., & Kowsigan, M. (2011). Efficient Scheduling in Computational Grid with an Improved Ant Colony Algorithm. International Journal of Computer Science and Technology, 2(4), 317-321.

Ramesh, D., & Vardhan, B. V. (2016). Analysis of crop yield prediction using data mining techniques. *International Journal of Research in Engineering and Technology, 4*(1), 470–473.

Ranganathan, P., Leech, P., Irwin, D., & Chase, J. (2006, June). Ensemble-level power management for dense blade servers. In ACM SIGARCH *Computer Architecture News, 34*(2), 66–77. doi:10.1145/1150019.1136492

Recordon, D. & Reed, D. (2006). Open id 2.0: a platform for user-centric identity management. In *ACM workshop on Digital identity management* (pp. 11–16).

Rindflesch, T. C., Tanabe, L., Weinstein, J. N., & Hunter, L. (2000). EDGAR: Extraction of Drugs, Genes and Relations from the Biomedical Literature. In *Proceedings of Pacific Symposium on Biocomputing* (pp. 517–528).

Rish, I. (2001, August). An empirical study of the naive Bayes classifier. In IJCAI 2001 workshop on empirical methods in artificial intelligence (Vol. 3, No. 22, pp. 41-46). IBM New York.

Rosen, L., Carrier, L. M., Miller, A., Rokkum, J., & Ruiz, A. (2015). Sleeping with technology: Cognitive, affective, and technology usage predictors of sleep problems among college students. *Sleep Health, 2*(1), 49–56. doi:10.1016/j.sleh.2015.11.003 PMID:29073453

Rouse, M. (2017, July). Cloud Computing. *TechTarget*. Retrieved July 2017, from http://searchcloudcomputing.techtarget.com/definition/cloud-computing

Roy, S., Rudra, A., & Verma, A. (2014, September). Energy aware algorithmic engineering. In *2014 IEEE 22nd International Symposium on Modelling, Analysis & Simulation of Computer and Telecommunication Systems (MASCOTS)* (pp. 321-330). IEEE. 10.1109/MASCOTS.2014.47

Roy, S., Rudra, A., & Verma, A. (2013, January). An energy complexity model for algorithms. In *Proceedings of the 4th conference on Innovations in Theoretical Computer Science* (pp. 283-304). ACM.

Rudenko, A., Reiher, P., Popek, G. J., & Kuenning, G. H. (1999, February). The remote processing framework for portable computer power saving. In *Proceedings of the 1999 ACM symposium on Applied computing* (pp. 365-372). ACM.

Sabnisa, S. K., & Awale, R. N. (2016). Statistical Steganalysis of High Capacity Image Steganography with Cryptography. *Procedia Computer Science*, *79*, 321–327. doi:10.1016/j.procs.2016.03.042

Saif, H., He, Y., & Alani, H. (2012). Semantic Sentiment Analysis of Twitter. In *International Semantic Web Conference ISWC 2012* (pp. 508-524). 10.1007/978-3-642-35176-1_32

Saini, H., & Saini, A. (2014). Security Mechanisms at different Levels in Cloud Infrastructure. International Journal of Computer Applications, 108(2).

Salerno, S., Sanzgiri, A., & Upadhyaya, S. (2011). Exploration of attacks on current generation smartphones. *Procedia Computer Science*, *5*, 546–553. doi:10.1016/j.procs.2011.07.071

Samson, T. (2012). Splunk Storm Brings Log Management to the Cloud. Retrieved from https://www.infoworld.com/article/2615403/managed-services/splunk-storm-brings-log-management-to-the-cloud.html

Sánchez, D., Martín-Bautista, M. J., Blanco, I., & de la Torre, C. J. (2008, December). Text knowledge mining: an alternative to text data mining. In *IEEE International Conference on Data Mining Workshops ICDMW '08* (pp. 664-672). IEEE.

Sánchez, D., Martín-Bautista, M. J., Blanco, I., & de la Torre, C. J. (2008, December). Text knowledge mining: an alternative to text data mining. In *IEEE International Conference on Data Mining Workshops ICDMW '08* (pp. 664-672). IEEE. 10.1109/ICDMW.2008.57

Sandhu, R. S., Coyne, E. J., Feinstein, H. L., & Youman, C. E. (1996). Role-based access control models. *Computer*, *29*(2), 38–47.

Satyanarayanan, M. (2010). Mobile computing: the next decade. In *ACM Workshop on Mobile Cloud Computing Services: Social Networks and Beyond.*

Satyanarayanan, M. (2010). Mobile computing: the next decade. In *Proceedings of the 1st ACM Workshop on Mobile Cloud Computing & Services: Social Networks and Beyond (MCS).*

Satyanarayanan, M., Bahl, P., C'aceres, R., & Davies, N. (2009, October). The Case for VM-Based Cloudlets in Mobile Computing. *IEEE Pervasive Computing*, *8*(4), 14–23. doi:10.1109/MPRV.2009.82

Satyanarayanan, M., Bahl, P., Caceres, R., & Davies, N. (2009). *The case for vm-based cloudlets in mobile computing*. Pervasive Computing.

Sauerwalt, R. (2017). *Benefits of Cloud Computing*. IBM. Retrieved July 2017, from https://www.ibm. com/cloud-computing/learn-more/benefits-of-cloud-computing/

Savitz, E. (2012). Gartner: 10 critical tech trends for the next five years. *Forbes*. http://www.Forbes. Com/sites/ericsavitz/2012/10/22/gartner-10-critical-tech-trends-for-the-next-five-years

Savitz, E. (2012). Gartner: Top 10 strategic technology trends for 2013. URL http://www. forbes.Com/ sites/ericsavitz/2012/10/22/gartner-10-critical-tech-trends-for-the-next-five-years

Sawale, G.J. (2013, April). Use of Artificial Neural Network in Data Mining For Weather Forecasting. *International Journal of Computer Science And Applications, 6*(2).

Schaathun, H. G. (2012). *Machine Learning in Image Steganalysis*. Hoboken: Wiley-IEEE Press. doi:10.1002/9781118437957

Schintler, L. A., & Kulkarni, R. (2014). Big data for policy analysis: The good, the bad, and the ugly. *The Review of Policy Research, 31*(4), 343–348. doi:10.1111/ropr.12079

Sensorly. (2016). Retrieved from http://www.sensorly.com/

Shakeri, E., & Ghaemmaghami, S. (2014). An Extended Feature Set for Blind Image Steganalysis in Contourlet Domain. *The ISC International Journal of Information Security*, 6(2), 169-181.

Shakeri, H., Poggi-Corradini, P., Albin, N., & Scoglio, C. (2016). Modulus of families of loops with applications in network analysis. arXiv preprint arXiv: 1609.00461

Shakeri, H., Poggi-Corradini, P., Albin, N., & Scoglio, C. (2016). Modulus of families of loops with applications in network analysis. arXiv preprint arXiv:1609.00461

Shen, Z., Subbiah, S., Gu, X., & Wilkes, J. (2011). Cloud Scale: elastic resource scaling for multi-tenant cloud systems. In *ACM Symposium on Cloud Computing*.

Shi, Y. Q., Xuan, G., Yang, C., Gao, J., Zhang, Z., Chai, P., . . . Chen, W. (2005). Effective steganalysis based on statistical moments of wavelet characteristic function. In *Proceedings of IEEE International Conference on Information Technology: Coding and Computing* (Vol. 1, pp. 768–773). 10.1109/ ITCC.2005.138

Siegel, E. (2013). *Predictive analytics: The power to predict who will click, buy, lie, or die*. John Wiley & Sons.

Siemens, G. (2012, April). Learning analytics: envisioning a research discipline and a domain of practice. In *Proceedings of the 2nd international conference on learning analytics and knowledge* (pp. 4-8). ACM.

Simonite, T. (2013). Facebook launches advanced AI effort to find meaning in your posts. *Tech. Review*. http://www.technologyreview.com/news/519411/facebook-launches-advanced-ai-effort-to-find-meaning-in-your-posts

SimpleTuition. (n.d.). Retrieved October 2, 2015 from http://www.simpletuition.com/

Simpson, W. A. (1996). *PPP challenge handshake authentication protocol.* CHAP.

Singh, Y., & Chauhan, A. S. (2009). Neural Networks In Data Mining. *Journal of Theoretical and Applied Information Technology.* Retrieved from http://www.jatit.org/volumes/research-papers/Vol5No1/1Vol5No6.pdf

Smith, L. I. (2002). A tutorial on principal components analysis. *Cornell University, 51*(52), 65.

Sociallipstick. (n.d.). Under the covers of oauth 2.0 at Facebook. Retrieved from http://www.social-lipstick.com/?p=239

Software-Systeme. (n.d.). Hardware Monitor. Retrieved 2015-07-01 from http://www.bresink.com/osx/HardwareMonitor.html

Somani, U., Lakhani, K., & Mundra, M. (2010, October). Implementing digital signature with RSA encryption algorithm to enhance the Data Security of cloud in Cloud Computing. In *2010 1st International Conference on Parallel Distributed and Grid Computing (PDGC)* (pp. 211-216). IEEE. 10.1109/PDGC.2010.5679895

Song, X., Liu, F., Zhang, Z., Yang, C., Luo, X., & Chen, L. (2016). 2D Gabor filters-based steganalysis of content-adaptive JPEG steganography. *Multimedia Tools and Applications.*

Stanford Center for Biomedical Informatics Research. (2016). Retrieved September 2016 from www.protege.stanford.edu

Stuedi, P., Mohomed, I., & Terry, D. (2010, June). Wherestore: Location-based data storage for mobile devices interacting with the cloud. In *Proceedings of the 1st ACM Workshop on Mobile Cloud Computing & Services: Social Networks and Beyond.* ACM.

Subashini, S., & Kavita, V. (2011). *A survey on security issues in service delivery models of cloud computing. Elsevier Journal of Network and Computer Applications.*

Sumathi, C.P., Santanam T., & Umamaheswari, G. (2013). A Study of Various Steganographic Techniques Used for Information Hiding. *International Journal of Computer Science & Engineering Survey, 4*(6).

Sun, S.-T. & Beznosov, K. (2012). The devil is in the (implementation) details: an empirical analysis of oauthsso systems. In *ACM conference on Computer and communications security* (pp. 378-390).

Sun, S., Bao, Y., Luc, M., Liu, W., Xie, X., Wang, C., & Liuc, W. (2016). A comparison of models for the short-term prediction of rice stripe virus disease and its association with biological and meteorological factors. *Acta Ecologica Sinica, 36*(3), 166–171. doi:10.1016/j.chnaes.2016.04.002

Swagota Bera, S. Subramanya Sikhar, AtulDwivedi. (2016). An efficient blind steganalysis using higher order statistics for the neighborhood difference matrix. In Proceedings: of wireless communications, signal processing and Networking (WiSPNET).

T.A. Press. (2015). Research it: 5 Things to Know About Apple's Medical Apps. Retrieved from http://www.nytimes.com/aponline/2015/03/11/technology/ap-us-tec-apple-researchkit.html

Taboada, M., Anthony, C., & Voll, K. (2006). Methods for creating semantic orientation dictionaries. In roceedings of the Fifth International Conference on Language Resources and Evaluation LREC'06, Genoa, Italy, pp. 427-432.

Taboada, M., Brooke, J., Tofiloski, M., Voll, K., & Stede, M. (2011). Lexicon-based methods for sentiment analysis. Computational linguistics, 37(2), 267–307. doi:10.1162/COLI_a_00049

Tamai, K., & Shinagawa, A. (2011). Platform for location-based services. *Fujitsu Scientific and Technical Journal, 47*(4), 426–433.

Tan, Z., Chu, D., & Zhong, L. (2014). Vision: cloud and crowd assistance for GPS urban canyons. In Proceedings of the fifth international workshop on Mobile cloud computing & services (pp. 23-27). ACM. doi:10.1145/2609908.2609950

Tang, S., Yuan, J., & Li, X. (2012). Towards optimal bidding strategy for amazon ec2 cloud spot instance. In *IEEE 5th International Conference on Cloud Computing* (pp. 91–98). 10.1109/CLOUD.2012.134

Tannahill, B. K. (2014). Big Data Analytic Techniques: Predicting Renewable Energy Capacity to Facilitate the Optimization of Power Plant Energy Trading and Control Algorithms.

Tavel, P. (2007). *Modeling and Simulation Design*. AK Peters Ltd.

Teng, W.-G., & Chen, M.-S. (2005). Incremental mining on association rules. In *Foundations and Advances in Data Mining* (pp. 125–162). Springer. doi:10.1007/11362197_6

Thakur, S., & Chaurasia, A. (2016, January). Towards Green Cloud Computing: Impact of carbon footprint on environment. In *2016 6th International Conference on Cloud System and Big Data Engineering (Confluence)* (pp. 209-213). IEEE.

The World Bank (Education Data). (n.d.). Education. Retrieved October 4, 2015 from http://data.worldbank.org/topic/education

Thiagarajan, A., Ravindranath, L., LaCurts, K., Madden, S., Balakrishnan, H., Toledo, S., & Eriksson, J. (2009). Vtrack: accurate, energy-aware road traffic delay estimation using mobile phones. In *ACM Conference on Embedded Networked Sensor Systems* (pp. 85–98). 10.1145/1644038.1644048

Thinkcerca. (n.d.). Teach Critical Thinking Through Argumentative Writing. Retrieved September 2, 2015 from http://www.thinkcerca.com/

Tim Jones, M. (2013). Process Real-Time Big Data with Twitter Storm. Retrieved from https://www.ibm.com/developerworks/library/os-twitterstorm/

Toldinas, J., Štuikys, V., Ziberkas, G., & Naunikas, D. (2015). Power awareness experiment for crypto service-based algorithms. *Elektronika ir Elektrotechnika, 101*(5), 57–62.

Trace the Face. (n.d.). Restoring Family Links. Retrieved September 29, 2015 from http://familylinks.icrc.org/europe/en/Pages/Home.aspx

Tran, V. N. N., & Ha, P. H. (2016, December). ICE: A general and validated energy complexity model for multithreaded algorithms. In *2016 IEEE 22nd International Conference on Parallel and Distributed Systems (ICPADS)* (pp. 1041-1048). IEEE. 10.1109/ICPADS.2016.0138

Tsai, J.-L., & Lo, N.-W. (2015). A Privacy-Aware Authentication Scheme for Distributed Mobile Cloud Computing Services. *IEEE Systems Journal, 9*(3), 805–815. doi:10.1109/JSYST.2014.2322973

Tsai, P. S. M., Lee, C.-C., & Chen, A. L. P. (1999, April 26-28). An efficient approach for incremental association rule mining. In *Proceedings of the 3rd Pacific-Asia Conference on Methodologies for Knowledge Discovery and Data Mining (PAKDD '99)*, Beijing, China (pp. 74-83). 10.1007/3-540-48912-6_10

Tumanov, A., Cipar, J., Ganger, G. R., & Kozuch, M. A. (2012). alsched: algebraic scheduling of mixed workloads in heterogeneous clouds. In *ACM Symposium on Cloud Computing*. 10.1145/2391229.2391254

Urgaonkar, B., Shenoy, P., & Roscoe, T. (2002). Resource overbooking and application profiling in shared hosting platforms. *ACM SIGOPS Operating Systems Review, 36*, 239-254.

Ushahidi. (n.d.). Retrieved October 4, 2015 from http://www.ushahidi.com/

Ustimenko, V., & Wroblewska, A. (2013, July). On some algebraic aspects of data security in cloud computing. In Proceedings of Applications of Computer Algebra ACA 2013 (p. 155).

Van Dijk, M., Juels, A., Oprea, A., Rivest, R. L., Stefanov, E., & Triandopoulos, N. (2012, October). Hourglass schemes: how to prove that cloud files are encrypted. In *Proceedings of the 2012 ACM conference on Computer and communications security* (pp. 265-280). ACM.

Vaquero, L. M., & Rodero-Merino, L. (2014). *Finding your Way in the Fog: Towards a Comprehensive Definition of Fog Computing*. HP Laboratories.

Verma, A., Dasgupta, G., Nayak, T. K., De, P., & Kothari, R. (2009, June). Server workload analysis for power minimization using consolidation. In *Proceedings of the 2009 conference on USENIX Annual technical conference* (pp. 28-28). USENIX Association.

Verma, S., & Bhattacharyya, P. (2008). Incorporating Semantic Knowledge for Sentiment Analysis. In *Proceedings of ICON-2008: 6th International Conference on Natural Language Processing*.

Vidhya, A. (2018). Beginners Guide to Topic Modeling in Python. Retrieved March 2017 from https://www.analyticsvidhya.com/blog/2016/08/beginners-guide-to-topic-modeling-in-python/

Voloudakis, D., Karamanos, A., Economou, G., Vahamidis, P., Kotoulas, V., Kapsomenakis, J., & Zerefos, C. (2014, September 22). Prediction of climate change impacts on cotton yields in Greece under eight climatic models using the AquaCrop crop simulation model and discriminant function analysis. *Journal of Agricultural Water Management, 147*, 116–128.

Wang, H., Xu, Z., Fujita, H., & Liu, S. (2016). Towards felicitous decision making: An overview on challenges and trends of Big Data. *Information Sciences, 367*, 747–765. doi:10.1016/j.ins.2016.07.007

Wang, P., Wei, Z., & Xiao, L. (2016). Pure spatial rich model features for digital image steganalysis. *Multimedia Tools and Applications, 75*(5), 2897–2912. doi:10.100711042-015-2521-9

Wang, P., Wei, Z., & Xiao, L. (2016). Spatial rich model steganalysis feature normalization on random feature-subsets. *Soft Computing*.

Wang, W., Li, B., & Liang, B. (2012). Towards optimal capacity segmentation with hybrid cloud pricing. In *IEEE 32nd International Conference on Distributed Computing Systems* (pp. 425–434). 10.1109/ICDCS.2012.52

Wang, Y., Wu, J., & Yang, W. S. (2013). Cloud-Based Multicasting with Feedback in Mobile Social Networks. *IEEE Transactions on Wireless Communications, 12*(12), 6043–6053. doi:10.1109/TWC.2013.102313.121508

Wei, W., & Gulla, J. A. (2010). Sentiment Learning on Product Reviews via Sentiment Ontology Tree. In *Proceedings of the 48th Annual Meeting of the Association for Computational Linguistics ACL '10*, Uppsala, Sweden (pp. 404–413).

Welikala, R. A., Fraz, M. M., Dehmeshki, J., Hoppe, A., Tah, V., Mann, S., ... Barman, S. A. (2015, July). Genetic algorithm based feature selection combined with dual classification for the automated detection of proliferative diabetic retinopathy. *Computerized Medical Imaging and Graphics, 43*, 64–77. doi:10.1016/j.compmedimag.2015.03.003 PMID:25841182

Westfeld, A., & Pfitzmann, A. (1999). Attacks on steganographic systems. In *Proceedings of Third International Workshop on Information Hiding*, Dresden, Germany, September 28–October 1 (pp. 61-75).

Westfeld, A. (2001). F5 – A Steganographic Algorithm. In International workshop on information hiding, *LNCS* (Vol. *2137*, pp. 289–302). doi:10.1007/3-540-45496-9_21

Wright, A. (2009). Get Smart. *Communications of the ACM, 52*(1), 15–16. doi:10.1145/1435417.1435423

Wu, H., Wang, Q., & Wolter, K. (2013). Mobile Healthcare Systems with Multi cloud Offloading. In *IEEE 14th International Conference on Mobile Data Management* (pp. 188-193). 10.1109/MDM.2013.92

Xin, L., Chen, G., & Yin, J. (2016). Content- adaptive steganalysis for color images. *Security and Communication Networks, 9*(18), 5756–5763. doi:10.1002ec.1734

Xu, T., & Cai, Y. (2007, November 7-9). Location anonymity in continuous location-based services. In *Proceedings of the 15th ACM SIGSPATIAL International Conference on Advances in Geographic Information Systems (ACM SIGSPATIAL GIS 2007)*, Seattle, WA.

Yang, F., Shanmugasundaram, J., Riedewald, M., & Gehrke, J. (2006). Hilda: A high-level language for data driven web applications. In *IEEE International Conference on Data Engineering* (pp. 32).

Yang, J. H., & Lin, P. Y. (2016). A Mobile Payment Mechanism with Anonymity for Cloud Computing. *Journal of Systems and Software, 116*(June), 69–74.

Yang, D., Xue, G., Fang, X., & Tang, J. (2012). *Crowdsourcing to smartphones: incentive mechanism design for mobile phone sensing.* In *ACM MobiCom*. doi:10.1145/2348543.2348567

Yaqoob, I., Hashem, I. A. T., Gani, A., Mokhtar, S., Ahmed, E., Anuar, N. B., & Vasilakos, A. V. (2016). Big data: From beginning to future. *International Journal of Information Management, 36*(6), 1231–1247. doi:10.1016/j.ijinfomgt.2016.07.009

Yenkar, V., & Bartere, M. (2014). Review on "Data Mining with Big Data". *International Journal of Computer Science and Mobile Computing, 3*(4), 97–102.

Yi, S., Hao, Z., Qin, Z., & Li, Q. (2015). Fog Computing: Platform and Applications. In *IEEE Workshop on Hot Topics in Web Systems and Technologies (HotWeb)*, Washington, DC. 10.1109/HotWeb.2015.22

Yi, S., Li, C., & Li, Q. (June 2015). A Survey of Fog Computing: Concepts, Applications and Issues. In *Workshop on Mobile Big Data (Mobidata '15)*, Hangzhou, China (pp. 37-42). ACM. 10.1145/2757384.2757397

Yoshida, H. (1999). *LUN security considerations for storage area networks (Paper-XP, 2185193).* Hitachi Data Systems.

Youseff, L., Butrico, M., & Da Silva, D. (2008). Toward a Unified Ontology of Cloud Computing. In *Grid Computing Environments Workshop, GCE'08*. IEEE. 10.1109/GCE.2008.4738443

You, T. H., Peng, W. C., & Lee, W. C. (2007, May 11). Protecting moving trajectories with dummies. In *Proceedings of the International Workshop on Privacy-Aware Location-Based Mobile Services (PALMS)*, Mannheim, Germany.

Yuan, W., & Nahrstedt, K. (2003, October). Energy-efficient soft real-time CPU scheduling for mobile multimedia systems. *Operating Systems Review, 37*(5), 149–163. doi:10.1145/1165389.945460

Yuasa, H., Satake, T., Cardona, M. J., Fujii, H., Yasuda, A., Yamashita, K., . . . Suzuki, J. (2000). U.S. Patent No. 6,085,238. Washington, DC: U.S. Patent and Trademark Office.

Yu, S., Wang, C., Ren, K., & Lou, W. (2010, March). *Achieving secure, scalable, and fine-grained data access control in cloud computing. In 2010 proceedings IEEE Infocom.* IEEE.

Zafer, M., Song, Y., & Lee, K. (2012). Optimal bids for spot vms in a cloud for deadline constrained jobs. In *IEEE 5th International Conference on Cloud Computing* (pp. 75–82). 10.1109/CLOUD.2012.59

Zaman, S., & Grosu, D. (2011). Combinatorial auction-based dynamic vm provisioning and allocation in clouds. In *IEEE Third International Conference on Cloud Computing Technology and Science* (pp. 107–114). 10.1109/CloudCom.2011.24

Zhang, H., Ping, X. J., ManKun, X., & Wang, R. (2014). Steganalysis by subtractive pixel adjacency matrix and dimensionality reduction. *Science China. Information Sciences, 57*(4), 1–7. doi:10.100711432-014-5073-0

Zhao, Q., & Bhowmick, S. S. (2003). Sequential pattern mining: a survey (technical report). CAIS, Nanyang Technological University, Singapore.

Zhu, W., Luo, C., Wang, J., & Li, S. (2011). Multimedia cloud computing. *IEEE Signal Processing Magazine*, *28*(3), 59–69. doi:10.1109/MSP.2011.940269

Zikopoulos, P., & Eaton, C. (2011). *Understanding big data: Analytics for enterprise-class Hadoop and streaming data*. McGraw-Hill Osborne Media.

Zohreh, S., Saeid, A., Abdullah, G., & Buyya, R. (2013). Heterogeneity in Mobile Cloud Computing: Taxonomy and Open Challenges. *IEEE Communications Surveys and Tutorials*, (99): 1–24. doi:10.1109/SURV.2013.050113.00090

Zong, H., Liu, F., & Luo, X. (2012). Blind image steganalysis based on wavelet coefficient correlation. *Digital Investigation*, *9*(9), 58–68. doi:10.1016/j.diin.2012.02.003

About the Contributors

Periasamy Karthikeyan was born in Dindigul, Tamilnadu, India in 1981. He is currently working as an Assistant Professor in Thiagarajar College of Engineering, Madurai from 2007 onwards. He has completed the Ph.D. programme in Information and Communication Engineering under Anna University, Chennai, Tamilnadu, India in the year 2015. He published 13 papers in refereed international journals and conferences. He received the B.E. degree in Computer Science and Engineering from Madurai Kamaraj University, Madurai, Tamilnadu, India in the year 2002. He also received his M.E. degree in Computer Science and Engineering from Anna University, Chennai, Tamilnadu, India in the year2004. His research interests include optimization algorithms, ad hoc networks, engineering education and mobile cloud computing.

M. Thangavel is an Assistant Professor presently working in the Department of Information Technology at Thiagarajar college of Engineering, Madurai. He presently holds 3 years of Teaching and Research experience in Thiagarajar college of Engineering, Madurai and 2 years of Teaching and Research experience in Madras Institute of Technology, Anna University - Chennai. He graduated as a B.E. Computer Science and Engineering from M.A.M College of Engineering, Trichy (Anna University - Chennai) and as an M.E. Computer Science and Engineering from J.J. College of Engineering and Technology, Trichy (Anna University - Chennai) and Pursuing his PhD from Madras Institute of Technology, Chennai under Anna University - Chennai. He is a Gold Medalist in UG and Anna University - First Rank Holder with Gold Medal in PG. His specialization is Cloud Computing, and Information Security. His Areas of Interest include DNA Cryptography, Ethical Hacking, Compiler Design, Computer Networks, Data Structures and High Performance Computing. He has published 5 articles in International Journals, 8 book chapters in International Publishers, 14 in the proceedings of International Conferences and 3 in the proceedings of national conferences /seminars. He has attended 38 Workshops / FDPs/Conferences in various Higher Learning Institutes like IIT, Anna University. He has organized 21 Workshops / FDPs /Contests/Industry based courses over the past 5 years of experience. He has been recognized by IIT Bombay & SAP CSR as SAP Award of Excellence with cash reward of Rs.5000/- for the best Participation in IITBombayX: FDPICT001x Use of ICT in Education for Online and Blended Learning. He shows interest in student counseling, in motivating for better placements and in helping them design value-based life-style.

* * *

A. Sheik Abdullah is working as Assistant Professor, Department of Information Technology, Thiagarajar College of Engineering, Madurai, Tamil Nadu, India. He completed his B.E (Computer Science and Engineering), at Bharath Niketan Engineering College, and M.E (Computer Science and Engineering) at Kongu Engineering College under Anna University, Chennai. He has been awarded as gold medalist for his excellence in the degree of Post Graduate. He is pursuing his PhD in the domain of Medical Data Analytics, and his research interests include Medical Data Research, E-Governance and Big Data. He has handled various E-Governance projects such as automation system for tracking community certificate, birth and death certificate, DRDA and income tax automation systems. He has published research articles in various reputed journals and International Conferences. He has been assigned as a reviewer in Various reputed journals such as European Heart Journal, Proceedings of the National Academy of Sciences, Physical Sciences (NASA) and so on. He has received the Honorable chief minister award for excellence in E-Governance for the best project in E-Governance. Currently he is working towards the significance of the medical data corresponding to various diseases and resolving its implications through the development of various algorithmic models.

A.M. Abirami is a Computer Science Engineer from Bharathiyar University, Coimbatore where she awarded the B.E. degree with first class distinction in 1999. She then served as a Software Engineer in Tata Consultancy Services Ltd. from 1999 – 2006 where she worked as a QA member. She did her M.E. degree from Anna University Tirunelveli with first class distinction in the year 2010. Since 2010, she is working as Assistant Professor in Department of Information Technology, Thiagarajar College of Engineering, Madurai. She is pursuing research in Text Analytics using Semantic Web Technologies. She is interested in improving Teaching Learning methodologies of Engineering Education. She has attended Wipro's MISSION 10x workshop to set up the Active Learning Environment in the class and earned "Cambridge International Certificate for Teachers and Trainers." She has been given training on Outcome Based Education and is the active participant in Curriculum Design and Development of UG/PG courses of Department of Information Technology, TCE. She has been selected and nominated as "Master Trainer" by Anna University Chennai and NASSCOM for conducting FDP on "Foundation Skills for Integrated Product Development" and in turn to students for the Course "Engineering Design". She has attended IIT Bombay's FDPs for the use of ICT tools in Engineering Education during May-June 2016. She has implemented many Active Learning Strategies while teaching Data Structures, Programming and Software Engineering courses to UG students.

Sanjay P. Ahuja has a Ph.D. in Computer Science and Engineering from the University of Louisville. He is a full professor in the School of Computing within the College of Computing, Engineering, and Construction at the University of North Florida and was the FIS Distinguished Professor in Computer and Information Sciences from 2010-2014. His research expertise is in Cloud Computing, Computer Networks, Distributed Systems, and performance evaluation and benchmarking. He is a Senior Member of the IEEE and a member the SPEC Cloud Working Group. He is the faculty advisor to the Upsilon Pi Epsilon Computer Science Honor Society.

Usha B. A. has been working in R V College of Engg from 2006. Interested in the fields of information security, software engineering, compiler design, system software and database management systems.

Priyanka Chinnaiah is completed her M.E Computer Science and Information Security in Thiagarajar College of Engineering, Madurai, Tamil Nadu, India. Her area of interest is Cloud Computing.

Prasenjit Choudhury is an assistant professor in the Department of Computer Science and Engineering at National Institute of Technology, Durgapur, India. He completed his PhD in Computer Science and Engineering from the same institute. He has published more than 40 research papers in international journals and conferences. His research interest includes Wireless Network, Data Analytics, and Recommendation systems.

Stephen Dass is currently pursuing an M.Tech (by research) in the Vellore Institute of Technology University. He received his M.S. in software engineering (5 year integrated course) from Vellore Institute of Technology. His current research interests include big data analytics, internet of things, cryptography, network security, multimedia and cyber crime. He is the author/co-author of papers in international journals and conferences.

Pijush Dutta Pramanik is a PhD Research Scholar in the Department of Computer Science and Engineering at National Institute of Technology, Durgapur, India. He has acquired a range of professional qualifications in the field of Information Technology namely MIT, MCA, MBA(IT), MTech(CSE), and MPhil(CS). He is actively engaged in research in the domains of Internet of Things, grid computing, fog computing, crowd computing and recommendation systems. He is passionate about technical writing and working on a number of such projects. He can be reached at pijushjld@yahoo.co.in.

AbdElRahman ElSaid is a research assistant at the Computer Science Department, University of North Dakota.

Hongyu Guo is an Associate Professor of Computer Science at the University of Houston - Victoria. He received his Ph.D. degree from the University of Florida. His research interests include computer vision, machine learning, artificial intelligence and data mining.

Priyanka Dhoopa Harish is currently working as a Software Engineer at Synopsis, California. Prior to this, she worked as a Software Development Engineer at Deutsche Bank, North Carolina. She received her Master of Science in Computing and Information Sciences degree in Fall 2015. Priyanka was working as a graduate research assistant under the guidance of Dr. Swapnoneel Roy at UNF from January 2014 - August 2015 and also worked as graduate teaching assistant during spring 2015. The research work performed by her has resulted in the conference publications in the field of Computer Security and Energy Aware Computing. She has participated in IEEE conferences like ACM SIGCOMM-2014 held at Chicago, GREENCOM-2014 held at Taipei and also, she was awarded with a travel grant to participate in the workshop, N2WOMEN at ACM SIGCOMM. Priyanka has worked for 4 years as a Software Engineer at IBM Software Labs, where she was responsible for developing the testing framework for database application tools using technologies such as Java J2EE, Perl, C and IBM DB2.

Wen-Chen Hu received a PhD in Computer Science from the University of Florida in 1998. He is currently an associate professor in the Department of Computer Science of the University of North Dakota. He is the Editor-in-Chief of the International Journal of Handheld Computing Research (IJHCR), the general chairs of a number of international conferences, and associate editors of several journals. In addition, he has acted in more than 100 positions as editor and editorial advisory/review board member of international journals/books, and track/session chairs and program committee member of international conferences. Dr. Hu has been teaching more than 10 years at the US universities and in over 10 different computer/IT-related courses, and advising/consulting more than 100 graduate students. He has published over 100 articles in refereed journals, conference proceedings, books, and encyclopedias, and edited more than 10 books and conference proceedings. His current research interests include handheld/mobile/smartphone/tablet computing, location-based services, web-enabled information system such as search engines, electronic and mobile commerce systems, and web technologies.

Prabhu J. received his PhD (Computer science and Engineering) and Master of Computer Science and Engineering from Sathyabama University Chennai, Tamil Nadu, India and he received the B.tech degree from the Department of Information Technology, Vellore Engineering College, Affiliated to Madras University in 2004 located at Vellore, Tamil Nadu, India. . He worked as an Assistant Professor in various Engineering colleges for more than 10 years. Now he is working as an Associate Professor in School of Information Technology and Engineering VIT University, Vellore, Tamil Nadu, India. His Research interests are software testing, Software Quality Assurance, Software metrics and big data.

Hemalatha Jeyaprakash received a B.E and a ME degree in Computer Science and Engineering under Anna University Chennai in 2007 and 2013. She is currently pursuing the Ph.D. degree in Information and Communication Engineering with Anna University, Chennai, India. In July 2013, she joined the Department of Computer Science and Engineering at P.S.R Engineering College, Sivakasi. India. Her research interests include Digital steganography, Steganalysis, Machine Learning and Image Processing. She has published more papers in reputed International Conferences and Journals.

K. Rohini did her Bachelors of Engineering in Computer Science and Engineering from K.L.N College of Information Technology in 2016. She is currently pursuing Master of Engineering in Computer Science and Information Security at Thiagarajar College of Engineering. Her research interests include data engineering, Cloud computing and Cryptography.

K.S. Suriya did her Bachelors of Engineering in computer science and engineering from Kalasalingam Institute of Technology in 2015. She is completed her Master of Engineering in computer science and information security at Thiagarajar College of Engineering in 2017. Her research interests include Data mining, Cryptography and Network Security.

Naima Kaabouch is currently full professor in the Department of Electrical Engineering, University of North Dakota, USA. She received her B.S., M.S., and Ph.D. all in Electrical Engineering from the University of Paris 11 and the University of Paris 6, Paris, France, in 1982, 1986, 1990, respectively. Dr. Kaabouch's research interests include wireless communications and networking, cybersecurity, sensing, signal/image processing, and autonomous and smart systems. She has published over 140 peer reviewed journal and proceedings articles. She is also the co-editor of 3 books and 1 handbook. Dr. Kaabouch is the recipient of numerous research and teaching awards, including the 2010 University of North Dakota Faculty Star Award and the 2016 Outstanding Faculty Award in Teaching, Research, and Service.

M. Sandeep Kumar is currently pursuing an M.Tech (by research) in the Vellore Institute of Technology University. He received his M.S in software engineering (5 years integrated course) from Vellore Institute of Technology University. His Current research interests include big data analytics, IOT, Recommender systems, Virtualization and Data analytics. He is the author/co-author of papers in international journals and conferences.

M.K. Kavitha Devi received her under graduate and graduate degrees in computer science and engineering, and her Ph.D. Degree in information and communication engineering in 1994, 2004 and 2011, respectively. Her research focuses on recommender systems, information security & hiding, cloud computing, and big data. She has received the Best Computer Science Faculty Award in 2014 from Association of Scientists, Developers and Faculties (ASDF). She has published more than 20 refereed Journal and International Conference papers in these areas. She is the reviewer in referred journals including IEEE Intelligent Systems and Springer - Journal of The Institution of Engineers (India): Series B. She organized faculty development programs, workshops and conferences. Under her guidance, 10 PhD scholars from Anna University, Chennai are working in her area. Currently, she is an Associate Professor in the Department of Computer Science and Engineering, Thiagarajar College of Engineering, Madurai, India.

Brojo Kishore Mishra is an Associate Professor (IT) and the Institutional IQAC Coordinator at the C. V. Raman College of Engineering (Autonomous), Bhubaneswar, India. Received M.Tech and Ph.D. degrees in Computer Science from the Berhampur University in 2008 and 2012 respectively. Currently he is guiding PhD research scholars at Biju Pattnaik University of Technology, Odisha. His research interests include Data mining and big data analysis, machine learning, Soft computing, Evolutionary computation. He has already published more than 40 research papers in internationally reputed journals and referred conferences, 7 book chapters, has edited 1 book, and is acting as a member of the editorial board/associate editor / Guest editor of various International journals. He served in the capacity of Keynote Speaker, Plenary Speaker, Program Chair, Proceeding chair, Publicity chair, Special session chairperson and as member of programme committees of many international conferences. He was associated with a CSI funded research project as a Principal Investigator. He is a life member of ISTE, CSI, and member of IEEE, ACM, IAENG, UACEE, and ACCS.

Sushruta Mishra is working as an assistant professor in C.V. Raman College of Engineering, BBSR. He has more than 6 years of teaching experience in the academics field with several research publications to my credit.

Kowsigan Mohan received his B.TECH degree in Information Technology from Anna University in 2008 and M.TECH Information Technology in Anna University in 2011. He is pursuing his PhD in Anna University. He is currently an Assistant Professor in Department of Information Technology in Sri Krishna College of Technology, Coimbatore. He has published many papers in many reputed journals and conferences. His main research interest includes Cloud Computing, Grid Computing, Soft Computing and Internet of Things.

Sunil Mohapatra is an Asst. Prof. in the Dept. of Computer Science & Engineering, C.V. Raman College of Engineering, Bhubaneswar.

Sneha Narendran is a research scholar at Sri Krishna College of Technology, Coimbatore, India. She has published many research articles in reputed conferences/journals. Her area of interest includes Cloud Computing and Internet of Things.

P. Balasubramanie is currently working as a Professor in the Department of Computer Science & Engineering, Kongu Engineering College, Tamilnadu, India. He is one of the approved supervisor of Anna University Chennai and guided 26 PhD scholars. Currently he is guiding 10 Ph.D scholars. He has published 203 articles in national/international journals. He has published 11 books with reputed publishers. Three of the books published are used as text/reference books by many of the leading universities in India. He has completed one AICTE research promotion scheme (RPS) as a Principal Investigator. Currently he is working in a UGC minor research project as a principal investigator. He has received a 13 lakhs grant from various funding agencies like AICTE, CSIR, DRDO, NBHM, ICMR and so on and organised 21 SDP/ STTP/ Seminar/ workshops for the benefit of faculty members and research scholars. So far, he has received 14 awards. He is actively involved in training and consultancy activities. His field of specialization includes cloud computing, datamining and networking.

Saurabh Pal is an assistant professor in the department of Computer Science & Engineering and Information Technology at Bengal Institute of Technology, Kolkata. He has more than 10 years of teaching experience in the field of computer science and engineering. Saurabh Pal has received B.Sc degree from University of Calcutta, India, in 1998, M.Sc degree in Information Technology from Allahabad Agricultural Institute – Deemed University, India, in 2006 and Master of Technology – Information Technology degree from Jadavpur University, India, in 2010. Presently he is pursuing PhD in Computer Science & Engg from NIT, Durgapur, India. He has published his research work in many International Journals and Conferences. His primary research area includes education technology, mobile computing, context aware computing, semantic web and natural language processing.

Parkavi R started her research in mobile learning and is currently working as an Assistant Professor in the Department of Information Technology, Thiagarajar College of Engineering, Madurai, India. She completed her B.Tech (Information Technology) in Sree Sowdambika College of Engineering and M.E (computer science and engineering) at Thiagarajar College of Engineering. She firmly believes that improving m-learning will enhance the teaching-learning process thereby improving the potential excellence in educational institutions.

Shiva Shankari R A is a graduate in information technology from Thiagarajar college of engineering with special interest in Text Mining domain.

Siddharth Rajesh is a research scholar in Sri Krishna College of Technology, Coimbatore, India. He has published many research articles in reputed conferences/journals. His area of interest includes Cloud Computing and Internet Of Things.

G. R. Kanagachidambaresan received his BE degree in electrical and electronics engineering from Anna University in 2010 and ME Pervasive Computing Technologies in Anna University in 2012. He has completed his PhD in Anna University. He is currently working as an Associate Professor in the Department of CSE in Veltech Rangarajan Dr Sagunthala R&D Institute of Science and Technology, Avadi, Chennai. His research includes IoT and Wireless Networks.

Swapnoneel Roy is an assistant professor with the School of Computing, University of North Florida. His research interests are computer security, green computing, and algorithms. He earned his PhD in computer science and engineering from the University at Buffalo. He serves as the faculty advisor to the AITP Club, UNF's only hacking club.

S. Geetha Received the B.E., and M.E., degrees in Computer Science and Engineering in 2000 and 2004, respectively, from the Madurai Kamaraj University and Anna University of Chennai, India. She obtained her Ph.D. Degree from Anna University in 2011. She has rich teaching and research experience of 15+ years. She has published more than 60 papers in reputed international conferences and refereed journals. She joins the review committee for IEEE Transactions on Information Forensics and Security and IEEE Transactions on Image Processing. Her research interests include steganography, steganalysis, multimedia security, intrusion detection systems, machine learning paradigms and information forensics. She is a recipient of University Rank and Academic Topper Awards in B.E. and M.E. in 2000 and 2004 respectively. She is also the proud recipient of ASDF Best Academic Researcher Award 2013.

S. Pudumalar is working as Assistant Professor in the Department of Information Technology at Thiagarajar College of Engineering, Madurai. She received her UG and PG degrees with the specialization of Computer Science and Engineering. She has a passion for teaching as well as Research. She is an active member of pedagogical activities including Curriculum Design and Teaching Learning Process. Her recent publication on Engineering Education includes Effectiveness of Mobile Learning at TCE, India: A Learner Perspective in IEEE International Conference T4E2015. Her current research interests include predicting the chances of offering scholarship to students.

S. Sujitha is doing her research in software defined networks, and currently working as Assistant Professor in the Department of Information Technology, Thiagarajar College of Engineering, Madurai, India. She has done her Masters in computer science and engineering, Government College of Engineering, Tirunelveli, India.

Soumya Sahoo is continuing as an Asst. Prof in CSE dept. at C.V Raman College of Engineering.

S. Raghu Talluri was born in Vijayawada, India on March 31, 1992. After finishing his school in 2009, he studied computer science in Jawaharlal Nehru Technological University (JNTU). He is pursuing his Masters in computer science at the University of North Florida and working as a software engineer at CSX Technology.

Index

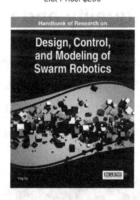

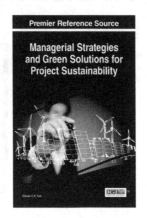

Printed in the United States
By Bookmasters